“Our Little *Monitor*”

OUR LITTLE
MONITOR

“Our Little *Monitor*”

The Greatest Invention of the Civil War

Anna Gibson Holloway and Jonathan W. White

The Kent State University Press · Kent, Ohio

Library of Congress Catalog Card Number 2016054989
ISBN 978-1-60635-314-1
Manufactured in Korea

Library of Congress Cataloging-in-Publication Data

Names: Holloway, Anna Gibson, author. | White, Jonathan W., 1979- author.
Title: "Our Little Monitor" : the greatest invention of the Civil War / Anna Gibson Holloway and Jonathan W. White.
Description: Kent, Ohio : The Kent State University Press, 2017. | Series: Civil War in the North | Includes bibliographical references and index.
Identifiers: LCCN 2016054989 (print) | LCCN 2016056728 (ebook) | ISBN 9781606353141 (hardcover : alk. paper) | ISBN 9781631012648 (ePub) | ISBN 9781631012655 (ePDF)
Subjects: LCSH: Monitor (Ironclad) | Hampton Roads, Battle of, Va., 1862. | Virginia (Ironclad) | United States--History--Civil War, 1861-1865--Naval operations.
Classification: LCC E595.M7 H65 2017 (print) | LCC E595.M7 (ebook) | DDC 973.7/5--dc23
LC record available at https://lccn.loc.gov/2016054989

22 21 20 19 18 5 4 3 2 1

Contents

Tables and Illustrations

Acknowledgments

Anna Gibson Holloway's Acknowledgments

If someone had told me twenty years ago that I would one day trade in wooden ships for ironclads, and square sails for steam, I would have told them that they were crazy. Clearly they did not know me well—I mean, my world revolved around sixteenth- and seventeenth-century vessels.

That was before I met the *Monitor*.

This curious little ironclad and the men who built her, served on her, and died with her, as well as the men and women who discovered, recovered, and now maintain and conserve her have become as much a part of my everyday existence no matter how many miles and fathoms, or decades and centuries, separate us.

And yes, the *Monitor* is a she, no matter what the current Navy custom is today. To me it seems somehow wrong to take that pronoun away from "our little *Monitor*." Relegating her to an "it" somehow removes the soul from a vessel, though she was not a delicate girl by any means. She drank, smoked, belched, roared, reeled, and staggered like a drunk man, if you read the words others used about her. She went by the names "Ericsson's Folly," "tin can," "rat trap," "cheesebox." Yet she became the hope of a nation, the home for some 108 men over her brief life above the waves and the nursery for countless creatures aquatic over the course of a century and a half, serving proudly as America's first National Marine Sanctuary under the auspices of the National Oceanic and Atmospheric Administration.

She first came into my life in 2000, when I became director of education at The Mariners' Museum in Newport News. Oh, I knew of her already to be sure, but I did not visit the nineteenth century often in those days. Little did I know that she and her officers and crew would become as familiar as old friends and long-lost members of my family. To the 108 men who sometimes called themselves "The *Monitor* Boys," I give my eternal thanks.

Eternal thanks also go to my co-author, Jonathan White. We first met after an epic bidding war over a *Monitor* "sad iron" on eBay several years ago. Despite the fact that I won the coveted iron, and despite the fact he drove up the price exponentially, I count him as one of my most treasured colleagues and friends. He and his students have enhanced this project in ways I could never have imagined. He also brought me back to the right side of the podium for a few years when I served as adjunct faculty at Christopher Newport University. The students I had the privilege to teach in those few years continue to inspire and amaze me.

But my part of this work would never have seen the light of day had it not been for Carol Sheriff and Jim Whittenburg from the Department of History at the College of William and Mary. They had been there with me at the beginning of my "gradual school" career and were determined to see me through to the end. They, along with Scott Nelson, convinced me to switch time periods, and dissertation topics, midstream. And they were right to do it! I cannot thank them enough for all of their continued support, cheerleading, and expertise, as well as the rest of the faculty, staff, and students of the Lyon Gardner Tyler Department of History.

My colleagues at The Mariners' Museum went above and beyond any call of museum duty to make it possible for me to be a part of the *Monitor*'s story. Thanks to Mary Ann Cleary and John Hightower, for seeing my potential as curator of the *Monitor,* and Tim Sullivan and Dr. Bill Cogar, for making sure that this work could get done, as well as the incredible staff there at the museum and my colleagues, past and present, at NOAA's Monitor National Marine Sanctuary. Thanks to Dr. John Broadwater for his assistance and insightful comments in preparing this manuscript, and in teaching me to love the little cheesebox. Thanks as well to David Alberg, Tane Casserly, Joe Hoyt, and Jeff Johnston from NOAA; Captain Bobbie Scholley, Captain Chris Murray, Chief Warrant Officer Rick Cavey, and the deeply missed Master Chief Master Diver Jim Mariano (who left this world far too soon); and all the gang at MDSU TWO for letting me tag along on some of the expeditions (and not laughing at my sad little seasick self), as well as providing me access to these national treasures. Thanks also to the former and current staff of The Mariners' Museum Library and Archives, especially Ben Trask, Bill Barker, Tom Moore, Bill Edwards-Bodmer, and Dr. Jay Moore, for helping me paw through primary source documents from the nineteenth, twentieth, and twenty-first centuries. The late Budge Weidman, founder of the Civil War Conservation Corps at the National Archives, provided invaluable research assistance early on, as did the staff of the Manuscript Division of the Library of Congress.

One of my fabulous volunteers at The Mariners' Museum, Lona Ross, likely does not realize how important all of her incredibly insightful questions were to me in preparing for this. I thank her for keeping me on my toes with the minutiae of the nineteenth century. Similar thanks go to Tom and Nancy Lee Clark (we miss you, Nancy) for their support and laughter through the years. Speaking of laughter, I owe so much to Mariners' Museum collections technician Cindi Verser for her love of early telegraph history, pea-shooting toys, and things that look like the *Monitor,* which is truly infectious. Our story here was made far better by her historical stalking.

Extremely special thanks go out to David Krop, Marcie Renner, Curtiss Peterson, Wayne Lusardi, Eric Nordgren, Erin Secord, Susanne Grieve, Eric Schindelholz, Pedro Goncalves, Elsa Sangouard, Will Hoffmann, Tina Gutshall, Gary Paden, Michael Saul, Kate Sullivan, Gerry Hanley, and all of the staff and volunteers of the *Monitor* Conservation Project in years past for all of the phone calls in the past decade and a half that began with the words, "Anna, you need to come over here and *see* this!"

Big ironclad thanks go to my co-curator Jeff Johnston from NOAA, along with Len Soccolich, Judy Vannais, and Scott Guerin of the design firm of DMCD as part of our initial *Monitor* Center team. But so many more were so essential to its initial and continuing success: David Lenk, the groovy John Quarstein, Chris Voll (who brought his vision of the as-built turret to life in the galleries), Priscilla Hauger, John Cannup, Susan Berg, Josh Graml, Jeanne Willoz-Egnor, Sara Johnston, David Dwyer, Lyles Forbes, Nick Brown, Richard Ormond, George Sawyer, Johnny Lawson, Sidney Moore, Claudia Jew, John Pemberton, Greg Vicik, Jason Copes, Erin Lopater, Megan Evans, Bruce Hagerman, David Jones, Roger Brown, Mike Dunning, Rachel Conley, Tracey Neikirk, Tangela Shepard, Rhonda Todd, Kim Gove, Barbara Wright, Lauren Furey, Wisteria Perry, Mark Arduini (who helped get the pop culture section rolling back in 2001), Dan Maher, Gary Egan, Justin Lyons, Karen Owen, "Little" Mary Helen Hilton, Marge Shelton, Joe Tvelia, Teri Johnson, Mary Brevard (alas, Joe and Teri and Mary—we miss you all so much), Marc Marsocci, Helen Myers, Fred Wallace, Dan Archibald, Alison Dressler, Kimberly Hansin, Mita Vail, Andrea Bear, Two Rivers Studios (thanks, Tim, MK, and Sara), Pyramid Studios (thanks, Dixie and Bruce), Batwin + Robin, our incredible exhibit editor Susannah Livingston, the dream team of Harold and Edith Holzer, along with John O'Keefe and Tim Mulligan (John and Tim also gone too soon). These and a cast of thousands all played or continue to play major roles in creating the USS *Monitor* Center exhibition. Their good humor, incredible skills, and willingness to do some pretty bizarre things for the sake of the *Monitor* are the stuff of legend. I cannot thank them enough.

Bill Still—a *Monitor* legend himself—has pointed the way to many overlooked collections and connections (over excellent drinks, I might add) over the years, as has Bill Dudley. Cathryn Newton and Norm Cubberly have helped me build a bridge to the discovery of the *Monitor* with their prose and their poetry. The Battle of Hampton Roads Weekend family of Fran DuCoin, Bill Finlayson, George and Janice Weinmann, George Buss, and so many more—along with the Naval History Mutual Admiration Society of Matt Eng, Charles Wexler, Laura June Davis, and others have helped to keep the ride fun. Extra special thanks go out to Craig Symonds (and MaryLou) and Jim Delgado (and Ann) for their support throughout the years (making sure I had the right beard on Lincoln and the right information on the shipwreck) and for their willingness to read and comment on this manuscript. Their attention to detail and love of the *Monitor* have made this book all the better. If there are any errors—the fault is ours, not theirs. Thanks also to Myra King for willingly agreeing to read an early draft when she really didn't have to.

I jumped ship from The Mariners' Museum and took up a berth in the Park History Program of the National Park Service just as this initial manuscript was completed. Thanks so much to my colleagues Robert Sutton, John Sprinkle, and Lu Ann Jones, and especially my shipmate Kelly Spradley-Kurowski in the Maritime Heritage Program, for their amazing support as I learn a whole new vocabulary of acronyms up here in Washington, D.C.

Of course, the greatest support comes from friends and family, for though they may not have been there in the gallery or at the computer every day with me, the constant of their friendship, love, and support is what sustained me through this massive project. Special thanks go to Anne Marie Millar (my mysterious twin sister on both stage and screen who has never managed to escape the Civil War no matter how hard she tries) and Alex "the Awesome Intern" Ruble for being my daily cheering section, and to others around the world (Addie, Lexy, and Melody—it loves its!) who sent their best thoughts and encouragement online. I raise a glass of the finest port to the wonderful J. Michael Moore (founding member of the Riverwalk Historical Society), with whom I have spent many fine hours discussing the finer points of ironclad goodness. Michael has been a great friend over the years, even while constantly reminding me that his museum has the *Monitor*'s tablecloth and mine did not.

Immense thanks go to Duane and Pat Holloway for their love and friendship, and for accepting me into their brood and cheering me along. And while mere words seem too lacking, I would like to thank my parents, Tom and Greta Gibson, for . . . well, for absolutely everything. I would not have made it this far without them. They went above and beyond for me countless times with their love, support, friendship, and discussions of recipes, and I only wish that they, along with Duane, could still be here to see this book released.

Finally, I want to thank my husband, Jim, for loving me and the kitties. His patience, humor, gourmet cooking, and ukulele serenades have sustained me throughout my shift from sail to steam, from shot to shell, and from wood to iron in the many years of *Monitor* madness. I can think of no one else with whom I would rather sail, or in this case *steam* away.

Jonathan W. White's Acknowledgments

First, I owe a debt of gratitude to Anna for allowing me to join her in this project. I am convinced that no one in the world knows more about the *Monitor* or the Battle of Hampton Roads than she does, and it has been a joy to learn from her as we have worked on this book together. *"Our Little* Monitor" is derived from her dissertation and her years of hard work at The Mariners' Museum, and she deserves the full credit. I have valued her friendship over the years and can (almost) honestly say that I am not bitter about losing the *Monitor* iron to her on eBay (although it would have been a nice addition to my collection). I look forward to future conversations about the *Monitor* over glasses of Short Fuse at the Oozlefinch Craft Brewery at Fort Monroe (see chapter 5). The research in this book, after all, helped inspire that spectacular IPA.

My friend and former student Chris Chappell and my current students Daniel Glenn and Emily Risko were all extremely helpful in the research and transcriptions in this book. Jesse Spencer, Christopher Newport University's InterLibrary Loan specialist, tracked down a number of items for me that greatly facilitated the research. Trevor Plante at the National Archives in Washington, D.C., always goes above the call of duty to facilitate my research. And the staff at The Mariners' Museum Library—Bill Barker, Jay Moore, Tom Moore, Jennifer Anielski, Bill Edwards-Bodmer, and Patti Hinson—were always welcoming and helpful whenever I came to do research. I also am grateful for how they have helped so many of my students gain experience working in a world-class archive.

Claudia Jew and Brock Switzer of The Mariners' Museum performed a herculean feat, tracking down dozens of high-resolution images for us to include in this book, most of them at the last minute. For that we are truly grateful. David Gerleman, Christian McWhirter, and Stacy McDermott Pratt of the Papers of Abraham Lincoln also provided images from the National Archives.

I thank the Department of Leadership and American Studies, Dean Bob Colvin of the College of Social Sciences, and the Office of the Provost at Christopher Newport University for supporting research trips to the Huntington Library (in San Marino, California), the Abraham Lincoln

Presidential Library and Museum (in Springfield, Illinois), and the National Archives (in Washington, D.C.). Will Underwood, Mary Young, and Chris Brooks at the Kent State University Press have been wonderful to work with, and we appreciate their enthusiasm for this project. Indeed, we cannot express enough gratitude to the Press for permitting us to use so many images in this volume. Craig Symonds, Jim Delgado, and the anonymous readers for the Press all gave the manuscript a close reading and offered exceptional advice.

My parents, Bill and Eileen White, have always supported and encouraged my love of history. One Christmas when I was a teenager they gave me a Battle of Hampton Roads puzzle. At the time I didn't know anything about the *Monitor,* but it piqued my interest. Many years later, in 2011, I loaned it to Anna for an exhibit at The Mariners' Museum called "Up Pops the *Monitor.*" I look forward to one day doing the puzzle with my daughters.

Finally, I thank my wife, Lauren, for her support during all of my many writing projects. When we first moved to Newport News in August 2009, we visited the USS *Monitor* Center and were astounded by the quality of the exhibits (I didn't know Anna yet, nor that she was the driving force behind it). Lauren allowed me to purchase a painting of the Battle of Hampton Roads in September 2009 that still hangs in our living room today. Now when we talk about monitors, however, our conversations more often have to do with whether or not our two beautiful daughters are sleeping ("Honey, have you seen the monitor?"). Charlotte (born in 2013) learned how to walk at the USS *Monitor* Center and loves meeting Abe (the marvelous George Buss) there every March at the Battle of Hampton Roads Weekend. We (or at least, I) hope that Clara (born 2016) will follow in her footsteps.

Introduction

On the afternoon of March 8, 1862, the Confederate ironclad ram *Virginia,* built upon the burned-out hulk of the steam screw frigate *Merrimack,* crawled slowly into Hampton Roads to challenge the Union blockade of the Confederate coastline. Before nightfall, the *Virginia* had wreaked havoc upon the Union blockading fleet: the USS *Cumberland* lay at the bottom of the Roads, her flags still defiantly flying while the surrendered USS *Congress* blazed ominously in the harbor until exploding spectacularly in the early morning hours of March 9. The USS *Monitor*—a vessel of a radical new design and completely untried in battle—arrived too late to make a difference on the 8th, but met the *Virginia* on the morning of the 9th in a contest that signaled the first time ironclad had met ironclad in combat. While their four-and-a-half-hour battle ended in a draw, it changed much of the future course of naval warfare.

Within days of the engagement, navies around the world were declaring an end to wooden construction and moving forward with their own ironclad building programs—many of which predated both the *Monitor* and the *Virginia.* Furthermore, the *Monitor*'s rotating gun turret design freed vessels from the strictures of broadside tactics by allowing the guns, rather than the entire vessel, to be turned, ushering in a new element of battleship design. Neither the *Virginia* nor the *Monitor* lived out that year, however. The *Virginia* was destroyed in May 1862 by her own crew to keep her from enemy hands, while the *Monitor* succumbed to a nor'easter on New Year's Eve off the coast of Cape Hatteras.

In 1978, just five years after the discovery of the Civil War ironclad USS *Monitor*'s wreck site, Lieutenant Edward Miller, USN, optimistically proclaimed in his work *U.S.S. Monitor: The Ship That Launched a Modern Navy,* that "only now can the complete story of the USS *Monitor* be written." Miller knew that only through the investigation of the archaeological remains of the vessel could she truly be understood. Yet by the end of his work he acknowledged that to write the truly complete story would require a recovery and conservation effort that was beyond the technological and financial capabilities of the research teams and agencies involved with the *Monitor* at that time. He concluded the volume with the hope that the discovery of the site "will not be the end of the *Monitor* story, but only a new beginning."[1]

On March 9, 2007, the National Oceanic and Atmospheric Administration (NOAA) and The Mariners' Museum opened the USS *Monitor* Center in Newport News, Virginia—a few short miles from the scene of the first battle between ironclads 145 years earlier. This state-of-the-art facility features an 18,000-square-foot exhibition, as well as a 20,000-square-foot conservation lab where the artifacts from the USS *Monitor*'s wreck site (NOAA's Monitor National Marine Sanctuary) are undergoing conservation. Here, large artifacts from the Union ironclad steamship *Monitor* sit in their baths of deionized water and chemical, slowly releasing 140 years' worth of chlorides as visitors look on through the windows of the Batten Conservation Facility. The slow reclamation of the iconic portions of this vessel stands in stark contrast to the frenzied efforts to complete construction of the ship within 100 days in late 1861 and early 1862. Conservators take pains to stop the corrosion brought on by decades in the harsh environment of the Atlantic Ocean. Moving slowly and carefully, they disassemble that which workmen assembled in foundries throughout the Northeast more than a century and a half ago. These young men and women are the first to lay eyes on what has been hidden since 1862.

Though seemingly mute, 210 tons of the *Monitor*, including the gun turret, guns, engine, and condenser have offered up volumes of information about the construction, modification, and ultimate destruction of the vessel. Previously unknown makers' marks emerge from meticulous cleaning. Dropped tools and personal items remind the staff that here in these iron walls lived men of flesh and blood. The connection between past and present is palpable.

The *Monitor* that lives within those tanks and tubs, and within the galleries of The Mariners' Museum is not the *Monitor* of March 9, 1862. Daily use, modification, and improvements made from that day until her sinking give us the evolving understanding of life lived in this "sub-aquatic system of naval architecture," as her inventor John Ericsson called her. The *Monitor* in those tanks and tubs is also the snapshot of a moment—a devastating moment that took the lives of 16 men and took the "pet of the people" down 240 feet into the dangerous waters of the aptly named Graveyard of the Atlantic in the early morning hours of December 31, 1862.

Through the artifacts themselves, and through the archival records, the *Monitor* of 1862 emerges—familiar, yet foreign. The boys who served below deck left us a documentary record that describes what they experienced during their time on the ship they affectionately called "Our Little *Monitor.*" The turret, too, serves as a time capsule that tells the ship's story in a way that the survivors could not. This volume is an attempt to bring those two stories together—that of the survivors, and that of the surviving artifacts.

Part 1 of this book gives a narrative history of the *Monitor,* from conception, to construction, to military service, to sinking, and finally to recovery and conservation. This is a unique history in that it draws from a wide array of sources, including textual, photographic, and archeological records. Part 2 tells the story—from launch to demise—through the unadulterated words of those who experienced the *Monitor* firsthand. In making our selections, we wanted to give readers the opportunity to become immersed in particular individuals' voices and perspectives, so we have broken Part 2 into six short chapters, each one reproducing previously unpublished letters and journal entries from a particular writer (or set of correspondents) for a particular time period.

Notes on the Text

In transcribing and editing the letters Part 2, we have kept the writers' grammar and spelling as close to the originals as possible. In a few instances we have inserted words in brackets to ensure that readers understand their meaning, and in chapter 9 we normalized the punctuation. Words that could not be deciphered are either noted as illegible or followed by a bracketed question mark or a bracketed guess with a question mark.

PART ONE

The *Monitor* in History and Memory

CHAPTER 1

The Origins of the CSS *Virginia*

On December 20, 1860, just six weeks after the election of Abraham Lincoln, South Carolina voted to secede from the Union. In Charleston the secession convention issued the following ordinance, which read in part: "We, the people of the State of South Carolina, in convention assembled, do declare and ordain . . . that the union now subsisting between South Carolina and other States, under the name of the 'United States of America,' is hereby dissolved."[1] South Carolina was the first of the states to leave the Union, and it would lobby other southern states to secede. By the time of Lincoln's inauguration on March 4, 1861, Mississippi, Florida, Alabama, Georgia, Louisiana, and Texas had followed suit.

Early on the morning of April 12, 1861, Confederate general Pierre Gustave Toutant Beauregard ordered the bombardment of Union-held Fort Sumter in Charleston Harbor. Sixty-eight men, under the command of Major Robert Anderson, held the fort for thirty-four hours before eventually surrendering in the face of a hopeless situation. One observer wrote: "All the pent-up hatred of the past months and years is voiced in the thunder of these cannon."[2] With these shots, the American Civil War—the bloodiest, most divisive conflict the country has ever known—was truly under way.

On April 15, 1861, President Lincoln called for 75,000 volunteers from loyal citizens to put down the rebellion. Originally called to serve for only ninety days, these men and boys poured into Union town centers throughout the spring and summer of 1861, their uniform buttons polished and their bands merrily playing—fired with patriotic enthusiasm.[3]

Virginians were split, politically and ideologically, over the issue of secession. But when Lincoln called for volunteers to fight their southern brethren, many in Virginia felt they had to take a stand. On April 17, 1861, Virginia seceded, soon to be followed by Arkansas, North Carolina, and

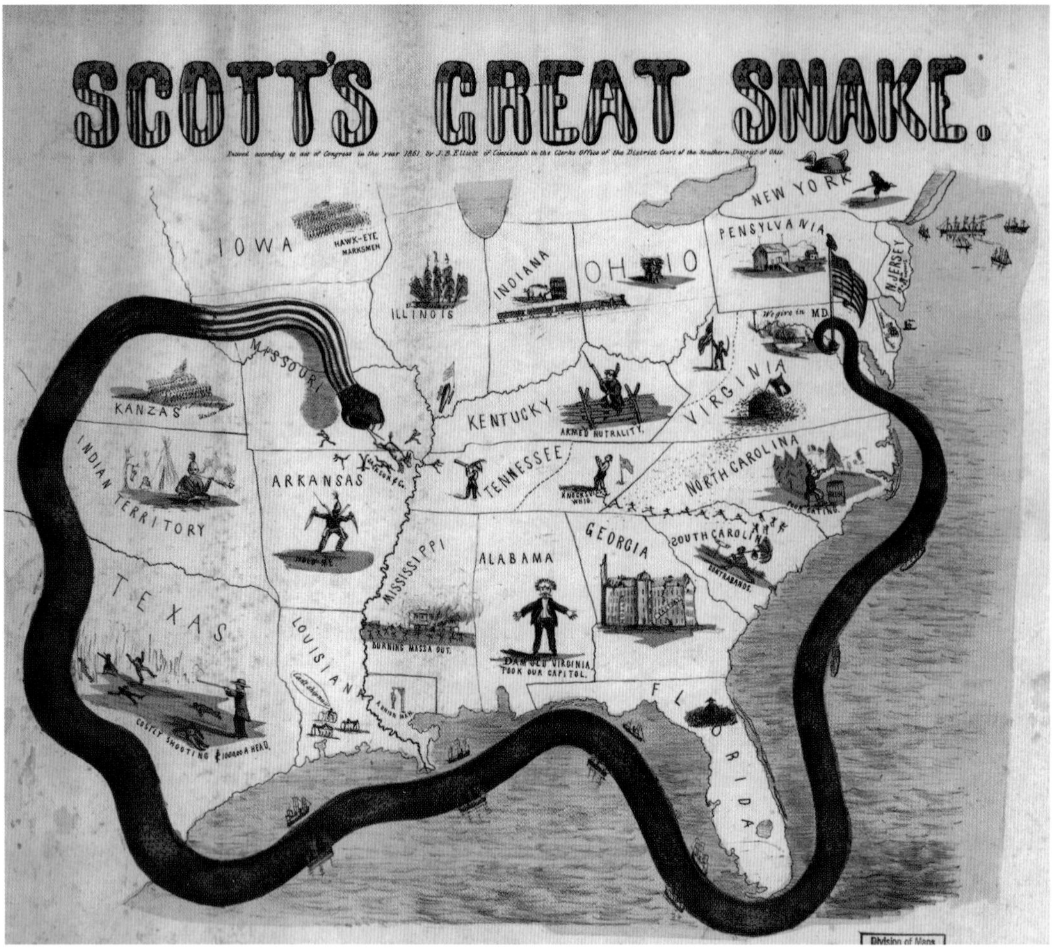

Fig. 1. Scott's Great Snake. Union general Winfield Scott's "Anaconda Plan" sought to strangle the Confederacy. (Library of Congress)

Tennessee. Virginia governor John Letcher wrote to U.S. Secretary of War Simon Cameron, "I have only to say that the militia of Virginia will not be furnished to the powers at Washington. . . . You have chosen to inaugurate civil war, and having done so, we will meet it in a spirit as determined as the Administration has exhibited toward the South."[4] With the loss of Virginia, the fight for control of Hampton Roads began in earnest.

Union war strategists knew that the Confederacy would have to rely on continual, steady trade with Europe in order to acquire the manufactured goods needed to conduct a modern war. Looking to cut off such trade, Lincoln issued a proclamation on April 19 "to set on foot a blockade of the ports" of South Carolina, Georgia, Alabama, Florida, Mississippi, Louisiana, and Texas—all states that had joined the Confederacy. The blockade of Virginia and North Carolina followed on April 27.[5]

The central, burning question for Lincoln was how to restore the Union. His general in chief, Winfield Scott, realized that the Union would have to attack and invade the South, and that therefore the Confederates would be fighting close to home and close to their sources of supply. Scott needed time to expand his tiny regular army to attack, but above all he needed to cut off the Confederate supply lines. Scott proposed to put the squeeze on the South by enforcing a naval blockade that stretched over 3,500 miles of coast from Virginia to Mexico and up the Mississippi from New Orleans to New Madrid Bend. This so-called Anaconda Plan could only succeed over time: the South would not starve overnight, so patience was an essential part of Scott's strategy. While the South suffocated, he reasoned, the Union army would attack and triumph.

The State of the Navy in 1861

On March 7, 1861, Abraham Lincoln appointed Gideon Welles to be secretary of the navy. Welles, however, was not a naval man as such, though he had been chief of the navy's Bureau of Provisions and Clothing from 1846 until his attention turned to his (failed) campaign for the Senate in 1850. In fact, Lincoln was far more interested in Welles for his politics than his webbed feet. The son of a shipping merchant, Welles was a lawyer, a journalist, and a politician. Also, as a newly minted Republican, Welles had avidly supported Lincoln's nomination at the 1860 Republican Convention in Chicago, though it may have been as much to keep William H. Seward from the nomination as it was to secure it for Lincoln. Welles, like many former Democrats, had been opposed to Seward on the grounds that Seward stood for wasteful government spending, an "imperial" federal government, and was an advocate for stronger ties to Great Britain. Lincoln, nonetheless, appointed his onetime rival Seward as his new secretary of state. Welles, Lincoln reasoned, would provide a good balance to the Whiggish notions of Seward and others within his cabinet. Also of importance, Lincoln specifically wanted "a man of democratic antecedents from New England."[6] Welles became a favorite with political cartoonists and was dubbed the "Rip Van Winkle of the Navy Department," in part because of his enormous white beard but also for his secrecy and avoidance of the press.[7] In contrast, Welles's assistant secretary, Gustavus Vasa Fox, appointed to that post in August 1861, had a great deal of naval experience. Fox had served in the navy, passing as midshipman in 1838. He had also spent time as part of the U.S. Coastal Survey (the organization that would later become a primary component of the National Oceanic and Atmospheric Administration, or NOAA).[8]

The navy these men inherited in 1861 was not exceptional, but neither was it moribund. Younger officers, though unable to advance as rapidly through the ranks because of the tenure system, were not bound so much by naval custom as were their elders. They would be the generation to accept the new technologies in ways the older officers, who had spent their entire careers on wooden sailing vessels, could not. In addition, the Naval Academy had been established in 1850 at Annapolis expressly for the training of new naval officers. So at mid-century American naval officers were well trained—and spent the majority of their time on exploratory or diplomatic missions.

By 1861 the U.S. Navy had ninety ships, but only fifty-two were considered serviceable. Of those, only four were in northern waters where they could be easily deployed against the rebellion. Four vessels were in Pensacola, Florida, and one was in the Great Lakes. Twenty-four vessels were spread out around the world, in the Mediterranean, the Pacific, off the coast of Africa and Brazil, and in the Caribbean. The rest were laid up "in ordinary," which meant that they were undergoing repairs of some sort or were simply mothballed.[9] Furthermore, this was a deepwater navy, ill suited to coastal and harbor engagements, which would be precisely what they would encounter during the war to come.

In the Confederacy there effectively *was* no navy. There was, however, a secretary of the navy, for President Jefferson Davis had appointed former Florida senator Stephen Russell Mallory to that post in February 1861. In the 1850s Mallory had been the chairman of the U.S. Senate Naval Affairs Committee and an active backer of naval reform. Mallory was a visionary and had followed the developments in the Crimea closely. Shortly after his appointment, he wrote that the Union "has built a navy; we have a navy to build."[10] This new navy would need to be composed of "a class of vessels hitherto unknown to naval service," combining steam power, devastating ordnance, and iron sides if it was to be effective.[11]

The Confederacy also had a large pool of naval officers from which to draw. Nearly three hundred officers had resigned their commissions and "gone south." Unfortunately, they had few crew members to command. Most career sailors hailed from the North, and the Confederacy's problems were compounded by the fact that for some time now the South had relied almost exclusively on northern ships to carry cargo.

The South also had no large vessels. What did exist, however, was a large number of coastal and riverine craft. The only private shipyard in the Confederacy was in New Orleans. The other two were federally controlled—Gosport Navy Yard in Portsmouth, Virginia, and Pensacola Navy Yard in Florida. There were no major foundries save one, the Tredegar Ironworks in Richmond, Virginia.

The South had rail transport, but only ten ports had rail connections to the interior, and of these only six had interstate rail. All but Norfolk

Fig. 2. This ca. 1862 map features the southeastern part of Virginia from the Chesapeake Bay and York River to the Blackwater River. (Library of Congress)

had shallow waters, thus keeping larger vessels from entering directly. The infrastructure of the roads system in the Confederacy was also substandard, with very few paved roads. Even the Confederacy's population was lacking in comparison to the North: there were 9 million people in the Confederacy, but 3.5 million were enslaved. The Union had a population of roughly 23 million, the vast majority of whom were free. Even though barred from active service in the Union army until 1863, blacks were able to serve in the Union navy, though limited initially, at the outbreak of the war, to the lowest pay rating of "boy."[12] Both the Union and the Confederacy desired control of the deepwater harbor of Hampton Roads. For the Union, it offered access to the southern Atlantic coast—a target of Scott's Anaconda Plan. In addition, rivers running into the Roads offered direct links to crucial Confederate sites: the Elizabeth River provided an avenue to Gosport Navy Yard, and the James River led directly to the Confederate capital city of Richmond. For the Confederates, control of Hampton Roads meant direct access to the Union capital of Washington, D.C., and to Baltimore, an important industrial and shipping center within the Union.

Gideon Welles understood that Gosport Navy Yard would be a tempting target for pro-secession Virginians. Therefore, Welles ordered Flag Officer Garrett J. Pendergrast, commander of the USS *Cumberland,* to keep his ship in Gosport "and, in case of invasion, insurrection, or violence of any kind, to suppress it, repelling assault by force." At the same time, however, Welles ordered the navy yard's commander, Charles Stewart McCauley, to remove all public property from Gosport—in this case, any of the warships "in ordinary" there that were laid up in the dockyard with their ordnance, masts, sails, and rigging removed and the upper deck roofed over to protect the interior spaces. At Gosport this included the *Merrimack,* the *Germantown,* the *Plymouth,* and the *Dolphin.* McCauley was to prepare the vessels in the yard for departure. Welles was particularly keen to have the *Merrimack* moved to Philadelphia to keep her from harm's way, for though she was undergoing repairs, she was still a formidable weapon that Welles wanted to keep for the Union, and out of the hands of the Confederacy.[13]

On April 14, 1861, Commander James Alden and U.S. Navy chief engineer Benjamin Franklin Isherwood arrived at Gosport Navy Yard to find that McCauley had done very little. Alden had orders to take command of the USS *Merrimack* and bring her to Philadelphia if it appeared that evacuating the navy yard was the only recourse. But Union naval officials still held out hope that the yard and the vessels and material within it could be saved. Assessing the situation, Isherwood immediately set to work reassembling the *Merrimack's* engine. He had crews working at a

Fig. 3. The USS *Merrimack* prior to conversion to the CSS *Virginia*. (The Mariners' Museum, Newport News, Virginia)

feverish pace around the clock. Meanwhile, Welles continued to apply pressure to the hapless McCauley to protect the navy's assets at the yard. The worst thing that could happen, in Welles's estimation, would be to allow the yard, with its drydock, to fall into enemy hands.[14]

Isherwood completed repairs to the USS *Merrimack* on April 18. But the Virginia legislature had passed the ordinance of secession the day before. Accordingly, Virginia governor John Letcher ordered Major General William Booth Taliaferro of the Virginia Militia to Norfolk to occupy Gosport Navy Yard. Citizens in Norfolk and Portsmouth created an impromptu vigilance committee and began placing disruptions to navigation off Sewell's Point to hinder Union access into and out of the yard.[15] Other citizens created a ruse to make McCauley believe that vast numbers of troops were arriving by train—a ruse carried out by William Mahone, who was chief engineer of the Norfolk and Petersburg Railroad. Mahone's biographer wrote that "by means of his Railroad control, [Mahone] used his stock so as to convey the idea reinforcements were continually arriving to the rebels, sending locomotives, away, quietly, to return, as noisily, blowing their whistles and ringing their bells, as if drawing after them loads of fresh troops and supplies."[16] Though Isherwood proclaimed the

Fig. 4. The destruction of the Gosport Navy Yard at Norfolk, as depicted in *Harper's Pictorial History of the Civil War* (1894). (The Mariners' Museum, Newport News, Virginia)

frigate ready for sea, yard commander McCauley denied approval for the *Merrimack* to leave Gosport.

On April 20 Virginia militia forces began advancing on the yard. Although the Union had done a great deal of work to rescue as much as possible, the plan ultimately shifted to one that would destroy the yard and its drydock so that the Confederates could not use these assets against the Union. (One New Yorker wrote to Welles, begging him, "for God's sake mine and totally destroy the dry dock there and destroy all the shipbuilding materials and apparatus. The want of a dock will seriously damage the traitors.") Ships that had been nearly ready for departure were instead scuttled and burned to keep them out of Confederate hands. McCauley, confused, despondent, and possibly drunk, refused to leave Quarters A and had to be physically carried out by fleeing troops. Though Union naval officers tried their best to ensure the utter destruction of the yard, Confederate sympathizers captured the two men tasked with blowing up the drydock (Captain H. G. Wright of the Corps of Engineers and Commander John Rodgers of the U.S. Navy) and rendered useless the kegs of powder they had planted. The yard was damaged but not destroyed.[17]

The USS *Pennsylvania, Germantown, Raritan, Columbia,* and *Dolphin* burned, while the *Delaware, Columbus,* and *Merrimack* burned and sank at their moorings in the conflagration. Union forces chose not to destroy the *United States* (she would become the Confederate receiving ship *Confederate States*), principally because they considered her too old and decrepit. However, they also spared her out of veneration for her years of service, as she was the first of the original six frigates commissioned in the U.S. Navy in 1797. The USS *Cumberland,* built as a frigate in 1842, had been converted (or "razeed") into a sloop of war in 1857 and was certainly serviceable. Having her decks cut down allowed her to carry more powerful guns and be more efficient under sail. Thus transformed, and equipped with new rifled guns, she had become a formidable vessel and one that Welles was anxious to save. Union sailors towed her to safety by the eerie light of the burning navy yard.[18] One sailor aboard the *Cumberland* wrote home that it was "the greatest fire I ever saw."[19] Under that same light, the Virginia State Navy moved in.

And what of McCauley? Despondent, he was placed on board the *Cumberland.* By the end of 1861 he was retired, having been promoted to the rank of commodore. McCauley never forgot the chaos of the final days at Gosport, however. The loss of ships and matériel was troubling enough to him, but the resignation of his officers and their subsequent service with the Confederacy hurt him deeply. He recalled, "I could not believe it possible that a set of men, whose reputations were so high in the Navy, could ever desert their posts, and throw off their allegiance to the country they had sworn, to defend and protect." Welles was understandably disappointed by McCauley's actions in April 1861. He later wrote, "The fidelity and patriotism of Comodore [*sic*] McCauley, who was in command of the yard, were unquestioned and his reputation as a good and efficient officer all admitted.... Subsequent events proved him faithful but his energy and decision had left him, and he proved unequal, in almost every respect, to this occasion."[20] McCauley's obituary also stands as a sad testimony to the bitter end of a once glorious career. On May 23, 1869, the *New York Times* posted a brief notice about McCauley's death, stating, "The Congressional Committee appointed to investigate the affair failing to exonerate him entirely from blame in the matter, he felt that his honor as an officer had been wounded, his reputation blemished, the effect of which was to plunge him into the deepest melancholy, and causing disease of the heart, of which he died." The war would have many casualties who did not die in battle. McCauley was one such.[21]

Debate would arise among observers at the time about who was to blame for "the disgrace at Norfolk," as *New York Tribune* editor Horace Greeley called it. Senator John P. Hale of New Hampshire, the chairman of the Naval Committee, issued a report castigating Welles for not sending reinforcements to Norfolk. "The committee can but regard this as a negligence and dereliction of official duty of the gravest character," wrote Hale. "That it was a part of that fatal policy of temporization and negotiation with armed and causeless rebellion against the rightful authority of the laws, and of scrupulous tenderness toward seditious citizens, which seems to have actuated the government at that time, renders this remissness scarcely less excusable." Following Hale's lead, Greeley wrote a few years later in his history of the war, *The American Conflict* (1866), "Thus ended the most shameful, cowardly, disastrous performance that stains the annals of the American Navy."[22]

Secretary Welles took exception to the criticisms of politicians and newspapermen. "In the light of subsequent events the performance may be condemned," he wrote in a private reflection on the first few months of the war. "It was certainly unfortunate and disastrous. There were feebleness and incapacity in McCauley, and treachery and infidelity on the part of his subordinates—matters shameful indeed, but I am aware of no evidence of cowardice, even in the pusillanimous commander." Moreover, Welles noted that Congress had not made any provision for the situation (he did not mention that Congress was out of session from March 4 until July 4, 1861). Men like McCauley did not yet "realize that such a tornado was upon them, and at the commencement they hesitated to be the first to imbrue their hands in the blood of their countrymen." Then, with obvious rage at the hypocrisy of those who spoke but would not fight, he concluded, "Mr John P. Hale and Mr Horace Greeley might have done differently and saved the yard and public property and Norfolk." Welles continued, "The misfortune was bad enough when truly and fairly stated, but aggravated by the misrepresentations and exaggerations of reckless and unscrupulous men like Hale, and the partizan fictions of Greeley, great injustice is done to officers of undoubted patriotism."[23]

In late April 1861 a Virginia "secessionist" wrote in the Confederate-friendly *Baltimore Exchange,* "There are now twelve [Union] vessels of war in the Roads, and Norfolk and the James River ports are for the present effectually blockaded. Commodore Pendergrast who is in command, is universally detested by the inhabitants of this place."[24] Federal forces also had control of the tip of the Virginia Peninsula on the north side of Hampton Roads, from Camp Butler at Newport News Point to Fortress Monroe at Old Point Comfort. Confederate forces controlled the peninsula from Newmarket Creek westward and had constructed three major lines of fortifications to protect Richmond. Confederates also controlled the south side of Hampton Roads, including the towns of Norfolk and Portsmouth. In the aftermath of the destruction of Gosport, the Virginia State Navy (which would shortly be subsumed into the Confederate navy on June 8, 1861) had acquired several damaged yet serviceable pieces of war matériel; scores of pieces of ordnance, three damaged Union ships, the *Merrimack, United States,* and *Germantown;* and claimed for itself the finest granite dry dock in the country.

The sunken *Merrimack* posed a significant interference with navigation in the waters near the navy yard for the Virginians, who immediately seized control of the yard following the Union departure. Thus the new commandant, French Forrest, entered into a contract on May 18, 1861, with the Portsmouth-based firm of B & J Baker & Company to raise the hull. On May 30 brothers Barnabas and Joseph Baker, along with their nephew Alexander, successfully raised the burned-out hull of the *Merrimack* from the Elizabeth River. Barnabas, who lived in Portsmouth, and Joseph, who lived in Berkeley, were specialists in salvage and "submarine diving." Employing divers who used heavily weighted, surface-supplied diving suits, they were able to repair holes in the hull of the vessel, whereupon they used a steam pump on one of their tugs to pump the water out. As the *Richmond Daily Dispatch* reported on June 1, 1861:

> The celebrated wreckers, the Bakers, of whom I have heretofore made mention, have been engaged for the last four days in making the necessary preparations for raising the steam frigate Merrimac—the same splendid specimen of naval architecture which the vandals, under Pendergrast and company left in flames, and which was burnt to the water's

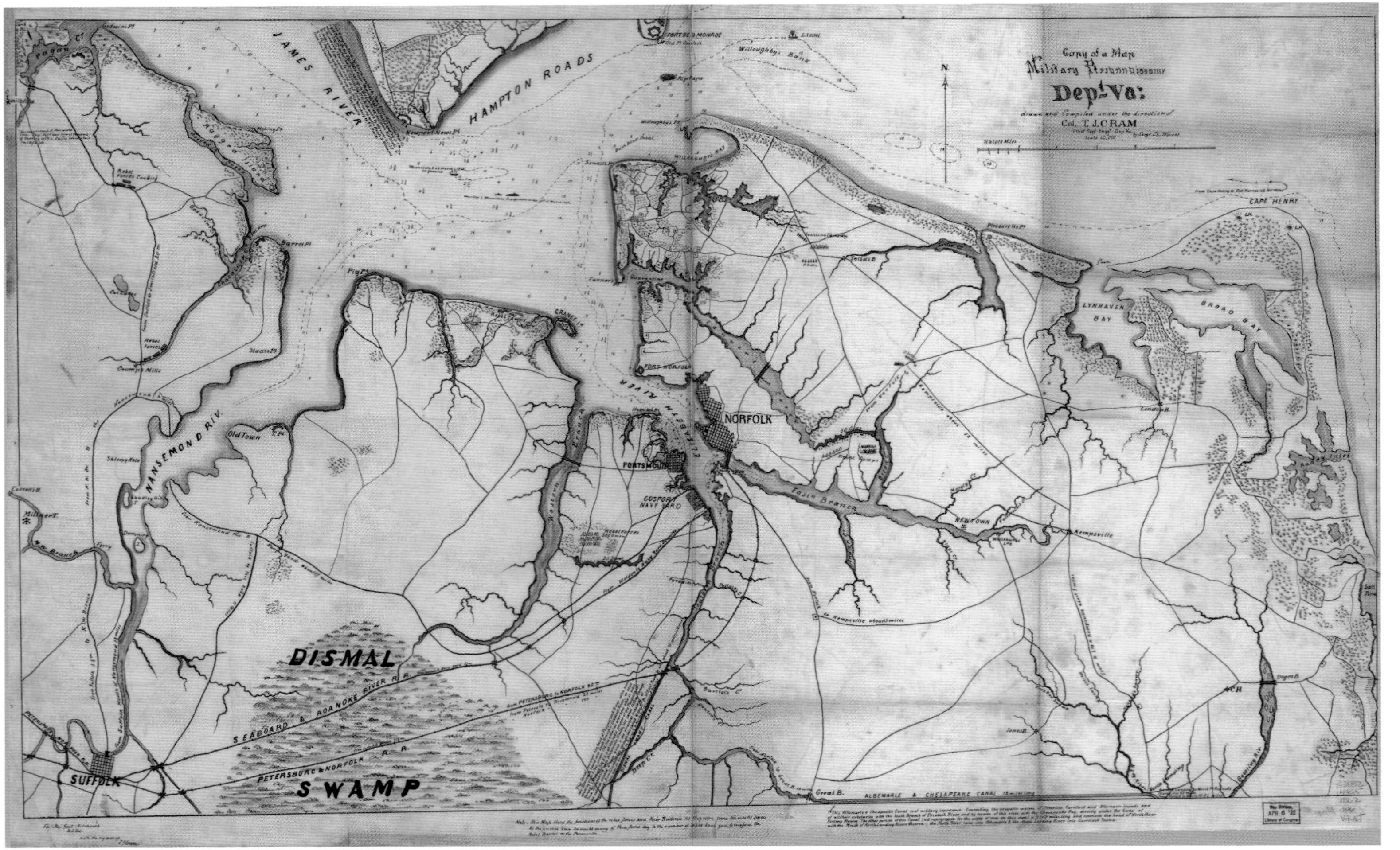
Copy of a Map
Military Reconnoissance
Dept. Va:
drawn and Compiled under the direction of
Col. T. J. CRAM
JAMES RIVER
HAMPTON ROADS
FORTRESS MONROE
Willoughbys Bank
CAPE HENRY
LYNHAVEN BAY
BROAD BAY
NORFOLK
PORTSMOUTH
GOSPORT NAVY YARD
FORT NORFOLK
ELIZABETH RIVER
Eastn Branch
NEW TOWN
Kempsville
NANSEMOND RIV.
Old Town
DISMAL
SWAMP
SEABOARD & ROANOKE RIVER R.R.
PETERSBURG & NORFOLK R.R.
SUFFOLK
ALBEMARLE & CHESAPEAKE CANAL
Great B.

edge. Yesterday morning, at five o'clock, four steam pumps were put in motion, the holes battened and leaks having been previously stopped, and indeed, every preparation made preparatory to the operation of pumping. The four pumps discharged one hundred and sixty barrels of water each minute, or forty barrels each.

Fig. 5. Map of military reconnaissance, Department of Virginia. This map from ca. 1862 features the locations of the grounded *Minnesota,* as well as the *Monitor* and *Virginia* locked in close combat on March 9, 1862. (Library of Congress)

The report added that "the damage to the engine is not of a serious character. Under the superintendence and management of Chief Engineer Michael Quinn, this splendid machinery will be rendered as fit for service as before."[25] Confederate naval constructor John Luke Porter ordered the hull moved to the dry dock, and found that the "bottom of the hull, boiler and heavy and costly parts of the engine [were] . . . but little injured."[26]

"A Class of Vessels Hitherto Unknown to Naval Service"

Confederate secretary of the navy Stephen Russell Mallory knew that no ordinary vessel would be able to break the Union blockade. Mallory had studied European naval technology, including ironclads, and he urged Confederate president Jefferson Davis to "adopt a class of vessels hitherto unknown to naval service."[27] Since time was short, Mallory began a two-pronged effort to obtain ironclads. Some he would try to purchase in Europe. Others he would have built within the Confederacy. However, if the Confederate navy was to build its own ironclad, it first needed a design. In a meeting with Mallory in late June 1861, ordnance expert Lieutenant John Mercer Brooke presented an idea for an ironclad with submerged ends and a sloped casemate, or shield, housing a battery of powerful rifled guns. At the same meeting, naval constructor John Luke Porter presented a model (likely a paper plan) of a floating steam battery, which also featured a casemate design. Porter's plan offered nearly 360 degrees of firing ability from a gun deck that could accommodate six XI-inch Dahlgren smoothbores.

William Price Williamson, a naval engineer who had also resigned his commission in the U.S. Navy, was present at the meeting as well to give advice on propulsion for the nascent ironclad. "By unanimous consent," Brooke later wrote in his journal, the three men, with Mallory's blessing, agreed on a design that combined elements of both Brooke's and Porter's concepts. Porter offered to draft the new plan. Only one problem remained, however. The Confederacy had no quick way to produce a suitable engine to power an ironclad of any design. But it did have the engine salvaged from the *Merrimack.* Though that engine was designed for a deep draft frigate, and not Brooke and Porter's floating battery, Williamson suggested that perhaps the *Merrimack* herself could be converted into an ironclad.[28]

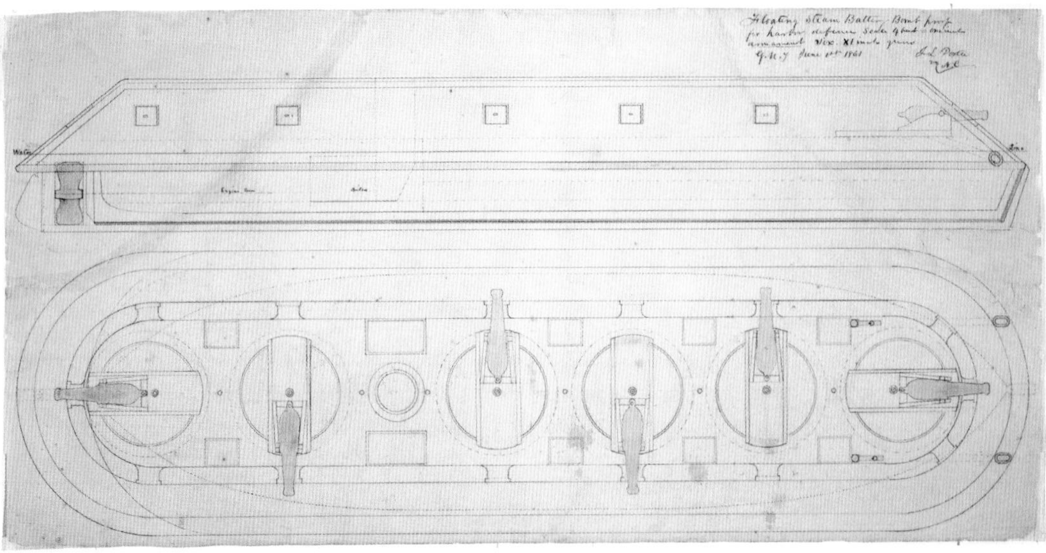

Fig. 6. John Luke Porter's original plan for an ironclad vessel, seen here, differed significantly from the way the *Virginia* was ultimately built. (The Mariners' Museum, Newport News, Virginia)

Returning to Portsmouth, Porter set about adapting Brooke's concept to the *Merrimack* while Williamson surveyed the engines. By July 11, 1861, the ironclad project was officially under way; Secretary Mallory issued orders to French Forrest at Gosport to "build, equip, and fit [the *Merrimack*] in all respects according to her designs and plans. . . . you will see that the work progresses without delay to completion."[29] The projected launch date for the converted vessel was November 1861.

The first task was to remove the burned portions and assess the overall condition of the hull. Finding the hull sound, workmen then began the process of cutting the hull down to a straight line about three feet above the waterline. This would provide the platform upon which they could construct the casemate. Meanwhile, Williamson had the task of overhauling the engine. Since this same engine had caused the *Merrimack* to be at Gosport for repairs, Williamson was already aware of its shortcomings. His task was made even more difficult by the fact that the engine had spent some time at the bottom of the Elizabeth River. Components needed to be cleaned or replaced and re-lubricated. It was vitally important that the engine work as well as possible, given its history. For, unlike the original *Merrimack,* which used sails as her principal means of motive power, this new ironclad would have only an engine to power the vessel.[30]

Another task involved trying to ascertain how thick the iron needed to be to withstand U.S. naval ordnance. Accordingly, ordnance officer John Mercer Brooke ordered tests, since he was relatively sure that one-inch-thick plate, the thickest the nearby rolling mill at Tredegar was able to produce, would not be enough to protect the converted *Merrimack.* A test conducted on Jamestown Island in early October 1861 showed that

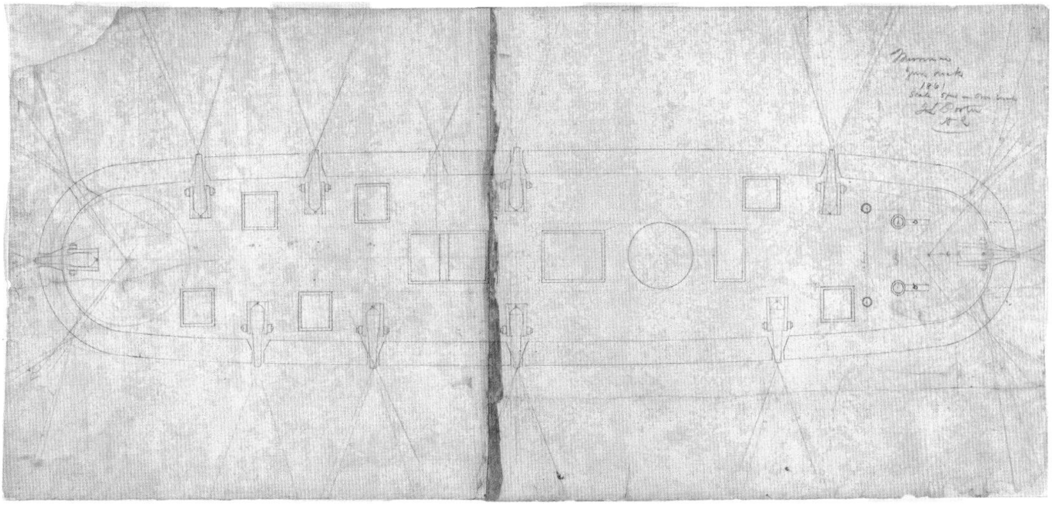

Fig. 7. Design for the CSS *Virginia* by John Luke Porter. (The Mariners' Museum, Newport News, Virginia)

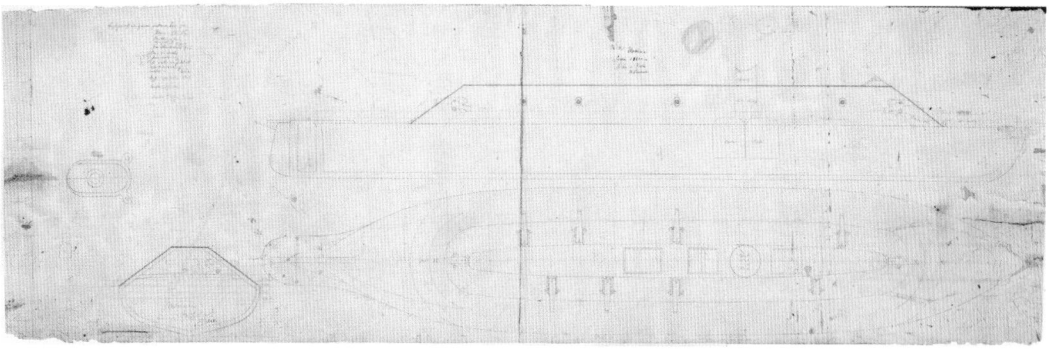

Fig. 8. Another of John Luke Porter's designs for the CSS *Virginia.* (The Mariners' Museum, Newport News, Virginia)

AMERICAN COLORTYPE CO.
2. "MERRIMAC" IN DRY DOCK, BEING CONVERTED INTO THE IRON BATTERY "VIRGINIA."
FROM ORIGINAL PAINTING BY B. A. RICHARDSON.

Fig. 9. Postcard, ca. 1906, depicting the *Merrimack* in dry dock during her conversion. (The Mariners' Museum, Newport News, Virginia)

he was correct: solid shot from an 8-inch Columbiad shattered an iron plate and traveled five inches into the wood backing of the target. From this, Brooke calculated that two two-inch-thick layers of iron, backed by nearly two feet of wood, would be needed for the casemate. Tredegar was forced to retool its machinery to produce the thicker plate, which then had to be shipped from Richmond to Norfolk. This was the cause of many delays to the production schedule: transportation by land down the peninsula or on either the James or York River was impossible because of the Union Army at Fortress Monroe and the Union navy's blockading fleet in Hampton Roads. The material thus took a circuitous route from Richmond, down into North Carolina, then back up to Gosport from the south. Delays were further compounded by the Confederate army's penchant for commandeering some of these railcars and dumping the iron pieces over the side in favor of room for troop and other material transport.[31]

Despite these delays, the *Merrimack* continued to evolve. The sloped casemate of the nascent *Virginia* would become the feature that would define Confederate ironclads (as well as some Union ironclads) throughout the war. The new vessel's casemate was 170 feet long, beginning 29 feet from the bow. The walls of the casemate would be 28 inches thick, constructed in five layers of 8 by 8-foot sections of timber and iron. The layers were arranged from interior to exterior thus: 4 inches of oak board laid horizontally, 8 inches of yellow pine studs laid vertically, 12 inches of white pine studs laid horizontally, and 2 inches of iron plate laid horizontally; finally, the exterior showed 2 inches of iron plate laid vertically.[32] The alternating horizontal and vertical layers made it resilient and nearly impossible to penetrate. The layers of wood could provide shock absorption, and additional "knees" (brackets of live oak) were added to the design to fit under the original *Merrimack* gun deck, which supported the weight of the casemate. The roof and the casemate walls worked together like an arch, protecting both guns and gun crew.

Naval constructor Porter calculated that all of this would require a thousand tons of iron. However, by the summer of 1861, Tredegar Ironworks in Richmond had already used up its prewar supply of iron in the construction process. To continue supplying Gosport with materials, hundreds of tons of old tools, obsolete guns, and railroad iron had to be melted down and rolled into plate to armor the converted vessel. (For tables showing the specifications of the *Merrimack* and *Virginia* before and after conversion, see the appendix.)

The still-unfinished Confederate ironclad was finally christened, launched, and commissioned as the CSS *Virginia* on February 17, 1862. Even with her new design, many people, including the ironclad's own crew, continued calling the *Virginia* by her old U.S. Navy name, the *Mer-*

rimack. But *Virginia* was her name, "not *Merrimac*," wrote Confederate colonel Charles Norris, for that had "a nasal twang equally abhorrent to sentiment and to melody, and meanly compares with the sonorous sweetness of '*Virginia*.' She fought under Confederate colors, and her fame belongs to all of us; but there was a peculiar fitness in the name we gave her. *In* Virginia, *of* Virginia iron and wood, and *by* Virginians was she built, and in Virginia's waters, now made classic by her exploits, she made a record which shall live forever."[33]

The CSS *Virginia* may not have been the ironclad that Brooke, Porter, Williamson, and Mallory had initially envisioned, but she was menacing nonetheless. Her design included a number of features that made her a formidable warship—one capable of taking on the powerful Union navy single-handedly. The sloping armor of her casemate design was a radical departure from the more upright walls of wooden warships. Angling the sides was a simple strategy for deflecting shot and preventing it from penetrating the casemate's walls—and it worked. The principle of sloped sides can still be seen in today's armored tanks, stealth planes, and the U.S. Navy's latest guided missile destroyer, USS *Zumwalt*.[34]

Brooke specified that the *Virginia*'s bow and stern should be submerged two feet to improve her buoyancy and speed, just as he had thought in his original proposal. The design also protected the ship from enemy fire, for nothing could be seen of her afloat but the casemate itself. Mallory observed, "The novel plan of submerging the ends of the ship and the eaves of the casemate was the peculiar and distinctive feature. . . . It was never before adopted."[35] Because her deck was designed to be almost awash when at sea, Brooke devised a rough breakwater on the bow to keep water from splashing into the bow gunports.

While the *Virginia* was to be a very modern vessel, the weapon mounted on her bow was quite ancient—a ram. Though long obsolete as a naval weapon, when steam propulsion replaced wind power, naval engineers reconsidered the use of the ram. Mallory knew that ramming could be a devastating offensive tactic and that "even without guns the [*Virginia*] would be formidable."[36]

Displacement, too, was a critical calculation, but in this, unfortunately, Porter was mistaken in his estimates. When the *Virginia* was launched in February 1862, the armored shield barely reached below the water's surface. As the ship consumed both fuel and ammunition in the course of combat, she would ride even higher in the water, perhaps even exposing the wooden hull to enemy fire. Executive Officer Catesby ap Roger Jones complained, "We are least protected where we need it most."[37] Problems continued to crop up in the construction: the last-minute addition of the ram resulted in a cracked flange, and the connection between the new

Fig. 10. Commander Catesby ap R. Jones. (Naval History and Heritage Command)

casemate and the existing hull was not a good fit. All of these weaknesses would have serious consequences in battle.

Placement of the guns on the gun deck was problematic as well. The sharp slope of the casemate meant that while there was a comfortable seven feet of headroom running down the length of the deck, the headroom tapered off sharply to port and starboard. Furthermore, in order to allow room for recoil and loading, the guns had to be staggered along the two broadsides.[38] Ten guns could fit on the deck this way, but handling the guns during combat would be difficult. Still, the *Virginia* would be equipped with the most devastating battery the Confederates could muster. Her engines may have been weak, but her guns would not be. In fact, the Confederates kept some of the *Merrimack*'s original IX-inch Dahlgrens as part of the CSS *Virginia*'s battery, and they supplemented these with other IX-inch Dahlgrens that had been cast at Tredegar and were on hand at Gosport.[39] The six Dahlgrens were already powerful guns, but Brooke made them even more deadly to wooden vessels by modifying two of them to fire hot shot. A special furnace was installed in the engine room to heat solid shot to a cherry red (around 1500° F) for the guns during combat.

Four more guns rounded out the battery. At both the bow and stern was a 7-inch Brooke rifle (actually a banded and sleeved IX-inch Dahlgren) on modified pivot mounts. In the broadsides there were two 6.4-inch Brooke rifles that were modified 32-pounders. This new "Brooke" gun was the type of advanced weapon the Confederates would need to confront the Union navy. Superior in "strength, precision, and range" to any other cannon available in America, the Brooke gun owed its success to the banding of the gun at the breech, which prevented it from bursting when fired.[40] The 32-pound guns on the *Virginia* were prototypes for the 6.4-inch Brooke rifle. Brooke installed the 7-inch rifles of his own design in the CSS *Virginia*'s bow and stern, each mounted on a semicircular pivot that allowed the gun to be aimed through one of three gunports at the ends of the casemate. This arrangement offered greater flexibility in aiming the gun without having to turn the ship.

With intelligence that the Union was tentatively stepping into ironclad design, Brooke also designed a flat-headed, wrought-iron, elongated shot, or bolt, for use in his rifled cannon, a weapon that could punch a hole through armor plate. But in the rush to complete the CSS *Virginia,* Brooke instructed Tredegar Iron Works to concentrate on producing explosive shells instead. After all, he reasoned, the *Virginia*'s first engagement would be with wooden ships.

Steering the new ironclad would not be easy, although it would not be radically different from any large sailing vessel. Porter designed a pilothouse at the forward end of the vessel, a conical cast-iron structure protruding from the top of the casemate. However, he had to compromise ease of viewing with protection for the men within the structure. Access to the pilothouse was via a ladder on the gun deck. While Porter's plans clearly show the positioning of the ladder, the operation of the forward pivot gun made the construction of a fixed ladder impossible. It is likely that a rope ladder was used instead. When the *Virginia* was under way, the platform might hold the captain and his lieutenant, as well as one or two pilots. An auxiliary steering wheel may have been installed within the pilothouse, with steering ropes running aft to the original tiller/rudder mechanism of the old *Merrimack,* but there is no documentary evidence to that effect. Principal steering would have taken place aft, with an iron wheel constructed for the new ironclad. Instructions from the pilothouse would have been relayed either by speaking tube or by crew runners whose job was to convey instructions from the pilothouse to the wheel.[41]

The ironclad had her weaponry. She now needed a commanding officer.

Believing that the secession of Maryland from the Union was imminent, Captain Franklin Buchanan—first superintendent of the United States Naval Academy, Mexican War hero, and commandant of the Washington Navy Yard when the war broke out—resigned his commission in the U.S. Navy on April 22, 1861, and waited for Maryland to become part of the Confederacy. Recent events in his home state had certainly led him to that belief. There had been bloodshed on Pratt Street in Baltimore three days earlier, on April 19, as citizens sympathetic to the Confederate cause attacked a Massachusetts regiment. The regiment had responded with gunfire, killing twelve. The press had had a field day, and all signs pointed toward a Confederate Maryland. Buchanan, reflecting on it later, even said that at the time "the belief was general throughout the state that she was virtually OUT of the Union." When Maryland's secession did not come to pass, however, Buchanan requested reinstatement in the U.S. Navy. Secretary Welles immediately rejected the request. Later that year Buchanan chose to join the Confederate navy.[42] Appointed as flag officer for the Confederate fleet in Hampton Roads on February 24, 1862, his flag vessel would be the *Virginia.*

While there was an excellent pool of former U.S. Navy officers from which to choose, ordinary sailors were harder to find. When recruiting stations in Norfolk and Richmond failed to yield the 320 men needed to

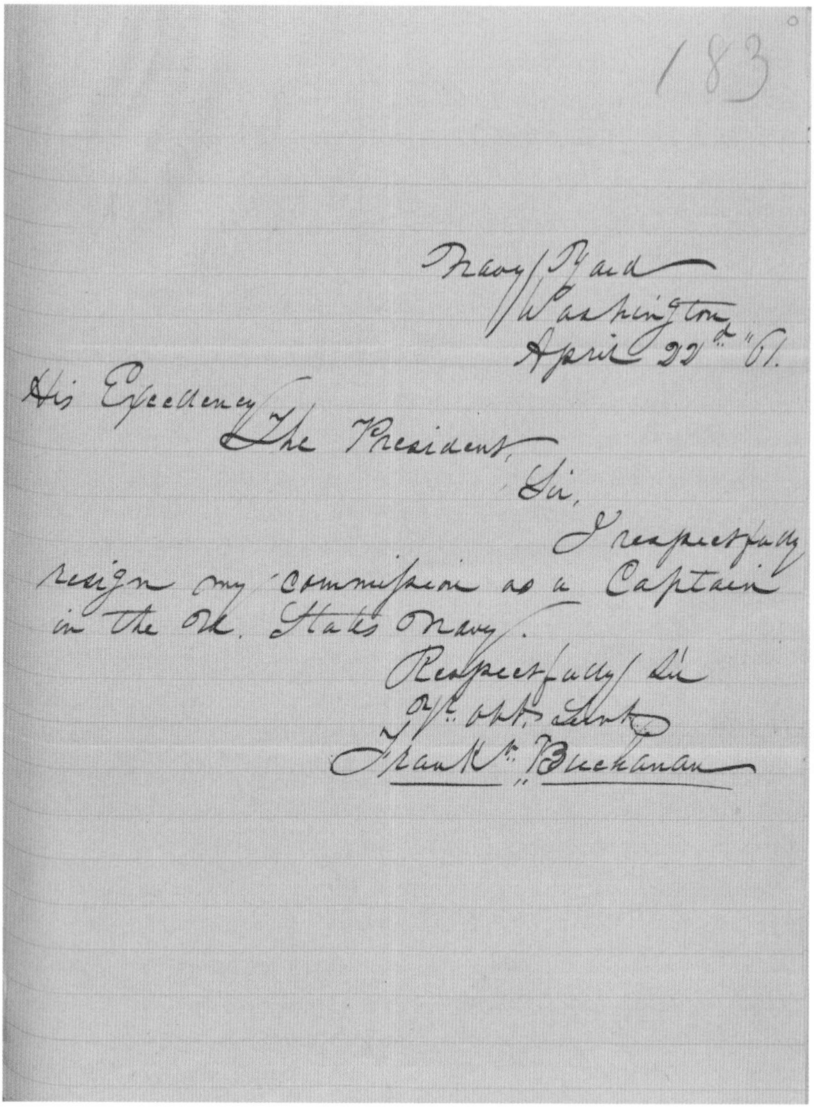

183

Navy Yard
Washington
April 22nd '61.

His Excellency
The President,
Sir,
I respectfully resign my commission as a Captain in the U. States Navy.
Respectfully Sir
Yr. obt. Servt.
Frankn. Buchanan

Fig. 11. Resignation letter from Franklin Buchanan to Abraham Lincoln. (National Archives)

man the CSS *Virginia,* they reached out to artillerymen from nearby Confederate army units. Finally, on March 6, 1862, the last contingent was mustered when Captain Thomas Kevill and his United Artillery Company (Company E, 41st Virginia Volunteer Infantry) volunteered to go on board the ironclad Steamer *Virginia.* Kevill's artillery unit began life as the United Fire Company, which Kevill had created before the war to provide the businesses of downtown Norfolk with a fire department. Many downtown business owners and employees were members of this volunteer fire department, and their membership transferred from the United Fire Company to the United Artillery on April 19. Stationed at Fort Norfolk, Kevill's Company supplied the final 31 crew members needed to complete

Fig. 12. Men who served on the *Virginia,* from left to right: Thomas Kevill, William R. Jarvis, Elsberry Valentine White, Charles B. Oliver, Charles J. Creekmur, James E. Barry, and Andrew J. Dalton. (The Mariners' Museum, Newport News, Virginia)

Fig. 13. Capt. Thomas Kevill of the 41st Virginia Infantry, who volunteered to serve aboard the CSS *Virginia* two days before the Battle of Hampton Roads. Most of the other men from the 41st who enlisted with him served under his command at Gun #9 aboard the *Virginia.* (The Mariners' Museum, Newport News, Virginia)

the *Virginia*'s complement. Kevill asked for 31 volunteers, and the entire company stepped forward. Therefore, Kevill chose 31 men "whom he thought best qualified, by physical strength, to do the heavy work which was required of them." One of these men was Isaac Huff Walling, a professional diver from New Jersey, who was detailed to work with B & J Baker & Company in their ongoing work at the navy yard.[43]

Throughout the entire conversion process, Union authorities were kept abreast of the activities at Gosport from an unlikely source. One Union official reported in March 1862 that "the most valuable information we received in regard to the Merrimack and the operations of the rebels came from the colored people." In fact, one black woman named Mary Louvestre played a daring role in these reconnaissance efforts. At great risk she traveled to Washington, D.C., to personally deliver plans for the *Virginia* to Secretary of the Navy Gideon Welles. "Not a word would she communicate in the presence of any one," wrote Welles ten years later in support of her pension application, "but when we were alone she informed me she was from Norfolk, told me the condition of the vessel, and took from her clothing a paper, written by a mechanic who was working on the 'Merrimac,' describing the character of the work, its progress and probable completion." Welles reported that the information she provided proved reliable. "If the government is paying for service of this description, I am aware of none more meritorious than thanks this poor colored woman whose zeal and fidelity I remember and acknowledge with gratitude."[44]

CHAPTER 2

"The Navy Department Will Receive Offers . . ."

The knowledge that the Confederates were building an ironclad, coupled with the lobbying of well-heeled northeastern foundry and railroad owners, prodded the Union into action. With the backing of Congress, the Navy Department took out advertisements in a number of newspapers across the Northeast in early August 1861. The *Boston Daily Journal, New York Enquirer, Philadelphia Evening Bulletin, New York Times,* and *Baltimore Clipper,* among others, ran notices through the second week in August requesting proposals for ironclad steam vessels:

> The Navy Department will receive offers from parties who are able to execute work of this kind, and who are engaged in it, of which they will furnish evidence with their offer, for the construction of one or more IRON-CLAD STEAM VESSELS-OF-WAR, either of iron or of wood and iron combined, for sea or river service, to be of not less than ten nor over sixteen feet draught of water; to carry an armament of from eighty to one hundred and twenty tons weight, with provisions and stores for from one hundred and sixty-five to three hundred persons, according to armament, for sixty days, with coal for eighty days. The smaller draught of water, compatible with other requisites, will be preferred. The vessel to be rigged with two masts, with wire rope standing rigging, to navigate at sea.
>
> A general description and drawings of the vessel, armor and machinery, such as the work can be executed from, will be required.
>
> The offer must state the cost and the time for completing the whole, exclusive of armament and stores of all kinds, the rate of speed proposed, and must be accompanied by a guarantee for the proper execution of the contract, if awarded.

Persons who intend to offer are requested to inform the Department of their intention before the 15th August, instant, and to have their propositions presented within twenty-five days from this date.[1]

With the advertisement in the appropriate publications, all Gideon Welles needed was a group to review any forthcoming proposals. Welles knew that he could not empanel men like Chief Naval Constructor John Lenthall, who had expressed the opinion of many naval officers when he said in the spring of 1861 that "the necessarily large size, the cost and the time required for building an iron cased steam vessel is such that it is not recommended to adopt any plan at present."[2] For the ironclad project to be successful, the panel would require men who had no known opposition to the construction of ironclads. Accordingly, on August 8 Commodore Joseph Smith, Commodore Hiram Paulding, and Commander Charles Henry Davis found themselves to be members of the Ironclad Board of the U.S. Navy. Though extremely experienced naval officers, these three were by no means experts on ironclad technology. But because they had not expressed any overt opposition to the concept, they fit Welles's requirements.

Fig. 14. Commodore Joseph Smith. (Library of Congress)

Joseph Smith was the senior member of the Ironclad Board. Born in Boston in 1790, Smith had already distinguished himself during the Battle of Lake Champlain in 1814, fought in the Second Barbary War in 1815, and by 1861, at the age of seventy-one, he had been tirelessly commanding the navy's Bureau of Docks and Yards for fifteen years. Smith understood the need for technical innovations in naval construction from a practical standpoint. However, he may also have had a personal interest in outfitting the Union navy with the best current technology had to offer. His son, also named Joseph, was in the U.S. Navy, currently stationed in Hampton Roads as executive officer of the USS *Congress,* uneasily waiting to see what was to become of his former ship, the *Merrimack,* in the hands of the Confederacy. The elder Smith was keenly watching the situation as well.

Hiram Paulding was born the same year as the venerable frigate USS *Constitution*—1797. Therefore, it was fitting that his first berth was on that same vessel when he entered the service as a midshipman in 1811 at the age of fourteen. A veteran of the Battle of Lake Champlain in 1814, he continued his ascension within

Left: **Fig. 15.** Commodore Hiram Paulding. (Library of Congress)

Right: **Fig. 16.** Captain Charles Davis. (Naval History and Heritage Command)

the U.S. Navy, serving in the Mediterranean, Pacific, Caribbean, and South Atlantic before entering what he believed would be his last service before retirement: commander of the Home Squadron. But the impending sectional crisis kept him active, and the navy required his services in Washington, D.C. Working in the Navy Department, his career became inextricably linked to current and future events in Hampton Roads. Paulding had been placed in charge of the evacuation of Gosport in April 1861, though his efforts came too late to save the yard.[3] Following his service with the Ironclad Board, he found himself commandant of the New York Navy Yard, where ironclads would eventually become a standard sight during his tenure there. Whatever his personal opinion of ironclads and steam-powered vessels, his professional life from 1861 onward was dominated by them.

Commander Charles Davis was not Welles's first choice for the Ironclad Board, his extensive technological experience notwithstanding. Welles had hoped that ordnance expert Commander John Dahlgren would fill that role. But Dahlgren requested that he be relieved of this particular duty, for the same reason he had turned down the position of ordnance chief—paperwork got in the way of research, experimentation, and development.[4] Davis, who was already begrudgingly engaged in Navy Department business in Washington, D.C., was tapped for the job instead.

Born in Boston in 1807, Charles Davis was a scholar with a penchant for adventure. While a student at Harvard University, he had received an offer to enter the navy as a midshipman and leaped at the chance for practical experience. (Davis would eventually receive his degree, in 1841.) He was assigned to the frigate *United States,* first encountering the vessel at Gosport Navy Yard in Portsmouth, Virginia, in 1823, where he also first served with then lieutenant Hiram Paulding. After seventeen years of active service at sea, Davis began work on the Coastal Survey and eventually the *Nautical Almanac,* which he was working on in 1861 when war broke out. Both a sailor and a mathematician, Davis was certainly an appropriate substitute for Dahlgren—and although he was the youngest member of the board, he would prove to be its most skeptical member.[5]

By early September 1861 the Ironclad Board had received sixteen proposals, many of them promising. The preeminent clipper-ship builder, Donald McKay of Boston, had actually submitted his design to the navy earlier in 1861, before the specifications were published in August. Despite not conforming explicitly to the requirements listed in the advertisement, the group felt his design had great merit. Nevertheless, the board rejected McKay's proposal because of the $1 million price tag he demanded. McKay soon mounted a press campaign to criticize the Ironclad Board for its shortsightedness. In a letter dated January 24, 1862, but not printed in the *New York Times* until March 23, 1862, McKay stated incredulously that "it appears, then, that, for the future, our fleets will be constructed, not after the well-known principles of naval architecture, but the wildest schemes may be adopted in the construction of our ships, if they are only offered under a guarantee! Such a course will make us the laughing-stock of the whole world, and yet, it appears that our Navy Department intends to curry out the same system on a larger scale in the construction of the twenty iron-cased vessels lately voted (?) to be built by Congress!"[6]

Edward Sabine Renwick, a successful mechanical engineer with wide-ranging interests, presented a "novel" design that the board believed would "attract the attention of scientific and practical men."[7] However, questions of stability and feasibility plagued Renwick's proposal, and the board wanted experts to review the plan. Like McKay's proposal, the greatest failing of Renwick's was its price tag of $1.5 million.[8]

Designer Charles Whitney and Thomas Fitch Rowland, owner of Continental Ironworks in Greenpoint, Brooklyn, had submitted a plan for an ironclad vessel to the navy in April 1861, which was included among the proposals sent to the Ironclad Board; however, their proposal was not accepted for fear that it could not bear the weight of the armor.[9] Despite this setback, Rowland soon found himself very much involved in the ironclad program, as Continental Ironworks would be one of the principal contractors with the U.S. Navy in ironclad construction.

Locomotive designer William Norris of Philadelphia submitted an iron ship with no armor, while Henry Dunham of New York wanted $1.2 million for a proposal that had neither drawings nor specifications. Other plans with missing information were similarly rejected. The board's response to the proposal submitted by William Kingsley of Washington, D.C., was the most terse. One can imagine its surprise at receiving a proposal for a "*rubber-clad* vessel, which we cannot recommend." After much debate, the three officers chose two proposals for construction. Both designs represented only a moderate departure from a traditional warship. One of these would be named USS *New Ironsides,* the other USS *Galena.*[10]

Merrick and Sons of Philadelphia used the basic design of the British ironclad *Warrior* as inspiration for the USS *New Ironsides.* The Ironclad Board considered this plan "the most practicable one for heavy armor." With a projected price of $225,000 and a completion time of nine months, the *New Ironsides* was a bargain, and with an angled casemate made of four and a half inches of iron plate, a submerged ram, and a battery of sixteen heavy guns, the *New Ironsides* would eventually become the most powerful of the Civil War ironclads.

The iron gunboat USS *Galena* was to be a 210-foot-long, sail-rigged vessel with six guns mounted in broadside. Designed by Samuel H. Pook of Connecticut, son of the successful naval architect Samuel M. Pook, she would feature a curved, sloped casemate, 3⅛ inches of iron plate, and an unarmored deck. While the four months' projected construction time seemed unrealistic, the price of $235,250 was extremely attractive. The conservative *Galena* was the sort of vessel that would appeal to the Ironclad Board, but she had a secret advantage, too: Pook's design was submitted by Cornelius S. Bushnell, a powerful Connecticut financier with connections in Congress.[11]

Fig. 17. Cornelius Bushnell. (The Mariners' Museum, Newport News, Virginia)

Bushnell had long been acquainted with the sea, having worked on coasting vessels as a boy. By the age of sixteen he was master of a sixty-ton schooner. He dabbled in the grocery business in his early twenties but made his fortune by investing in the struggling New Haven & New London Railroad. Realizing that a connecting route between New York and Boston would be highly lucrative, he invested in connecting the New Haven & New London to the Stonington line and on to Boston, contracting with Erastus Corning and John Flack Winslow of the Albany Ironworks in Troy, New York, and with John Griswold, owner of the Rensselaer Ironworks, also in Troy. Only thirty-two years old at the outbreak of the Civil War, Bushnell was a millionaire with a desire to aid the Union while still serving his own financial interests. On April 18, 1861, he joined the Washington Clay Guards, a unit made up of non-District residents for the immediate protection of the White House and President Lincoln in the days following Fort Sumter. Bushnell, along with the rest of the volunteers, was discharged two weeks later when reinforcements arrived. Abraham Lincoln "cheerfully" signed the discharge.[12]

Bushnell took great interest in the affairs of the U.S. Navy and was well acquainted with Gideon Welles. Upon receiving word about the Confederates' conversion of the *Merrimack* into an ironclad, Welles quickly drafted a bill to be put before Congress that would authorize the construction of ironclad steam vessels for the Union navy to combat the Confederate threat. The bill was largely ignored, however, and Welles determined that a businessman of some influence might better be able to persuade members of Congress to support the bill. Therefore, Welles enlisted fellow Connecticut native Cornelius Bushnell to carry the bill personally to Capitol Hill and use his influence with Connecticut congressman James E. English to move it forward. English was a member of the Naval Committee and also represented Bushnell's district in Connecticut. With Bushnell's influence and English's backing, the bill soon passed both House and Senate and was quickly signed by Lincoln.[13]

In fact, with his insider knowledge that Congress was preparing to authorize the creation of an ironclad board, Bushnell submitted Pook's design for the *Galena* on June 28, 1861, just days before the vote. Congress approved the bill on July 4, 1861, authorizing $1.5 million for the construction of ironclad vessels. Bushnell, who owned a shipyard in Connecticut, was more than ready to offer his services as soon as the navy required them, and he maintained a residence at the Willard Hotel in Washington, D.C., throughout the summer in order to monitor the progress of the new Ironclad Board.

Bushnell was not the only businessman spending time in D.C. hoping for a contract with the navy. Cornelius Delamater also sought favor with the Navy Department during the summer of 1861. A successful New York businessman, Delamater had taken a small company, the Phoenix Foundry, and transformed it into a major ironworks that dominated the waterfront between 13th and 14th Streets in Manhattan. The Cornelius H. Delamater ironworks was one of the largest such establishments in New York, and certainly the largest under a sole proprietor.[14]

Delamater's particular friend was the Swedish engineer John Ericsson, with whom he had partnered on many projects and with whom he commiserated on the deplorable treatment Ericsson had received at the hands of the U.S. Navy following the *Princeton* affair of 1843 (described below). Both Delamater and Ericsson believed that much of the blame for Ericsson's continued blacklisting emanated from the mouth and pen of Benjamin Franklin Isherwood, chief of the Naval Bureau of Steam Engineering. In the summer of 1861 Delamater traveled to Washington in part to seek a contract with the navy, but in fact he also desired to figuratively "finish off Mr. Isherwood if possible, which I think I owe it to my country to do."[15] In a letter to his friend Ericsson, Delamater remarked that he had met with Secretary Welles twice but had "no expectation of any contract or immediate good to result to me or to us from my present stay."[16] Delamater was not one to give up, however, and continued to visit D.C. throughout the summer, staying at the Willard Hotel. There he grew well acquainted with his fellow petitioners, including Cornelius Bushnell.

Fig. 18. John Ericsson. (Library of Congress)

Despite Bushnell's insider knowledge and influence, the Ironclad Board questioned the seaworthiness of Bushnell's *Galena*. "The objection to this vessel," they wrote in their report, "is the fear that she will not float her armor and load sufficiently high, and have stability enough for a sea vessel. With a guarantee that she shall do these, we recommend on that basis a contract."[17] Though the date is not recorded, Bushnell was leaving the Willard a few days prior to September 13, 1861, when he chanced upon Cornelius Delamater on the hotel steps. Bushnell confided that he had a contract for the *Galena* but that the plans needed review. Delamater suggested that Bushnell consult with Delamater's friend, John Ericsson, in New York City.[18]

Born on July 31, 1803, in Värmland, Sweden, Ericsson had been a child prodigy. By the time he was eight he was working alongside his engineer father on a national canal project, and at sixteen he was put in charge of six hundred men and also drew up plans for a cross-country canal. In 1826, after serving seven years in the Swedish army, Ericsson immigrated to London to look for better opportunities. There, in partnership with John Braithwaite, he produced designs for engines that ran on heat rather than steam and he also created a steam-screw propeller for the British Royal Navy (which they ultimately rejected in favor of one created by a British-born citizen).[19]

In 1836 Ericsson married nineteen-year-old Amelia Byam, but by 1839 he had fallen on difficult times, having even spent some time in debtors' prison. Now he felt it was time to move on, especially since his work in England was not going unnoticed on the other side of the Atlantic. Indeed, Ericsson's talents had caught the eye of American naval officer Robert F.

Stockton, who invited him to come to the United States in 1839. Amelia stayed behind in London, and while she eventually joined Ericsson in New York, she returned to England shortly thereafter and never saw her husband again, though they never divorced.[20]

Ericsson's relationship with the U.S. Navy appeared promising, but it came to an abrupt end with the *Princeton* tragedy.

At Stockton's urging, Ericsson had designed the experimental USS *Princeton*. Commissioned in 1843, the *Princeton* was the first steam-screw warship in any navy. Ericsson had first received a patent for his propeller design in 1836. His improved design from 1839, still used by navies around the world, allowed for the ship's propulsion system to be positioned entirely within the hull. The *Princeton* also incorporated several other of Ericsson's innovations. It was the first warship with machinery entirely below the waterline, the first to burn anthracite coal, and the first to use fan blowers for the furnace fires.

John Ericsson's innovative propulsion system for the *Princeton* included two vibrating lever engines, three tubular boilers, and a six-bladed screw propeller, fourteen feet in diameter. The introduction of propellers revolutionized steamship propulsion, as they were much more efficient and less liable to damage than the cumbersome paddlewheel.[21]

Two new guns were placed on the *Princeton* as well. The first, the massive, wrought-iron "Oregon," designed by John Ericsson, featured a strengthened breech that increased the safety of the gun and protected it against explosion. Large iron hoops had been heated and placed around the breech. Upon cooling, they contracted, forming a tight seal. The massive pressures found within the gun upon firing were easily contained, and ordnance officers fired the gun over one hundred times before it was proofed for a fifty-pound charge. Robert Stockton designed the second gun, called the "Peacemaker." While similar in appearance to Ericsson's gun, it had neither the same safety features nor the extensive proofing of the "Oregon." The breech had additional metal added to it but no banding, and the gun had only been fired five times before being placed on the *Princeton* for demonstration.[22]

Ericsson was invited to demonstrate his new model vessel for the naval hierarchy, but Stockton, "who was not disposed to share the credit of success," according to Ericsson's biographer, William Conant Church, left Ericsson at the dock in New York and proceeded to Washington, D.C., without him. Over two hundred guests were on board the USS *Princeton* on February 28, 1844, including President John Tyler and his cabinet. Captain Stockton fired the two new 12-inch shell guns to impress the dignitaries. The trip went without incident—until it was decided to fire the "Peacemaker" a final time. The gun, taxed beyond its capabilities, burst when fired, killing seven, including the secretary of state and the secretary of the navy, and wounding twenty, including Stockton himself.

Stockton immediately requested an inquiry, wishing to exonerate himself. Accordingly, the members of the inquiry convened on board the *Princeton* on March 5, 1844, and began questioning Stockton, as well as other experts and eyewitnesses.[23] Stockton invited Ericsson to the inquiries concerning the incident, but as Stockton had anticipated, Ericsson declined, reasoning that he was innocent. Ericsson wrote, "I must be permitted to exercise my own judgment in this matter, and I have to state most emphatically that since Captain Stockton is in possession of an accurate working plan of his exploded gun my presence at Washington can be of no use."[24]

Though the normal course of events would have required Ericsson to be subpoenaed, Stockton was able to ensure that Ericsson's wish not to attend was honored. Given that Ericsson's knowledge as an engineer would have proven the fault lay with Stockton, it is not surprising that Stockton did not want Ericsson to attend. Yet he used Ericsson's absence as proof that the Swedish inventor was culpable. Inexplicably, the navy and the president absolved Stockton of the blame for his role in the failure of his gun, and the president even asked Stockton to build a similar gun to the "Peacemaker" following the inquiry. Stockton shifted the fault to Ericsson. He also ensured that the U.S. Navy did not pay the Swedish engineer for his work on the *Princeton,* and the tragic incident resulted in bad relations between the navy and Ericsson for almost twenty years.

The episode also contributed in small part to the navy's reluctance to build steam-screw warships for another ten years, though the propulsion system had no bearing upon the tragic accident. The fact that it was associated with John Ericsson was enough. Ericsson's original propeller was removed from the *Princeton,* though the vessel quietly received another propeller of Ericsson's design a few years after the incident.[25] The naval officers involved in the inquiry also expressed concerns over the use of experimental weapons, thus creating another impediment to quick progress within the U.S. Navy.[26]

Stung by this betrayal, Ericsson returned to some earlier ideas, including his "caloric" (hot air) engine and something he mysteriously called a "sub-aquatic system of naval warfare." Always ahead of his time, Ericsson had envisioned an ironclad steam-powered warship as early as 1826, but it was not until the outbreak of the Crimean War in 1853 that he finished his design. In September 1854 he submitted a full set of plans to Napoleon III of France, who turned them down. Undaunted, Ericsson set his drawings aside and waited. The essential elements of what would become the USS *Monitor* were already apparent in this revolutionary

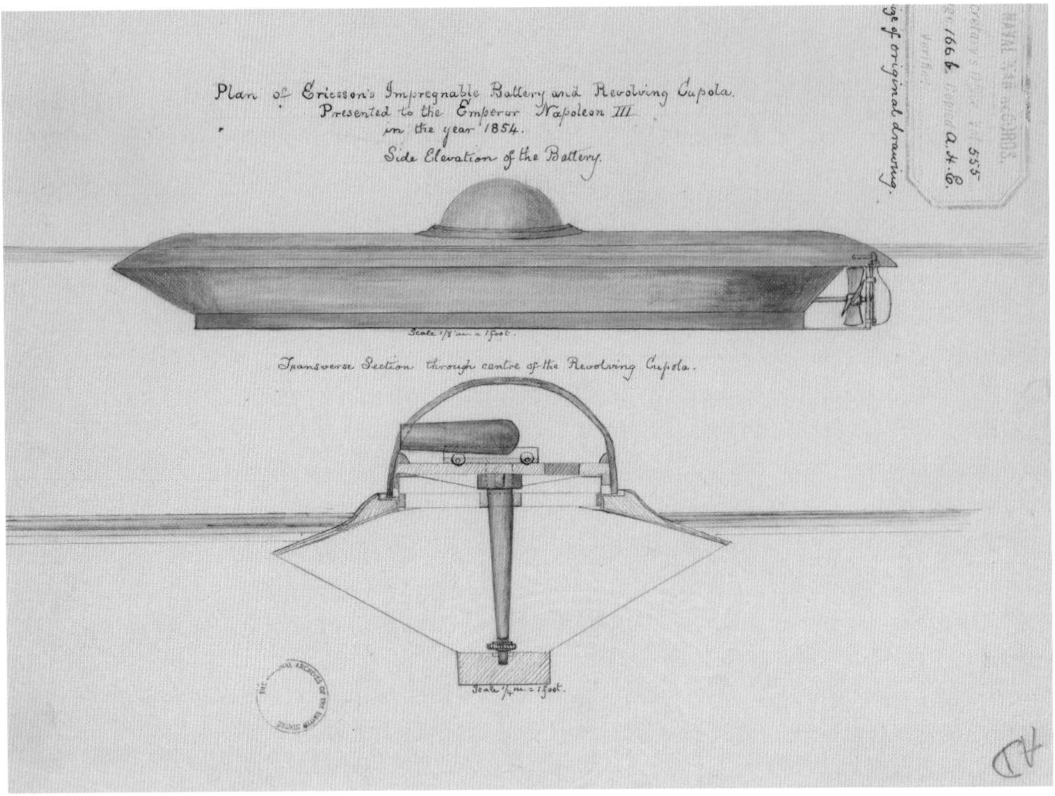
Plan of Ericsson's Impregnable Battery and Revolving Cupola.
Presented to the Emperor Napoleon III
in the year 1854.
Side Elevation of the Battery.
Transverse Section through centre of the Revolving Cupola.

Fig. 19. John Ericsson's original design for an "impregnable battery and revolving cupola," which Ericsson presented to Napoleon III of France in 1854 during the Crimean War. (National Archives)

design. The vessel was to be constructed entirely of iron, with all of her machinery and living quarters located underwater. Only the deck and a semi-globular revolving gun turret—the ship's most radical feature—would ride above the waterline.[27]

Upon hearing of the Union navy's desire for ironclad designs in August 1861, Ericsson quickly drafted a letter to offer his services and enclosed drawings of his novel ship. Dated August 29, 1861, the letter outlined the Swede's successes, making no mention of the *Princeton.* Ericsson, who had addressed the letter to Lincoln and not to the Ironclad Board, told the president that "attachment to the Union alone impels me to offer my services at this fearful crisis—my life if need be—in the great cause which Providence has called you to defend."[28] But neither the letter nor the plans found their way into the Ironclad Board's deliberations.

Bushnell arrived in New York the following day, August 30, and visited Ericsson at his office on Franklin Street in lower Manhattan. Bushnell laid out the plans for the *Galena* and Ericsson agreed to examine them, telling Bushnell to return the next day for an answer. Accordingly, on August 31, Ericsson informed Bushnell that the *Galena* "will easily carry the load you propose and stand a six-inch-shot at a respectable distance."

Ericsson then asked Bushnell if he had time to look at Ericsson's own design. Bushnell recalled that Ericsson then "produced a small, dust-covered box" within which was a model and a plan for his "sub-aquatic system of naval warfare." Also in the box was a medal and letter of thanks from Napoleon III. Bushnell was impressed with what he saw and begged Ericsson to loan him the model and plan to bring them before the navy for consideration. Ericsson agreed, and Bushnell immediately left for Hartford, Connecticut, where he knew Gideon Welles was staying. Upon seeing the model, Welles "was favorably impressed" and urged Bushnell to "lose no time" in returning to Washington to bring the model before the Ironclad Board.

The Ironclad Board was not pleased when it learned that the ship Bushnell was promoting belonged to John Ericsson. But Bushnell would not give up on Ericsson's strange design. He used his friendship with Welles and his acquaintance with Secretary of State William H. Seward to gain a meeting with both President Lincoln and the Ironclad Board on September 13, 1861. When Bushnell arrived at the White House, Lincoln's secretary William O. Stoddard remarked that he "was a massive, vigorous, fine-looking man." Lincoln, who took a keen interest in war technology, was impressed with Ericsson's pasteboard model, which had a moving turret and tiny guns. According to Stoddard, "Mr. Lincoln made a careful study of what was said to resemble a cheese-box on a raft, and he ordered a board of naval officers to get together and examine it." Bushnell later recalled that the president held the model in his hand and said, "All I have to say is what the girl said when she stuck her foot into the stocking. It strikes me there's something in it."[29]

Commodore Smith and Commodore Paulding were willing to consider Ericsson's proposal, but Captain Davis adamantly refused, even with the president's endorsement. He told Bushnell to "take the little thing home and worship it, as it would not be idolatry, because it was in the image of nothing in the heaven above or on the earth beneath or in the waters under the earth."[30]

Bushnell realized the only way to truly persuade the board was for Ericsson to explain his strange vessel in person, for, as Bushnell reasoned, "Ericsson is a full electric battery himself." Bushnell left for New York to persuade Ericsson to come to Washington, but Ericsson adamantly refused to speak with the navy. Bushnell had to play to Ericsson's vanity to get the imperious Swede to Washington, later recalling that he told Ericsson, "Paulding says that your boat would be the thing to punish those Rebels at Charleston." He continued with the praise: "You have a friend in Washington—Commodore Smith. He worships you. He says those plans are worthy of the genius of an Ericsson." Then Bushnell slyly mentioned that "Captain Davis wants a little explanation in detail which I could not give." But Ericsson *could* explain, and he told Bushnell, "I will go to-night!" With that, Bushnell "knew that the success of the affair was assured." Ericsson and Bushnell left for Washington immediately.[31]

To Ericsson's surprise, when he arrived at the Navy Department on September 15, 1861, he not only found that was he not expected but that his plan had also already been rejected. Bushnell had conveniently left that bit out. When Ericsson inquired as to the reasons for the rejection, Commodore Smith replied that because of the vessel's apparent instability, "it would upset and place her crew in the inconvenient and undesirable position of submarine divers."[32]

Ericsson chided the board for its lack of vision, and though his words are now lost, those present recalled that he ended his soliloquy with the stirring admonition, "Gentlemen . . . I consider it to be your duty to the country to give me an order to build the vessel before I leave this room." Bushnell recalled that Ericsson "carried the Board and Secretary Welles as if by storm," and the board, clearly moved by Ericsson's impassioned speech, conferred briefly and asked him to return at 1:00 P.M. Prompt as always, Ericsson returned at the appointed hour to find Commodore Paulding alone in the boardroom. Paulding asked Ericsson a few more questions about buoyancy and stability, to which Ericsson responded in full; Paulding declared afterward that "I have learnt more about the stability of a vessel from what you have now said than all I knew before."[33] But Ericsson still did not have a contract, and the board continued to deliberate. He was asked to return at 3:00 P.M., at which time he found Gideon Welles awaiting him, along with a promise for a contract.

CHAPTER 3

Building the *Monitor*

On September 21, 1861, Commodore Joseph Smith sent a brief letter to John Ericsson informing him that the Ironclad Board had "reported favorably on your proposition for an iron-clad gunboat." For Ericsson, the merits of his gunboat were self-evident, and he did not need three superannuated naval officers to tell him this. The letter's tacit acknowledgment that he stood to regain his favorable standing with the U.S. Navy was most important to Ericsson. However, Smith sullied the sentiment by adding that "there seems to be some deficiencies in the specifications" and that "some changes may be suggested." Knowing that he had added fuel to Ericsson's caloric fire, Smith closed the letter with the request that Ericsson had "better come on and see to the drawing of a contract," adding, almost as though in sotto voce, "if we can mutually agree."[1]

Despite the rocky beginnings with the Ironclad Board, it seemed as though there might be civil negotiations between Ericsson and Smith at the outset of the formal relationship. Even as Smith was penning his letter to Ericsson on September 21, Ericsson was writing a letter to Smith that bordered on congenial. Ericsson wrote excitedly that he intended "to furnish a condenser for making fresh water," as well as ships' boats—including "an India rubber boat to be folded up and carried below, to be used in case of need after the destruction of the deck boats." He also mentioned that he had been paying particular attention to "the construction of a temporary rigging to be put up in case of need."[2] Ericsson then dashed off a letter to Bushnell authorizing the battery's primary financial backer to "amend and complete my specifications of an impregnable floating battery, in accordance with any request of Commodore Smith." Ericsson added that he was ready "to comply with any modification he [Smith] may see fit." To Smith he wrote that "Messrs. Winslow and Griswold from Troy" were hard at work executing "the contract for building the battery."

Winslow and Griswold were the same gentlemen with whom Bushnell had worked on the railroad extension project before the war. He now turned to them for assistance in the two ironclad contracts in which he was involved. John Flack Winslow was not only the managing partner of the Albany Ironworks, he was also an investor in the Rensselaer Ironworks; both firms would be subcontracted to supply the angle and bar iron and the spikes and bolts needed to assemble Ericsson's vessel. John Griswold, with controlling interest in the Rensselaer Ironworks, oversaw the project's complex financing and navigated the political waters in which the project was already embroiled.[3] Winslow, Griswold, and Bushnell also put up seed money in return for a quarter interest in the enterprise and an equal share in any later Ericsson ironclads. There was no written agreement regarding shares between the four. Winslow later recalled that "it was simply a verbal agreement and nothing more."[4]

Ericsson had claimed he could deliver an ironclad in ninety days, but Ericsson had already been hard at work even before the contract was signed on October 4, 1861. Ericsson himself, confident that nothing would go awry with the negotiations, had already begun work on the engine that would power his gunboat. He hastened to add that the government had no need to worry about his overeagerness to begin the project, for the engine "will do for driving our propeller vessels should it not be wanted for war purposes."[5] Thus the compact, low-profile, vibrating side-lever engine was already taking shape at Delamater's foundry. To further streamline the construction, Ericsson ordered significant modifications to his original plans. A conventional pair of Dahlgren smoothbore guns in the turret replaced the steam-powered gun and torpedo he had hoped for. The globular cupola soon became a cylindrical turret, and the sloping deck became a nearly flat deck—just as unconventional, but much easier to construct.

Still wary of Ericsson, navy officials wanted to make sure that he and his partners would bear all the risk if the ironclad project failed. The contract drawn up on October 4, 1861, for Ericsson's "Iron Clad Shot-Proof Steam Battery," gave the navy ample opportunity to get out of paying for the ship. The navy's description of the contracted vessel also showed a stubborn adherence to old technology and a lack of confidence in Ericsson's radical vision. For the navy's part, officials provided Ericsson with an additional ten days to build his gunboat. Ericsson had claimed that he needed ninety days—the navy offered one hundred. In that time, Ericsson was to build an

> *Iron Clad Shot-Proof Steam Battery* of iron and wood combined on *Ericsson's* plan; the lower vessel to be wholly of iron and the upper vessel of wood; the length to be one hundred and seventy-nine (179) feet, extreme breadth forty-one (41) feet, and depth five (5) feet or larger if the party of the first part shall think it necessary to carry the armament and stores required, the vessel to be constructed of the best materials and workmanship throughout, according to the plan and specifications hereunto annexed forming a part of this contract.[6]

The contract acknowledged Ericsson's considerable experience with ship design, unsurprising given its principal authors—John Griswold, John Winslow, and Cornelius Bushnell. Items that Ericsson had mentioned to Smith from the original advertisement also appeared, including the "*Masts, Spars, Sails* and *Rigging.*" This rigging was far more substantial than the "temporary rigging . . . in case of need," however. The contract specified that the rigging must be of "sufficient dimensions to drive the vessel at the rate of *six knots* per hour in a fair breeze of wind." Yet in all of Ericsson's letters written to Smith and Bushnell concerning the contract, Ericsson made no mention of his dismay about the robust nature of the rigging.[7] Ultimately, though Ericsson himself had first mentioned the possibility of rigging, it appears that he ultimately chose to ignore that particular stipulation in the contract, and the topic did not come up again until after the vessel's launch.

The changes to the contract upon which the navy insisted included the stipulation that Ericsson, Bushnell, Winslow, and Griswold assume the entire financial risk of the undertaking. In this respect, one former *Monitor* crewman recalled, the contract for the ironclad was "a veritable iron clad too."[8] The document read: "When the work shall have progressed to the amount of Fifty thousand dollars in the estimation of the Superintendent of the vessel on the part of the United States, that sum shall be paid to the party of the first part," in this case John Ericsson as principal and John Griswold, John Winslow, and Cornelius Bushnell as sureties. Thereafter, the syndicate would receive similar payments, minus 25 percent held in reserve, which would "be retained until after the completion and satisfactory trial of the vessel, not to exceed ninety days after she shall be ready for sea."[9]

Very little in the contract was unexpected, and as one *Monitor* crewman later recalled, "the risks were readily and most gladly accepted."[10] Yet there was one provision that had been in the early drafts of the contract that gave John Winslow pause. The navy would only consider the vessel acceptable—and thus pay the investors the full amount—if it was successfully tested under enemy fire for ninety days after she was ready for sea. While on the surface this was a reasonable request, there were concerns about its interpretation. Cornelius Bushnell explained to Joseph Smith:

> Captain Ericsson, Griswold, and myself were better pleased with the wording of your contract for Ericsson's Battery, than with the one executed and sent forward, but Mr. Winslow had an idea that the three months, in the last clause might be construed by other parties than yourself, as allowing three months to test the vessel in active service under the enemies fire before the Government would be justified in paying for, or accepting the same.[11]

This addition to the contract and the attendant risk the investors would have to bear proved almost too much for Winslow, who considered withdrawing his support. Bushnell remained calm, as there were other investors waiting in the wings—or so he reported to Smith. But Bushnell and Ericsson both desired to keep Winslow within the fold. Ericsson, for his part, agreed with the stipulation but insisted that he would support the contract revision for the sake of retaining Winslow. Ericsson was supremely confident in his design. He wrote to Smith on October 2: "It is hardly necessary for me to say that I deem your decision to test the impregnable battery under the enemy's fire, before accepting, perfectly reasonable and proper. If the structure cannot stand this test, then it is indeed worthless."[12] Discussions between Bushnell, Ericsson, Griswold, and Winslow ensued, and Ericsson was pleased to report on October 4 that "Mr. Winslow after mature reflection, now admits the propriety of your testing the battery under the enemy's fire."

Fig. 20. Thomas F. Rowland, ca. 1883. (The Mariners' Museum, Newport News, Virginia)

To save time, nine contractors and an unknown number of subcontractors worked simultaneously in at least seven different cities to produce the components for assembly at Continental Ironworks in Greenpoint, Brooklyn.[13] The plan for a vessel submitted by Continental's young owner, Thomas Fitch Rowland, may have been rejected by the Ironclad Board, but his services were needed nonetheless. It was an incredibly complex manufacturing process—but then, this would be no ordinary ship. As a member of the *Monitor*'s crew would later recall, "Thus the war for the moment was being carried on not at Hampton Roads but at Norfolk and Brooklyn, and the victory was to depend, not only upon the bravery of the officers, but upon the speed of the mechanics. It was a race of constructors."[14]

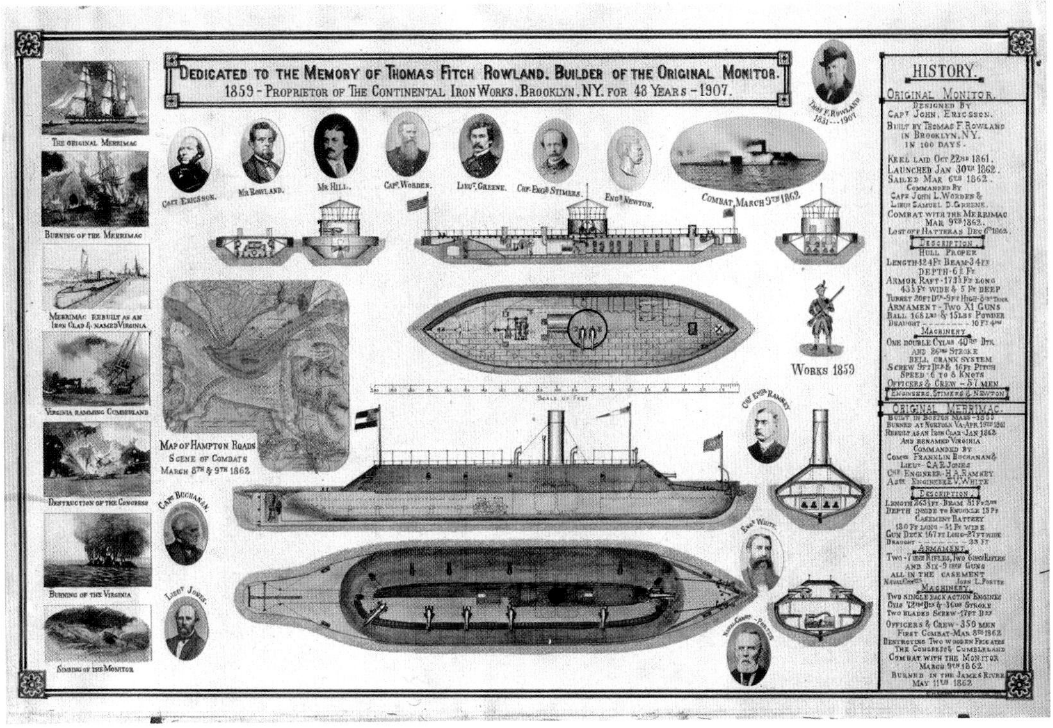

Only the industrial capabilities of the Union made it possible to even consider building an experimental vessel in one hundred days. (In contrast, the conversion of the *Merrimack* to the *Virginia* took nearly nine months.) Ironworks throughout New York State worked to manufacture the raw and finished materials needed to build Ericsson's battery. Yet New York boasted no foundry capable of rolling the 192 plates needed for the most important feature of the vessel—the rotating gun turret. The turret was composed of eight layers of one-inch-thick iron.[15] The thickness of the iron was not an issue for the New York companies; rather, the problem was the nine-foot length of each plate. The only foundry within the Union capable of rolling plates up to ten feet in length was in Baltimore—Abbott and Sons in the Canton area of the city. Thus, Thomas Rowland of Continental Ironworks, with Charles Whitney acting as his agent, subcontracted with Abbott to make

Fig. 21. This 1908 print, a commemorative history of the *Monitor* and *Virginia,* was dedicated to the memory of Thomas Fitch Rowland, proprietor of the Continental Ironworks in Brooklyn from 1859 until his death in 1907. (The Mariners' Museum, Newport News, Virginia)

Fig. 22. Horace Abbott. (*Baltimore: Past and Present* [1871])

the plates. Horace Abbott, originally from Massachusetts, had purchased the Canton Ironworks foundry in Baltimore in the 1830s because of its proximity to both marine and rail transport. Abbott maintained an office in New York in order to take advantage of lucrative contract opportunities in the North, however.

Table 1 is based upon William Still's 1988 study of the known contractors on the *Monitor* project; it shows the principal companies involved in the *Monitor*'s construction along with the elements they supplied. However, there were many more companies scattered throughout the Northeast that all had a part to play in rushing the vessel to completion. Stephen H. Muller of Troy, New York, has also added a great deal to our understanding of the substantial role that the ironworks in Troy played in the construction of the *Monitor*.[16] In 2004 Captain William R. Porter donated a heretofore unknown collection of receipts from John Griswold's papers to The Mariners' Museum, revealing the names of several more companies who supplied services or smaller items. Finally, maker's marks found by Mariners' Museum conservators have added new information to the list (see table 2).

Table 1: Principal *Monitor* Companies

Company	Supply to *Monitor*	Location
Holdane & Company	125 tons armor plate, bar and angle iron	New York City
Albany Ironworks	Angle and bar iron, spikes, bolts—hull plates, floor plates, deck plates, midships bulkhead	Troy, N.Y.
Rensselaer Ironworks	Angle and bar iron, spikes, bolts—hull plates, floor plates, deck plates, midships bulkhead	Troy, N.Y.
Niagara Steam Forge	Port stoppers	Buffalo, N.Y.
H. Abbott & Sons	Armor plate for turret	Baltimore, Md.
Novelty Iron Works	Assembled turret	New York City
Delamater Iron Works	Main engine, boilers, propeller, other machinery	New York City
Clute Brothers Foundry	Turret engines, gun carriages, anchor windlass, engine room grates	Schenectady, N.Y.
Continental Ironworks	Assembled vessel	Greenpoint, Brooklyn, N.Y.

Source: Still, *Monitor Builders*.

Table 2: Additional *Monitor* Suppliers

Company	Supply to *Monitor*	Location
James Gregory	Brass valves[17]	New York City
Eagle Steam Saw Mill	Timber	Greenpoint, Brooklyn, N.Y.
Black & Secor	Screw bolts	New York City
Thomas Peterson	Installed boilers	Greenpoint, Brooklyn, N.Y.
H. R. Worthington	Supplied bilge pumps	New York City
George A. Kingsland	Carpenter; built ship house	Greenpoint, Brooklyn, N.Y.
E. W. Barstow	Anchor and anchor chain	New York City
Bussing, Crocker & Co.	Screws and bolts, insurance	New York City
Chrisman & Durbin	Iron plate (possibly boilermakers)	Jersey City, N.J.
E. Bootman & Son	Painters (31 Corlears St.)	New York City
B. K. Dickerman/ J. W. Southack	Ship's furniture—cabinetmakers located at 196 Broadway	New York City
Wm. D. Andrews & Brothers	Unknown articles[18]	New York City
Benjamin Pike Jr.	Unknown[19]	New York City
E. S. Hidden/E. Williams	Unknown[20]	New York City
J. W. Atwater	Unknown service (83 South Street)[21]	New York City
Thomas M. Shepard	Unknown service[22]	New York City
E. V. Haughwout & Co.	Possibly china and ceramics, other domestic furnishings. Maker's marks on ceramics found on *Monitor* match known maker's marks for unfired ceramics used by Haughwout for custom orders.	New York City
Smith, Hegeman & Co.	Possibly iron	New York City
Victor Giroud	Engine room clock	New York City[23]
John Powers	Tri-cock valve assemblies on main steam engine, manometers	New York City[24]
William Sewell	Manometers	New York City
McNabb, Carr, and Company	Brass valves[25]	New York City
John A. Kernochan	Wholesale iron	New York City
Alfred B. Sands/ L. H. Tooker	Unknown[26]	New York City

Source: Unless otherwise noted, information is derived from the USS *Monitor* Design and Construction Collection (MS335), TMM.

One hundred days was a short time in which to construct this new vessel, however, and Commodore Smith had been counting each one down. The engine, already under construction before the contract was signed, was one of the first systems to be successfully tested on the vessel. By late December 1861 the engine had been installed inside the hull of the ship, and on December 31, the chief engineer at the navy yard, Alban C. Stimers, wrote to Commodore Smith that "the engines and propeller of the Ericsson Battery have been operated by steam this day, and . . . their performance was highly satisfactory."[27] Although construction was moving along, it was not fast enough to satisfy Smith. Under pressure to deliver an ironclad vessel to Hampton Roads before the *Merrimack* could be completed, Smith was clearly anxious. His communications to Ericsson and Stimers, which had been friendly yet formal through most of the construction, became more terse. On January 14 Smith telegraphed a single sentence to Ericsson: "The time for the completion of the shot-proof battery according to the stipulations of your contract, expired on the 12th instant."[28] The following day, Smith sent an equally brief communication to Lieutenant John L. Worden, who had recently been released by the Confederates in a prisoner exchange. Worden had the dubious distinction of being the first prisoner of war of the conflict, for his role in delivering the orders to reinforce Fort Sumter to the commanding officers in Pensacola. In fragile health as a result of his captivity, he nonetheless had been tapped for a special assignment. Smith's letter read: "I enclose a copy of the contract with Captain J. Ericsson, 95 Franklin Street, New York, for an ironclad battery, for your information and government as commander of said battery."[29] The vessel may not have been completed, nor had she been named, but she had a commanding officer.

Her name was not long in coming, however. John Ericsson, as the titular owner of the ship until she proved herself successful under enemy fire, had the honor and responsibility of naming his ironclad. (He told a correspondent in 1874, "The Monitor was private property on going into the battle at Hampton Roads. The government had however a lien on the vessel, having advanced a certain part of the contract amount. The Monitor was not accepted by the Navy Department, nor fully paid for, until after the successful conflict."[30]) He chose the name *Monitor* in order to convey a sense of both observation and warning. In a letter dated January 20, Ericsson explained his thinking to Assistant Secretary of the Navy Gustavus Vasa Fox:

> In accordance with your request, I now submit for your approbation a name for the floating battery at Greenpoint. The impregnable and aggressive character of this structure will admonish the leaders of the

Southern Rebellion that the batteries on the banks of their rivers will no longer present barriers to the entrance of the Union forces. The iron-clad intruder will thus prove a severe monitor to those leaders. But there are other leaders who will also be startled and admonished by the booming of the guns from the impregnable iron turret. "Downing Street" will hardly view with indifference this last "Yankee Notion," this monitor. To the Lords of the admiralty the new craft will be a monitor, suggesting doubts as to the propriety of completing those four steel clad ships at three and a half million apiece. On these and many similar grounds, I propose to name the new battery, "Monitor."[31]

By January 24, 1862, the guns were still not on board, and John Worden indicated that while he would be able to sight them within the turret, it would take three or four days to do so properly. The first gun arrived on the twenty-fifth, and Smith was reassured that the launch of the *Monitor* would take place on January 29, provided the weather and tide cooperated.[32] Ultimately, the launch occurred on January 30 at 9:50 A.M. during a steady drizzle. A large crowd had assembled at Greenpoint to watch the curious vessel move down the ways, despite the fact that there had been little notice about the event. Only a shell of the turret was on board—one quarter of the plates—nor were all the coal and stores, so the vessel would float high. But more important than that to most observers was the fact that she would float at all. Ericsson and a small group stood on the deck, in defiance of the naysayers (though a small boat was kept next to them in case the vessel "should make a dive to the bottom"). Both Stimers and Ericsson sent telegrams to Smith informing him of the successful launch, while the *New York Times* reported that "yesterday morning, the Ericsson battery was launched from the ship-yard of Mr. T.F. ROWLAND, Greenpoint. L.I. Notwithstanding the prognostication of many that she would break her back or else swamp, she was launched successfully." The *New York Tribune* noted that "the assemblage cheered rapturously" as the "strange-looking craft glided swiftly and gracefully into its new element." This included the tepid cheers of those "who had lost money by bets on the certainty of her sinking." Crews on vessels attending the event fired salutes in honor of the successful launch. The *New York World* reported that "it was very evident to the dullest observer, that the battery had not the slightest intention of sinking."[33] The remainder of the turret was brought on board on January 31, and the work on the battery continued around the clock.

A private communication from Ericsson to Smith reveals vulnerability not normally seen in the imperious Swede. He admitted to Smith that he was worried about the amount of freeboard (the amount of the hull

Fig. 23. This depiction of the launch of the *Monitor* appeared in *Harper's New Monthly Magazine* in September 1862. (The Mariners' Museum, Newport News, Virginia)

above the waterline) the new ship would expose. He had calculated eighteen inches of freeboard, but admitted to Smith that "I do not see how we ever can get down so deep as not to show 21 inches of vessel out of the water."[34] Stimers was not concerned, however, and with the distribution of coal and ordnance, the vessel did display the eighteen inches that Ericsson had predicted. Smith added to Ericsson's stress by thanking him for his letter, and adding, "She is much needed *now.*"[35]

Though Smith took an intense interest in the vessel, he had not actually seen her, as his office was in Washington, D.C. Therefore, his instructions to Worden on February 6 were based on his knowledge of the contract language, which required certain features to be present on the vessel. He instructed Worden to "inspect her outfits; see to the rigging, sails, ground tackle, boats, stores, and to the vessel generally." Smith further reminded Worden that the vessel would not be accepted by the navy until she had proved herself under fire, after which Worden was to "report in full upon her performance, as the acceptance of the vessel will depend principally upon your certificate."[36] A week later Smith reminded him once again of the necessity of the vessel to carry "spars and sails which shall propel her six sea miles per hour with a fair wind."[37] There is no record of Worden's reply.

The press was flocking to Greenpoint to get a look at the newly named *Monitor.* Detailed descriptions appeared in several northern papers from reporters who were allowed to swarm all over the vessel. Before giving particulars, however, one correspondent to the Burlington, Vermont, *Weekly Free Press* gave his initial perceptions of the battery:

> Of the appearance of the vessel as a whole it is difficult to give an adequate impression in a few words. It is in fact unlike anything that ever floated on Neptune's bosom. The impression at a short distance is that of insignificance and harmlessness; but on standing upon its deck and looking upon it more closely, the impression is that of great power and invulnerability. The description of the Leviathan of the Scriptures very adequately expresses the feeling which this sea monster excites.[38]

Despite Smith's attempts at secrecy, the world was interested in the *Monitor* and the virtual tours given by the various reporters left very little to the imagination. The most defining feature of the newly named *Monitor* was her rotating gun turret, which was first put into operation on February 17, 1862. Both Alban Stimers and John Flack Winslow sent their observations to Smith, with Stimers reporting that the turret turned at two and a half revolutions per minute under twenty-five pounds of steam.[39] On February 25, 1862, Lieutenant John Worden made the first entry in his new vessel's logbook. It read:

> Remarks 25th February 1862
>
> Comes in with fine weather
> At 3 o clock P.M.
> Received crew from Receiving Ship
> North Carolina
> Vessel put in commission
> by Capt. Almy[40]
>
> This day ends with
> clear cold weather[41]

The U.S. Navy had taken provisional possession of Ericsson's *Monitor.* A volunteer crew, culled from the men awaiting assignment on board the receiving ship *North Carolina,* stepped on board their new home that same day.

Just what was this vessel that now resided at the Brooklyn Navy Yard? She was a strange craft, nearly a submarine, with only her signature turret visible at any distance. The turret seemed to most observers to be the real novelty of the vessel, but John Ericsson, by no means a humble man, never claimed credit for inventing it. He attributed the original concept for a round defensive turret to the ancient Greeks. His associates in the construction of the new battery, however, were worried about possible infringement on a more recent turret design. Theodore Ruggles Timby, an American inventor, held a patent on the turret concept. Born in Dover, New York, in 1822, Timby first conceived of the rotating gun turret when he was nineteen years old. Between 1841 and 1848 Timby presented his plans to a variety of U.S. government officials, including U.S. senator and Smithsonian regent Jefferson Davis of Mississippi, but no one in the government showed any active interest. In 1856 Timby sought an audience with Emperor Napoleon III of France to promote his turret concept, but the emperor was also uninterested. Concurrent with Timby's efforts, Cowper Coles, a captain in the British Royal Navy, had put his own turret design into action near Sebastopol. The protective turret sat atop a raft and worked well enough that Coles drafted plans and applied for a patent as early as 1859.[42]

These previous turrets and their patents had not gone unnoticed. Recognizing that Timby had a patent, Ericsson's financial backers arranged, in 1862, to pay Timby a royalty for every turret constructed on an Ericsson vessel. Coles's patent, held in Great Britain, was simply ignored by Winslow, Bushnell, and Griswold. Timby never received all of the money due to him, however, and long after the war, newspaper articles continued to appear that sought to set the record straight about Timby's invention of the turret.[43]

Composed of 192 one-inch-thick iron plates, the *Monitor*'s turret stood 9 feet high and had an external diameter of 21 feet, 4 inches. The plates, to be bolted and riveted together in eight concentric layers, were rolled at Abbott in Baltimore and shipped to Brooklyn for assembly. Conservators at The Mariners' Museum have discovered Roman numerals engraved on the tops of the recovered turret plates but have not yet been able to determine whether these numbers were placed on the turret plates at Abbott for use by crews in Brooklyn for reassembly or if they served another purpose.

A central shaft supported the turret from below and provided the means by which the turret could be raised. This shaft rested on a wedge-shaped "key," which was drawn inward by means of turning a large bolt with a wrench. When fully engaged, the key could raise the turret $2\frac{3}{4}$ inches, leaving enough space between the turret and the brass ring on which it sat for the turret to turn freely.[44] The innermost course of iron plate in the turret sat a half-inch lower than the other seven courses, thus concentrating the turret's weight on a smaller area and producing a watertight seal. Inside the turret, Ericsson designed a set of diagonal braces that could be tightened with large turnbuckles. This bracing was needed to keep the turret from sagging on its central shaft. The original plans for the turret indicated only one set of these diagonal courses, which ran from the center of the roof of the turret diagonally down to points in the deck to the starboard and port. When the turret was recovered in 2002, archaeologists discovered a second set of diagonal braces running fore and aft. Because this second set of braces does not appear in the presentation plan of the *Monitor* (given to Continental Ironworks owner Thomas Fitch Rowland following the completed construction of the vessel), this has led NOAA and Mariners' Museum staff to believe that these braces were a last-minute addition before the vessel left New York.

The turret was powered by two small steam engines mounted directly below the deck beams, each at a 45-degree angle to the centerline of the vessel. As initially designed, a crank handle mounted on the starboard bulkhead of the turret controlled the starting, stopping, and reversal of the turret. This appears to have been the mechanism in use during the March 9, 1862, battle, based on official reports, but no archaeological evidence of this mechanism exists within the turret. A brass plate housing a lever and bearing the words "Left," "Stop," and "Right" has been excavated, however, and may indicate a later change in the turret mechanism.

Two gunport shutters dominated the forward bulkhead of the turret, covering the scalloped gunports. These massive, coffin-shaped structures were pierced with holes, to allow the shafts of gun tools to pass through the shutters so that gun crews servicing the guns would not be exposed to potential enemy fire. The cylindrical nature of the turret dictated that each shutter would have to swing inward, toward the other by means of block and tackle, effectively allowing only one gun to be fired at a time.[45] The gunports also afforded the best, yet deadliest view. Safer sight holes pierced the turret's sides in three locations—directly opposite the gunports and at the ten and two o'clock positions to either side of the gunports.

The *Monitor* was armed with two XI-inch Dahlgren shell guns that were located inside the revolving gun turret. The cast-iron guns were over thirteen feet long with a bore diameter of eleven inches. Each gun weighed approximately nine tons. Rear Admiral John A. Dahlgren designed the guns, numbers 27 and 28, which were manufactured at Robert P. Parrott's West Point Foundry in Cold Springs, New York, in 1859.

Though guns had been ordered for the vessel, delays in construction had allowed other naval officers the opportunity to appropriate them. Fearing that the lack of designated guns for the vessel would absolve the contractors from the strictures of the contract, Smith ordered that guns be taken from another vessel to be used on the *Monitor*. Thus, guns 27 and 28 were removed from the gunboat *Dacotah* in order to arm the *Monitor*.[46]

Though he wanted to equip his vessel with these powerful guns, Ericsson faced a major design challenge because of them. Physics dictated that a thirteen-foot-long gun needs an equal amount of room for recoil. However, the turret was only twenty feet in diameter in its interior. Though Ericsson initially wished to saw off the muzzles of the guns to accommodate them within the turret, Dahlgren himself objected to the danger this could impose upon the gun crews within the turret. Thus, Ericsson was required to design two gun carriages that could arrest the recoil motion of the guns within the small interior of the turret. These carriages, built of iron, wood, and brass components, each had a friction gear that allowed a series of iron fins on the underside to clamp together on wooden friction slides. Wheels mounted vertically were paired with horizontal rollers to slide on the iron rails the carriages were mounted upon.[47] The friction gear, properly employed, was capable of arresting the recoil of the gun safely.

Thin sheets of iron served as mantelets, or shields, to keep the nuts and bolts holding the turret plates together from becoming shrapnel within the turret while under fire. These mantelets gave the interior of the turret a smooth appearance. Whitewash on the interior surfaces took advantage of available light, which streamed in through the railroad rails that made up the roof overhead. These rails could be covered with a series of thin iron plates perforated with holes to provide ventilation while under fire or in heavy weather. Tubes attached to the vent holes on the two XI-inch Dahlgren guns within the turret allowed the noxious fumes of the guns to be vented out under these conditions.

The turret was designed to have up to twenty-four awning stanchions attached to its roof to provide shade and shelter from the elements, as well as a rope lifeline to keep the crew from tumbling off in heavy seas. Extant photos of the *Monitor*, taken in July 1862, show twelve stanchions deployed to hold the canvas awning, which was hoisted up a central support to create an umbrella-like effect. This awning, and the stanchions, could be easily removed and stowed below when the ship went into battle. Two sliding hatches for external access were in the roof above, and hatches for access from below were in the wooden decking of the turret. In order to access these hatches, the turret had to be turned to align these hatches with openings in the deck below. A ladder attached to the outside of the turret allowed access to the weather deck from above.

The turret was a formidable structure. A reporter from the *Daily National Intelligencer* of Washington, D.C., stated that "the gunner inside a defence of this character will feel as secure as an ancient Knickerbocker in his easy chair while heavy balls are striking all about him, within a few feet outside, with all the force which the enemy's best guns can give them."[48]

The vessel itself was 173 feet in length and 41 feet, 6 inches in the beam, with a draft of 10 feet, 6 inches. Her upper hull (or deck) was wooden, clad in two layers of thin iron plate, and her lower hull and keel were constructed of iron plate and angle iron bolted or riveted together. The weather deck consisted of two layers of half-inch-thick iron plate spiked to a backing of 14 by 7-inch pine planks. At the bow and stern the deck formed overhangs, which protected the anchor well at the bow and the propeller and rudder assemblies at the stern. Both anchor and propeller could be accessed by removing plates on the main deck if in need of service.

Besides the turret, the most striking feature on the weather deck of the *Monitor* was her rectangular iron pilothouse. Within this small structure, the commander had only a half-inch slit through which to view the world. Ericsson had located the pilothouse at the bow about fifty feet forward of the turret. Unfortunately, this arrangement effectively limited the *Monitor*'s ability to fire her guns dead ahead. Ericsson would later admit that "*excepting the omission* to place the *pilot-house* on the top of the turret, the original *Monitor* was a *perfect* fighting machine."[49]

Though a machine, the *Monitor* would be the home to between fifty-eight and sixty-three men at any given time throughout her career. The accommodations for these men, however, were not the norm for a traditional naval vessel. On every warship in the U.S. Navy, a certain physical hierarchy obtained. The commanding officer lived farthest aft, in the largest and finest quarters. Just forward of him, his officers found their accommodations. Living amidships were the petty officers and the aptly named young "midshipmen," while the common sailors slept on the orlop or gun decks, and in the forecastle, or "before the mast."[50] However, because part of the ingenuity of the design of the *Monitor* lay in the placement of all systems save ordnance below the waterline, the engine had to be placed aft, in the space traditionally allotted to the commanding officer. Thus, Ericsson threw naval tradition aside in his design and placed the captain's quarters as far forward as possible, just abaft the anchor well and pilothouse. Officers would live abaft the captain in small, yet well-appointed cabins to the starboard and port of the officers' wardroom. A wooden bulkhead would separate these officers from the berth deck where the crew and a few unfortunate junior officers lived. Ericsson was aware that this unorthodox layout might be a difficult thing for seasoned officers to bear. Therefore, he outfitted the officers' quarters quite elegantly, and at his own expense.

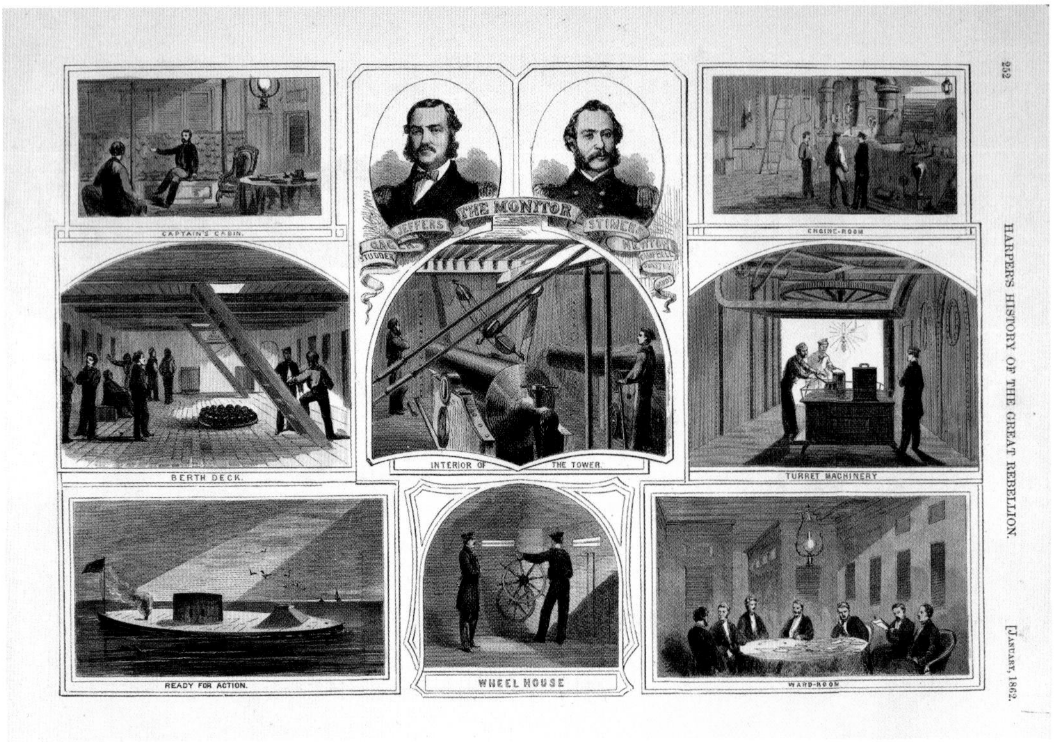

Fig. 24. Readers of *Harper's Weekly* were captivated by these images of the *Monitor's* interior when they first appeared in the April 12, 1862, edition. They were later reprinted in *Harper's History of the Great Rebellion* (1866). (The Mariners' Museum, Newport News, Virginia)

The presentation plan of the *Monitor* shows some detail of the interior of the officers' quarters, including elaborately decorated wood paneling with darker wood trim. But to get a clearer picture of the absolute Victorian excess that prevailed within these small quarters, it is necessary to turn to the writings of the men who lived there. William F. Keeler, the paymaster of the vessel, provides the most detailed description. A forty-year-old businessman from Illinois, Keeler became acting assistant paymaster on the *Monitor,* where he kept the ship's accounts, ordered provisions, and issued pay to the crew. He was a keen observer with free time on his hands, and he wrote seventy-nine letters to his wife, Anna, in 1862 alone. These letters now offer us a window on the world of the *Monitor.*

Hoping she would be able to picture his daily life, Keeler sent a sketch to his wife. He wrote, "Here is a plan that will give you a little idea [of how my room looks]—A is my desk, B is the door let down to write on, the iron chest is placed underneath, C is the door, D is the shelf in which is my washbowl, underneath is another shelf in which holes are cut (remember that at sea nothing is placed on a shelf, but in it) for my slop jar . . . &c &c all of nice white ware with '*Monitor*' . . . in gilt letters."

No detail was too small for Keeler: "Over the wash bowl is a small shelf for hair brush, comb &c. . . . [and] a large looking glass in a gilt frame. The floor . . . is covered with oil cloth, . . . a tapestry rug & . . . a fine, soft goat's

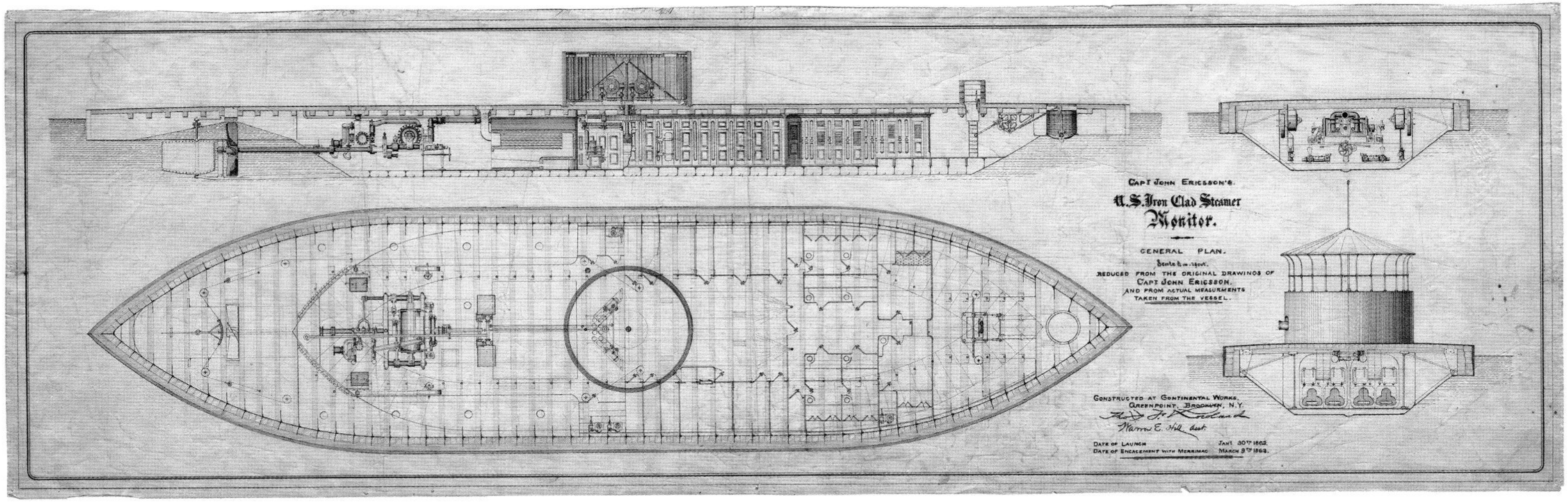

Capt John Ericsson's.
U.S. Iron Clad Steamer
Monitor.
General Plan.
Reduced from the original drawings of
Capt John Ericsson,
and from actual measurments
taken from the vessel.
Constructed at Continental Works,
Greenpoint, Brooklyn, N.Y.
Warren E. Hill, asst.
Date of Launch Jan. 30th 1862.
Date of Engagement with Merrimac March 9th 1862.

Fig. 25. John Ericsson's original presentation plans for the *Monitor.* (The Mariners' Museum, Newport News, Virginia)

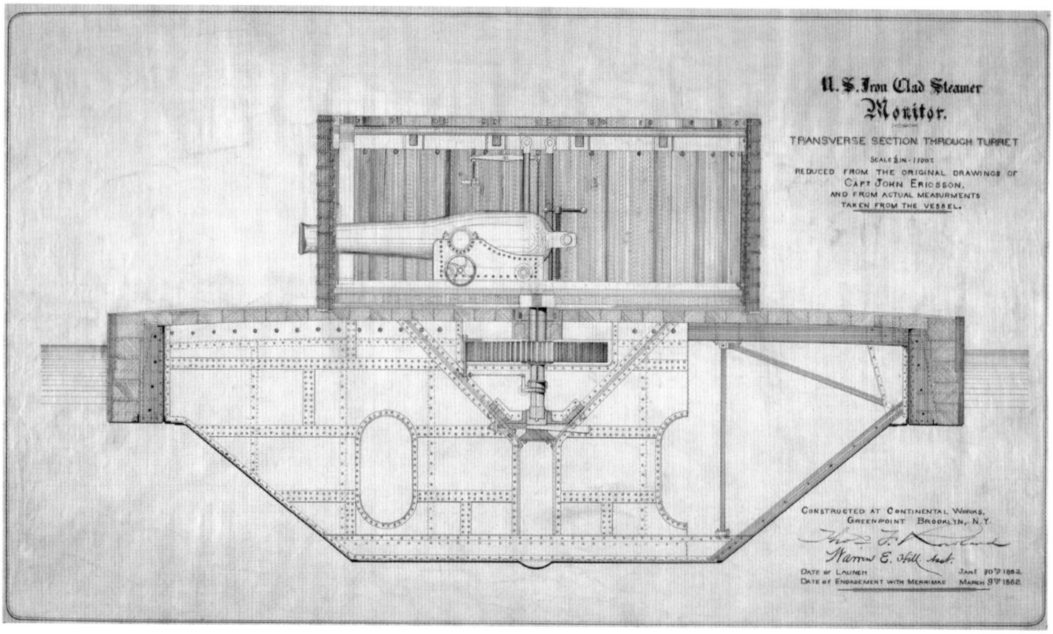
U. S. Iron Clad Steamer
Monitor.
TRANSVERSE SECTION THROUGH TURRET
REDUCED FROM THE ORIGINAL DRAWINGS OF
CAPT JOHN ERICSSON.
AND FROM ACTUAL MEASURMENTS
TAKEN FROM THE VESSEL.
CONSTRUCTED AT CONTINENTAL WORKS,
GREENPOINT BROOKLYN, N.Y.
DATE OF LAUNCH
DATE OF ENGAGEMENT WITH MERRIMAC
MARCH 9TH 1862

Fig. 26. Transverse section of John Ericsson's original presentation plans for the *Monitor.* (The Mariners' Museum, Newport News, Virginia)

hair mat." Keeler continues: "F.F. are two closets, . . . but they are so high up & so far back that it is unhandy to get at them. Under the berth are four drawers. [They] . . . are all of black-walnut, the curtains are lace and damask, or an imitation I suppose."[51]

To improve ventilation for the wardroom and the cabins that flanked it, Ericsson designed the space with short partitions and doors with louvered panels. Unfortunately, the features that permitted air to circulate also allowed voices to carry. Keeler complained, "While writing now, every word spoken . . . around the ward room table is as audible as if they were seated by my elbow." Poor privacy-starved Keeler wrote a few weeks later, "I had to laugh when [you said] . . . you hope I will be allowed to read it in quiet, for in the Cabin were [several men] . . . discussing iron clad ships." In the room next to him were "a half dozen, alternately spouting Shakespeare, criticising the Opera, Theater, & other places not quite as reputable, while another in a room at my side is exercising his lungs by reading in a loud tone the 'personals' of the 'N.Y. Herald' interspersed with intended witticisms."[52]

It was difficult to provide natural light within the vessel. Therefore Ericsson installed a series of oil lanterns every six to nine feet along the port and starboard sides of the vessel. Elegant brass sconces to hold them were purchased ready-made from suppliers in New York, such as E. V. Haughwout in lower Manhattan.[53] William Keeler described the lighting in the staterooms: "The only objection is they are too dark. I have all my writing to [do] by candlelight & lamps are always burning in the ward room.

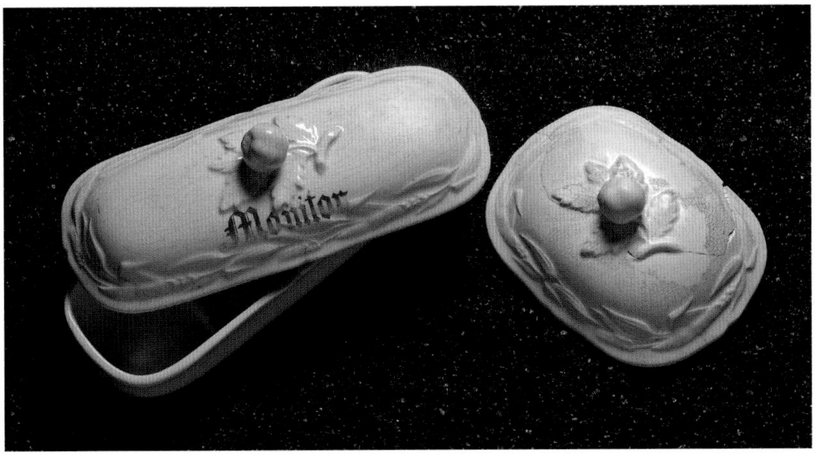

Fig. 27. A dish from the *Monitor*, likely removed when she was at the Washington Navy Yard for repairs. (The Mariners' Museum, Newport News, Virginia)

If the sun ever shines again it may light us up a little better." A series of decklights, six-inch-diameter holes set into the deck with thick glass in iron frames, let light into each stateroom. The wardroom had two of them. The decklights were often covered with water when the deck was awash, but the light got through anyway, and according to Keeler, "when the sun shines bright it is sufficiently light to read and write without difficulty."[54] The decklights could be opened to allow in fresh air when conditions allowed, and at least once Keeler found his decklight used as a mailbox when a fellow officer delivered Keeler's mail through the opening.[55]

In contrast to the damask and lace of the officers' quarters, the berth deck was a utilitarian space of sixteen feet by twenty-five feet, stretching from the staterooms to a point beneath the turret. This was where the crew of about forty-nine men slept in hammocks, taking turns keeping watch.[56] Oil lamps provided most of the light, for there were no deck lights to let daylight into the crew's quarters. When the upper hatches were opened, the crew enjoyed more light and air. Storerooms, including the powder magazine and the shell room, bordered the berth deck. Sitting just twenty feet away from Keeler's elaborate cabin, fireman George Geer wrote to his wife, Martha: "I have for my desk a water pail turned upside down." In another letter, Geer apologized for not writing more, saying, "If you could see how I am writing this you would not expect a very long one. I am on the Hammocks, where I cannot sett up strait and can hardly move my arms."[57]

Another feature of the *Monitor* was a concession to the men who would have to live in this machine. Ericsson equipped his vessel with below-the-waterline toilets, designed to keep the men safe from both the enemy and the elements when nature called. These "heads" bore no resemblance to any marine head that had come before: these were the first flushing toilets ever installed below the waterline on a ship. Ericsson's system of a pump and waste tube allowed waste to be safely discharged into the sea. The men found it important to follow the precise operating directions; this toilet could turn into an unwelcome bidet if the proper sequence was not followed, which the ship's first surgeon found out, much to his embarrassment.[58] The commanding officer had a private head in his cabin, while the officers' head was located amidships on the port side. The crew shared two heads located amidships on the starboard side.[59]

A central iron bulkhead divided the berth deck from the galley and the engine room. The engine, its attendant boilers and condenser, and the two small Worthington bilge pumps took up much of the aft half of the vessel. On either side of the engine, large iron bunkers held the eighty tons of hard anthracite coal the vessel was able to carry—forty tons per side.

The design of the vessel's 400-horsepower engine, referred to as "a vibrating side-lever engine," was a favorite of John Ericsson's and had proven successful in his earlier ships. Before Ericsson developed this engine design in the 1840s, steam engine pistons had operated in a vertical motion and had taken up a great deal of space. In a warship, these engines were vulnerable to enemy fire, since they rose above a vessel's waterline. Ericsson's design allowed the pistons to move horizontally. This meant that the height of the equipment was greatly reduced and the new engine could be mounted below the waterline—and safe from enemy fire. Sitting on a raised, diamond-plate floor, the engine dominated the space and left very little room for movement around it. Small walkways allowed the engineers access to the brass oil cups that could be found attached to every part of the engine needing lubrication. Hard tallow, placed in the cups, would melt with the engine's heat and the liquid fat could drip in slowly.[60] Paint traces found on recovered pieces indicate that the engine room was very likely a colorful place. The diamond plating appears to have been painted a royal blue, while the engine may have been red or green. Bright brass pieces, including the steam gauge, the silver-faced clock, and the elegantly curved brass reversing wheel dominated the face of the engine, along with the brass engine register. After cleaning off the marine growth on the register, conservators at The Mariners' Museum discovered that the face of this piece had the word "MONITOR" engraved on it in elaborate script, with "1862" engraved below the dials. This was the first object bearing the vessel's name to be recovered from the wreck site (see fig. 94).

On March 3, 1862, the *Monitor* was ready for her sea trials. The logbook for that day read thus:

> Remarks March 3/62
> From Midnight to 4 AM. Weather light & clear wind from N
> G Frederickson

From 4 to 8 AM. Wind & weather same J. Webber

From 8 to Meridian weather thick from N.E. at 10 AM. A board of commission composed of Com. Gregory Chief Eng Garvin Naval Cons Hart came on board to witness the trial trip at 10:30 AM hove up Anchor & started from yard under full head of steam & proceeded down Harbor in Tug Boat Rapid wind N.E.

Louis Stodder

From Meridian to 4 PM at 20 minutes past. First of firing blank cartridges 2nd a stand of grape, 3rd with canister with a full charge of powder 2:15 with 30 lbs steam making 50 Revolutions turned with helm hard a starboard turned in 4 min 15 sec within a compass of 3 times her length & proceeded towards the yard against a strong ebb tide vessel going at the maximum speed of 6 & 1/4 knots an hour Greatest no of rev's attained 64

G Frederickson

From 4 to 6 PM thick rainy weather with strong N.E. wind Came (to) anchor at Navy Yard with 5 fathoms water & 20 fathoms of chain

J. Webber

From 6 to 8 PM Wind and weather same at 6 PM put L. Murray in irons

Louis Stodder

From 8 to Midnight thick rainy weather strong N.E. wind At 9 PM released ward room steward at: 10 PM Norman McPherson & John Atkins deserted taking the ship's cutter & left for parts unknown so ends this day

G Frederickson[61]

The *Monitor* had been taken out for a test spin, quite literally, the morning of March 3. Turret turning, guns working, the new crew put her through her paces, steaming around in circles she "turned with helm hard a starboard . . . in 4 min 15 sec within a compass of 3 times her length," master's mate George Frederickson had written while he stood the afternoon watch. Commodore Francis H. Gregory, chief engineer Benjamin F. Garvin, and naval constructor Edward Hartt had come on board to observe this experimental vessel's trial run. The undercurrent of this visit does not come through in the log book entry, however. But given the events of a week prior, one can imagine John Ericsson's head spinning just as surely as his turret over this visit.

The week before, on February 26, a defect had been found in the steering gear, and now that defect sent the *Monitor* "first to the New York side then to the Brooklyn & so back & forth across the river, first to one side then to the other, like a drunken man on a side walk, till we brought up against the gas works with a shock that nearly took us from our feet," recalled paymaster William Keeler.[62] It also kept the *Monitor* away from Hampton Roads a few more days until Ericsson could correct the problem.

The press stood by to report on what they had now dubbed "Ericsson's Folly," and there were some naval personnel in the naval yard who intimated that they would have to pull the ironclad into drydock and install a rudder that they knew would work—a steering mechanism *not* of Ericsson's design. But given that he still owned the vessel, Ericsson was not willing to allow this to happen. According to his biographer, William Conant Church, he turned bright red at the suggestion and roared, "The *Monitor* is MINE, and I say it shall not be done. Put in a new rudder! They would waste a month in doing that; I will make her steer just as easily in three days."[63] The navy observers were there to make sure that he followed through with that boast.

But testing the new steering mechanism was not the only excitement that day. While the logbook reported that the guns were tested that afternoon, what is not reported is what actually happened during the test firing. As previously noted, the XI-inch Dahlgrens in the *Monitor*'s turret each weighed approximately 9 tons, were 13 feet long, and fired a 165-pound shot. Such a gun needed approximately twice its length for recoil room, or 26 feet. The turret, however, was only 21 feet in its interior diameter.

The gun carriages within the turret were two of a kind, custom made for the *Monitor* and the *Monitor* alone. Friction gears tightened with a handscrew served to stop the recoil if operated properly. Unfortunately for Alban Stimers, who was to demonstrate the working of the guns, Ericsson had not made the braking mechanisms uniform. As Stimers turned the screw on carriage number one to the right to increase the friction, his action produced precisely the opposite effect, and upon firing, one massive Dahlgren leaped backward from its carriage and smashed its cascabel into the turret bulkhead. Assuming erroneously that the second carriage must be a mirror image of the first, Stimers reversed his action and sent the second Dahlgren crashing into the turret bulkhead as well. Before she had even seen battle, the *Monitor* had two large dents *inside* her turret. Those same dents remain there to this day and are a testament to human error that can still be seen on the mantelets, which have been removed from the turret's interior for conservation.

While all of this was occurring in the turret, the wardroom steward had taken a bottle for a spin as well. The log indicates that he was put in chains during the first dogwatch that day and released only at nine that evening. Others' words are needed to fill in the story, however. Paymaster William Keeler wrote to his wife about the goings-on in his strange new home:

> It was a dismal rainy day & our wet iron decks were anything but comfortable to stand upon. We had an awning fitted over the top of the turret, running up to a point in the center like a tent & under this we managed to keep pretty dry, going down below occasionally to warm. Commodore Gregory & other notables from the Yard were with us & arrangements were made on board to give them a dinner suited to the occasion. The preliminaries were all right, but unfortunately we found upon seating ourselves at the table that "the wisest plans of mice & men gang aft aglee" . . . for to sum it all up in one short sentence, the Steward, upon whom it all depended, was drunk. I suppose he had been testing the brandy & Champaine before putting it upon the table. As may be supposed it was a decided failure—the fish was brought in before we had finished the soup, & Champaine glasses were furnished us to drink our brandy from & vice versa.[64]

Fig. 28. This dent in the turret bulkhead was discovered during the August 2011 excavation season by conservators after having removed marine concretions. (Photo by Anna Gibson Holloway)

The log reveals the name of the steward: Lawrence Murray, a thirty-four-year-old native New Yorker who stood five feet, six inches tall, with striking blue eyes, a fair complexion, and a singularly bald head. According to Keeler, Murray "yelled & hollowed & begged & plead . . . [but] was pretty well sobered before he was released & appeared a good deal humbled & mortified." Yet he was back at the bottle the next day—and was "ironed & shut up in one of the chain lockers."[65]

The log entry at ten o'clock that evening indicates that Norman McPherson and John Atkins, two of the volunteer crew members, expressed their discomfort with being on an experimental vessel by stealing the ship's boat and leaving "for parts unknown."[66] It seems that the test voyage had not inspired a great deal of confidence in some of the crew. While the *New York Times* reported only the successes of the day, one negative comment noted that "the compass in the iron pilot-house did not work altogether satisfactorily, but no difficulty is apprehended with regard to being able to adjust it."[67]

Fig. 29. The *Seth Low.* (The Mariners' Museum, Newport News, Virginia)

All of this excitement had occurred before the vessel ever left New York, but that same day she finally received orders to head south. A dispatch from Hiram Paulding instructed Lieutenant Worden to "proceed with the *Monitor* under your command to Hampton Roads and on your arrival report to the senior naval officer there," adding, "when the weather permits."[68] The weather remained difficult for the next two days, though, and the *Monitor*'s departure was delayed until March 6.

Though Ericsson had designed the *Monitor* to be a seagoing vessel, no one was willing to take any chances with her. Accordingly, on Thursday, March 6, the *Monitor* left the navy yard under tow. The steam tug *Seth Low* towed her to sea, in company with the steamers *Sachem* and *Currituck.* By four in the afternoon they had left New York Harbor and were heading south. However, Gideon Welles had issued new orders to the *Monitor* at the advice of General George Brinton McClellan, who felt that the *Monitor* could best benefit the Union by clearing the Potomac River in advance of McClellan's planned troop movements. McClellan was preparing to move troops south to Urbanna and then proceed overland to Richmond. Welles telegraphed the navy yard in New York with orders for the *Monitor* to "proceed immediately to Washington," but the message arrived two hours after the *Monitor* had left. A vessel carrying the new orders raced to reach the *Monitor* but was unsuccessful.[69] The message did reach Commodore John Marston in Hampton Roads, however.

Executive Officer Samuel Dana Greene recalled that "on the following day a moderate breeze was encountered, and it was at once evident that the *Monitor* was unfit as a sea-going craft." The log indicates initially a Force 4 on the Beaufort Scale, but it is somewhat telling that after a point the officers of the watch ceased trying to estimate what force the wind was. This was perhaps in part due to the fact that the men were desperately trying to keep their vessel afloat. Compounding their difficulties, the leather belts of the engine had grown sodden and stretched with the influx of seawater into the engineering spaces. With stretched belts, the ventilators were unable to blow. Noxious fumes began to fill the engine room. Alban Stimers told his father, "Engineers commenced to stagger and the men to tumble down. I sent them all out and remained awhile alone trying to get the blower going but I soon began to find myself getting very limber in the legs." Stimers decided to evacuate the turret. Climbing the ladder, he "managed to reach [the top of the turret] just as my strength gave out and I tumbled over upon the turret deck at full length." Surgeon Daniel C. Logue recalled that second assistant engineer Albert Campbell, third assistant engineer Robinson Hands, and four firemen were found "in a state of total unconsciousness on the floor of the fire-room. They were immediately removed to the turret deck where restoratives were applied successfully." Most of the crew ended up on top

Fig. 30. Paymaster William F. Keeler, standing. Before leaving the Brooklyn Navy Yard, Paymaster Keeler had his photograph taken in his new uniform. "I felt awkward enough at first in mine," he wrote to his wife, Anna, because "it seemed like every one was looking at me." Keeler felt rushed by the photographer and was unhappy with the portrait. "I wanted to select my own attitude and put on spectacle frames, but the artist said it was unnecessary. I am sorry now that I did not insist on having my own way." A second portrait of Keeler appears in fig. 31.

Fig. 31. Paymaster William F. Keeler, sitting. (U.S. Naval Academy Museum)

of the turret on that impossibly long night. Paymaster William Keeler wrote that "things for a time looked pretty blue, as though we might have to 'give up the ship,'" while Samuel Dana Greene said of his first five days underway on the *Monitor,* "I think I lived ten good years."[70]

As the *Monitor* steamed south, Commodore John Marston of the USS *Roanoke* and Union naval commander in Hampton Roads received his own telegram from Gideon Welles. It read:

> Send the *St. Lawrence, Congress,* and *Cumberland* into the Potomac River. Let the disposition of the remainder of the vessels at Hampton Roads be made according to your best judgment after consultation with General Wool. Use steam to tow them up. I will also try and send a couple of steamers from Baltimore to assist.
>
> Let there be no delay.[71]

Welles sent this message on March 7. He then sent a second message telling Marston to await additional orders carried by Assistant Secretary of the Navy Gustavus Vasa Fox, who was traveling to Hampton Roads on the eighth.

CHAPTER 4

The Battles of Hampton Roads

March 8, 1862

The same storm that nearly sank the *Monitor* on her trip south also kept the CSS *Virginia* in her berth. It was not until the morning of March 8, 1862, that the weather appeared acceptable for taking the Confederate ironclad out into Hampton Roads. With workmen still aboard, the commanding officer, Franklin Buchanan, ordered his crew to ready the ersatz vessel for a cruise. Most believed that this cruise would be a shakedown test, but Buchanan had confided to his officers that he intended to take the vessel directly into battle. As the crew cast off the mooring lines, the workmen, who had been installing the fore and aft gunport shutters leaped to the dock. The *Virginia* was underway. Those observing her departure kept eerily silent, as some of the crew recalled years later. As the *Virginia* neared Craney Island, Commander Buchanan reportedly said, "Sailors, in a few minutes you will have the long looked for opportunity of showing your devotion to our cause. Remember that you are about to strike for your country and your homes. The Confederacy expects every man to do his duty. Beat to quarters!" Then he reminded them that "the whole world is watching you today."[1]

Privately, Buchanan must have had mixed feelings. Like many others in this war he would soon be opening fire upon his own flesh and blood. His brother, Thomas McKean Buchanan, was the paymaster on board the USS *Congress.*

As the *Virginia* steamed down the Elizabeth River, both banks were crowded with people. Many were just curious about the ship's strange appearance. One Alabamian observed that she looked like "a powerful battery resembling the roof of a house as seen on the water."[2] Some refused to

Fig. 32. The interior of the CSS *Virginia* during the Battle of Hampton Roads, from the French publication *Le Monde Illustré,* ca. 1862–1865. (Library of Congress)

believe in her, shouting, "Go on with your old metallic coffin!" Those with a richer sense of history realized that the day had finally come—that "here was to be tried the great experiment of ram and iron-clad in naval warfare."[3]

Saturday, March 8, 1862, was laundry day for the crews of the Union's North Atlantic Blockading Squadron in Hampton Roads, Virginia. The rigging of the wooden vessels was festooned with blue and white clothing, drying in the late winter sun. Shortly after noon, the quartermaster of the USS *Congress,* which was anchored off Newport News Point, saw something strange through his telescope. He turned to the ship's surgeon and said, "I wish you would take the glass and have a look over there, Sir. I believe *that thing* is a'comin' down at last."[4]

The men of the North Atlantic Blockading Squadron, who had grown weary of waiting for the *Virginia* to come out, now scrambled to prepare for battle. In the panic of the moment, and with the tide at ebb, several vessels ran aground, including the USS *Congress* and the USS *Minnesota.* (Confederate artillerist Stephen Dodson Ramseur would claim credit for running the *Minnesota* aground with his well-aimed cannonading.[5])

The USS *Cumberland* was Buchanan's first target. With his guns firing at the wooden ship, Buchanan rammed the *Cumberland* on her starboard side. The hole below her waterline was large, and the ship immediately be-

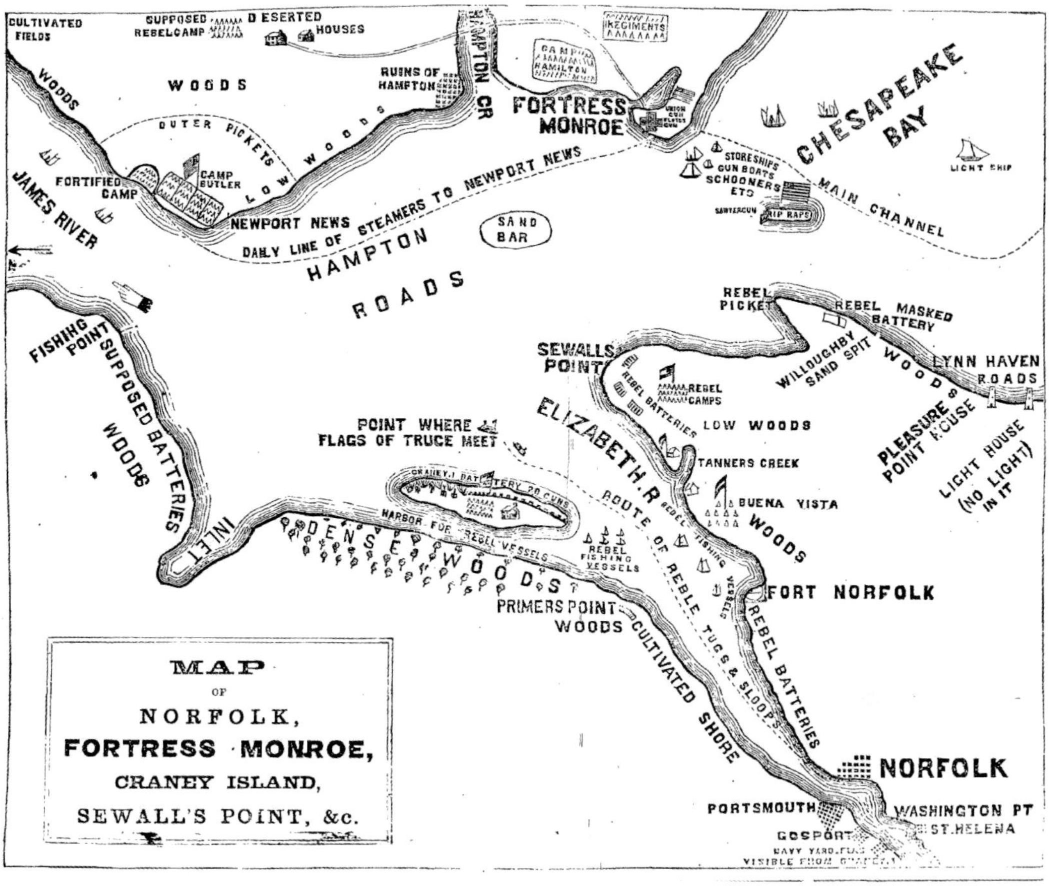

gan to sink, nearly taking the *Virginia* with her (and, unbeknownst to Buchanan, separating the ram from the *Virginia*). Marine Daniel O'Connor, who survived the sinking of the *Cumberland,* described the agony and frustration of the scene in a letter home a few days later:

> At said time [3:00 P.M.] the *Cumberland* [was] sunk by the *Merrimack* driving a hole through her that you could drag your body through, with her prow right on the starboard bough. None of our shots did not have any effect on her. She came about 50 yards of us before she fired a shell & every shell she fired killed some. I was first loder [*sic*] of the cabin guns & being always on the portsides I had a chance to see every shell she fired. . . . She came alongside twice and you could hear them cheer but you could not see them. I hear them laugh, which was aggravating to us in that perdicament.

Fig. 33. "Map of Norfolk, Fortress Monroe, Craney Island, Sewall's Point, &c.," printed in the *Philadelphia Inquirer,* March 10, 1862.

According to O'Connor, an officer from the *Virginia* asked Lieutenant George Upham Morris to surrender the *Cumberland.* But Morris retorted,

Fig. 34. George Upham Morris, commander of the *Cumberland*. (The Mariners' Museum, Newport News, Virginia)

"Dam[n] you, you coward you have made a slaughter house of the ship. We will sink with our colours first." "Sink it is," replied the Confederate.

Several men from the *Cumberland* attempted to board the *Virginia* to attack her, "but it was no go," recalled O'Connor. "We could not board her. You could not step on the quarter deck without walking through blood. Mens legs in one place arms in another. The poor fellows that were wounded all got drowned." Lieutenant Morris soon thereafter shouted to his crew, "All hands save your selfs" as the ship continued to slip beneath the waves. O'Connor must have experienced an incredible adrenaline rush at that point as he realized how tenuous his situation had become:

> The ship was turning over then. As I was praying one of the guns she struck me on the shou[l]der & nocked me down. All the guns was running in. I picked myself up as quick as possible & got out the porthole just as the water was commencing. When I got out on the side I took my coat off & was in the act of taking my shoes off when I found myself up to my neck in the water. I would not trust to the boats. There was so many getting into them I thought they would go down so I struck out for shore.[6]

O'Connor was one of the lucky ones. He was eventually picked up by another boat and taken safely to the shore. Others were not so fortunate. Scores of Union sailors from the *Cumberland* died at their guns or went down with their ship, guns still firing and flags still defiantly flying. Evidence of the *Cumberland*'s wreckage would remain in Hampton Roads for months, and soldiers gathered souvenirs from among the items that washed onto the shore.[7] In late May a Union surgeon discovered the body of a sailor from the *Cumberland* floating by the beach. He recalled:

> About sundown last night I was walking on the beach quietly smoking my pipe, when I saw something which proved to be the body of a man floating on the water just at the edge of the shore. I pulled it up on the beach, covered it with seaweed, and then reported the incident. Meanwhile I returned to watch, walking up and down in the moonlight, or standing by the mound of seaweed, thinking of the poor nameless thing beneath,—thinking in ways that a month since were unknown to me. Since coming here death has faced me at every turn and in every conceivable form; yet my own future, my happiness, and my activity seem assured to me. Did that poor fellow look forward as confidently, I won-

Fig. 35. "CSS *Virginia* Attacking USS *Congress,*" painting by Alexander Charles Stewart, ca. 1862–1875. (The Mariners' Museum, Newport News, Virginia)

> dered? Possibly, and yet I cannot think he felt quite as safe as I. Then, was I homesick? Only the moon and the stars and the night could testify. . . . The arrival of the provost marshal forced me back again to the existing facts. He recognized the body as that of one of the unfortunates who was drowned when the "Cumberland" was sunk by the "Merrimac."[8]

Months later, a Union nurse on her way to Fort Monroe would call the still-visible remains of the *Cumberland* a "fit monument—grave and monument as well of heroes."[9]

The *Virginia* broke free from the *Cumberland* and steamed slowly into the James River. The men on the stranded *Congress* began to cheer, thinking they had been spared the same horrific fate. That cheer was cut short, however, when they saw the *Virginia* make her ponderous turn.[10]

The *Virginia*'s withering firepower tore into the *Congress* for nearly two hours. With most of the crew dead or wounded, including the commanding officer, the next in command, Lieutenant Commander Austin Pendergrast, surrendered the *Congress.* One of the gunners recalled the emotion upon the *Congress* about the time of the surrender. "Our little powder boy, a lad of only thirteen years of age, would bring us ammunition, with the tears streaming down his cheeks," he wrote. "He had pure grit and stuck to his duties like a man." Although the order to cease firing had come, this gunner noted, "My gun was loaded at the time, and, although the order had been given to cease firing, I pulled the lanyard and fired what proved to be the last shot ever fired on board the fated 'Congress.'"[11]

Enraged that Union shore batteries were firing upon the white flag, Buchanan ordered the *Congress* to be set afire. He then climbed onto the top deck of the *Virginia* and began personally firing back at the shore with a rifle. Buchanan quickly became a target, taking a bullet in the leg. Wounded, he turned command over to his executive officer, Lieutenant Catesby ap Roger Jones, who returned the *Virginia* to her moorings that evening. Falling darkness and a receding tide had saved the steam frigate USS *Minnesota* from the same fate as the *Congress* and *Cumberland.*

Thousands of Union and Confederate soldiers and civilians watched the action of March 8 from their respective shorelines, and Union sailors stared in wonder from their vessels. A few ran away in terror. Private Asher Williams of the 11th New York Volunteers was court-martialed for "shamefully abandoning his post in the face of the enemy" and running to Fort Monroe when the *Virginia* appeared. Asher later claimed that he "saw her fire into and sink the Cumberland, and fire into the Congress," but that he "then met a lady who asked me if I would . . . accompany her into the woods as she thought she was in danger." But the court did not believe him, and he was sentenced to hard labor at Fort Wool for the remainder of his enlistment, with a ball and chain attached to his leg.[12]

Unlike Private Asher, most spectators on the shorelines watched in amazement. One Georgia soldier was "enlivened by watching the CSS *Virginia* destroy Union ships." Colonel R. E. Colston of the 16th Virginia Infantry, commanding a Confederate brigade on the south side of the James River and overseeing the shore batteries at Craney Island, later recalled "a curious incident" from that first day of the battle—an effect now known as "acoustic shadows." "The cannonade was visibly raging with redoubled intensity; but, to our amazement, not a sound was heard by us from the commencement of the battle," he later wrote. "A strong March wind was blowing direct from us toward Newport News. We could see every flash of the guns and the clouds of white smoke, but not a single report was audible."[13]

At Fortress Monroe the opposite was nearly true. While some of the battle could be seen from the ramparts, much was obscured. Fourteen-year-old telegrapher John O'Brien heard the battle begin and sent a message to George D. Cowlam, the operator at Newport News Point. Cowlam confirmed that the *Merrimack* had come out. John's older brother Richard, also monitoring the telegraph for traffic, found himself listening to a live account of the battle as the news clicked through the office in American Morse code. As he recalled,

> 'Tis Cowlam, and this is what he telegraphs: "She is steering straight for the 'Cumberland'"—a pause—"The 'Cumberland' gives her a broad-

> side"—waiting at the fort—"She keels over"—suspense—"Seems to be sinking"—anxious watching—"No; she comes on again"—great anxiety—"She has struck the 'Cumberland' and poured a broadside into her. God! the 'Cumberland' is sinking"—breathless suspense—"The 'Cumberland' has fired her last broadside."

Cowlam's office at Newport News Point afforded him a front-row seat to the battle, but it was not without peril. Shells from the conflict "shrieked about his quarters, and two tore through his office."[14]

Night

The mood in Hampton Roads was one of disbelief and, for some, resignation. Major General John E. Wool of the U.S. Army kept Washington informed of events via the telegraph, the problematic new lines of which had been repaired late in the day. The news that he sent to Secretary of War Edwin M. Stanton at 8:30 P.M. from Fortress Monroe was bleak:

> The *Merrimack* came down from Norfolk to-day, and about 2 o'clock attacked the *Cumberland* and *Congress.* She sunk the *Cumberland,* and the *Congress* surrendered. The *Minnesota* is aground and attacked by the *Jamestown, Yorktown* and *Merrimack.* The *St. Lawrence* just arrived and going to assist. The *Minnesota* is aground. Probably both will be taken. That is the opinion of Captain Marston and his officers. The *Roanoke* is under our guns.[15]

Wool continued, ominously: "It is thought the *Merrimack, Jamestown,* and *Yorktown* will pass the fort to-night." Secretary Stanton took this news to heart, reportedly peering out the window of the White House to see if the Confederate ironclad and her consorts had already arrived on the Potomac, stating in an alarmist fashion that it was "not unlikely we shall have a shell or cannonball from one of her guns in the White House before we leave this room." Confederate sympathizers in the North, by contrast, were jubilant and hopeful as the rumors trickled north. "Great excitement in town," wrote one woman who was traveling in Baltimore on March 9. "[It is] reported that the ironclad ship, the *Merrimac,* created havoc at Old Point among the Federal ships—Heaven grant that it may be true."[16]

Had the men of the *Monitor* not been aware of the impending completion of the reconfigured *Merrimack,* the scene that greeted them in Hampton Roads would have been something nearly inconceivable to them—more akin to a chapter out of a fantastical novel than a safely blockaded harbor. Even before the incredible destruction was visible to them, the officers and crew heard the distant sounds of booming guns as the *Monitor* approached the mouth of Chesapeake Bay at three in the afternoon.[17] Paymaster William Keeler recalled, "As we neared the harbour the firing slackened & only an occasional gun lit up the darkness." Yet the horror of the day's events had sent civilians into a panic, and Keeler noted that as the *Monitor* drew closer to the scene, "vessels were leaving like a covey of frightened quails & their lights danced over the water in all directions."[18]

At seven in the evening, a local pilot sent to bring the ironclad into the harbor confirmed what the men already suspected—the *Virginia* had come out and had had her way with the Union fleet. The news seemed to slow time instantly for the crew. William Keeler wrote that the *Monitor* "crept slowly on & the monotonous clank, clank, of the engine betokened no increase of its speed" while the "moments were hours." Yet within the hour the *Monitor* came to anchor off Fortress Monroe, whereupon Lieutenant John Worden reported to Commodore John Marston on board the *Roanoke.* Despite having received orders to send the Union ironclad immediately to Washington for the defense of the capital, Marston determined that the best way for the *Monitor* to protect Washington was to engage with the *Virginia* in Hampton Roads. Marston ordered Worden to render assistance to the grounded *Minnesota,* still trapped on Hampton Flats. Worden immediately sent a message to Secretary Welles, stating that "I arrived at this anchorage at 9 o'clock this evening, and am ordered to proceed immediately to the assistance of the *Minnesota,* aground near Newport News."[19]

Therein lay a problem. The *Monitor* would need a pilot to guide her to the *Minnesota* through the difficult waters of Hampton Roads. Despite drawing slightly less than eleven feet, the *Monitor* was still at risk of running aground. Yet there was no pilot to be found willing to guide the *Monitor* to the *Minnesota* and remain with the ironclad throughout whatever action might come the following day. (It was later reported in the press that "after the *Monitor* arrived twenty Baltimore pilots refused to take her to Newport News, excusing themselves because they did not know the channel when, at any other time, they would have jumped at the chance."[20]) Acting Volunteer Lieutenant N. Goodwin of the U.S. bark *Amanda* detailed his own acting master, Samuel Howard, to the *Monitor.*[21] With a skilled and willing pilot on board, Worden quickly had the *Monitor* under way and reached the side of the *Minnesota* by ten o'clock that night.[22] Young John O'Brien at Fortress Monroe watched the "dim outline of a queer, barge-like craft come into the Roads." He raced to the telegraph office to find his brother Richard already sending dispatches concerning her arrival.[23]

News of the *Monitor*'s arrival quickly spread among Union forces. Major General Wool sent the news to Brigadier General Joseph K. Mansfield that "the ironclad Ericsson battery *Monitor* has arrived and will proceed to take care of the *Merrimac* in the morning." That news was relayed to Secretary Stanton in Washington. Assistant Adjutant General W. D. Whipple sent General Wool the reassurance that the *Monitor* "has infused new life into the men" on shore.[24] The men on the *Minnesota* were perhaps a bit more skeptical, and Lieutenant Samuel Dana Greene, who was sent on board the *Minnesota* to inquire of Captain G. J. Van Brunt what manner of assistance the *Monitor* might render to the stranded vessel, recalled that "an atmosphere of gloom pervaded the fleet, and the pygmy aspect of the newcomer did not inspire confidence among those who had witnessed the destruction of the day before."[25] Nevertheless, Captain Van Brunt wrote in his official report, dated March 10, 1862, that "all on board felt that we had a friend that would stand by us in our hour of trial."[26] The real question on all minds, however, was whether the *Monitor*'s presence would make any difference against the seemingly unstoppable might of the Confederate monster.

Fig. 36. Executive officer Samuel Dana Greene. (The Mariners' Museum, Newport News, Virginia)

The burning *Congress* provided an eerie backdrop to the fevered activities that night in Hampton Roads, along with the "considerable noise" floating across the water from Confederate celebrations at Sewell's Point.[27] Observers on the French vessel *Gassendi* reported that "everything" for the Union fleet "seemed desperate on the evening of the 8th . . . everything was in confusion at Fort Monroe."[28] Most desperate of all was the *Minnesota*'s situation. Men from the bark *Amanda* had commandeered the *America,* whose captain and crew had refused to render assistance, and had taken the steam tug to the *Minnesota,* where, from 11:00 P.M. to 4:00 A.M., they attempted, unsuccessfully, to pull the frigate to safety. Despite the fact that "seven or eight guns had been thrown overboard and some others spiked [on the *Minnesota*]," more ammunition was brought on board for the pending engagement. Personal possessions such as bags and hammocks were placed on the USS *Whitehall* in the event that the *Minnesota* had to be abandoned and scuttled. Making the situation seem even more desperate, the *Minnesota* remained under fire until after midnight; however, this fire did not come from the enemy but from the *Congress,* which lay broadside to the *Minnesota.* Exploding munitions on the doomed vessel occasionally sent shot flying as though the unseen hand of an enemy was still firing. "By chance," recalled Joseph McDonald, who was stationed on the tug *Dragon,* which lay next to the *Minnesota,* "we escaped injury."[29]

Around 12:40 A.M. the flames of the *Congress* reached the ship's powder magazine, and the whole of Hampton Roads was treated to a dreadful fireworks show. Alban Stimers called it "the most magnificent pyrotechnic display it is possible to imagine."[30] William Keeler recalled that it was "a scene of the most terrible magnificence. She was wrapped in one sheet of flame, when suddenly a volcano seemed to open instantaneously, almost beneath our feet & a vast column of flame & fire shot forth till it seemed to pierce the skies. Pieces of burning timbers, exploding shells, huge fragments of the wreck, grenades & rockets filled the air & fell sparkling and hissing in all directions."[31] Despite being over two miles from the dying vessel, the explosion was so intense it "seemed almost to lift us out of the water," Keeler wrote. *Monitor* crewman David Ellis marveled at the brilliant colors, "not unlike the colors of the rainbow."[32] The explosion was felt for miles around.

Having barely survived the first test of the *Monitor*'s seakeeping capabilities, the men were eager to have a chance to test out her fighting prowess, and with the heightened senses that come with adrenaline and lack of sleep, the men prepared their untried vessel for the battle that they were certain would come in the morning. David Ellis summarized years later what he believed most of the men were thinking in those overnight hours: "We were about to enter a crisis; a life and death grapple, with a huge and victorious antagonist, possessing extraordinary powers of aggression." Though the men had not yet seen this antagonist in person, they had seen what she could do. The worry was compounded by what the men had experienced in their sea trials and their trip south. Would she stand the test? they wondered. What if she behaved as badly in battle as she had done in the storm? [33]

The men of the *Monitor* got very little rest that night. As Alban Stimers later recalled, "Just as our men were getting to sleep we were hailed from the 'Minnesota' to say that they were getting afloat and we were directly in her channel and must get out of the way. So we weighed our anchor and came to, a little to one side—but she did not float—and it was half past five o'clock when we finally turned in." Another crewman recalled "laying down where we could get a chance." But sleep would be short-lived. By seven in the morning the men were awake for breakfast.[34] They quickly readied their vessel for battle, first covering the deadlights with their iron covers, then removing the blower pipes and smokestacks. The *Monitor* would have as low a profile in the water as possible.

March 9, 1862

Upon first light on March 9, the men of the *Monitor* got their first close-up look at the *Minnesota,* whose ravaged sides towered over the tiny ironclad. The men of the *Minnesota* also got their first real look at the *Monitor.* Desperation mounted on board the frigate, and "the men were clambering down into the smaller boats—the guns were being thrown overboard & everything seemed in confusion." Bags and hammocks, barrels and provisions went over the side of the *Minnesota,* "some of which went into the boats & some into the water, which was covered with barrels of rice, whiskey, flour, beans, sugar, which were thrown overboard to lighten the ship."[35]

Just after dawn on March 9, the men of the *Virginia* tucked into a hearty breakfast made all the more festive by two jiggers of whiskey for each man.[36] In contrast, the *Monitor*'s exhausted crew sat together on the berth deck eating hardtack and canned roast beef, washing it down with coffee. Crewman John Driscoll recalled that

> Capt. Worden came down from the turett [*sic*]. He addressed the crew of 38 men all told besides the officers. He reminded us that we had all volunentered [*sic*] to go with him that now haveing [seen] what the Merrimac had done and from all appearances was now capeable [*sic*] of doing and that the fate of the Cumberland may soon be ours that if any one regretted the step he had taken he would put him on board the Roanoke.

Despite their fatigue, the crew leaped to their feet and gave Worden three cheers. Not a single man took Worden's offer.[37]

Soldiers and civilians on both sides of the water rushed to the shorelines to watch the engagement. "I tried to get a pass to go down there Sunday morning to see them fight, but could not get no pass," wrote one Georgia soldier to his brother. But that did not stop him. "I run away and went. They had a guard on the bridge, so I could not cross. I give a niger a half a dollar to carry me across in a bateau and then I had to walk some six miles." When he finally got to the scene of the action, he found the beach "covered for miles up and down the bay [with people] witnessing the great fighting."[38]

As the morning fog lifted and the dark bulk of the *Virginia* appeared to be moving toward the *Minnesota,* Lieutenant Worden of the *Monitor* inquired of Captain Van Brunt what his intentions were. Van Brunt replied, "If I cannot lighten my ship off I shall destroy her." Worden assured Van

MONITOR
THE FIRST NAVAL CONFLICT BETWEEN IRON CLAD VESSELS.
MERRIMAC

Fig. 37. "The First Naval Conflict Between Iron Clad Vessels," Charles Parsons, artist, was published in 1862 by Endicott & Co., New York. (The Mariners' Museum, Newport News, Virginia)

Brunt that he and the *Monitor* would "stand by you to the last if I can help you." Van Brunt curtly replied, "No Sir, you cannot help me." The exact words that the men of the *Minnesota* called out to the "little pigmy" *Monitor* are unrecorded, but William Keeler wrote that "we slowly steamed out of the shadow of our towering friend no ways daunted by her rather ungracious replies."[39]

Intense fog early on that morning delayed the *Virginia*'s assault upon the stranded *Minnesota,* so it was not until eight o'clock that the men on the *Virginia* could make out the ravaged hull of the *Minnesota.* They also saw what appeared to be "a shingle floating in the water, with a gigantic cheesebox rising from its center" sitting alongside the frigate. The *Virginia* fired the first shot—a warning of sorts—through the *Minnesota*'s rigging shortly before 8:30. The *Minnesota* returned fire, as did the cheesebox. Confederates who had been following the northern newspapers knew then that the cheesebox was the anticipated "Ericsson's Battery." Observers on shore, such as Sallie Brock Putnam, recalled that the *Monitor* was "of midnight hue, which, like a thing of darkness, moved about with spirit-like rapidity."[40]

Lieutenant Worden watched the approaching battle from the deck of the *Monitor.* Daniel C. Logue and William Keeler, who, as surgeon and paymaster respectively, were considered "idlers" who stood no watch, were able to climb atop the turret to survey the scene. A second shot from the

Virginia "howled over our heads & crashed into the side of the *Minnesota,*" recalled Keeler. Worden, ascending the turret to return to his pilothouse found the two men—neither of whom had seen battle—and sternly warned them: "Gentlemen, that is the *Merrimac,* you had better go below."[41] Not waiting for a second warning from their soft-spoken commander, the two quickly complied, with Worden following after. The iron hatch cover was put in place, effectively sealing the men inside their vessel.

What the men remembered most about the moments before the battle was the silence. The morning was serene. "Not a ripple could be detected or a sound heard . . . everything seemed so still, so peaceable, so serene, as if soothed and tranquilized and beautiful by a special benediction from heaven," recalled crewman David Ellis.[42] "Every one was at his post, fixed like a statue," Paymaster William Keeler remembered of the morning of March 9, 1862. "The most profound silence reigned" on board the USS *Monitor,* and "if there had been a coward heart there its throb would have been audible, so intense was the stillness."[43]

Worden took his place in the pilothouse, along with the pilot, Samuel Howard, and quartermaster, Peter Williams, who steered the vessel throughout the battle. In the turret the executive officer, Samuel Dana Greene, assembled his gun crews—eight men per gun. Bos'un's mate John Stocking and seaman Thomas Lochrane served as gun captains. Acting master Louis Napoleon Stodder assisted Greene, while Alban Stimers, who was on board as an observer, personally worked the turret gear. Acting master John J. N. Webber commanded the powder division on the berth deck with the gunner's mate, Joseph Crown. Firemen John Driscoll and George Geer were positioned at the foot of the turret ladder, where they passed up shot to the gun crews above.[44] In the engine room the chief engineer, Isaac Newton, commanded the working of the engine, along with engineers Albert Campbell and Robinson Hands.

The nagging questions about the vessel's capabilities intensified, and with good reason: the turret mechanism was already rusty from the seawater that had poured in during the voyage, the speaking tube between pilothouse and turret was completely disabled early in the action, and the men had not been drilled at the guns and thus "were not prepared to act in concert." To make matters even more precarious in the face of the *Virginia*'s ten powerful guns, the nineteen men inside the turret knew that because of the peculiar installation of the gunport shutters, only one gun could be run out at a time.[45]

To the astonishment of Captain Van Brunt on the *Minnesota,* the *Monitor* moved directly toward the *Virginia,* placing herself between the ironclad and her prey.[46] By putting his vessel in this position, Worden was risking being hit by both combatants, as both were firing ricochet shots.[47] The men in the turret, as well as below, waited in suspense in the dim light of the interior for the first shot to strike the *Monitor.* The "infernal howl . . . of the shells as they flew over our vessel was all that broke the silence & made it seem still more terrible," wrote Keeler. As the *Monitor* came alongside the hulking iron casemate, Greene in the turret asked permission to fire. Keeler relayed the request and returned with the reply, "Tell Mr. Green [*sic*] not to fire till I give the word, to be cool & deliberate, to take sure aim & not waste a shot."[48] Within yards of the *Virginia,* Worden called all stop to the engines and sent the command to Greene to "commence firing!" Greene then "triced up the port, ran out the gun, and, taking deliberate aim, pulled the lockstring."[49] The eerie silence within the *Monitor* was thus finally broken with the report of her first XI-inch Dahlgren, which jarred the crew considerably but nonetheless "was music to us all."[50]

The *Monitor* was now being tested under enemy fire, just as the contract had specified. The officers and crew of the *Monitor* were forced to improvise, given their difficult interior layout and the broken speaking tube. Paymaster Keeler and captain's clerk Daniel Toffey, both landsmen, were tasked with relaying communications between the pilothouse and the turret, a 150-foot round-trip each time. This was a risk, as their inexact understanding of maritime order or custom could potentially result in a devastating miscommunication. But there was no one else to spare for this duty, as each man on the crew had a specific task and the disabling of the speaking tube had not been anticipated.

A "rattling broadside," which could have easily as come from the *Minnesota* as the *Virginia,* soon slammed into the turret.[51] Alban Stimers recalled that this "first shot which struck the turret created quite a sensation among the gunners." Stimers looked over the guns and then turned to the gunners: "Did the shot come through?" he asked. "No sir, it didn't come through, but it made a big dent, just look a there sir!" Hoping to alleviate any fears among the men, Stimers looked at the wall of the turret and then replied, "A big dent, of course it made a big dent—that is just what we expected, but what do you care about that so long as it keeps out the shot?" The gunner replied, "Oh! it's all right then of course sir."[52]

The gunners now showed more confidence, since they knew that "the shots did not penetrate; the tower was intact and it continued to revolve."[53] At one point, a shot from the *Virginia* caused a slight panic. "Three of us were knocked down in the turret by leaning against the inside just where a shot struck upon the outside," Stimers told his father. "I was one of the three, but as I only had my hand against it I immediately jumped up again and did not leave my duties. The other two were somewhat stunned for a couple of hours, but were not injured."[54] But this was the extent of the harm incurred by members of the crew. Engineer Albert

LITH BY HATCH & CO. 29 WILLIAM ST. NEW YORK
Cumberland
Monitor
Minnesota. Merrimac
Yorktown
THE SPLENDID VICTORY OF THE ERICSSON BATTERY MONITOR,
Disabling the Rebel Battery "MERRIMAC" 10 Guns, & Steamers Jamestown & Yorktown,
IN HAMPTON ROADS, MARCH 9TH 1862.

Fig. 38. "The Splendid Victory of the Ericsson Battery *Monitor,*" published in 1862 by Hatch & Co., New York. (The Mariners' Museum, Newport News, Virginia)

Campbell later told his wife triumphantly that "we were hit twice from the *Minnesota* . . . but it don't make much difference who fires at us."[55] Ericsson's prescient inclusion on the interior of the turret of the thin metal mantelets ensured that the nuts, bolts, and rivets holding the eight layers of iron plate together did not turn into more "friendly fire" within the confines of the twenty-one-foot cylinder.

Unfortunately for the men inside, the turret proved difficult to *stop* revolving once in motion. Though Stimers attempted to start and stop the turret on Greene's command, the level of accuracy in aiming that was desperately required could not be achieved with the "novel machinery," which had never been tried in battle. The conventions applied to traditional broadside tactics soon went by the wayside as well. Though the men had carefully marked the stationary portion of the deck beneath the turret with chalk marks to indicate starboard and port bearings, and bow and stern, the marks were soon obliterated by both the movement of battle and the sweat that fell from the gunners "like rain."[56] Worden, who was stationary in the pilothouse, continued to give commands in the traditional way. When relayed Greene's query, "How does the *Merrimac* bear?" Worden's reply of "on the starboard beam" was of little use.[57]

Eventually Greene, Stimers, and the gun crews settled on a method of dealing with their perplexing "revolving drum." They let it continue to revolve, firing "on the fly" when the enemy target came in sight, then stopping it and reloading when the gunports were turned away from the enemy. At two and a quarter rotations per minute, there was no danger of dizziness. For observers on shore, at least, the turret was an absolute marvel to watch, and its movements belied the confusion and frustration within. Confederate signal corps officer William Norris recalled as he watched the battle that "during all this time, the *Monitor* is whirling around and about like a top, and by the easy working of her turret, and her precise and rapid movement elicits the wonder and admiration of all."[58]

Though the men may have admired the machinery, the rotation of the turret was frustrating to the crew of the *Virginia* as well. This was an entirely new kind of warfare. Lieutenant John R. Eggleston of the *Virginia* recalled that "we never got sight of her guns except when they were about to fire into us. Then the turret slowly turned, presenting to us its solid side, and enabled the gunners to load without danger."[59] Thus the *Monitor's* gunports became the particular target that the *Virginia's* gun crew focused upon, as that seemed to be the most vulnerable point upon the armored drum—though at the time the *Virginia's* gunners did not realize *how* vulnerable. Because of the limited space within the *Monitor* herself, the crew was small—so small that had a shot entered the turret, this "would have ended the fight, as there was no relief gun's crew on board."[60] Dents seen in the photographs taken by James Gibson in July 1862, and indeed upon the actual turret itself, show that most of the *Virginia's* fire was trained upon that area.

The *Virginia's* first shots fired deliberately at the turret were grapeshot rather than solid shot or exploding shell. Despite being the object of enemy fire, the men within the turret wanted to see what was happening. Though ordered not to, one of the gunners simply could not help himself and stuck his head out of the gunport for a view of the Confederate ship. Unharmed, he drew his head back in and with a broad grin reported that "the d—d fools are firing canister at us."[61] In fact, there was very little solid shot on board the *Virginia,* as she had no need for it against the wooden walls of the Union fleet at Hampton Roads. Nor did she have the armor-piercing bolts designed for the Brooke rifles on board. These bolts were not yet ready, nor had it been thought that she would need them.

Seeking to find any sort of vulnerability on the *Monitor,* several of the crewmen on board the *Virginia* took up rifles and were ordered by Lieutenant Hunter Davidson to "take one of those guns and shoot the first man that you see on board of that Ship." Gunners Richard Curtis and Benjamin Sheriff took "positions at the bow port," Curtis on the starboard side

Fig. 39. Swedish-Americans embraced John Ericsson and his *Monitor* with great zeal. This pullout poster depicting the Battle of Hampton Roads—suitable for framing—appeared in the magazine *Nya Verdlens* (New Worlds) in Chicago in 1877. (The Mariners' Museum, Newport News, Virginia)

and Sheriff on the port side, "both on our knees, but not in prayer." Having come directly alongside the *Monitor,* Curtis peered right into one of the gunports, looking for a target.[62] Sheriff frantically called out, "look out Curtis, look out Curtis," which Curtis "was doing with all my might." But "while looking for that man I saw one of her guns coming slowly out of her ports and looking me squarely in the face, Sheriff and myself thought it was time to move, which we did quickly. Saw no man, fired no gun."[63]

Eventually many of the gun crews on the *Virginia* stopped firing their guns altogether. Taking a quick turn through the gun deck, Lieutenant Jones found Lieutenant Eggleston's division at ease. When Jones asked, "Why are you not firing, Mr. Eggleston?" Eggleston responded with frustration, "Why, our powder is very precious . . . and after two hours incessant firing I find that I can do her just about as much damage, by fashing [snapping] my thumb at her every two minutes and a half."[64]

After about two hours of battle, it became necessary to replenish the ammunition in the turret. This necessitated having the turret hatches aligned with the deck hatches below. Worden moved his ship away from the *Virginia* to accomplish this task. He also had an intense need to know how well his vessel had weathered the battle so far. To the surprise of his officers and crew, Worden appeared in the turret, climbed out and descended to the weather deck below. Alarmed by this bold move, and worried for Worden's safety, a crewman called out, "Why Captain, what's the trouble?" Worden replied, "I can't see well enough from the pilot house.... I will go back, but I wanted to get a moment to take in the whole situation." He quickly returned to the safety of the turret, however.[65] Completing the rearming of the turret, Worden swung the *Monitor* back into battle.

When the *Monitor* withdrew, Lieutenant Jones seized the moment to bear down upon the *Minnesota.* Jones apparently had not conferred with his pilot, however, and the move caused the *Virginia* to run hard onto the Middle Ground shoal. Upon returning to battle, Worden brought his vessel near to the grounded *Virginia* and began to fire relentlessly into her, attempting to find a chink in her armor. Had Worden known precisely the construction of the *Virginia*'s armor, or had he been privy to the amount of coal burned the day before, he might have been successful. The *Virginia*'s load had been so lightened from the day before that a shot "between wind and water" would have taken her down quickly.[66] Fearing the worst, Jones and his engineers

> had to take all chances. We lashed down the safety valves, heaped quick-burning combustibles into the already raging fires, and brought the boilers to a pressure that would have been unsafe under ordinary circumstances. The propeller churned the mud and water furiously, but the ship did not stir. We piled on oiled cotton waste, splints of wood, anything that would burn faster than coal. It seemed impossible the boilers could long stand the pressure we were crowding upon them. Just as we were beginning to despair there was a perceptible movement, and the *Merrimac* slowly dragged herself off the shoal by main strength. We were saved.[67]

Finally safe, and assessing the situation, Jones realized that while the *Monitor*'s armor made her invulnerable to shot, her "sub-aquatic" nature could potentially be her undoing. His approach was twofold. First, he attempted to ram the vessel, reasoning that she might be vulnerable below the waterline. Jones was not aware that the *Virginia*'s ram had gone down with the *Cumberland* the day before, and he prepared the *Virginia* for ramming. This was no easy task, however, as it took nearly half an hour just to maneuver the vessel into ramming position and required over a mile of sea room to build up enough momentum to make the collision deadly. On board the *Monitor* the men realized what Jones was planning and were worried. Like the men on the *Virginia,* they knew how vulnerable their own lower hull was. Though iron, the hull was merely a half-inch thick, and the men had seen the results of the *Virginia*'s ram upon the *Cumberland*—her flags still defiantly flying as she rested on the bottom of Hampton Roads. Not knowing the size of the presumed ram on the *Vir-*

NAVAL BATTLE BETWEEN THE CONFEDERATE VESSELS "MERRIMACK," "YORKTOWN" AND "JAMESTOWN," AND THE FEDERAL WOODEN FRIGATES "CUMBERLAND" AND "CONGRESS."—SINKING OF THE "CUMBERLAND," AND VICTORY FOR THE CONFEDERATE NAVY, MARCH 8TH, 1862.
FIGHT BETWEEN THE "MONITOR" (TWO GUNS) AND THE CONFEDERATE RAM "MERRIMACK" AND GUNBOATS "YORKTOWN" AND "JAMESTOWN," CARRYING TWENTY-FOUR GUNS.—DEFEAT OF THE CONFEDERATE RAM AND GUNBOATS, AND RESCUE OF THE UNITED STATES STEAMER "MINNESOTA." HAMPTON ROADS, VA., MARCH 9TH, 1862.

Fig. 40. These hand-colored engravings of the Battle of Hampton Roads on March 8 and 9 were produced ca. 1890. (The Mariners' Museum, Newport News, Virginia)

ginia, they braced for the impact. But the *Monitor* was a nimble craft, and able to veer away, received only a glancing blow, the results of which can be seen in James Gibson's photos, which were taken four months later.

Thus far in the battle, cannon fire had not worked, small arms had not worked, and ramming had not worked against the *Monitor.* But Jones had another plan. He called for volunteers to board the *Monitor.* Their weapons would be peacoats and grenades, the coats used to "blind" the pilothouse. Since there was no access to the outer deck (except via the top of the turret), it would be nearly impossible for a *Monitor* crewman to remove the coat. Grenades tossed down the funnels or into the turret would wreak havoc within. Since the *Monitor* drew near the *Virginia* yet again, the volunteers stood ready to leap aboard. Realizing this—or perhaps hearing the call of "boarders away!"—Worden, who did order the two Dahlgrens double shot with canister, was able to quickly veer away, thus thwarting the plan.

The gunners on the *Virginia* took the opportunity, as the *Monitor* was turning, to continue shelling the *Minnesota.* The tug *Dragon,* which was stationed alongside the *Minnesota,* was ordered to cast off, as it was interfering with the *Minnesota*'s return fire from the lower tier of her guns.

Fig. 41. This chromolithograph, "The 'Monitor and Merrimac': The First Fight between Ironclads," by Julian Oliver Davidson (1853–1894), was widely reproduced in the late nineteenth and early twentieth centuries. (The Mariners' Museum, Newport News, Virginia)

Just as the *Dragon* pulled away a shell from the *Virginia* hit the boiler on the tug, wounding three men severely. One man on board the *Dragon* "had very long hair and whiskers." When the explosion took place, "these were burnt completely off in an instant," recalled one of his comrades, "but in the great commotion he did not miss them, and was unhurt." Later, on the deck of the *Minnesota,* one of his comrades turned to him and said, "Joe, where's your hair?" The poor sailor "looked more bewildered than ever as he put his hands up to find only a bald pate in place of his flowing locks of a few moments before."[68]

By now the *Monitor* had completed her turn and made for the *Virginia*'s fantail. While attempting her own ramming maneuver, the *Virginia*'s rifled stern gun fired directly into the *Monitor*'s pilothouse at a range of ten yards. The blast tore open the structure, cracking one of the huge iron "logs" and lifting the top. Lieutenant Worden, though protected somewhat by the heavy iron logs, took the full force of the explosion in the face. Though stunned and temporarily blinded, Worden gave the order to "sheer off" with the helm to starboard.[69] Paymaster Keeler and surgeon Logue helped Worden from the pilothouse, and Keeler ran to relay the news to Greene, who left the turret to assess the situation. Still standing at the foot of the pilothouse ladder, Worden told his officers, "Gentle-

Fig. 42. Thomas C. Skinner painted "Battle between *Virginia and Monitor*" between ca. 1935 and 1950. (The Mariners' Museum, Newport News, Virginia)

men I leave it with you, do what you think best. I cannot see, but do not mind me. Save the *Minnesota* if you can."[70] He turned command of the *Monitor* over to Greene and was led to his stateroom, where he was attended upon by surgeon Logue. The officers conferred and determined to return to battle, despite their wounded leader and damaged pilothouse. However, because the *Monitor* had veered off into shoal water while the men assessed the damage, the distance between the two ironclads was now over a mile. To Greene it appeared obvious that the *Virginia* was in retreat. Keeler wrote that "she seemed inclined to haul off & after a few more guns on each side, Mr. Greene gave the order to stop firing as she was out of range & hauling off." Anxiety over their wounded leader, combined with Worden's continued concern over the safety of the *Minnesota,* caused Greene to abandon the chase and return to the side of the *Minnesota*—to both protect it and to evacuate Worden from the *Monitor* so that he could receive proper treatment for his wounds.[71]

Catesby Jones on the *Virginia,* seeing the *Monitor* out of action and heeding the warnings of his pilot that the tide was receding, made a course for Gosport in order to repair the damage done to his vessel. Both sides claimed victory. *Virginia* gunner Richard Curtis recalled that as they headed back to Portsmouth he "looked once more through the port and saw the 'Monitor' going as fast as she could toward Fortress Monroe, she had given up the fight."[72] On the other side of the water, Union soldiers along the shoreline cheered the *Monitor*'s success. "If it had not been for the Erricson [*sic*]," wrote Lieutenant William Monegan of the 10th New York Volunteers, "the Merrimac would have knocked us all to pieces, as none of our shot would have effect on her Iron roof."[73]

Washington, D.C.

Tensions were high in Washington, D.C., on March 9, 1862, as northern civilians anxiously awaited the results of the battle. Secretary of War Stanton immediately ordered the news of the battle to be made public so that merchants could be aware of potential dangers to their commercial activities. One man observed, "For a great part of the morning the panic at Willard's [Hotel] was intense. Nothing was too wild to be believed in the way of theory and suggestion." Accounts vary as to how Lincoln reacted to reports from the front. According to Lincoln's assistant secretary, William O. Stoddard, "The President has been reading, with keen enjoyment, an all but continuous telegraphic account of the remarkable encounter between the *Monitor* and the *Merrimack-Virginia.* The monster which was destroying our ships has been met and beaten by another monster, Bushnell's and Ericsson's and the President's own, and the story of the fight sounds as nearly like a story of a miracle as one could expect to hear in these degenerate days." Lincoln's private secretary, John Hay, observed things a bit differently, however. "Stanton was fearfully stampeded," wrote Hay in his diary. "He said they would capture our fleet, take Ft Monroe, be in Washington before night. The President thought it was a great bore, but blew less than Stanton. As the day went on the news grew better. And at four oclock the telegraph was completed and we heard of the splendid performance of the Monitor." That night, Hay would call the *Monitor* "one of the pluckiest things on record."[74]

Sitting at his home in Washington, D.C., Benjamin Brown French, the commissioner of public buildings, wrote in his diary: "The stirring times in Hampton Roads last Saturday & Sunday rather stirred us up here for two or three days." Even "in the most favorable light possible[,] it was a sad affair," he wrote, since at least two hundred "of our brave men were sent to 'Davy Jones's locker' at one fell swoop of what was once our eagle of the seas [the *Merrimack*]—now changed, alas, in consequence of our own folly, into a poor beast of a rebel ram—*but,* yes, *butt,* he can, as the *Cumberland* and *Congress* found to *their* cost, and considerably to the cost of this Government." Still, French saw some hope in that moment. "Had it not been for the Providential arrival of the tough little *Monitor*

God only knows what the result would have been. All praise to Capt. Erricson [*sic*]."[75]

One of the many killed on the first day of the battle was Lieutenant Joseph Smith, the commander of the *Congress.* Back in Washington, Smith's father, Commodore Joseph Smith of the Ironclad Board, could not contain his grief upon hearing word that the *Congress* had surrendered. "Joe's dead. The *Congress* struck her flag," he sadly told the family living next door to him on Ninth Street. When one of the neighbors tried to say something reassuring, Smith simply replied, "No, my boy would never surrender. If the flag's down, then Joe's dead."[76]

As naval battles went, the engagement on March 9 was largely uneventful. The two ironclads danced a slow pas de deux with one another for four hours, testing their capabilities and their armor.[77] The significance of the two-day battle lay not so much in who won the field on the final day, however. The immediate importance for the Confederates was that they had destroyed Union vessels and kept the James River from becoming an easy roadway for the Federals to attack Richmond. For the Union, the blockade, though battered, had been maintained.

The two vessels had also fought before an international audience that day. Members of the Lincoln administration immediately recognized the global significance of what had transpired. Secretary of the Navy Gideon Welles felt that "the performance, power, and capabilities of the *Monitor,* must effect a radical change in naval warfare," and he sent a recommendation to Congress for establishing a dockyard for building "an Iron Navy."[78] Stoddard similarly observed that March 9 was "a costly day for Europe. Probably it is the costliest sea-fight ever fought, for it compels all the old nations to put away their existing navies and build new ones, and each of the new ships will be a worse drain upon depleted treasuries than would a squadron of the old."[79]

Political leaders in the Old World knew that the battle of March 9 would have immense implications for the future of warship design. Within days of the battle, Lord Richard Lyons, the British minister to the United States, sent two dispatches to Lord John Russell, the British foreign minister, reporting on the fight between the ironclads. In April Charles Francis Adams, the American minister to Great Britain, reported from London that the "battle between the Merrimack and our vessels has been the main talk of the town ever since the news came, in Parliament, in the clubs, in the city, among the military and naval people. The impression is that it dates the commencement of a new era in warfare, and that Great Britain must consent to begin over again." British leaders hoped to gather whatever information they could about the new American class of vessels. In May 1862 a member of the British legation in Washington traveled to Fort Monroe to examine the *Monitor*. His full memorandum, which detailed the specifications of the *Monitor* as best he could, was immediately sent to Lord Russell in London.[80]

Steam-powered ironclad vessels made more impervious to both shot and shell soon took the place of the wooden walls of the great Age of Fighting Sail. Steam power and the revolving gun turret would assure that the graceful white wings of sailing ships would give way to the black coal smoke that broke the ships free from old broadside tactics.

CHAPTER 5

"The Pet of the People"

The *Monitor* in Popular Culture

The appearance of the *Monitor* did much to shore up flagging spirits in the Union. The "90 day war" had now been going on for nearly a year. Her "victory" over the "rebel monster" was one that she shared in equally with her men. The officers and crew of the little ironclad were celebrated, to be sure. In July Congress passed a resolution "Expressive of the Thanks of Congress to Lieutenant J. L. Worden of the U.S. Navy, and to the Officers and Men Under His Command in the Monitor" for their "skill and gallantry" in the fight with the *Virginia.*[1] But in an even more important way, the vessel herself became a celebrity in her own right. While ships have always been assigned human attributes, the *Monitor* seems to have been credited with even more sentience than most and was lauded in the same way a human hero would be.

The public on both sides of the conflict in America, and indeed, on both sides of the Atlantic, could not get enough information about the vessels and their officers and crew. Engravers in America, England, and France rushed to get images of the fight to the curious masses, often letting speed get in the way of accuracy (something that continued to gall John Ericsson). Editors in the South commented on the inaccuracies in the northern press as well (inaccuracies concerning the "victory" of the *Monitor* and the "defeat" of the *Virginia,* that is) and printed sensational pieces in which the Union naval officers of the *Congress* and *Cumberland* were portrayed as guileless buffoons. All of this was represented as "positive fact."[2] The weekly illustrated newspapers, such as *Harper's* and *Leslie's* in America, had published pictures of the battle by March 22, and the *Illustrated London News* in England followed the next week. The *Penny Illustrated Paper* followed suit in early April, allowing those less affluent in London to also see the two strange vessels that were on everyone's mind.

Ch. Vernier
23
_ Eh ! mais ...., dites-donc monsieur John-Bull ...., et le trône du Mexique ?.....
_ Laissez-moi donc tranquille !........ goddem !........ j'ai bien d'autres chats à fouetter !......
et le Monitor !....... et le Merrimac à surveiller !!......

Fig. 43. In this cartoon, a man who appears to be future Mexican emperor Maximilian, says, "Hey! Sir, tell me about John Bull and the throne of Mexico?" while the Englishman (possibly John Bright) replies, "God damn it! Leave me alone! I have other stuff to do . . . having to keep on an eye on the Monitor and the Merrimac." (Collection of Jonathan W. White)

On the morning of March 10, 1862, major newspapers across the Northeast, as well as some in the South, carried a variety of early reports about the Battle of Hampton Roads—stories that would grow in length, and accuracy, in the coming days and weeks. But that early news was enough to inspire one man to quickly insert a reference to the two ironclads in a speech that he was scheduled to give that evening. Thus it was that at the first annual commencement of the Bellevue Medical College, the first recorded popular culture reference to the *Monitor* occurred. That evening "one of the finest audiences ever collected" gathered at Irving Hall in New York City to celebrate the new graduates and listen to remarks from several faculty members, the class valedictorian, and to the spirited speech by a Dr. Chapin that concluded the evening. Chapin used the newspaper headlines to make his point, "that whatever difficulty would arise, science would meet it." To thunderous applause, Chapin declared that whenever "some portentous *Merrimac* of evil [came] floating out on the waters of our humanity . . . there was always some Ericsson Battery . . . some scientific *Monitor* to beat it back."[3]

By March 11 the *Monitor* and *Merrimack* were already being used to sell products. Sleeper's of Philadelphia offered the first ad (and likely the first poem) using the ironclads as a marketing tool:

The *Monitor*'s a noble craft
Of Excellent construction
She forced the *Merrimack* to leave
To save herself destruction

The *Monitor* did fairly win
The fame she has acquired
And Sleeper for umbrellas has
A fame to be desired.[4]

Not to be outdone, other companies in Philadelphia entered the poetic fray with their own doggerel. Charles Stokes's One Price Clothing Store provided a longer poem, entitled "An 'Ironic' Idyl" (pun fully intended), which made a much more logical connection between the ironclads and his product than did Sleeper's.

I'll sing a song of modern times;
Of a battle fought in Southern climes,
    By "iron clads,"
By which one "Mac," not "beth" or "duff,"
Was whipped, though made of stronger stuff
    Than SHAK[E]SPEARE's lads.

The "Merri-mac." With coat of mail,
Showered on our ships her iron hail
    Of shells and balls;
Until a foeman crossed her track—
The "Monitor"—who drove her back
    Within her walls.

The story's known; it proves full well
That *well-clad* ships, or men, will tell
    In daily strife.
Thus STOKES', 'neath the Continental,
Clothes men with power that will be felt, all
    Through their life.[5]

This was followed on the March 15 by ads from Philadelphia clothiers Towne Hall and Oak Hall. The first included a poem entitled, "Latest Intelligence":

The Rebels are straying
Away from Manassas,
With bleating and braying
Like chastened jackasses

The *Monitor* punches
The stout *Merrimac*
Belaboring the monster
With whack after whack

The President's message
Doth stir up the nation
To the Border States help
In *E*-mancipation

The Rebels now wonder
And look for the crash
When our great anaconda
Shall grind them to smash

Mid all their derangements
We cheerfully sing
Of OAK HALL'S[6] arrangements
OF CLOTHES FOR THE SPRING

The second included a poem entitled "The Monitor and Merrimac," by "the Bard of Towne Hall":

A ship constructed
By Rebels bold,
The "Merrimac" by name,
Came out to meet
The Yankee fleet,
Unchecked by fear or shame

Her iron side
The balls aimed
Which at her ribs did knock

They would rebound
With rattling sound
Like brickbats from a rock

But to attack
The "Merrimac"
The "Monitor" came out;
She (hard shelled too)
In minutes few,
The Rebel ship did rout

The ships are best
In iron dressed;
But *men* who broadcloth wear
Should make a call
At TOWNE HALL
To view the armor there.[7]

While the merchants in Philadelphia liked to versify, those elsewhere enjoyed puns. In a piece entitled "The 'Merrimac' and the 'Monitor,'" a cobbler wrote in the Cleveland *Plain Dealer,*

> The *Merrimac* came out of her hole on Saturday and after sinking one Federal ship and capturing another, she went back into Norfolk a Merrier-mac. On Sunday morning she tried to repeat the experiment, but she caught a Tartar in the *Monitor,* which sent her back with a flea in her iron plated ear, a sadder and a wiser Mac—"Dixie" might as well give up. They can no more compete with the Yankees in the matter or iron ships than they can hope to rival the elegant boots and shoes manufactured by MCGUIRE, Ontario street.[8]

The instant notoriety of the two ironclads ensured that by merely invoking their names, readers would know what was meant by the reference. In the March 17, 1862, edition of Zanesville, Ohio's *Daily Courier,* a writer breathlessly extolled the talents of the magician Professor Anderson, who was to appear in Zanesville later in the month. Anderson was touted as being to magic what Napoleon was to war, what Thalberg was to piano, and that he was, in fact, "the best man in his trade—a *Monitor* among the gunboats."[9]

The *Monitor,* in the space of a few short hours, had gone from being "Ericsson's Folly" (or a "tin can," "rat trap," "iron coffin") to a celebrity. Most famously called a "cheesebox on a raft" by an eyewitness to the battle (an

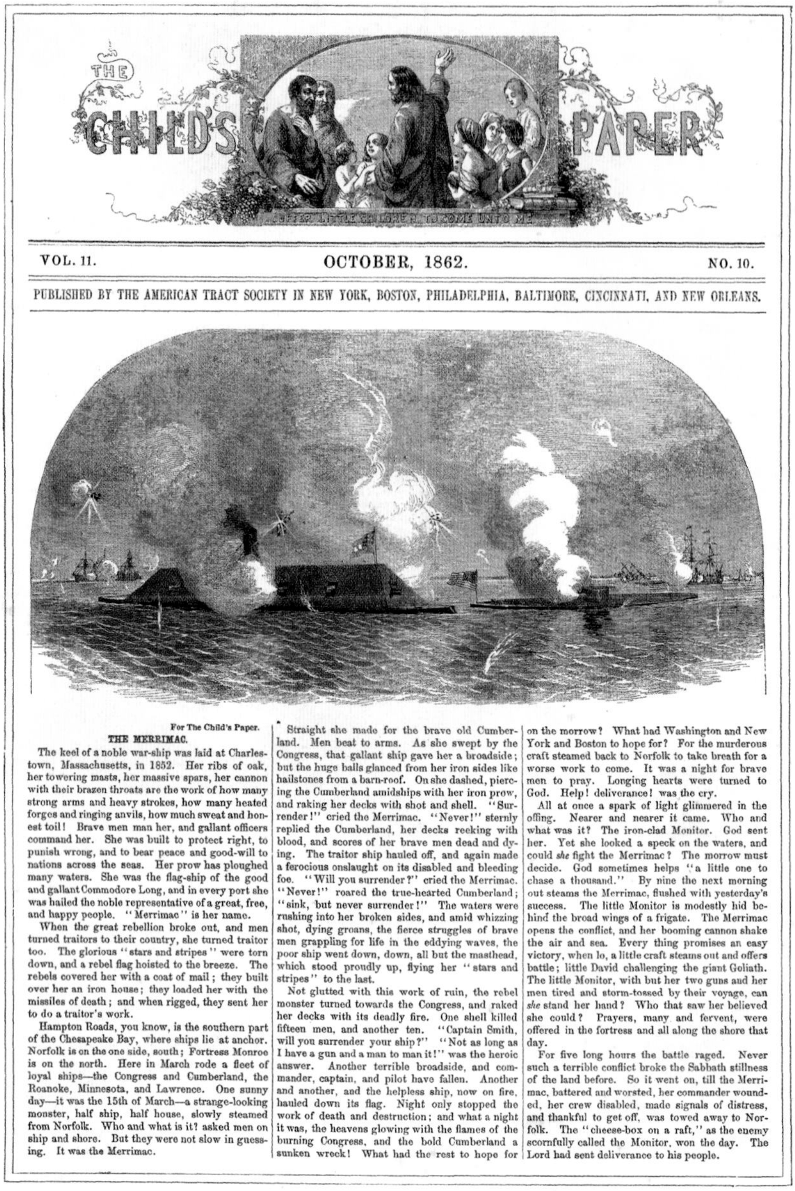

THE CHILD'S PAPER

VOL. II. OCTOBER, 1862. NO. 10.

PUBLISHED BY THE AMERICAN TRACT SOCIETY IN NEW YORK, BOSTON, PHILADELPHIA, BALTIMORE, CINCINNATI, AND NEW ORLEANS.

For The Child's Paper.

THE MERRIMAC.

The keel of a noble war-ship was laid at Charlestown, Massachusetts, in 1852. Her ribs of oak, her towering masts, her massive spars, her cannon with their brazen throats are the work of how many strong arms and heavy strokes, how many heated forges and ringing anvils, how much sweat and honest toil! Brave men man her, and gallant officers command her. She was built to protect right, to punish wrong, and to bear peace and good-will to nations across the seas. Her prow has ploughed many waters. She was the flag-ship of the good and gallant Commodore Long, and in every port she was hailed the noble representative of a great, free, and happy people. "Merrimac" is her name.

When the great rebellion broke out, and men turned traitors to their country, she turned traitor too. The glorious "stars and stripes" were torn down, and a rebel flag hoisted to the breeze. The rebels covered her with a coat of mail; they built over her an iron house; they loaded her with the missiles of death; and when rigged, they sent her to do a traitor's work.

Hampton Roads, you know, is the southern part of the Chesapeake Bay, where ships lie at anchor. Norfolk is on the one side, south; Fortress Monroe is on the north. Here in March rode a fleet of loyal ships—the Congress and Cumberland, the Roanoke, Minnesota, and Lawrence. One sunny day—it was the 15th of March—a strange-looking monster, half ship, half house, slowly steamed from Norfolk. Who and what is it? asked men on ship and shore. But they were not slow in guessing. It was the Merrimac.

Straight she made for the brave old Cumberland. Men beat to arms. As she swept by the Congress, that gallant ship gave her a broadside; but the huge balls glanced from her iron sides like hailstones from a barn-roof. On she dashed, piercing the Cumberland amidships with her iron prow, and raking her decks with shot and shell. "Surrender!" cried the Merrimac. "Never!" sternly replied the Cumberland, her decks reeking with blood, and scores of her brave men dead and dying. The traitor ship hauled off, and again made a ferocious onslaught on its disabled and bleeding foe. "Will you surrender?" cried the Merrimac. "Never!" roared the true-hearted Cumberland; "sink, but never surrender!" The waters were rushing into her broken sides, and amid whizzing shot, dying groans, the fierce struggles of brave men grappling for life in the eddying waves, the poor ship went down, down, all but the masthead, which stood proudly up, flying her "stars and stripes" to the last.

Not glutted with this work of ruin, the rebel monster turned towards the Congress, and raked her decks with its deadly fire. One shell killed fifteen men, and another ten. "Captain Smith, will you surrender your ship?" "Not as long as I have a gun and a man to man it!" was the heroic answer. Another terrible broadside, and commander, captain, and pilot have fallen. Another and another, and the helpless ship, now on fire, hauled down its flag. Night only stopped the work of death and destruction; and what a night it was, the heavens glowing with the flames of the burning Congress, and the bold Cumberland a sunken wreck! What had the rest to hope for on the morrow? What had Washington and New York and Boston to hope for? For the murderous craft steamed back to Norfolk to take breath for a worse work to come. It was a night for brave men to pray. Longing hearts were turned to God. Help! deliverance! was the cry.

All at once a spark of light glimmered in the offing. Nearer and nearer it came. Who and what was it? The iron-clad Monitor. God sent her. Yet she looked a speck on the waters, and could *she* fight the Merrimac? The morrow must decide. God sometimes helps "a little one to chase a thousand." By nine the next morning out steams the Merrimac, flushed with yesterday's success. The little Monitor is modestly hid behind the broad wings of a frigate. The Merrimac opens the conflict, and her booming cannon shake the air and sea. Every thing promises an easy victory, when lo, a little craft steams out and offers battle; little David challenging the giant Goliath. The little Monitor, with but her two guns and her men tired and storm-tossed by their voyage, can *she* stand her hand? Who that saw her believed she could? Prayers, many and fervent, were offered in the fortress and all along the shore that day.

For five long hours the battle raged. Never such a terrible conflict broke the Sabbath stillness of the land before. So it went on, till the Merrimac, battered and worsted, her commander wounded, her crew disabled, made signals of distress, and thankful to get off, was towed away to Norfolk. The "cheese-box on a raft," as the enemy scornfully called the Monitor, won the day. The Lord had sent deliverance to his people.

Fig. 44. A children's story about the Battle of Hampton Roads appeared in the *Child's Paper,* October 1862. (Collection of Jonathan W. White)

epithet used warmly by the press), she quickly took on a personality that was more enduring in the public mind than the names and personalities of her officers and crew would ultimately be. She was the "low, black vixen of a craft" that took on the "Iron Satan."[10] She became "the pet of the people"—at least for the people of the Union. Indeed, for many she was the Union's nimble David to the Confederacy's bumbling Goliath, and this gave her a moral weight within nineteenth-century American culture. In October 1862 a religious magazine for children depicted the Battle of Hampton Roads as a morality tale. The *Merrimack* had been "a noble war-ship" intended for brave and gallant men, but "she turned traitor too." After the first day of the battle, "It was a night for brave men to pray." Fortunately, the *Monitor* arrived, and just like David against Goliath, "The Lord had sent deliverance to his people."[11] The *Monitor* was an answer to prayer.

SYMPATHY FOR THE EUROPEAN POWERS.

THERE is a great deal of affliction, just now, in the large "Powers" family of Europe, who have been brought to meditate upon the mutability of human affairs by that little one of the *Monitor* and *Merrimac.* In England, all the science of engineering and artillery practice is daily displayed upon fresh plates, like veal kidneys in a restaurant window. Five-inch plates, and *Warrior*-plates, and all sorts of plates as yet invented, are in such demand for experimenting on that the Queen's horses have been instructed to give up wearing iron shoes, and the poor creatures are to go shod with silver to their early graves—for what horse could survive such an insult? The shoes are to be taken to Shoeburyness

Fig. 45. This political cartoon of the *Monitor* thumbing her nose at Napoleon III of France appeared in *Vanity Fair,* May 17, 1862.

Both she and the *Virginia* appeared to have a life of their own and were quickly given both human and animal traits by the press and thus the public. Unlike the celebrated *Cumberland,* who was defined by the actions of her men, the ironclads appeared to be sentient, their men hidden behind thick iron plates, invisible to the observer.[12] The *Monitor*'s turret, seeming to turn of its own accord, would have given the appearance of a creature turning its head, the two eye-like gunports blinking alternately, her shells vexing the larger Confederate vessel like a "saucy kingbird pecking at a very large and very black crow." In contrast, the *Merrimack,* with her slow, inexorable forward motion, seemed to many observers to be evil, even reptilian. A. B. Smith, the pilot of the *Cumberland,* recalled that she was like a "half-submerged crocodile." She "steamed majestically along, as if conscious of resistless strength," wrote one observer about her appearance on March 8. Though the attack on the *Cumberland* was anything but silent, the *Merrimack* was observed to be quiet and deliberate, "with not a soul on board to be seen." Like a reptile, she struck viciously, repeatedly, with the guns of the *Cumberland* having no more effect on her than "the wooden arrows of the Indian," glancing ineffectively from "the hide of the crocodile."[13] Likewise, *Vanity Fair* magazine depicted her as a scaly dragon in what is likely the first editorial cartoon depicting the March 8 battle.[14] *Vanity Fair* also continued to emphasize the human qualities of the *Monitor* in subsequent issues. In the May 17, 1862, edition, a tiny *Monitor* standing on two legs thumbs her nose (or in this case, her turret) at Napoleon III of France.[15]

Decks of playing cards featuring the two ironclads appeared for sale on the streets of New York City before the summer of 1862, and Currier and Ives, along with other lithographers, rushed to get images of the battle onto the walls of the public (see, for example, figures 37 and 38 in chapter 4).[16] With no photographs of the battle or of the ships to use as

Figs. 46, 47, 48, and 49: These wartime playing cards, produced about 1862, were inscribed "To Commemorate the greatest event in naval history—The substitution of iron for wood." (The Mariners' Museum, Newport News, Virginia)

Clockwise from top left: **Fig. 46.** Playing card, an ace, featuring the *Monitor.* **Fig. 47.** Playing card, a 10, featuring the *Monitor.* **Fig. 48.** Playing card, an ace, featuring the *Virginia.* **Fig. 49.** Playing card, a 10, featuring the *Virginia.*

references, however, some of the early depictions were based on eyewitness accounts and wishful thinking. Although Hampton Roads was an amphitheater of sorts for the twenty thousand observers who watched the battles of March 8 and 9, not all of them had a clear view of the wide-ranging, smoke-filled engagements, so even those present were not quite sure what they had seen. The newspapers and printmakers would not let accuracy stand in the way of a sale, however, and they provided the public with a vast number of images from which to choose. Many featured the events of March 8 and 9 occurring simultaneously, so that the tragedy of the *Cumberland*'s sinking could be seen next to the ironclads engaged in battle.[17]

As fascinating as the ironclads were, however, the *Cumberland* held her own in public sentiment and became a tragic icon of the passing of an era. To many, this was the moment in which naval warfare forever changed. The wooden walls of the past were no match for the ironsides of the present, and future. Yet it was not merely this passing of the torch from wood to iron that drove poets to write of the *Cumberland.* Quite simply, the ship was not surrendered. She went down with flags flying and guns blazing. Lieutenant George Upham Morris's famous, and perhaps apocryphal, command, "Give them a broadside, boys, as she goes," captured the imagination of poets and artists like few other lines in the war. Immortalized first by Currier and Ives as a caption to their 1862 lithograph, "The Sinking Of The Cumberland By The Iron Clad Merrimac, Off Newport News, Va. March 8th 1862," the phrase was a rallying cry to Union supporters and troops alike as they wearied of Southern successes. Elizabeth T. Porter Beach was inspired by the event to write "The Last Broadside" in 1862. The poem begins:

Shall we give them a broadside, my boys, as she goes?
Shall we send yet another to tell,
In iron-tongued words, to Columbia's foes
How bravely her sons say "Farewell"?

Like other poets, Beach made particular mention of "The Star-Spangled Banner still floating above / as a beacon upon the dark wave." The poem was set to music by Frank Buckley soon thereafter, and the stirring and somewhat bombastic melody made its way onto the pianos in genteel parlors throughout the Northeast.[18]

Poet and portrait painter Thomas Buchanan Read similarly wrote in his poem, "The Attack":

Down went the ship! Down, down; but never down
Her sacred flag to insolent dictator.
Weep for the patriot heroes, doomed to drown;
Pledge to the sunken Cumberland's renown.
She sank, thank God! unsoiled by foot of traitor!

Read also wrote, as an accompaniment to relics presented to President Lincoln by the Shakespearean actor and orator James E. Murdoch, a piece entitled "The Piece of Halliard From the Flag of the Cumberland." The rope fragment was "a shred from off the halliards of our hope," and from a battle flag that had not been lowered.[19]

Likewise in 1862, Oliver Wendell Holmes, Sr., used the image of the sunken *Cumberland* with her flag still defiantly flying in a poem that exhorted young men who had not yet enlisted to go to war either never or now:

Never or now! roars the hoarse-throated cannon
Through the black canopy blotting the skies;
Never or now! flaps the shell-blasted pennon
O'er the deep ooze where the Cumberland lies![20]

Interestingly—and perhaps not surprisingly—the *Congress,* the other victim of the CSS *Virginia* on March 8, is hardly mentioned in any poems or songs, particularly northern ones, since she had surrendered, her flag struck, and the white flag hoisted. One anonymous poet referred to this tacitly—in a poem praising the *Cumberland:*

Your flag, the gamest of the game,
Sank proudly with you—not in shame
But in its ancient glory.[21]

March 8 received the most attention overall—whether in songs and poems specifically devoted to that day's action or paired with March 9. Understandably, there were more southern poems devoted to March 8 than 9. One of the finest is by Ossian Gorman of the 4th Georgia Volunteers and was dedicated to William Christian Hutter, a young lieutenant on board the CSS *Raleigh* who had been killed by shore fire from Union troops at Camp Butler that day. The poet celebrated the scene of "our fleet advancing fast, / Beneath the sun's auspicious smile," closing the sixty-one-line poem with a tribute to the *Virginia*'s commander, Franklin Buchanan, as well as Lieutenant Hutter:

  The breezy zephyrs onward roam,
And echoing volleys float afar,
  Disturbing Neptune's coral home.
The victory's ours, and let the world
  Record Buchanan's name with pride;
The crew is brave, the banner bright,
  That ruled the day when Hutter died.[22]

Not all southern poems were as reverent. One entitled "The Turtle" gently teased the *Virginia*'s look:

Caesar, afloat with his fortunes!
  And all the world agog

Straining its eyes
At a thing that lies
    In the water, like a log!
It's a weasel! a whale!
I see its tail;
    It's a porpoise! a pollywog!

Tarnation! it's a turtle!
    And blast my bones and skin,
My hearties! sink her,
Or else you'll think her
    A regular terror—pin!

The frigate poured a broadside!
    The bombs they whistled well,
But, hit old Nick
With a sugar stick!
    It didn't "phase" her shell!

Piff, from the creature's larboard—
    And dipping along the water,
A bullet hissed
From a wreath of mist
    Into a doodle's quarter!

Raff, from the creature's starboard—
    Rip, from his ugly snorter,
And the Congress, and
The Cumberland
    Sunk, and nothing—shorter.

Now, here's to you, "Virginia,"
    And you are bound to win,
By your rate of bobbing round,
    And your way of pitchin' in;
For you are a cross
Of the old sea-horse
    And a regular terror—pin![23]

The *Monitor* inspired writers in the North. Stephen C. Foster, working in New York, addressed his adopted city's pride in the Brooklyn-built *Monitor* in a broadside published in 1862 called "Better Days are Coming."

It was truly a song of the moment—naive and patriotic. Foster wrote about McClellan in glowing words, for example, as the luster was still on "Little Mac." The last verse of the song was reserved for the *Monitor,* however.

> Here's health to Captain Ericsson, the Monitor and crew,
> Who showed the southern chivalry a thing they never knew;
> The Merrimac had slayed as St. Patrick did the toads,
> Till Worden with the Monitor came into Hampton roads.[24]

Foster continued the sentiments in another popular broadside, "That's What's The Matter":

> The Merrimac, with heavy sway,
> Had made our Fleet an easy prey:
> The Monitor got in the way;
>   And that's what's the matter!
> So health to Captain Ericsson,
> I cannot tell all he has done:
> I'd never stop when once begun:
>   And that's what's the matter!
> CHORUS—That's what's the matter
> The Rebels have to scatter;
> We'll make them flee
> By land and sea;
> And that's what's the matter.[25]

"Polkamania" swept the United States in the decades before the Civil War. Arriving on these shores in 1844, it seemed that anything could lend itself to becoming a polka. "The *Monitor* Polka" found its place alongside "The Secession Polka," "The Fortress Monroe Polka," "The Happy Contraband Polka," "Southern Rights Polka," "Battle Flag Polka," "Dixie Polka," and "Manual of Arms Polka."[26] Other composers wrote patriotic marches ("The *Monitor* Grand March"), and galops ("The Ericsson Galop"), while a popular broadside entreated Captain Ericsson with the musical plea, "Oh, Give Us A Navy Of Iron!" A new broadside ballad hit the streets of Philadelphia shortly after the March 9 battle. It boasted: "The Monitor went smack up to the Merrimac, and upon her sides played Yankee Doodle Dandy, O!"[27]

Likewise, the antiwar Copperhead newspaper, *The Crisis,* in Columbus, Ohio, printed a locally written song, sung to the traditional tune of "Yankee Doodle." In this, the ironclads are sentient and vocal as they contemplate one another:

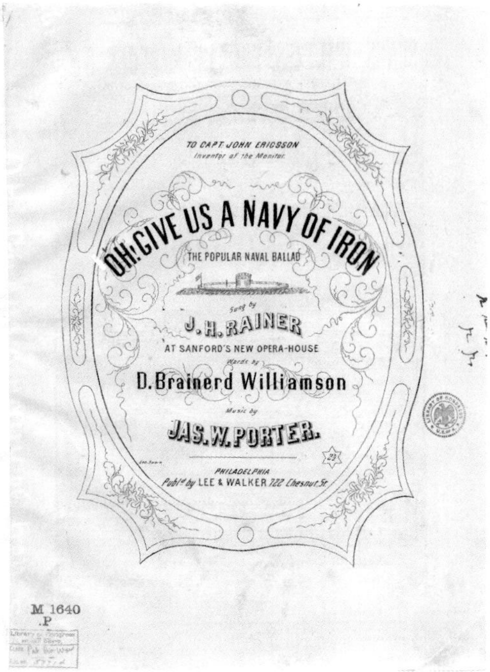

Fig. 50. The "Monitor Polka," written by G. Weingarten in 1862, was published in New York by H. B. Dodsworth. (Library of Congress)

Fig. 51. "Oh! Give Us A Navy of Iron," written in 1862 by D. Brainerd Williamson and James W. Porter, was published by Lee & Walker in Philadelphia. (Library of Congress)

Fig. 52. The "Monitor Grand March," written in 1862 by E. Mack, was published by Lee & Walker in Philadelphia. (The Mariners' Museum, Newport News, Virginia)

The Merrimac, a vessel bold,
  The pride of *Dixie's* nation,
Came out to strike our men of war
  With awe and consternation.
She was a mighty animal,
  All cased with railroad iron,
And had a lot of smashing guns
  Already fixed for firing.
    Yankee Doodle, &c.

She saw the frigate Cumberland,
  Lying there at anchor;
She let her have some balls of iron,
  Which gave to her the canker.
Then starting up with all her might,
  She struck a bee-line at her,
And stove a hole into her side,
  And made the sailors scatter.
    Yankee Doodle, &c.

Then turning to the Congress said,
  I'll to the bottom send her;
Pitched in and fought a round or two,
  And forced her to surrender.
Then in the heighth [*sic*] of pride she said,
  I'm monarch of the ocean,
And looking round she saw a craft
  She called a Yankee notion.
    Yankee Doodle, &c.

There is a raft, I do declare,
  A Yankee cheese box on it;
It is not worth an idle thought,
  I will not stop to comment.
Just then a flash, and then a bang,
  That filled their hearts with wonder,
And iron balls came 'gainst her sides,
  Like heavy claps of thunder.
    Yankee Doodle, &c.

They fought, but no impression made,
  One could not hurt the other;

Says Merrimac, this plan wont do,
I guess I'll try another.
She run into the Monitor,
And broke her iron snoodle;
Keep off or else you'll get the worst,
Says little Yankee Doodle.
Yankee Doodle, &c.

The Monitor then run around,
While Merrimac was thinking,
And put a ball into her stern,
Which set the monster sinking.
She run away, and steam tugs came,
And towed her in a kiting,
Thus ends the tale of Merrimac
And Yankee cheese box fighting.
Yankee Doodle, &c.[28]

Southern scribes were no less eloquent, though far fewer song lyrics are extant; a broadside issued in late March focused on the terror the *Virginia* had inspired in Washington. In it, Seward warns Lincoln that "Jeff. is out in the Merrimac, / He's laid the 'Congress' on her back; / And driven the 'Cumberland' off the track, / And will chase US yet out of Washington." In the song, Mary Todd Lincoln hints at her own Confederate sympathies and threatens to "turn out Old Butler and shiver the blade / Of each thieving Yankee who's making this raid / On my comfort and peace in Washington."[29]

Songs about the battle were not merely a nineteenth-century phenomenon, however. Recent compositions include folksinger Bob Zentz's "The Battle of Hampton Roads"; radio personality (and great-grand-nephew of John L. Worden) Eric Worden's "Iron is King"; Greenpoint Brooklyn indie pop band Bishop Allen's "The *Monitor*"; also from Greenpoint, the shoegaze band Titus Andronicus's 2009 album entitled "The *Monitor,*" with the song "Battle of Hampton Roads"; and the 2015 release by Swedish metal band Civil War, "U.S.S. *Monitor.*"[30]

The Battle of Hampton Roads quickly inspired parades, panoramas, polytechnicrons, and polymoramas throughout the nation. Perhaps fittingly, the first recorded parade was initiated by the very men who helped build the *Monitor.* On Saturday, March 29, 1862, four hundred workmen from Corning, Winslow and Company and the Rensselaer Ironworks in Troy, New York, formed a torchlight procession through the town to celebrate the success of the vessel they built. A banner featuring a visual

Fig. 53. A *Monitor* float in a Grand Army of the Republic parade. The *Monitor* became a popular subject for parade floats as early as 1862. In this photograph an officer in the GAR sits on a horse-powered *Monitor* with his feet inside the gun turret. (The Mariners' Museum, Newport News, Virginia)

representation of the March 9 battle (likely based on the *Harper's* or *Leslie's* engravings) was mounted in a wagon, along with the likenesses of John Ericsson, John Winslow, and John Griswold, and the phrase, "Honor to whom honor is due!"[31]

Union supporters around the country adopted the *Monitor* as a national symbol. On July 4, 1862, the supplement to the San Francisco *Evening Bulletin* excitedly reported that the "Fourth of July commenced earlier than usual this year. Instead of patiently waiting until midnight it went off half cocked on the evening of the third, as the sun sank." All night long in this West Coast city, thousands of miles removed from Hampton Roads, the firecrackers continued to crackle until finally at sunrise, as though the populace could not stand another moment of anticipation, the bells began tolling throughout the city—a joyous sound to all but those who had indulged too much the previous evening.

Over forty thousand flags festooned the city, and finally, by eleven in the morning, several divisions had organized themselves and made up a parade that stretched for blocks. Led first by military units, the parade also sported firemen, riggers, stevedores, and individuals from several other occupations, fraternal societies, and ethnic organizations. Wagons "loaded dangerously with brewers" followed giant milk cans in festooned

Fig. 54. This photograph most likely depicts members of the National Association of Naval Veterans of the United States at their Fifth Annual National Conference on August 13, 1892, in Boston. (The Mariners' Museum, a gift from Gregg Vaughan)

carts, while costumed children, brass bands, and the Sons of the Fenian Brotherhood marched loudly down the street. The fifth division of the parade appeared, "headed by Hunnewell's brass band, who before they get through the march may injure their lungs if they have not a care. 'The Union must and shall be preserved,' is the leading motto of this part of the long yet attractive pageant."

The pièce de résistance in this part of the procession, though, came lumbering slowly along in the rear: "a monster model of the famous *Monitor,* 41 feet long and 10 feet in the beam," which was almost one quarter the size of the original, still on duty in the James River in Virginia. To populate the ersatz ironclad with a crew, there were "any number of little jack tars" there to help man the "two big guns in the revolving turret." The float was well received, though its handlers found it "rather harder to handle in our streets than was its famous namesake in Hampton Roads." All this was followed by a parade of wagons, one of which bore the slogan "Pure Beef for friends of the Union—the points of our knives for its foes."[32]

The *Monitor* would continue to appear in parades during the Civil War, sometimes in more partisan contexts. In Columbus, Ohio, a grand procession held for the Republican candidate for governor in October 1863

Fig. 55. *Monitor* parade float made by the Patriotic Association of the Continental Ironworks, April 23, 1918. The original *Monitor* had been built at Continental Ironworks in Greenpoint, Brooklyn. (NOAA's Monitor National Marine Sanctuary)

Fig. 56. Reenactor portraying John Ericsson on a *Monitor* float in a July 4th parade in Manhattan in 1983. (NOAA's Monitor National Marine Sanctuary)

included a *Monitor* float. One woman in the audience observed it in wonder: "But the best of all was a *miniature 'Monitor'* on wheels, and a *large 'miniature'* it was too. I had no idea there was any 'machinery' connected with it, and you can imagine my surprise when it 'presented' its guns and fired right before our window." A "fine working model of the Monitor" was also included in Lincoln's second inaugural procession down Pennsylvania Avenue in March 1865. Festooned with flowers, flags, and other decorations, the two guns in the turret "fired at intervals" as four white horses pulled it down the street. *Monitor* floats would continue to appear in Fourth of July parades, Decoration Day (Memorial Day) commemora-

Fig. 57. This carte de visite shows children and adults gathered to watch the recreation of the Battle of Hampton Roads at the Sanitary Fair in Pittsburgh in 1864. (Naval History and Heritage Command)

tions, and Union veterans' encampments for more than a century after the Civil War.[33]

Patriotic citizens in the wartime North realized that the *Monitor* could be helpful in fund-raising efforts. During the latter half of the Civil War, the U.S. Sanitary Commission hosted fairs in cities throughout the North to raise money for soldiers and the war effort, and the *Monitor* played an important role in at least one of these massive events. The *Pittsburgh Gazette* reported on May 20, 1864, that one of the highlights of that city's upcoming fair would be a "miniature lake or canal, which has been made for the accommodation of the iron-clad 'Monitor' which is now being constructed at the Fort Pitt Works." The vessel was about eight feet long "and of sufficient capacity to carry a man, who will attend to the machinery and work her guns." Once the fair had opened to the public a Boston newspaper reported that it was "a perfect model of the original Monitor" and "a very pleasant object to contemplate." The miniature *Monitor* battled a miniature *Virginia,* with shore batteries around the pond firing as well. According to one report, "the noise of battle increases until the audience gets excited, and then the contestants pause for a breath, and afterwards renew the engagement." The exhibition was "literally jammed nearly all the time during the two or three weeks the fair lasted," recalled the person who had built the miniature, with spectators paying twenty-five cents apiece to see it. By the end of the fair the mini *Monitor* had raised about $75,000 of the $325,000 total raised by the fair.[34]

Models of the *Monitor* and *Virginia* were even popular overseas. In June 1862, a Paris correspondent to the *New York Evening Post* reported that a small clay model of the Battle of Hampton Roads could be seen

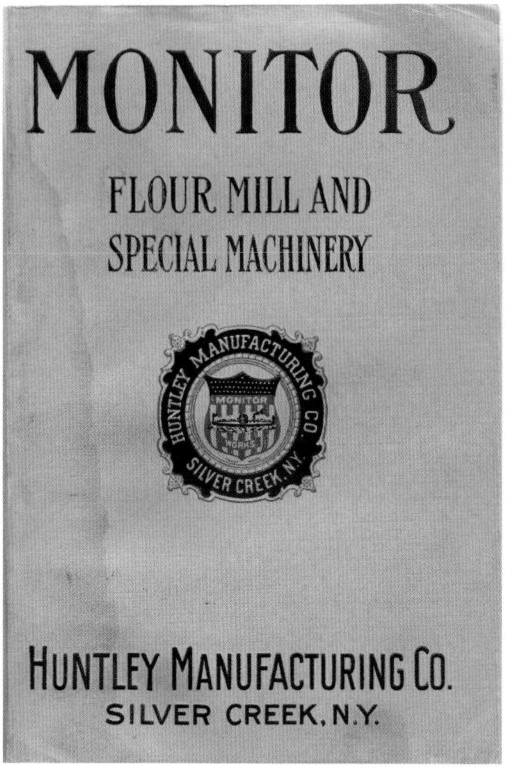

Fig. 58. A catalog for Monitor flour. (Collection of Anna Gibson Holloway)

Fig. 59. This trade card, ca. 1890, was one of several produced that featured the *Monitor* as part of a marketing campaign for Iron Clad Enameled Iron Ware. (The Mariners' Museum, Newport News, Virginia)

in a local shop window. Unlike other depictions of the battle, this rendering—"about as large as your hand"—took a humorous look at the two ships: "Two monkeys stand in mortal combat: both are costumed in large top boots and cavalier hats; out of the crown of monkey Merrimac's hat comes a steam pipe with a slight puff of smoke, he stands aiming a murderous blow with an immense spear at the very heart of monkey Monitor, whose cool and unmoved attitude, as he receives the attack, is inexpressibly comic; the edge of the spear is turned, it does not begin to penetrate and Monitor looks at his apish adversary with the funniest possible monkey expression, as it he were saying, 'Now, do tell; is that your best?'" The correspondent did not know the artist's name but reported that "he undoubtedly has great comic talent" and that the scene "would be greatly appreciated in your city could it be seen there."[35]

By the summer of 1862 the word "Monitor" was becoming part of the common parlance of Union soldiers. Troops stationed in North Carolina used an "armed car commonly called the Monitor." Near Folly Island, South Carolina, in May 1863, a few Union infantrymen pushed a two-foot-long plank into a river with "a fruit can placed on the board to

THE SATURDAY EVENING POST
59
The MONITOR TOP
makes this record possible
Of the hundreds of thousands of owners of General Electric Refrigerators NOT ONE has paid a cent for service.
SEALED IN STEEL
The Monitor Top—just look at it—scarcely bigger than a hat box—yet one of the most amazing—one of the most revolutionary—triumphs of modern engineering.
Scarcely bigger than a hat box—yet sealed within it is the entire mechanism that will operate a General Electric Refrigerator year in and year out, without a thought, without a worry, without so much as a drop of oil from you.
In the Monitor Top—sealed in steel and permanently oiled—is a mechanism so remarkable, so unbelievably efficient, that for three whole years not a single owner of a General Electric Refrigerator has paid a cent for service. Picture the comfort, the convenience—the economy in owning such a refrigerator!
Why not look at a General Electric Refrigerator this very day? Prices now start as low as $205 at the factory, and most people buy on our easy time payment plan. You'll find a model exactly suited to your own particular needs—a refrigerator of such quiet, efficient, and economical operation as you never dreamed of—ready to go to work for you tomorrow morning! Write for our illustrated booklet. Section S-6B, Electric Refrigeration Department, General Electric Company, Hanna Building, Cleveland, Ohio.
JOIN US IN THE GENERAL ELECTRIC HOUR, BROADCAST EVERY SATURDAY EVENING ON A NATION-WIDE N. B. C. NETWORK
GENERAL ELECTRIC
ALL-STEEL REFRIGERATOR
ELECTRIC WATER COOLERS • ELECTRIC MILK COOLERS • COMMERCIAL REFRIGERATORS

Fig. 60. Advertisement for a General Electric Monitor-top refrigerator. General Electric sold over one million of these refrigerators while the model was in production between 1927 and 1937. Early buyers also received a matching kitchen clock with their purchase, and they could even have matching salt and pepper shakers. GE proclaimed that their product "Makes it Safe to Be Hungry!" (The Mariners' Museum, Newport News, Virginia)

represent the Monitor turret." Meanwhile, out West a sketch artist for *Harper's Weekly* captured a humorous scene in the Army of the Mississippi: a drunken soldier being punished in camp by having to wear a barrel painted with the words, "Too fond of Whiskey." As might be expected, a crowd gathered around the poor fellow, whose head was poking out of the top of the barrel. One clever comrade doffs his cap and greets the convict, saying, "How are you, Monitor?" while another onlooker asks, "Where's the Merrimac?" The editors of *Harper's* opined, "Thus accoutred, the miserable fellow is the butt of the scoffs and jeers of his comrades for a day, and learns a lesson which ought to teach him the virtue of temperance for the rest of his life."[36]

Fig. 61. In June 1907 *Confederate Veteran* magazine announced that the Jamestown Exposition would contain a "spectacular reproduction" of the Battle of Hampton Roads through an electrified cyclorama that "will be as grand a sight as the human eye ever beheld." Also part of the exposition was the USS *Canonicus,* the last surviving ironclad of the Civil War, captured here in this photograph by a tourist. (Collection of Jonathan W. White)

During the war—and after—clothing itself became patterned after the *Monitor.* A gentleman could wear a *Monitor* checked shirt or a *Monitor* tie, while a lady could have a dress made from *Monitor* cloth that she could wear with her *Monitor* cloak and *Monitor* hat. Later in the century, she could add a pair of *Monitor* shoes to complete the ensemble. If she could not afford those styles from the store, she could make her own on a *Monitor* sewing machine. Wherever the clothes came from, they could be washed with a *Monitor* washboard and wrung out with a *Monitor* wringer, then dried by the *Monitor* stove. To remove wrinkles, a *Monitor* sad iron could be warmed up on a *Monitor* heater. One could have a meal made from *Monitor* flour, which might have been grown on a farm using *Monitor* rakes, *Monitor* seed drills, and *Monitor* windmills and pumps. Coffee ground in a *Monitor* grinder could be heated in a *Monitor* coffeepot, while perishable items could be stored in a *Monitor*-top refrigerator.

The two ironclad combatants at the Battle of Hampton Roads have remained household names for generations and have been ubiquitous in American culture. Children in 1866 could enjoy a game made by Milton Bradley that featured images of the battle that were illuminated by lantern light. In the 1880s, miners "got hold of a bonanza" of silver and copper in the Monitor and Merrimac Mines near Tucson, Arizona. In 1891, McCormick Harvesting Co. produced an advertisement featuring a large image of the battle with the tagline, "This fight settled the fate of the 'Wooden Walls' of the world and taught all nations that the War-Ship of the future must be—like the McCormick Harvester—a Machine of Steel." Local

Top left: **Fig. 62.** Memorial Day postcard. (The Mariners' Museum, Newport News, Virginia)

Top right: **Fig. 63.** Postcard featuring the Battle of Hampton Roads. (The Mariners' Museum, Newport News, Virginia)

Above: **Fig. 64.** Decoration Day postcard. (Collection of Anna Gibson Holloway)

Center right: **Fig. 65.** This trade card featuring the Battle of Hampton Roads, produced by McLaughlin's Coffee of Chicago about 1889, was part of a series of "peculiar war ships of the world." (The Mariners' Museum, Newport News, Virginia)

Bottom right: **Fig. 66.** This tobacco card, number 2 in the "Celebrated Ships" series produced by Will's Cigarettes in Bristol and London, England, features the Battle of Hampton Roads. John Ericsson—and even Ericsson's home in New York—were also featured on tobacco cards. (The Mariners' Museum, Newport News, Virginia) communities continued to commemorate the Union's famous warship. When, for example, Trenton, New Jersey, put a model of the *Monitor* in a city lake during the summer of 1898, a local newspaper reported, "no doubt it will attract a large number of visitors." A similar model was on display at the Washington Navy Yard about this time, while visitors to the Jamestown Exposition in 1907 flocked to see the *Canonicus,* the last survivor among the Civil War monitors.

References to the Battle of Hampton Roads continued to appear in American popular culture throughout the twentieth century, in postcards, advertisements, comic books, and souvenirs. On the big screen, the story of the *Monitor* and *Virginia* was celebrated in films such as *The Confederate Ironclad* in 1912, *Hearts in Bondage* in 1936, and *Ironclads* in 1991—and Daniel Day-Lewis also appears to be standing on a monitor-style vessel in the dream scene of Steven Spielberg's 2012 blockbuster, *Lincoln.* Families sitting at home could also catch references to the famous battle in some of their favorite television shows. In a 1965 episode of *Gilligan's Island,* Gilligan asks the Skipper, "Which one is it, the *Monitor* or the *Merrimack?*" when a Japanese submarine from World War II arrives at the castaways' island. A 1973 episode of the animated sitcom *Wait Till Your Father Gets Home* humorously used the battle as a metaphor for a conflict between neighbors.

Perhaps most fittingly, the *Monitor* has inspired coffee and other adult beverages for more than a century, or been used to advertise them. In the late nineteenth and early twentieth centuries, several cigarette and cigar manufacturers, as well as at least two liquor producers, used images of the Battle of Hampton Roads to push their products. In the 1890s J. C. Childs & Co. advertised "Monitor Blend" pure rye whiskey as a "scientifically blended" and "Excellent Product of the Still [that] has MEDICINAL and TONIC VIRTUES," while in the 1930s, Seagram's issued a magazine ad casting its gin as an "American Original" just like the two "American Originals" that "revolutionized the navies of the world." More recently, the Hampton Roads area has seen a renewed interest in the *Monitor*'s connection to sailors' favorite libations. Founded in 2015 in Newport News, the Ironclad Distillery produces Ironclad Bourbon, as their website states, "in an historic warehouse within view of the old historic battle site." In 2016 the Oozlefinch Craft Brewery opened at Fort Monroe, with each of their beers inspired by some aspect of the fort's history. One beer, Short Fuse, was inspired by Lawrence Murray, a steward aboard the *Monitor* who found himself in deep water for his behavior while drunk (see chapters 3 and 6).

If one indulged too much in these *Monitor* brews, or suffered from other ailments, Dr. Ray Vaughn Pierce's "pleasant pellets" were sure to be

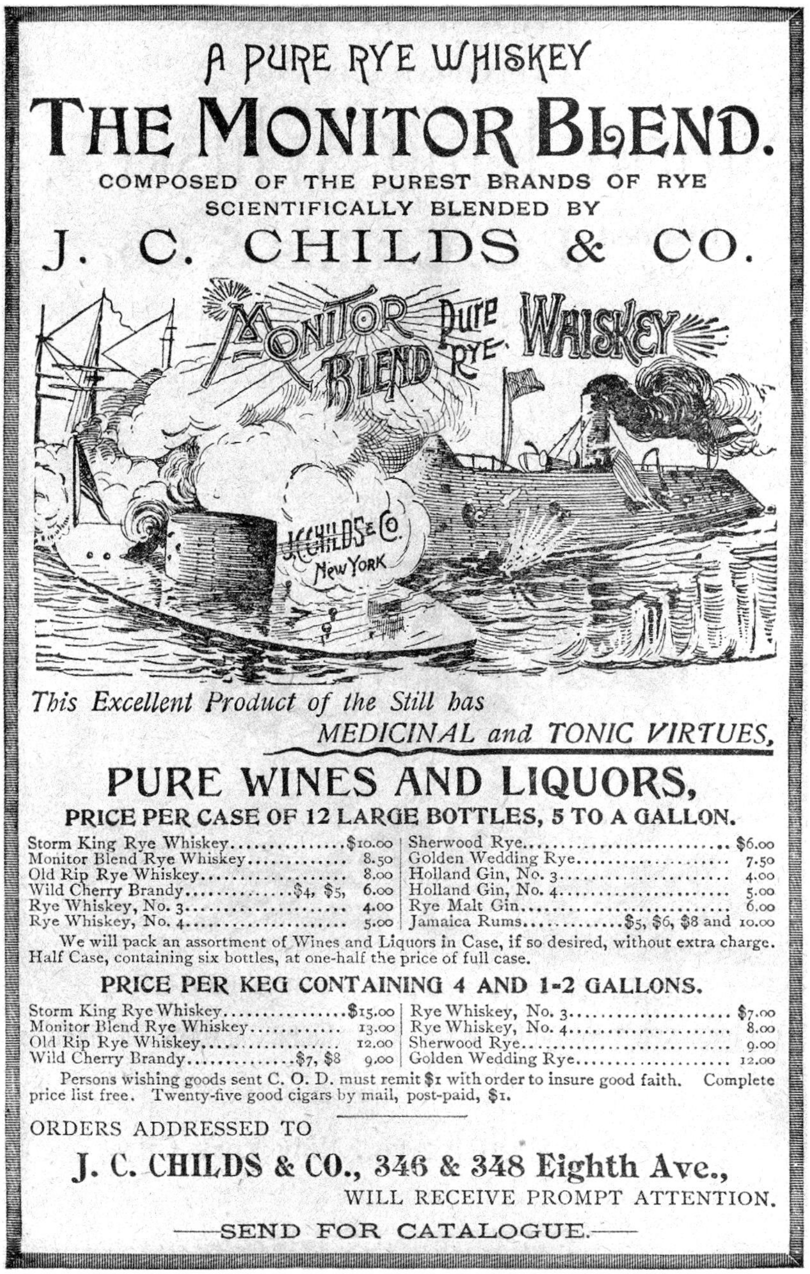

Fig. 67. Advertisement for Monitor Blend Whiskey. (The Mariners' Museum, Newport News, Virginia)

as effective as the *Monitor* in curing a whole host of ailments. In an advertisement that circulated in the 1890s and that featured the *Monitor* and the tagline, "Small But Effective," Dr. Pierce promised that his pills were "effective in conquering the enemy—disease." Whether a person was "grumpy, thick-headed and take a gloomy view of life," or suffered from "Sick Headache, Bilious Headache, Constipation, Indigestion, Bilious Attacks, and all derangements of the liver, stomach and bowels," Dr. Pierce's

American Originals
The first "ironclad" warships, the MONITOR and the MERRIMAC, were both American Originals. They revolutionized the navies of the world.
In Seagram's American Original–Ancient Bottle Gin–you can see the difference because it is naturally golden. You can taste the difference, too, because Seagram's Gin is naturally smoother, naturally dry-est. It is the result of an original process...the first basic improvement in gin making in 300 years.
Seagram's
Seagram's Ancient Bottle Gin
Ancient Bottle Distilled Dry Gin
Back in the famous Original Bottle of pre-war years
DISTILLED FROM AMERICAN GRAIN, 90 PROOF. SEAGRAM-DISTILLERS CORP., N.Y.

Fig. 68. Advertisement for Seagram's Gin. (The Mariners' Museum, Newport News, Virginia)

pellets would "clear up your system and start your liver into healthful action"—effective, just like that "little Monitor that met the Merrimac at Hampton Roads."[37]

CHAPTER 6

Aftermath of Battle

As the battle between the ironclads was raging on March 9, William H. Heiss, the assistant manager for U.S. government telegraph, was waging a battle of his own a few miles away at Cape Charles. "Boisterous weather" for several days had kept him from completing the damaged underwater telegraph cable that connected Fortress Monroe to the Eastern Shore and on to points north. Begun by the army with a military purpose in early February 1862, the telegraph line was also to be made available to news outlets in the North. However, a sixteen-mile section of cable had been lost following the recent gales and not yet recovered. While some dispatches had made it through the day before, the cable was finally made reliable on the ninth. Both the *New York Times* and the *Philadelphia Inquirer* of March 10, 1862, crowed, "Its completion at this opportune moment, to bring the news of the splendid victory of the *Monitor* and the disabling of the *Merrimac,* has saved the country from great anxiety and expense."[1] Indeed, thanks to this repair, the news of the battle between the two ironclads arrived in Washington, D.C., New York City, and beyond on the evening of March 9, just in time for the major newspapers on the East Coast to rush stories about the two days of battle onto their front pages.

Gustavus Vasa Fox, assistant secretary of the Union navy, had been one of the many thousands to witness the battle. His first telegram that evening was to Gideon Welles, reporting on the events of the day, adding that, though her commanding officer had been wounded in the battle, "the *Monitor* is uninjured and ready at any moment to repel another attack." A second telegram went out a few moments later, from Fox to Ericsson in New York, letting the inventor know that "your noble boat has performed with perfect success, and Worden and Stimers have handled her with great skill. She is uninjured." Fox then warned General McClellan that

A BOBTAIL BULL IN FLY-TIME.
(*Vide* the Howls of the British Parliament and Papers about the *Monitor*, &c.)

Fig. 69. "John Bull" has served as the personification of Great Britain since the early eighteenth century. In this cartoon, "A Bobtail Bull in Fly-Time," which originally appeared in *Harper's Weekly,* May 24, 1862, tiny flying American ironclads harass England's relationship with the Confederacy. (Special Collections & College Archives, Musselman Library, Gettysburg College)

the *Virginia* was undergoing repairs and might soon reappear: "She is an ugly customer, and it is too good luck to believe we are yet clear of her."[2] The young telegraph operators at Fortress Monroe steadily tapped out the messages that could now reach points north. Writers from the *New York Times,* meanwhile, also sent their reports with a Baltimore-bound boat, which left Fortress Monroe at eight in the morning.[3]

The *New York Times* headlines on March 10 shrieked the news: "Desperate Naval Engagements in Hampton Roads," along with eleven other subheadlines that took up more space than the actual article. The initial account of the battles of March 8 and 9, as reported by the *Times* observers, was printed with the caveat that it was based both on what the writer could see through a spyglass at eight miles' distance and from accounts gleaned from "a few panic-stricken non-combatants who fled at almost the first gun from Newport's [*sic*] News."[4] Later editions printed official telegrams from Fortress Monroe stating that "early this morning [the

Monitor] was attacked by the three vessels—the *Merrimac,* the *Jamestown* and the *Yorktown.* After five hours' contest they were driven off—the *Merrimac* in a sinking condition."[5] The *Philadelphia Inquirer,* in addition to reporting on the cable repairs, devoted the entire front page to the events in Virginia, complete with a map of Hampton Roads outlining both Union and Confederate positions and a dotted line showing the "Route of Reble [*sic*] Tugs & Sloops" out of Norfolk (see fig. 33 in chapter 4).[6]

Confederate newspapers naturally told a different story. The Monday, March 10, 1862, edition of the *Norfolk Day Book* bragged about the success of the *Virginia* with the headlines "The Hated Cumberland Sunk!" and "Large Number of Yankees Shot and Drowned!"[7] The *Macon Daily Telegraph* from Georgia reported on the "perfect success" of the resurrected *Merrimack,* which "dashed among the Federal craft like a porpoise in a shoal of herrings, scattering, sinking, burning and destroying everything within her reach." The appearance of the *Monitor* was downplayed, the Union ironclad being described as the "curious and formidable nondescript, Erricsson's [*sic*] floating battery," upon which the *Virginia* inflicted considerable damage. The *Monitor* was not a worthy opponent for the *Virginia,* as she was "in no respects a ship" and their meeting was "no fair test of the power of the ram," as the *Monitor* was more akin to a rock than an adversary. The editors then called for more "Merrimacs" to be built. It was clear that the ersatz ironclad *Virginia* had frightened the Union, and particularly the denizens of "Lincolndom." The editors of the *Macon Daily Telegraph* had also received copies of the *New York Herald*'s account of the battle in which the *Virginia* was said to have left in a sinking condition. The *Telegraph* made a point to report that she had, in fact, returned to Norfolk uninjured.[8]

The mail steamer *Arabia* made her normal run from New York to Liverpool via Queenstown and delivered the news to the British papers. Editions of the *New York Times, New York Tribune* and others made their way to London, Dundee, Sheffield, and beyond. The news became general throughout Britain by March 26, with most major papers having reported some version of the battle by the end of the month. The initial reports were repetitious of the American press, with little editorial comment. But by March 31 the commentary had begun to take over. Editors at the *London Telegraph* assessed the facts of the battle and declared that once the action was over and "the combatants had had enough . . . the Merrimac withdrew to Norfolk, and the Monitor to Fort Monroe, like Ajax and Hector, with divided honors." The commentary ended with an exhortation: "We must learn all about this great encounter, and give up, though with a sigh, the thought of ships less costly or complete than the Merrimac and her antagonist. It is fortunate we have already the beginning of our iron navy; we must forge and rivet the rest, at all convenient speed, for we cannot surrender the empire of the sea, and the little Monitor admonishes us that it must belong, for the future, to the best ironmongers."[9]

The same day in Parliament, while "the business [of the battle] was of no interest" in the House of Lords, the discussion in the House of Commons echoed the sentiments beginning to be expressed in the news. Monies that had been designated to improve shore defenses at Portsmouth seemed to be ill spent by some, who argued that funds should instead go to building a fleet of "small iron-plated vessels."[10] Though the debate was eventually dropped in that session, the panic seizing many in Britain was palpable. A commentator with the *Times* of London mocked the fear when he wrote, "We trembling English, who are thought at New York to be so terribly alarmed as to what will become of the 700,000 fighting men so soon as the war is over, and who are struck with fear lest they should all come over in the Merrimac and the Monitor and blot out this little island, may be re-assured now." Presumably the Americans would not have time to attack England, as they would be too busy collecting taxes that would be used to pay the already large war debt.[11] But the feeling was general that "in the present state of affairs, something should be done, and at once, if we desire to retain our ancient position among nations."[12]

Fears over imagined ironclad attacks seized the imagination of many, from Secretary of War Edwin Stanton's nervousness in Washington to the British acknowledgment that the English had, in fact, been admonished by the little *Monitor.* But these fears turned to laments of another kind. The romance of battle, if such a thing could be said to truly exist, seemed as vulnerable as the wooden walls of the *Cumberland* had proven to be in Hampton Roads.

The men themselves, though aware during the battle that they were, in fact, making history, understood that their role was somewhat different from that of fighting sailors of the past. Following the battle, routine on the vessel carried on as usual. Gustavus Vasa Fox came on board at the dinner hour, expecting to find a disabled vessel and lists of killed and wounded. Instead, he found the officers having a "merry party . . . enjoying some good beef steak, green peas, &c." Surprised, he exclaimed, "Well, gentlemen, you don't look as though you were just through one of the greatest naval conflicts on record." Samuel Dana Greene answered, half in jest, "No Sir, we haven't done much fighting, merely drilling the men at the guns a little."[13] Other members of the crew joked that one of their number, an "old deaf salt" who was on the berth deck, "innocently asked 'whereabouts the fighting was'" during the battle.[14]

But the men on the *Monitor* felt this subtle shift first—even before they left New York. There is a wistfulness that hovers around the edges of their letters home. In February William Keeler had assured his wife that her *"better half* [would] be in no more danger from rebel compliments than if he was seated with you at home." Continuing then, perhaps lamenting more for himself than to reassure his wife, he had said that "there isn't even danger enough to give us any glory—thick heavy plates & bars of iron on all sides above & below with two of the largest sized Columbiads in the tower."[15]

A month later, in another letter to his wife—a long narrative of the battle, stained with the sweat and dirt of the long days—Keeler wrote, "I experienced a peculiar sensation, I do not think it was fear, but it was different from anything I ever knew before. We were enclosed in what we supposed to be an impenetrable armour—we knew that a powerful foe was about to meet us—ours was an untried experiment & our enemy's first fire might make it a coffin for us all." Yet he ended the long report by saying, "I think we get more credit for the mere fight than we deserve, any one could fight behind an impenetrable armour—many have fought as well behind wooden walls or behind none at all." The credit, he felt, should go to their courage in actually volunteering to go to sea in an untried experimental vessel.[16] Keeler, though this was his first time in battle, was no stranger to sailing ships, having sailed around the world seeking his fortune in the 1840s and 1850s. His understanding of the enormity of what happened on March 9 must be seen through that lens.

In contrast, fireman George Geer had never been to sea for any extended period and had volunteered with the navy because he viewed it as having better benefits than the army. He wrote to his wife, Martha, "I often thought of you and the little darlings when the fight was going on and what would become of you should I be killed but I should have no more such fears as our ship resisted every thing they could fire at her as though they were spit balls."[17] His was the view of a young man who already understood steam and iron technology and accepted the vessel stoically, and without the longing for the past.

Public acknowledgment that the nature of warfare was changing came quickly in the days after the battle. A reporter for the *Times* of London wrote,

> Another point to be noticed is the apparently harmless character of a conflict between two of the new monsters. If the five hours' battle now on record is to be an example, the art of defence has gone beyond that of attack, and a sea fight will become more of an amusement than the tournaments between the mail-clad knights of old. There will be a great noise and smoke, a vast expenditure of powder, a deafening rattle of cannon balls on iron plates, a sickening smell of sulphur, and that is all.

Figs. 70, 71, 72. The war years were difficult for Martha Geer, wife of fireman George Geer. Not only did she have to take a job as a washerwoman to help make ends meet, but she also suffered from malnutrition and sadness. "You appear by all your letters to be very down hearted and unhappy," wrote Geer. "I expect when I come home I will find you as poor as a Crow with your anxiety and starving your self to be saving." In 1862 Geer asked Martha to send him a new photograph of her, but she was hesitant because she had had a tooth removed. In one letter he admonished her, "Give them *a good cleaning every morning"* and to "Get that nasty black off of them, or I [will] write you in *eve[r]y* Lettor to Clean them." Finally in September 1862, Martha sent her husband a copy of the second carte de visite she had taken. Although she may have looked careworn from the previous years' trials, George responded joyfully. "Your kind and ever welcom Lettor came to hand to day," he told her. "You say you do not know as the Picture will suit me. I can tell you it does suit me, to a dot. There is only one thing that would please me bettor, and that would be to see the Original. The Picture is all I could ask. It is you as perfect as can be, and I do not think you have altered much." (The Mariners' Museum, Newport News, Virginia)

Clockwise from top left: **Fig. 70.** Fireman George Geer. **Fig. 71.** Martha Geer, ca. 1860. **Fig. 72.** Martha Geer, ca. 1862.

> After all the gun powder has been burned, and all the shot and shell fired away, the two ships may be steered away from each other, to get a few flawed plates replaced, and a fresh supply of ammunition, preparatory to a fresh engagement. Is that to be the character of future sea fights?[18]

Mere days after the battle, Nathaniel Hawthorne visited the "Rat Trap," as he called the *Monitor.* With her coming he felt that "all the pomp and splendor of naval warfare are gone by." She signaled a sea change that would breed "a race of enginemen and smoke-blackened cannoneers, who will hammer away at their enemies under the direction of a single pair of eyes." Saddest of all, he felt, was that "heroism . . . will become a quality of very minor importance."[19]

Despite their near-instantaneous rise to fame as national heroes, the men of the *Monitor* knew something about their experience in battle that most Americans did not yet appreciate. Indeed, Hawthorne's observation aligned with what Keeler had written to his wife shortly before the battle—that there was not "danger enough to give us any glory." To be sure, Keeler was wrong in the short run: the officers and crew of the *Monitor* were almost universally hailed as saviors of the Union, and autograph seekers clamored for their signatures. But a few astute observers at the time recognized that iron walls required individuals to risk and to sacrifice less of their personal safety in naval warfare. Writing from Silver Spring, Maryland, on March 15, 1862, Elizabeth Blair Lee told her husband, "I am disgusted that the Officers & crew of the Monitor should be so noticed when those of the Cumberland are unmentioned[;] these were more exposed to danger—did their part nobly—& would have done it successfully had the Govt done their part at all."[20] Soon after the war, Herman Melville captured this new reality rather gloomily when he wrote of the battle of the ironclads in the poem "A Utilitarian View of the *Monitor*'s Fight," in his poetry collection *Battle-Pieces and Aspects of the War* (1866):

> Yet this was battle, and intense—
> Beyond the strife of fleets heroic;
> Deadlier, closer, calm 'mid storm;
> No passion; all went on by crank,
> Pivot, and screw,
> And calculations of caloric.

Melville ends with the pronouncement that "War shall yet be, but warriors / Are now but operatives."[21] The ironclad age may have made war efficient, but many of the men were not comfortable settling into their new role of "operatives."

Most Americans did not yet comprehend what Keeler, Lee, Hawthorne, and Melville understood about this new mode of warfare. Following the battle, the *Monitor* became a celebrity, a tourist attraction, and the object of a tug-of-war between the army and the navy. "We became a great lion," Alban Stimers told his father. "Distinguished people from all parts of the country came to see us and all were astonished that so small a vessel could do so much." These distinguished guests included Vice President Hannibal Hamlin and several U.S. senators with their spouses. And ordinary citizens climbed aboard for a look-see, too. After touring the *Monitor,* one sailor from the USS *Cambridge* wrote home excitedly, "I visited the 'Monitor' yesterday—one can get no idea of her from the illustrations [in the newspapers]." He then proceeded to describe what he saw in great detail.[22] But after a while, the attention got old. "Since the battle we have been litterally overrun with military officers," wrote engineer Isaac Newton to a friend in New York at the end of March. "In one day half a dozen Brigadier Generals & three Major Gens, in fact this visiting has become an intolerable nuisance—I have explained this vessel so often, that I smile involuntarily while repeating this stereotyped explanation—I can now hardly afford to be polite to anything less than a Brigadier Gen."[23] Tired of being a tour guide, William Keeler made a tongue-in-cheek suggestion to his fellow officers that they should produce "a guide book for the *Monitor* & hand a copy to each visitor as he arrives."[24]

The vessel still required repairs, and a new commanding officer as well. Thus, early on the morning of March 10, she repaired to Fortress Monroe and later in the day received Thomas O. Selfridge as her next commanding officer. Selfridge had been attached to the USS *Cumberland* when she came under the fire of the *Virginia* on March 8. He had survived by jumping overboard as the vessel was sinking. Now he found himself on the ironclad that had challenged the might of the rebel monster. He regaled the crew with his tales of the events of March 8 on board the doomed *Cumberland.*[25] But his appointment was brief, and he was relieved as soon as Lieutenant William N. Jeffers could arrive to take command of the ironclad. A brilliant ordnance officer, Jeffers was flag officer Louis M. Goldsborough's choice to be the new captain—and he would have the longest tenure of any commanding officer on the *Monitor.* Though he had not yet been aboard the *Monitor,* when he first took possession of her he felt he knew her, and he expressed his dismay at how the press had reported on the Union ironclad a bit *too* well. He remarked to a newspaper reporter who was on hand that if he (Jeffers) "knew as much of the *Merrimac* from newspaper descriptions and pictorial representations and diagrams as the rebels know of the *Monitor,* I would go up and sink her before sundown!"[26]

Because the Confederates had confounded General McClellan's Urbanna plan by moving forces to the Virginia Peninsula, McClellan opted to land instead near Fortress Monroe. McClellan had obviously not been able to neutralize the *Virginia* before she came out on March 8. But with the *Monitor* now on hand, McClellan reasoned that this would be easy. (In early April McClellan visited the *Monitor* and told Captain Jeffers "that if we would take care of the *Merrimac,* he thought he could do the rest."[27]) Yet neither McClellan nor Goldsborough wished to risk failure. Further complicating matters, President Lincoln himself had ordered that the *Monitor* not be risked in any fruitless confrontation with the *Virginia.*[28] Her weaknesses were now known. Yet the *Monitor*'s crew chafed under this restriction, feeling as though they were being treated in the same way that "an over careful house wife regards her ancient china set—too valuable to use, too useful to keep as a relic, yet anxious that all shall know what she owns & that she can use it when the occasion demands though she fears much its beauty may be marred or its usefulness impaired."[29] The ship had been placed in "a big glass case . . . for fear of harm coming to us."[30]

The *Virginia* seemed to taunt the men as she remained just out of their reach, "smoking, reflecting, & ruminating" each day until sunset, wrote Keeler, when "she slowly crawled off nearly concealed in a huge, murky cloud of her own emission, black & repulsive as the perjured hearts of her traitorous crew."[31] Some Union soldiers watched eagerly from the shorelines, hoping for another epic fight. "This morning the Merrimac made her appearance, in the James River with seven Gun Boats in Company with her, and as soon as it was known, Every Body made for the shore to see the Fun," wrote one Pennsylvania cavalryman. "I secured a good position on the top of a mast of one of the schooners laying at the wharf," adding that "the shores were Black with men and the Rigging of Shipping were crowded."[32] While many of the men on the ground were excited by the prospect of another major naval engagement, Union leaders were kept in a state of apprehension throughout the spring of 1862. Nobody was quite sure whether she would attack the wooden blockading vessels again or perhaps steam up the York River to destroy General McClellan's supply line; nor were they certain they could stop her.[33]

Meanwhile, the officers and crew of the *Monitor* now had to get used to their new commanding officer. While Keeler referred to Jeffers as a "cool, cautious, careful brave man," many members of the crew felt otherwise. The lack of action against the *Virginia* was wearing upon them, and the crew believed it to be the fault of Jeffers himself, rather than a result of following overly cautious orders. On April 24, 1862, the crew wrote a letter to Lieutenant Worden expressing their desire for his return:

Hampton Roads April 24th 1862
U.S. *Monitor*

To our Dear and Honored Captain,
Dear Sir,

These few lines is from your own crew of the *Monitor* with their kindest love to you their Honored Captain hoping to God that they will have the pleasure of welcoming you back to us again soon for we are all ready, able and willing to meet death or anything else only gives us back our own Captain again. Dear Captain we have got your pilot house fixed and all ready for you[34] when you get well again and we all sincerely hope that soon we will have the pleasure of welcoming you back to us again for since you left us we have had no pleasure on board of the *Monitor*. We once was happy on board of our little *Monitor* but since we lost you we have lost all that was dear to us. Still we are waiting very patiently to engage our antagonist if we could only get a chance to do so. The last time she came out we all thought we would have the pleasure of sinking her but we all got disappointed for we did not fire one shot and the Norfolk papers says we are coward in the *Monitor* and all we want is a chance to show them where it lies. With you for our captain we can teach them who is cowards but there is a great deal that we would like to write to you but we think you will soon be with us again yourself. But we all join in with our kindest love to you hoping that God will restore you to us again and hoping that your sufferings is at an end now and we are all so glad to hear that your eye sight will be spared to you again. We would wish to write more to you if we have your permission to do so but at present we all conclude by tendering to you our kindest love and affection to our dear and honored Captain.

We remain until death your affectionate crew.

The *Monitor* Boys[35]

Despite the sentiments of the men, Worden was not returned to the *Monitor,* and Jeffers would remain with the vessel until August.[36]

Meanwhile, Bushnell's ironclad, *Galena,* arrived in Hampton Roads the same day that the crew posted their letter to Worden, joining the other vessels in the Union blockade, which also included a small ironclad battery, the *Naugatuck,* a miniature offspring of the permanently stalled Steven's Battery project.[37] At a hundred feet in length, the *Naugatuck* carried a single large gun in its tower, a stationary, turretlike structure. While the men on the *Monitor* were happy to have the support, neither of these two ships appeared to be any sort of a match for the *Virginia.* Rear Admiral Goldsborough was unimpressed with the *Galena,* saying she was "beneath naval criticism."[38]

In the early morning hours of May 3, acting master Edwin Gager noted in the *Monitor*'s logbook that the sound of "heavy firing in the direction of Yorktown" was heard throughout the Roads, a sound that continued throughout the day.[39] This was the sound of the Confederate artillery masking Confederate troop movement. Having overestimated the Confederate force significantly, and lacking the Union gunboat support he had requested to attack the Confederate battery at Gloucester Point on the York River, McClellan believed that a siege was the only way to take Yorktown, and he set May 4 as his target date to begin.[40] The Confederates at Yorktown, under the command of General Joseph E. Johnston, used McClellan's anticipated hesitation as an opportunity to abandon the old colonial port, massing their forces farther west up the peninsula. Like William Mahone the year before, General John Bankhead Magruder had created a ruse to provide the illusion of a great number of troops, and many of the guns at Yorktown were nothing more than large wooden logs painted black. The Confederates had "magnified their defences and humbugged," wrote Fox to Goldsborough.[41]

President Lincoln arrived in Hampton Roads at ten in the evening on May 6, a not-so-subtle message that the president was growing increasingly impatient with his "Little Napoleon," General McClellan. Accompanied by Secretary of War Edwin Stanton and Secretary of the Treasury Salmon P. Chase, the men arrived in the USRCS *Miami*.[42] Acting Volunteer Lieutenant William Flye wrote in the *Monitor*'s log on May 7 that at "1 P.M. President Lincoln & suite came on board."[43] Lincoln, who was keenly interested in new technology and in the vessel he had approved in the fall of 1861, desired to see the *Monitor* for himself.[44] He had read with interest all of the official reports of the battle, and his questions to the officers and crew showed that he had studied their vessel in detail. The president did not stay long, however, on his first visit to the *Monitor*. As he and his party were departing, the cry went up that the "*Merrimac* was . . . coming around Sewall's Point apparently bound straight for us."[45] Yet, like so many other appearances of the Confederate ironclad, this was just another tease; still, Lincoln remarked that "the vessel must be destroyed if it took the whole navy to do it."[46] That evening, the president personally led a reconnaissance party onto the Norfolk shore, something that McClellan had failed to do, despite Lincoln's urging.

The weeks of inaction were finally over, and the men of the *Monitor* prepared their vessel for the bombardment of Sewell's Point with incendiary shells. The *Monitor* was joined by the *Seminole, Dacotah, Susquehanna, San Jacinto,* and *Naugatuck*. The fleet rained "an uninterrupted storm of iron . . . into the rebel defenses," wrote Keeler—except for the *Naugatuck,* which, far to the rear of the action, sent exploding shells into the midst of

Fig. 73. *Embarkation of Fort Monroe, May 10, 1862,* by G. Kaiser. President Lincoln, General Wool, and Secretary of the Treasury Chase stand in the foreground, while the *Monitor* and *Virginia* hover in the background of this wonderful artistic rendering of Fort Monroe as troops prepare for the capture of Norfolk. (The Mariners' Museum, Newport News, Virginia)

her own fleet. Captain Jeffers remarked to his paymaster, "Why the beggar . . . we are in more danger from him than the enemy."[47] Lincoln and his party remained far nearer the action than the tiny *Naugatuck.*

The attack was of short duration. The Confederate forces within the fortifications were small in number and were unable to return effective fire. Shelling continued throughout the following day, and the *Virginia* continued to be a menacing, yet distant, presence. Still under orders not to engage the Confederate ironclad directly, Jeffers left her alone, to the chagrin of his men, for they did not want the *Galena* or any of the other gunboats to be the vessel that destroyed the *Virginia.* Let them have the *Jamestown, Yorktown,* and *Teaser,* only save the "Big Thing," as the men called the *Virginia,* for the *Monitor.* They desired to once again take her on single-handed, "as a crowning glory to our career so finely commenced," wrote Keeler.[48]

Lincoln's personal reconnaissance had identified the Ocean View section of Norfolk as a likely spot to begin the invasion, and on the morning of May 10, 1862, Union forces landed on the shore and began moving inland. By five o'clock that afternoon they had reached downtown Norfolk, where the mayor, William Lamb, had staged an elaborate surrender ceremony that involved presenting the "keys to the city" to the Union commander—a ruse which allowed the Confederate army time to leave the town. A principal objective for the Confederates was to destroy the navy yard. In an eerie replay of the events of April 20, 1861, flames once again engulfed Gosport, this time set by Confederate hands. In the frantic rush, Confederate Major General Benjamin Huger neglected to inform Commander Josiah Tattnall, now in command of the CSS *Virginia,* that Norfolk had fallen earlier than anticipated.

The *Virginia* was now without a home, and Tattnall was faced with a dilemma. If he attempted to attack the Union fleet, he had some hope of destroying several vessels before being sunk, or worse, captured. He rejected this plan because of the risk of being taken. Making a run for the open waters of Chesapeake Bay was impossible because the only channel deep enough for his vessel's deep draft ran directly between the massive guns of Fortress Monroe and the artificial island Rip Raps (now Fort Wool). Though an ironclad, the *Virginia* could not withstand that withering fire. Some of the vessel's officers reportedly suggested that they abandon her to the enemy, wait for the celebration they knew would come, and then sink the ram with the carousing Union sailors on board. However, the only viable option was to lighten the vessel's load enough to allow her to pass over the James River bar and thus allow her to steam to Richmond for that city's defense.

Accordingly, all available material was taken off the ship, with the crew working well into the night throwing everything they could overboard. They had succeeded in gaining three feet of draft when the wind abruptly changed around midnight. The *Virginia*'s pilots opined that the westerly wind would drive the tide out more significantly and the vessel could never get past the bar. Only one course of action remained. Just as she had been destroyed to keep her from enemy hands a little over a year before, now the vessel again faced destruction by her own men. At two o'clock in the morning the call was given for the *Virginia*'s crew to "splice the main brace" by drinking a double ration of grog. Then Tattnall ordered the vessel run aground at Craney Island and the men told to evacuate. A small detachment rigged the vessel to explode and set her ablaze. As Richard Curtis, who had manned one of the *Virginia*'s guns, recalled, "Thus the finest fighting ship that ever floated on American waters at that time came to an untimely end at the hands of her friends, with no enemy within 8 or 10 miles of her—a sad finish for such a bright beginning."[49]

Early in the morning of May 11, 1862, fireman George Geer heard "a very large Explosion," telling his wife that "nothing could be seen of the Merimack [*sic*] after it."[50] The *Monitor* boys had been robbed of their chance to destroy the Confederate ironclad. They steamed up the Elizabeth River toward Norfolk. On the way, the *Monitor* crew got their first glimpse of what was left of the *Virginia*. Several collected souvenirs to send home (one piece was turned into a baseball bat in Massachusetts in 1866, while in the coming days black refugees in the area would collect burnt timber and other articles from the wreckage to build shelters and beds). Arriving in Portsmouth, the *Monitor*'s crew tied up at the *Virginia*'s old moorings in Gosport, under the curious and quietly hostile eyes of the locals. Lincoln and his retinue steamed past the *Monitor*, the president doffing his signature hat to the crew and bowing in thanks for their part in the action. After a brief conference, Goldsborough ordered Jeffers back to Hampton Roads and then on to Richmond the next day.[51]

On May 12 the *Monitor* and the *Naugatuck* began to move up the James River. While fortifications at Day's Bluff in Isle of Wight County lobbed a few shots at the *Monitor*, no one was harmed. Rendezvousing with the *Galena*, *Aroostook*, and *Port Royal* at Jamestown Island, the *Monitor* and *Naugatuck* led the fleet farther up river. As the width of the river began to close in, Confederate sharpshooters who haunted the banks of the James River became a principal concern. The men of the *Monitor* thus found themselves largely confined below. Anchoring at night, the fleet set a picket on shore, with the men of the various vessels standing two-hour picket duty throughout the night.[52]

While the two ironclads would not meet again in battle, their crews would meet once more at Drewry's Bluff. Catesby ap Roger Jones, who had commanded the *Virginia* against the *Monitor* on March 9, would face the Union ironclad again, commanding many of the same men. Leaving their burning vessel behind, several of the crew of the *Virginia* moved west, following the James River, to a bend a few miles downriver from Richmond. There, high on a bluff stood the fortifications known as Fort Darling, where the Confederates had placed several large guns. The *Virginia*'s consorts, the *Jamestown* and *Yorktown,* were found by the Confederates to be more useful as sunken obstructions to navigation than as gunboats. The Confederates had robbed the Union fleet of two more prizes, it seemed.

On May 15, 1862, the Union fleet began its attack on Fort Darling, situated high on Drewry's Bluff. Captain Jeffers, attempting to aim the guns more effectively, stationed himself behind a barricade of rolled-up hammocks atop the turret for part of the action.[53] Yet there was no possibility of claiming victory for the *Monitor* in this engagement; she and her consorts could gain no advantage over the fortification up on the bluff, nor could the *Monitor* elevate her guns far enough, a serious design flaw that would make turreted vessels ineffective against such high fortifications. The ventilation within the turret, though fine during the cool morning of March 9, was inadequate to handle the warm May day. Temperatures within the turret rose to an oppressive 140 degrees, and several of the gunners fainted from a combination of the heat and gases from the gunpowder and engine, as well as smoke and heat from lamps and the "emanations" from the sixty men who had been enclosed in the "fetid atmosphere" for hours. The *Monitor,* according to chief engineer Isaac Newton, proved to be "a mighty hot concern in warm weather."[54]

The *Monitor*'s sister ironclad, the *Galena,* engaged with the fortifications at Drewry's Bluff as well, but as Goldsborough had intimated, the *Galena*'s design proved to be entirely unable to withstand the plunging fire from the bluff and was pierced through seventeen times. The fleet was forced to retreat down the James. It was reported, though the story is perhaps apocryphal, that Lieutenant John Taylor Wood, formerly of the CSS *Virginia,* called out from the fortification: "Tell Captain Jeffers *that* is not the way to Richmond."[55]

The aftermath of the battle on board the *Galena* was a scene of horror to the men of the *Monitor* who went aboard to assess the situation. Body parts lay strewn throughout the gun deck, with brains and lumps of flesh spattered on the guns, tackle, and bulkheads. The *Monitor,* in contrast, sustained three hits to her turret and no casualties, though many men were reported ill the following day as a result of "river water & foul air in the ship." The crew also expanded by one, when during the night of May 16 a young black man rowed to the *Monitor* from the north shore of the James River. Thinking him to be a Confederate, the men standing watch fired a warning shot and sounded the alarm that a boarding party had been sighted. Twenty-four-year-old Siah Carter, an escaped slave from Shirley Plantation, called out to the crew, "O, Lor' Massa, oh don't shoot, I'se a black man Massa, I'se a black man," and they knew he posed no threat. Because of his knowledge of the area, Carter was taken aboard as a crew member—contraband of war—and rated as a cabin boy.[56]

The experience at Drewry's Bluff revealed the limitations of the *Monitor*'s design. While Alban Stimers had already relayed many of his observations to Commodore Smith and Secretary Welles in March and April, Captain Jeffers was eager to share his observations with Goldsborough and other navy officials because several other vessels of this type had been ordered as early as March 17 and were already being built. He began:

> First. With her present guns, she cannot engage another iron-plated vessel of good construction with advantage. The ball has not sufficient velocity to penetrate, and must rely on its smashing effects only. It would not penetrate, though it might shatter, an inclined side of four (4) inches, well backed with wood, or our own vertical side.[57]

The *Monitor*'s XI-inch Dahlgrens with their fifteen-pound charges were clearly not powerful enough to effect any damage on a Confederate ironclad. The next class of monitors under construction, the Passaic class, would carry an XI-inch and a XV-inch Dahlgrens in their larger turrets. Jeffers continued:

> Second. Although she manoeuvres very quickly, her speed is not six knots at a maximum. She must, therefore, as against a vessel, await the enemy's pleasure to close, and is much trammelled, as herein before stated, by the limitation of the field of fire to 220° of the 360°.

Jeffers had experimented with the turret's range of fire prior to moving up the James River. He found that the guns could not be fired forward any nearer than 30 degrees to either side of the pilot house without deafening the persons within. He told Goldsborough: "I tried this experiment myself, and the pain and stupefaction caused by the blast of the guns satisfied me that half a dozen similar discharges would render me insensible." Furthermore, he found that it was not prudent to fire aft within 50 degrees to either side of the boilers, as any mistake could cause the boilers to leak at best and explode at worst.

Jeffers further pointed out that this vessel design would only be effective against a fortification if both were at the same level, yet he felt that being a small target yielded a monitor-class vessel some level of safety. He also observed that "a solid shot, of ten-inch and higher calibres, fired with heavy charges, striking near the same spot half a dozen times at short ranges, would dislocate the turret plates, drive in fragments, and end by coming through." But most crucially, he wrote to Goldsborough, was her mode of ventilation, for "either in action or at sea, the loss of the vessel might readily be caused by *the failure of a leather belt.*"[58]

By June the *Monitor*'s logbook entries had become a litany of temperatures, and both the vessel and the men began to get cranky. On June 2, 1862, Acting Lieutenant William Flye noted that "at 5 am got underweigh [*sic*] & proceeded up the river followed by the rest of the fleet. At 8 am anchored in consequence of a derangement of the engine."[59] On June 12 Flye, standing the afternoon watch, wrote, "At 1 pm thermometer stood 142 degrees inside the galley, the door being open and the blowers of the engine being in action." By the next day at noon, acting master Louis Stodder was able to report that the "thermometer stood at 165 in the galley." On the fourteenth the engine was once again deranged and the temperatures soared. The celebrated flushing toilets heated to a fetid 131 degrees. A cool front brought some relief for the next several days, but at 1:30 A.M. on June 23, Stodder and his watch discovered a fire around the stovepipe of the galley. Though they were able to extinguish it, there was enough damage to take the galley out of commission for several days.[60] During this time, John Ericsson rather uncharacteristically sent a sympathetic note to his friend Isaac Newton, saying, "I admit that you have had a very severe trial and cannot imagine anything more monotonous and disagreeable than life on board the Monitor, at anchor in the James River, during the hot season."[61]

To make matters worse, Paymaster Keeler had initially miscalculated the timing of fresh provisions. Geer complained to his wife about how the paymaster was new and green and because of his inexperience they were having to use molasses in their coffee. Supplies did arrive, however, and while the men complained about all of the tasty "sesesh" beef walking around on the banks of the James, they did eventually manage to get fresh food throughout the summer. In fact, Keeler noted that "a portion of our iron deck has been converted into a stock yard containing just at present, one homesick lamb, one tough combative old ram, a consumptive calf, one fine lean swine, an antediluvian rooster & his mate, an old antiquated setting hen."[62]

The late spring and summer of 1862 were difficult ones for the *Monitor* boys. Unable to return fire effectively against shore batteries, suffering from the heat, bad food, and incessant mosquitoes, they found that they spent their time up the James River ultimately more to improve national morale than for any direct martial purpose. Chief engineer Isaac Newton quipped to his mother that "if that's the case moral effect must be pretty well strewed along the river in these parts from the number of times we have passed up & down." In the heat the officers were also chafing under the ultimate command of Rear Admiral Goldsborough, a man "whose principal qualifications are immense size, big feet & the faculty of using neat, heavy round oaths when the occasion permits," wrote Newton. What galled both officers and men was the fact that while they were sweltering on the James, Goldsborough was "quietly rusticating on board the *Minnesota* in Norfolk Harbor."[63]

The officers joined the lamentations of the crew over the command of Lieutenant Jeffers, whom they all agreed was an ordnance genius, but the praise largely stopped there. Newton wrote, "Although I acknowledge the professional ability of our commander I must say he is the personification of selfishness." George Geer, promoted by Newton to the rank of engineer yeoman following the Drewry's Bluff engagement, was less generous: Jeffers was a "damd old Gluttonous Hogg," he wrote Martha, adding that "I hope the curse of Hell will rest on him." For his part, Keeler lamented Jeffers's "extreme selfishness & his want of decisive energetic action," as well as the "most supreme contempt" Jeffers showed toward volunteer officers. Jeffers even managed to offend civilians around him. A nurse aboard another vessel on the James River wrote in her diary, "The Captain of the *Monitor* paid our Captains a visit just before tea. He took hardly any notice of me and none of Mrs. Willett, which we did not like."[64]

The fleet attempted to steam up the Appomattox River in late June in an attempt to destroy a railroad bridge at Swift Creek and thus cut off a critical supply route for the Confederates. Isaac Newton complained that "the inevitable *Monitor*" was going to be "dragged along up this dirty shoal river, gracious only knows for what purpose except to be stuck & abandoned."[65] On the evening of June 26, the *Galena* and the *Port Royal* took up a spectacular diverting fire so the small gunboats could achieve their objective. Yet the Appomattox proved too treacherous. The *Monitor,* together with three gunboats, "got in a perfect mess on the bar," recalled Newton, and several vessels ran aground. In addition, many in the small boats detailed to row ahead and set fire to the bridge feared that there might be Confederate sharpshooters along the banks of the river, which had narrowed considerably around the fleet as they steamed farther in. The assembled officers of the small fleet determined it was too dangerous to press on, and the fleet, once they had been refloated, in some cases had to steam backward out of the narrow river. One small steamer, the *Island Belle,* could not be refloated and was destroyed.

The mission was a failure. According to Keeler, "Four or five thousand dollars worth of ammunition expended, one Steamer . . . burned, a large quantity of whiskey drank, with what result? A number of people badly frightened & the corner of a house knocked off."[66] It was an ignominious chapter in the *Monitor*'s career, yet one that went largely unmentioned. Historian Chuck Veit writes that "in the end, all was for naught, and, had the story of the Appomattox River raid not been lost in the climax of the Seven Days Battles, any serious investigation of the failed raid would have resulted in rejoicing that it had not ended much the worse for the Navy and the nation."[67] One observer on another vessel in the James River captured the mood of the men on the *Monitor*. Following a thunderstorm on July 15, Union nurse Harriet Douglas Whetten wrote in her diary, "The Monitor looked like a black monster in the midst of the thick bronze waves. There was a look of Hell about her."[68]

There was at least one small success shortly after the Appomattox raid, however. In the final days before McClellan's retreat, the *Monitor* and the steamer *Maratanza* happened upon their old foe the CSS *Teaser* at Turkey Island in the James River. Commanded by Hunter Davidson, late of the CSS *Virginia*, the *Teaser* was transporting Confederate army officers to locations near Chaffin's Bluff on the James. Two shells from the *Maratanza* disabled the *Teaser*, and all on board leaped into small boats and "skeedadled" ashore, leaving papers and other war matériel on board. Among the items captured were diagrams of mines laid by the Confederates in the James River near Richmond, and of particular importance to the men of the *Monitor*, Hunter Davidson's private memorandum book, which outlined a clever attack plan on the *Monitor* that had been forthcoming. Diagrams of the *Monitor* were included, with written instructions on how the *Monitor* was to be "boarded from four tugs at the same time . . . by men carrying turpentine, ladders, fire balls, wedges, sheets of metal, chloroform &c."[69]

Ultimately, the Union did not take Richmond in the spring and summer of 1862. The *Monitor* had spent her time on the James, first supporting McClellan's advance, and then, with the failure of the Seven Days campaign in early July, his retreat. Her "moral effect" had not been enough. Yet the public still wanted to know more about her. From the entreaties of Confederate spy Rose O'Neal Greenhow to come on board to "see how you look inside," as she was being taken back to Richmond as part of a prisoner exchange, to continued coverage in *Harper's Weekly* and other newspapers, the *Monitor* and her men were celebrities.[70] Yet all of the images of the vessel to that point had been hand drawn, painted, or engraved. Therefore, as the Union fleet retreated down the James

Fig. 74. In July 1862 James F. Gibson captured this image, a stereograph of a 12-pound rifled cannon of the CSS *Teaser,* one of the first Confederate gunboats. (Library of Congress)

Fig. 75. The USS *Maratanza,* as she appeared immediately after her capture of the *Teaser.* James F. Gibson's photograph of the *Maratanza* was taken in July 1862. (Library of Congress)

River, Union photographer James F. Gibson came on board to document the celebrated ironclad and her crew. It was also hoped that Gibson's visit to the ironclad would coincide with President Lincoln's next visit.

Both Gibson and Lincoln visited the *Monitor* on July 9, 1862, as she lay anchored off Berkeley Plantation on the James River. Lincoln arrived at 7:45 A.M., before Captain Jeffers was awake. The president had a boat sent for Goldsborough to attend him on the *Monitor.* Lincoln and Welles were both frustrated with Goldsborough's lack of action and near refusal to provide appropriate naval support for McClellan's peninsular campaign. Welles had issued the order on July 6 to detach twenty-three vessels from Goldsborough's squadron to form a new James River flotilla. The flotilla would be under the command of the quixotic Captain Charles Wilkes, who would report directly to Welles. Goldsborough was furious at this slight, ultimately asking to be relieved of command.[71] Welles obliged him.

Fig. 76. James F. Gibson photographed the officers and crew aboard the deck of the *Monitor* on July 9, 1862. In this image, Captain William N. Jeffers sits alone next to an empty chair, a fair representation of his relationship with his men. It is possible that the empty chair was intended for Lincoln. (Library of Congress)

The meeting between Lincoln and Goldsborough was apparently brief, and both men left before Jeffers ever made his appearance. Captain Wilkes would be taking over as flag officer of the new flotilla that afternoon.[72] Gibson arrived in the afternoon as well, and though the president had left, the photographer took eight photographs of the men of the *Monitor,* the only known photographs of the vessel. Some of the shots seem composed in order to take in the still-visible battle damage on both the hull and the turret, while other shots were clearly taken to show the officers and crew. One image of the crew shows a young black man crouched in the foreground—possibly Siah Carter from Shirley Plantation. Next to him a makeshift galley sits on the weather deck, a remnant from the fire on June 23. Another crew shot shows the men more relaxed, some playing checkers while another reads the newspaper, seemingly unaware his portrait is being made. Three photographs show the officers in various combinations, joined by a lieutenant from the *Galena.* A final photograph shows Jeffers alone, a visual testament to his alienation from his men. Copies of the photographs were given to the men, some of whom sent them home to their families.[73] The fatigue and frustration are lined upon their faces.

William Keeler, on hearing of Wilkes's appointment in Goldsborough's stead, expressed his frustration with naval affairs to his wife: "A

Fig. 77. The turret of the *Monitor,* showing dents from the *Virginia.* Also shown are some of the *Monitor* officers. Left to right: Robinson W. Hands, Louis N. Stodder, Albert B. Campbell, and William Flye. (Library of Congress)

Fig. 78. Stereograph of the *Monitor* crew on deck. (Library of Congress)

great mistake is made in appointing superannuated old fogies whose life & energies are used up to these important commands when a younger man of life, energy & enterprise is so much needed."[74] To add to their woes, the news had been spread that the Confederates had been working upon a "*Merrimac* No. 2," known as the *Richmond.* Originally under construction at Gosport, her incomplete hull had been towed to Richmond in advance of the fall of Norfolk in May, and Confederate deserters had

Fig. 79. The *Monitor* crew relaxing on deck. (Library of Congress)

Fig 80. Stereograph of the officers of the *Monitor* (version 1). Back row, left to right: George Frederickson, Mark T. Sunstrom, Samuel Dana Greene, L. Howard Newman (executive officer of the USS *Galena*), Isaac Newton; middle row, left to right: Louis N. Stodder, William F. Keeler, William Flye, Daniel C. Logue; front row: Robinson W. Hands, Albert B. Campbell, Edwin V. Gager. (Library of Congress)

described her progress to the *Monitor* crew over the summer. Each puff of smoke on the horizon seemed to the men of the Union fleet to be a harbinger of the new Confederate naval threat. "*Merrimac*-on-the-brain" was a "disease" thought to be rampant among the Union navy command. The Confederate army for its part would occasionally shell the Union positions, and small shore batteries battered Union gunboats on patrol, further adding to the discontent.

Then in mid-July came the unkindest cut of all: the U.S. Congress passed an act banning spirituous liquor on board Union vessels unless for medicinal purposes.[75] The ban would take effect on the first of September, though

Fig. 81. Stereograph of the officers of the *Monitor* (version 2): Back row, left to right: Albert B. Campbell, Mark T. Sunstrom, William F. Keeler, L. Howard Newman (executive officer of the USS *Galena*); middle row: Louis N. Stodder, George Frederickson, William Flye, Daniel C. Logue, Samuel Dana Greene; front row: Robinson W. Hands, Edwin V. Gager. (Library of Congress)

any alcohol already on board at that time would be allowed. The grog ration would be a thing of the past, and for many men the slight raise in pay in exchange for the ration would be cold comfort. (Third assistant engineer George White thought it "a miserable law and our wise men in Congress had better devote their time to matters of more importance.") Bottles of hair tonic and bitters found in the wreck of the *Monitor* may be examples of attempts to circumvent this ruling. One day after the order went into effect, officer's steward Lawrence Murray, who had so fumbled the luncheon service during the *Monitor*'s sea trials on March 3, was granted leave and returned from his time ashore quite drunk. Upon coming aboard the *Monitor,* he seized an axe and tried to kill the paymaster's steward. Placed in chains on the deck, Murray rolled or jumped overboard (accounts differ), and his body was not recovered until September 5.[76]

Other changes were in store for the *Monitor.* On August 15 Captain Jeffers announced that he would be leaving for a position in which he would supervise the building of more ironclads. Clearly his recommendations to Goldsborough had borne fruit. On the eighteenth he was relieved of command by his replacement, Commander Thomas Holdup Stevens, late of the *Maratanza.*[77] On August 20, chief engineer Isaac Newton was also detached from the vessel. Like Jeffers, he would be overseeing the construction of more ironclads.[78]

Another assault on Drewry's Bluff or the Appomattox River seemed to be a real possibility for the *Monitor* in late August, and preparations were underway for the eventuality of both. However, on the twenty-eighth the fleet received orders to proceed down the James River to Hampton Roads, where they anchored, a few yards from the sunken *Cumberland,* on August 30.[79] The feeling of freedom of the salt air, and from being targets of Confederate sharpshooters, was palpable, although some men lamented that they could not assist the army. "It is a pity the Monitor is not a land as well as a water boat," third assistant engineer George H. White wrote his mother, "for it would require but a few of our 11 inch shell to settle their [Confederates'] hash."[80]

Several significant changes were in store for the officers and crew as autumn approached. Stevens was detached from the *Monitor* in mid-September, having "won the respect & esteem" of the men. In contrast to his predecessor, Jeffers, Stevens had made the vessel "seem like another place, his treatment of his officers & men has been so kind & pleasant."[81] John Pine Bankhead, a career navy man from South Carolina and a cousin to Confederate general John Bankhead Magruder, would be their new commander. With Bankhead's arrival, a new logbook was started. The old logbook was sent to the Navy Department.

CHAPTER 7

"The *Monitor* Is No More"

The late September days in Hampton Roads were pleasant ones for the crew of the *Monitor*. Fresh seafood abounded, and fresh vegetables and some fruits were still available. The men experimented with hand grenades in anticipation of the new *Merrimac*'s appearance. Despite the relative calm, it was with great relief that the *Monitor* was finally ordered to the Washington Navy Yard for repairs on September 30, 1862. Taken under tow of a small tug, *Rescue,* also badly in need of repairs, the *Monitor* slowly made her way to Washington. She arrived at the mouth of the Potomac on the morning of October 1 and sluggishly made her way up the river, anchoring at night for safety. The men were excited at the prospect of seeing Mount Vernon, though disappointed as it was obscured by trees.

On the morning of the third, the *Rescue* towed the *Monitor* to the mouth of the Eastern Branch (now known as the Anacostia River), and as though allowing her some dignity, the *Rescue* cast her loose. Thus the *Monitor* came in to the navy yard under her own power—as a conquering heroine—accompanied by a swarm of small vessels filled with onlookers. Steaming up to the wharf, she was received amid cheers and gun salutes. On hearing that the *Monitor* had arrived, yard workers streamed out of their workshops "to take a look at the 'cheese-box.'"[1]

The *Monitor*'s men were transferred to the U.S. steamer *King Philip* for accommodations, which were much more spacious than the ironclad they had inhabited for so many months. They looked in awe at the Capitol, Treasury, White House, Patent Office, and other landmarks, while it appeared that everyone in D.C. was clamoring to see their ship. The Washington *Daily Intelligencer* reported that "quite a fleet of sail and row boats, including not a few steam-tugs, crowded with the curious, have sought a landing, but have, in every instance, been ordered away."[2]

The town was consumed with *Monitor* madness. Even the town prostitutes celebrated the little ironclad by offering their services at brothels named "The Monitor" and "The Iron-clad Battery."[3]

The *Monitor* was turned over to the workmen in the navy yard the following Monday. Soon the men of the *Monitor* would be able to take a well-deserved leave and visit their loved ones. The crew was to receive 14 days' leave, and the officers were granted leave up to 4 weeks. However, curious citizens continued their efforts to catch a glimpse of the ironclad from small boats that swarmed the perimeter of the navy yard. On Saturday, October 6, before most of the officers and crew could begin their leave, the *Monitor* was opened to a select group of citizens. Keeler wrote that "the docks were lined with carriages—& it was in fact a perfect jam—no caravan or circus ever collected such a crowd." The men enjoyed the attention, especially that of the large number of ladies who came to see the ship, and the officers and crew were delighted to stand at the bottom of the steep ladders on board to greet the ladies—and look up their skirts. That evening, guards were stationed at the dock so that the officers and crew could eat their evening meal without the intrusions of the public.[4]

After dinner on Monday, October 6, Benjamin Brown French, the commissioner of public buildings, and three other companions went to the navy yard to tour the *Monitor*. "We got almost to her before we saw her, and such an insignificant looking craft for a war steamer I never saw or dreamed of," he wrote in his diary a few days later. "'A cheese box on a raft' expresses her appearance better than anything else, and those on board the *Merrimack* must have been utterly astonished to see such a *thing* come boldly up and give the monster battle, and still more so when they had to skedaddle off into Norfolk pretty essentially used up!" On board the vessel, French found General and Mrs. Nathaniel P. Banks, and the group "examined the wonderful craft—saw the very slight effect which the shot of the *Merrimack* had upon her iron sides, deck and turret." After spending another thirty minutes on the deck, French and his friends went aboard another vessel and toured some machine shops. "We left about sunset, after having our curiosity very much gratified," he wrote.[5]

Benjamin Franklin Isherwood, engineer in chief of the navy's Bureau of Steam Engineering, took advantage of the *Monitor*'s time at the yard to run a series of tests on the vessel's engine. The nemesis of Delamater and Ericsson, Isherwood likely wished to find fault with Ericsson's vessel and its Delamater-made engine.

Because of the public interest, as well as the close proximity of Confederate territory across the Potomac, guards were stationed at the *Monitor* work site around the clock. That duty was not without its perils. On the evening of October 27 Richard Carter, a watchman at the navy yard, tripped over one of the large ropes used to relaunch the *Monitor* and "was precipitated into the dock," leaving "an interesting family to deplore his sad fate."[6]

Navy officials tightened security during the repairs, but bowing to public pressure, they placed a small ad in the Washington *Daily Intelligencer* on Thursday, November 6, which read: "The 'MONITOR' will be open to the public this (Thursday) afternoon, from one o'clock until sunset. This is the only opportunity the public will have to see her. Passes will not be required at the navy yard gate." The same paper reported later that, once again, "all the city flocked to the Navy Yard" to see her.[7] Soldiers, sailors, and civilian men, women, and children all turned out to tour the celebrated ironclad. This time, however, most of the officers and crew were still on leave, not to return until later that night. Seeking souvenirs, the crowds took whatever they could remove, as there was very little security to stop them. Acting master Louis Stodder recalled that "when we came up to clean that night, there was not a key, doorknob, escutcheon—there wasn't a thing that hadn't been carried away."[8]

Everyone who could visited the *Monitor* that day, and because passes were not required, anyone was able to go aboard, including a young man named R. P. Compton. After touring the vessel Compton "went into one of the offices at the yard, and stated that he was a Southern man, that the South would be successful; and as for the Monitor, she was a d—d humbug." He was immediately arrested and placed in irons in the guardhouse.[9] Others with Southern leanings who may have visited kept their loyalties to themselves. (In fact, it is known that Robert E. Lee had at least one Confederate spy reporting back on the construction of other monitors in New York during this time.[10])

Rushing to complete the work on the vessel, workmen at the navy yard continued painting and installing woodwork and ironwork (and replacing those items that had been taken by the tourists) while officers and crew began moving ship's stores, coal, and their personal possessions back on board. Finally, on November 9, though "everything was tumbled aboard after a fashion," the *Monitor* left Washington, D.C., and returned south to her "old moorings off Newport News."[11]

The *Monitor*'s time at the Washington Navy Yard had yielded several changes to the vessel—and this, then, is the *Monitor* we know. On their return in early November, the men found that their ship had undergone a transformation. A telescopic smoke pipe some thirty feet in height had been installed and everything gleamed with fresh paint. The berth deck had been raised up significantly to afford storage space underneath, and the storage rooms to either side of the berth deck had been reduced by several feet, leaving far more room for living quarters. Additional blowers for ventilation had been installed, a result of Jeffers's observations over the summer. Iron cranes and davits had been affixed to the weather deck for new ship's boats. This arrangement was far preferable to towing boats or lashing them to the deck. New awnings had also been provided to shade both turret and weather deck. She was like a new vessel.

Newspapers reported that the dents in the turret had been marked with the names of the sources from whence they had come. Keeler wrote to his wife that they were marked "'Merrimac,' 'Merrimac's Prow,' 'Minnesota,' 'Fort Darling.'"[12] The guns that had been removed from the turret during a portion of the vessel's stay at the yard were also engraved. The starboard gun bore the name "Ericsson" on the breech, with the words "Monitor & Merrimac" beneath in smaller letters. The port gun, named "Worden," also bore the names of the two vessels in the March 9 battle. The engravings still exist, discovered on the Dahlgren guns in the turret in the fall of 2002. The marks on the dents on the turret have apparently not survived. Conservators at The Mariners' Museum completed the removal of marine concretion from the recovered turret in August 2011 and found no markings extant.

The changes to the vessel were not the only new things on board. There were new officers and crew as well. Some men had been officially detached from the vessel when she arrived in Washington while others sought to detach themselves in less official ways, deserting for better appointments, or through drunken mishaps.[13] Several new crewmen came on board in Washington, including Jacob Nicklis, a twenty-one-year-old from Buffalo, New York, who had volunteered for the *Monitor* with his friend Isaac Scott. Nicklis "did not want to volunter [*sic*] for her but all the rest of the boys from our place did so I joined with them."[14] In all, twenty men came on board to replace the crew that had either been reassigned or had deserted.[15] There were replacement officers as well. Dr. Daniel Logue had resigned his commission and had been replaced by Dr. Greenville Weeks, while the second assistant engineer, George H. White, was replaced with Samuel Augee (or Auge) Lewis, the third assistant engineer. Norman Knox Attwater came on board as acting ensign, and master's mate George Frederickson, who had been on board since before the ship had a name, was promoted to ensign as well.[16]

On Christmas Eve 1862, orders came in for Captain John Pine Bankhead to "proceed in tow of the *Rhode Island,* with the *Monitor* under your command, to Beaufort, N.C., and wait further orders. Avail yourself of the first favorable weather for making the passage." Though not stated, the anticipation was that the *Monitor* would then make her way to Charleston with a large Union fleet that would eventually include several of her daughters—turreted ironclads that had been built following her success in March 1862.[17] But the weather was uncooperative and departure would have to wait.

Christmas Day was spent in Hampton Roads, and both officers and crew observed the holiday with a combination of work and festive food and drink. Crewman Jacob Nicklis and his thirteen messmates pooled their money—"a dollar a piece"—to have an enjoyable Christmas feast, which consisted of "chicken stew & then stuffed Turkey mashed potatoes, & soft bread after this we had a plum pudding & some nice fruit cake, with apples for des[s]ert."[18] Some of the crew had leave to go ashore and encountered the crew of several British vessels that were in port. The men mingled together "on the best of terms till the parties got too much whiskey when a fight would have to decide who was the best man of the two." William Keeler, who was ashore and a witness to the brawl, said that by the evening "there seemed to be a sort of general mass, black eyes, bloody noses, & battered faces seeming to predominate."[19]

The next few days, while the crew waited for the weather to clear, they placed oakum between the turret and its brass deck ring, though they did not seal it with pitch—this despite Ericsson's insistence that the turret formed a watertight seal with the deck. Old naval customs died hard, it seemed. They bolted and caulked the gunport shutters, caulked the pilothouse slits, and secured iron covers over the deadlights. George Geer wrote to his wife that he sealed the hatches with "Red Lead putty and and [*sic*] the Port Holes I made Rubber Gaskets one inch thick and in fact had every thing about the ship in the way of an opening water tight." They needed to be cautious, for they were about to enter the area known as the Graveyard of the Atlantic. In the midst of the preparations, Albert Campbell, second assistant engineer, was injured while working on the engine and was removed from the ship. He would not make the trip south.[20] On December 28 Jacob Nicklis wrote to his father in Buffalo: "Do not answer this letter until you hear from me again which I hope will be shortly. They say we will have a pretty rough time a going around Hatteras but I hope it will not be the case."[21]

On December 29 two massive hawsers were passed from the *Monitor* to the vessel assigned for the ocean tow, the USS *Rhode Island*. The *Monitor*'s small boats were transferred to the consort vessel, where they could be kept safe.[22] At 2:30 P.M. John Bean, a local pilot, came on board the *Rhode Island*, and the two vessels got underway. The weather was clear and pleasant, and Captain Bankhead wrote that there was "every prospect of its continuation." As the *Monitor* was leaving Hampton Roads, her former commander, John Worden, was entering the roadstead in another monitor, the USS *Montauk.* The *Monitor* and *Rhode Island* passed Cape Henry at six o'clock that evening and thus entered the Atlantic Ocean.

Just before dawn on December 30, the USS *Monitor,* in tow of the USS *Rhode Island,* began to "experience a swell from the southward," and as the day progressed the clouds increased "till the sun was obscured by their cold grey mantle." Officers and crew amused themselves by watching three sharks swim alongside the ship. Soon, however, the sea began to break over the vessel, the waves white with foam. As the weather grew worse, the men were forced to go below decks, and at five that afternoon the officers sat down to dinner in the wardroom, joking about being free from their "monotonous inactive life."

As the *Monitor* prepared to round Cape Hatteras, waves hit the turret so hard it trembled. But the crew was elated: "Hurrah for the first iron-clad that ever rounded Cape Hatteras!" they cried. "Hurrah for the little boat that is first in everything!"[23] The air temperature began to rise into the seventies. The barometer, however, was falling.[24] By 7:30 P.M. one of the hawsers snapped, and the *Monitor* began rolling wildly. The increased motion forced out some of the oakum under the turret, and water started pouring in through the gaps.

The situation belowdecks was serious. The water level had risen to one inch in the engine room, and Captain Bankhead ordered engineer Joseph Watters to put the Worthington bilge pumps to work. Water had also reached the coal bunkers, and the coal was growing too wet to keep up the steam in the engines. The pressure, which normally ran at eighty pounds, had dropped to twenty pounds—dangerously low. The captain ordered the large centrifugal water pump into action. Mountainous waves crashed over the *Monitor*'s deck as the storm intensified. The pilothouse was almost continuously under water. Many of the men were on top of the turret. Bankhead "signalized several times to the *Rhode Island* to stop."[25] The engineers reported that the pumps were having no effect.

At 8:45 P.M., the *Rhode Island* stopped. For a moment the *Monitor* seemed to ride more easily, but the wind kept picking up. The waves now began "burying her completely for an instant, while for a few seconds nothing could be seen of her from the *Rhode Island* but the upper part of her turret surrounded by foam."[26]

At 10:00 P.M. the engineers told Bankhead that the water was more than a foot deep in the engine room—so deep that the blowers were spitting water. Surgeon Weeks later wrote, "The vessel's doom was sealed; for with [the fires'] extinction the pumps must cease, and all hope of keeping the *Monitor* above water."[27] The men organized a bucket brigade, but it did no good except to lessen the crew's panic. Weeks recalled that "some sang as they worked, and the cadence of the voices, mingling with the roar of the waters, sounded like a defiance to Ocean."[28]

For his part of the bailing, landsman Francis B. Butts stood in the turret, passing buckets from the lower hatchway to the men on top of the turret. Butts later recalled, "A black cat was sitting on the breech of one of the guns, howling one of those hoarse and solemn tunes which no one can appreciate who is not filled with the superstitions which I had been taught by the sailors, who are always afraid to kill a cat." Despite his fearful apprehensions, Butts grabbed the cat and shoved it into one of the guns, capping it off with wadding and a tampion. As he exited the turret a few moments later, he "could still hear that distressing yowl."[29]

At 10:30 P.M. Bankhead gave the order for the red distress lantern to be hoisted. The engines were slowed to preserve steam for the pumps. But the decrease in speed made the hawser taut, and the ironclad became unmanageable. Bankhead called for volunteers to cut the towline. Master Louis Stodder, bo'sun's mate John Stocking (aka Wells Wentz), and the quarter gunner, James Fenwick, climbed down the turret, but eyewitnesses said that Fenwick and Stocking were swept overboard and drowned. Stodder managed to hang on to the safety lines around the deck and cut through the hawser with a hatchet.

At 11:00 P.M. Bankhead sent the signal to the *Rhode Island:* "Send your boats immediately, we are sinking!" Commander Stephen D. Trenchard of the *Rhode Island* called for that ship's engines to be stopped and her boats "away to the rescue!" The first boat, a launch, was commanded by Ensign A. O. Taylor. The second, a cutter, was commanded by master's mate Rodney Browne. Watching from the deck of the *Monitor,* Weeks felt gratitude to the men of the *Rhode Island* for the danger they voluntarily placed upon themselves: "Their captain and they knew the danger; every man who entered that boat did it at peril of his life; and yet all were ready. Are not such acts as these convincing proof of the divinity of human nature?" Weeks later recalled that the *Monitor* boys "watched her with straining eyes, for few thought she could live to reach us," but as the rescue boat neared the *Monitor* they "thank[ed] God!" At about this same time Bankhead had the *Monitor*'s engines stopped as well. When the two boats from the *Rhode Island* reached the *Monitor,* Bankhead ordered Lieutenant Samuel Dana Greene "to put as many men into them as they would safely carry."[30]

To get to the rescue boats, the men had to cross the rolling, storm-swept deck. Keeler told his wife that what he saw that night would "appall the boldest heart." On January 6, 1863, he recounted the traumatic scene in harrowing detail:

> Mountains of water were rushing across our decks & foaming along our sides; the small [rescue] boats were pitching & tossing about on them or crashing against our sides, mere playthings on the billows; the howling of the tempest, the roar & dash of waters; the hoarse orders through the speaking of trumpets of the officers; the response of the men; the shouts of encouragement & words of caution:
>
> "the bubbling cry
> Of some strong Swimmer in his agony;"
>
> & the whole scene lit up by the ghastly glare of the blue lights burning on our consort, formed a panorama of horror which time can never efface from my memory.[31]

Men jumped from the deck of the *Monitor* into the rescue boats, but as the water swelled, some missed their target and soon were swept beneath the waves. "I was one of the last to jump, and by the time I did so there was too wide a space of sea showing between the ship's side and the small craft, and though I sprang with all the force I had in me I fell far short," recalled Weeks. "It was an awful sensation when I struck the water." Fortunately for Weeks, Lieutenant Greene was in the rescue boat looking out for Weeks. Seeing Weeks fall short, Greene reached over the side of the rescue boat and "grabbed me by my collar just in the nick of time."[32] Unfortunately for Weeks, his night of suffering was still young.

With both ships' power cut, the *Monitor* and the *Rhode Island* drifted dangerously close to one another. One of the launches was caught between them and suffered damage, but it remained afloat as sixteen men climbed in. The *Rhode Island* tried to pull away, but the hawser on the *Monitor* that Stodder had cut had become entangled in *Rhode Island*'s paddle wheel and was pulling the ships closer together. Sailors from the *Rhode Island* worked to cut the ships loose as they rolled heavily on the waves. Finally the lines were freed, and the *Rhode Island* began to drift away.

At midnight Ensign William Rodgers launched the third boat from the *Rhode Island.* The distance between the two ships had increased considerably, and Browne's cutter was almost unmanageable. As it approached the *Monitor,* it collided with Taylor's overloaded launch as it was trying to make its way to the *Rhode Island.* Surgeon Weeks, in the launch, reached out to the oncoming boat. The two boats scraped heavily as they passed, catching Weeks's right hand between the two, crushing three fingers and wrenching his arm "from its socket." Weeks's arm fell "helpless" at his side, but he was grateful to be alive. "We were saved," he later wrote, "and an arm was a small price to pay for a life."[33]

Shortly after midnight the water overcame the engine and the *Monitor*'s pumps stopped, and with them any hope of saving the ship. Bankhead reportedly said, "It is madness to remain here any longer . . . let each man save himself."[34] The boats from the *Rhode Island* were still coming to rescue the *Monitor*'s half-drowned crew, but it was clear that not everyone would make it in one trip. Desperate men had to cling to the top of the turret until the lifeboats returned.

Browne's cutter arrived soon after Bankhead's call to abandon ship. Browne recalled, "We had now got in my boat all of the *Monitor's* crew that could be persuaded to come down from the turret for they had seen some of their shipmates who had left the turret for the deck washed overboard and sink in their sight." Many of the men who did leave the foundering ship threw shoes, clothing, and possessions back into the turret so they would be able to swim if they needed to.[35] Those same possessions were found by conservators and archaeologists following the recovery of the turret in August 2002 (the remains of Butts's alleged black cat have yet to be discovered, however).

Paymaster William Keeler later gave a moment-by-moment account of his escape from the *Monitor*: "I divested myself of the greater portion of my clothing to afford me greater facilities for swimming in case of necessity & attempted to descend the ladder leading down the outside of the turret, but found it full of men hesitating but desiring to make the perilous passage of the deck." Keeler "found a rope hanging from one of the awning stanchions over my head & slid down it to the deck. A huge wave passed over me tearing me from my footing & bearing me along with it, rolling, tumbling & tossing like a merest speck." The wave carried Keeler "ten or twelve yards from the vessel" but when he came to the surface "the back-set of the wave threw me against the vessel's side near one of the iron stanchions which supported the life line; this I grasped with all the energy of desperation & . . . was hauled into the boat, into which the men were jumping one by one as they could venture across the deck."[36]

John Bankhead returned to his cabin for his coat, and other small personal possessions. He took "one lingering look and . . . left the Monitor's cabin forever." Master's mate George Fredrickson returned a watch he had borrowed from another officer, saying, "Here, this is yours; I may be lost." Some of the men refused to leave—or simply couldn't. Francis Butts recalled that engineer Samuel Lewis was too seasick to leave his berth.[37]

On board the *Rhode Island,* surgeon Samuel Gilbert Webber reset Weeks's arm and amputated parts of three fingers. Weeks came back to stand on deck with his *Monitor* shipmates, watching the sad drama unfold: "For an hour or more we watched from the deck of the Rhode Island the lonely light upon the Monitor's turret; a hundred times we thought it gone forever,—a hundred times it reappeared, till at last . . . it sank, and we saw it no more."[38]

THE WRECK OF THE IRON-CLAD "MONITOR."

Fig. 82. "The Wreck of the Iron-Clad 'Monitor'" appeared in *Harper's Weekly,* January 24, 1863. (The Mariners' Museum, Newport News, Virginia)

Browne and his men in the cutter were making "but slow progress" when the *Monitor*'s light disappeared for good. Then, turning back to the *Rhode Island,* they were horrified to see her "steaming away from us, throwing up rockets and burning blue lights—leaving us behind." Captain Trenchard searched for them all night and into the next day, when the search was abandoned and the *Rhode Island* steamed for Beaufort. Picked up by the schooner *A. Colby* the following day, Browne and his crew returned to the *Rhode Island* to be greeted by "hearty cheers."[39]

Forty-seven men were rescued from the USS *Monitor* before she slipped beneath the waves.[40] Sixteen were lost—either washed overboard while trying to reach the rescue boats or trapped inside the foundering vessel. Upon mustering the crew upon the *Rhode Island,* John Bankhead found the following men missing:

Landsman William Allen
Acting Ensign Norman Knox Attwater
Yeoman William Bryan
1st Class Boy Robert Cook
Landsman William H. Eagan
Quarter Gunner James R. Fenwick
Acting Ensign George Fredrickson
2nd Assistant Engineer Robinson Hands
Officer's Cook Robert H. Howard

1st Class Fireman Thomas Joice
3rd Assistant Engineer Samuel Augee Lewis
Coal Heaver George Littlefield
Landsman Daniel Moore
Seaman Jacob Nicklis
Boatswain's Mate John Stocking (aka Wells Wentz)
1st Class Fireman Robert Williams[41]

Fig. 83. "Loss of the 'Monitor,'" appeared in *Frank Leslie's Illustrated Newspaper* on January 24, 1863, and later in Frank Leslie's *The American Soldier in the Civil War* in 1885. (The Mariners' Museum, Newport News, Virginia)

NOAA archaeologists and Mariners' Museum conservators have found within the turret artifacts specifically associated with four of the sixteen men who perished. All are pieces of silver or silver-plated tableware, and all are of different patterns, indicating that they had likely been brought from home by the individual officers or crewmen. Among them is a spoon

Fig. 84. This postwar illustration of the sinking of the *Monitor,* titled "The Iron-Clad 'Monitor' Lost in a Storm off Cape Hatteras, Showing the Steamer 'Rhode Island' in the Distance," is from Marcus J. Wright's *Official and Illustrated War Record* (1898). (The Mariners' Museum, Newport News, Virginia)

bearing the intials "NKA." Norman Knox Attwater, acting ensign, who had come on board the *Monitor* in November 1862, originally hailed from New Haven, Connecticut, and was acquainted with William Keeler's father-in-law. There is also a fork with the name "G. Frederickson" engraved upon it. George Frederickson had been on the *Monitor* from the very beginning, initially rated as master's mate until his promotion to acting ensign in November 1862. Frederickson's hand was one of several to record entries in the log of the *Monitor,* and his young face peers out from several photos of officers taken by James Gibson in July 1862.

Three pieces of tableware recovered to date bear the initials "SAL" as well as the letters "USN." Samuel Augee (or Auge) Lewis of Baltimore had arrived to take up his commission as third assistant engineer in November 1862. William Keeler called him "a mere boy, nearly a cypher in our little society."[42] But poor Lewis's life came to an inglorious end only a month after his arrival. Recalling the events of December 30 and 31, 1862, Francis Butts wrote,

> I think I was the last person who saw Engineer S.A. Lewis as he lay seasick in his bunk, apparently watching the water as it grew deeper and deeper, and aware what his fate must be. He called me as I passed his door, and asked if the pumps were working. I replied that they were. "Is there any hope?" he asked; and feeling a little moved at the scene, and

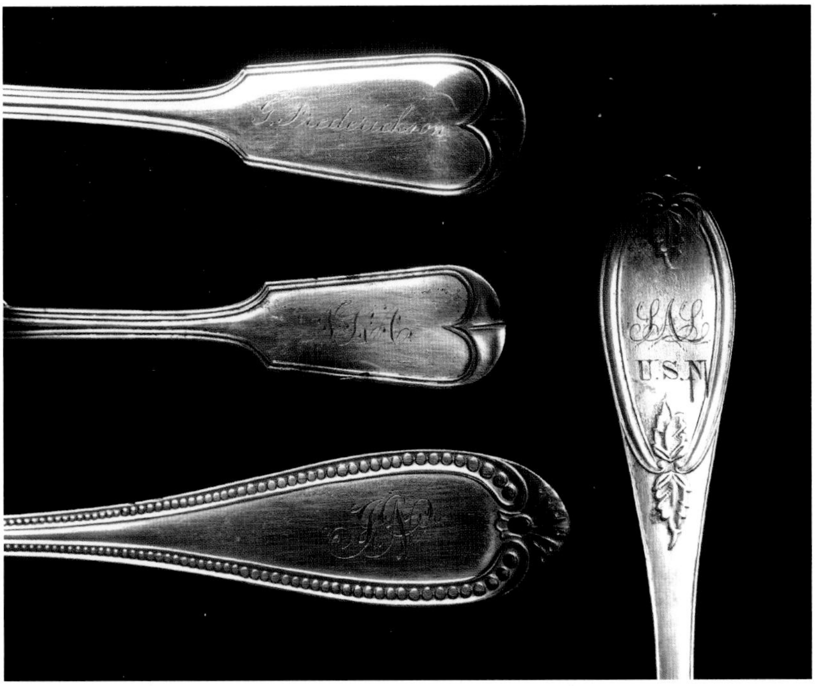

Fig. 85. Silver forks and spoons discovered during excavation of the turret. They belonged to master's mate George Frederickson, ensign Norman Knox Attwater, seaman Jacob Nicklis, and third assistant engineer Samuel Augee Lewis. (The Mariners' Museum, Newport News, Virginia)

knowing certainly what must be his end, and the darkness that stared at us all, I replied, "As long as there is life there is hope."[43]

A large silver spoon bears the initials "JN." This spoon is more than likely the property of Jacob Nicklis, the twenty-one-year-old sailor from Buffalo who had come on board the USS *Monitor* as Ship's Number 61 on November 7, 1862, when the *Monitor* was undergoing repairs at the Washington Navy Yard. According to his enlistment record, Nicklis, standing at 5 feet, 7 inches tall, had gray eyes, light-colored hair, and a "ruddy complexion." The son of a Buffalo tailor, Nicklis had enlisted in the navy at age sixteen and reenlisted in 1862 for a one-year term.[44]

Conservators and historians are still unsure how these pieces of tableware came to be in the turret. In all there are over thirty pieces, along with the remains of a drawer and a chest. It is possible that one or more of the men were trying to bring the ship's silver chest with them and then thought better of it. It is also possible that the chest fell into the turret sometime after the sinking, since the vessel turned over as it plummeted to the bottom. Either way, they are poignant reminders of the loss suffered by the *Monitor*'s crew.

The *Rhode Island* returned to Hampton Roads with the remaining crew from the *Monitor*, the *Rhode Island* crew sharing their warm clothing with the *Monitor* boys.[45] Upon arriving at Fortress Monroe, the survivors rushed to send letters home to assure their families and friends that they were safe. George Geer sent two letters, one to his wife Martha, which was brief and bereft of detail:

> U.S. Steamer Rhode Island
> Jany 2 1862 [*sic*]
>
> Dear Wife
> I am sorry to have to write you that we have lost the *Monitor,* and what is worse we had 16 poor fellows drownded. I can tell you I thank God my life is spaired. Besides the 16 we lost one boat that was sent from this Steamer with 11 se[a]men . . . missing. We have crused two days for them, and have given them up for lost. I have not time to write you any more, but do not worry. I am safe and well. Write to Troy and let them know I am safe.
>
> Your Loving
> Husband
> Geo S. Geer[46]

A second, longer letter, which went to Geer's brother, had more harrowing details of the sinking—details Geer wished to keep from his wife in order not to worry her.[47] In contrast, William Keeler spared no detail in his letter home, telling his wife, "The *Monitor* is no more. What the fire of the enemy failed to do, the elements have accomplished."[48]

CHAPTER 8

Discovery and Recovery

The same telegraph office at Fortress Monroe that had sent news of the *Monitor's* success the previous March now sent more sobering news, which spread quickly throughout both the Union and Confederacy. Upon learning of the sinking on January 3, 1863, Secretary of the Navy Gideon Welles expressed a personal sense of loss in his diary. "She is the primary representative of a class identified with my administration of the Navy," he wrote. "Her novel construction and qualities I adopted and she was built amidst obloquy and ridicule." Few naval men would have been willing to take the risk and responsibility of adopting such a novel vessel, he surmised. "But the Board which I appointed seconded my views, and were willing to recommend the experiment if I would incur the risk and responsibility." (Of course, Ericsson incurred the greatest financial risk.) "Her success with the Merrimac directly after she went into commission relieved me of odium and anxiety, and the men who were preparing to ridicule were left to admire."[1]

The news of the sinking in the press was wildly speculative and wrong, at first. Word that the *Monitor* had gone down off Hatteras in the early morning hours of December 31, 1862, reached the major newspapers by January 4, 1863. The front page headlines of the *New York Times* screamed "A Dreadful Disaster," "Foundering of the Monitor off Cape Hatteras," and, erroneously, "Two officers and Thirty-eight Men Lost." The *New York Herald,* while more accurate in its reporting, was no less emotional: "The Monitor Foundered! The Famous Iron-Clad Gunboat Lost Off Cape Hatteras. Four Officers and Twelve Men Missing." The paper also included a sketch of the *Monitor* lest anyone forget what she looked like. In the Midwest the *Daily Milwaukee News* was slightly more staid, running the headline "The Monitor Foundered off Cape Hatterass" on page 4. On page 3 of that same issue, the persistent ad for "The Little Monitor" coal and kerosene stove ran as it had for days.[2]

While the sixteen men were mourned by many throughout the Union, the *Monitor* herself was mourned far more publicly. On January 4, 1863, the *New York Herald* wrote a paean to "that invaluable 'cheese box on a raft' . . . this favorite little ship," ending with the statement that "her loss is the loss of the pet of the people."[3]

The news spread rapidly on January 5, traveling throughout the East Coast and upper midwestern states of the Union. Page 2 of the Providence *Evening Press* carried word of the sinking, but the standard Monitor Cooking Stove advertisement still held pride of place on page 1. Ads in the Portland, Maine, papers on January 7 and 8 touted a tableau at Deering Hall that would depict the battle between the *Monitor* and *Merrimack.* Like others, the ads were mute about the sinking, having been placed and typeset well before the event. But on January 8 a small article in the *Daily Eastern Argus* encouraged readers to attend the tableau if they wished to see the *Monitor* "as she really was," the past tense indicating awareness of her sinking. As is always the case in entertainment, the show must go on.[4]

A small ad in the January 9, 1863, edition of the *Hartford Daily Courant* was the first to use the tragedy to sell goods. Just four days after hearing the news of the sinking, Ford and Bartlett of Vernon, Connecticut, advertised that "THE MONITOR SUNK!—But the Ship of State still floats down the river of Time; and FORD & BARTLETT, in a small boat, are coming, too, with a few thousand dozen HOOP SKIRTS attached."[5]

A similar ad appeared on January 10, 1863, in the Providence *Evening Press.* The Monitor stove ad had now moved to page 3, and with its move, its message had changed: "STILL AFLOAT!" it declared, "OUR MONITOR HAS NOT SUNK." The ad went on to remind customers that "history has already made the name immortal, and the destruction of the original Monitor cannot destroy its prestige."[6] One could display a stove with that prestige in one's parlor. *Frank Leslie's* began running ads in the *New York Herald* on January 14, touting an upcoming issue that was going to feature "A beautiful engraving of THE LOSS OF THE MONITOR."[7] (See fig. 83.) Though she was gone, the little *Monitor* could still move products.

THE MONITOR SUNK!—But the Ship of State still floats down the river of Time; and FORD & BARTLETT, in a small boat, are coming, too, with a few thousand dozen HOOP SKIRTS attached. Specimens to be seen at Weatherby & Co.'s. Sample dozens sent at the lowest cash wholesale prices, and all orders promptly filled, by FORD & BARTLETT, Vernon, Ct.

WANTED IMMEDIATELY!—Fifty experienced Girls to work in a hoop skirt shop. Work clean and easy, and pay liberal Apply to FORD & BARTLETT, Vernon, Ct.
jan 8 2d*

Fig. 86. "The Monitor Sunk," an advertisement for hoop skirts that appeared in the Hartford *Daily Courant,* January 8, 1863.

Despite her fame, the Union navy chose not to search for the *Monitor.* Captain Bankhead's official report estimated that she had gone down in three hundred feet of water, making the wreck site far too deep for existing recovery methods.[8] In addition, the *Monitor* had only two guns and was not worth a major recovery effort even if the conditions had been slightly better. Thus, other than those Union navy crews looking for survivors immediately after the sinking, no one had actively searched for the vessel since December 31, 1862. "Our Little *Monitor*" was never forgotten, however.

In 1950, while testing General Electric's newly developed Underwater Object Locator (UOL) Mark IV south of the Cape Hatteras Light in North Carolina, the crew of a U.S. Navy vessel detected a submerged object approximately 140 feet in length. Because this general area had been identified as a likely resting place for the USS *Monitor*, the crew speculated that this could in fact be the lost ironclad. Unfortunately, strong currents prevented the deployment of any divers, so there could be no visual affirmation of the acoustic signal at that time.[9]

Although inconclusive, the UOL operation did generate enough interest for the Office of Naval History to open a "*Monitor* file." However, the navy chose not to pursue recovery at that time, and the press coverage of the navy's decision led to a new popular interest in the lost Union ironclad.[10] Raynor McMullen, a retired postal clerk from Michigan, organized the USS *Monitor* Foundation in Washington, D.C. McMullen offered a $1,000 reward to anyone who could locate and recover the *Monitor*. His offer once again drew the attention of the navy.[11] In an unusual move, Assistant Secretary of the Navy R. H. Fogler made the recommendation on September 30, 1953, that the *Monitor* be formally abandoned, as she was deemed no longer "essential to the defense of the United States," in large part because no one truly knew where she lay. Accordingly, she came under the auspices of the General Services Administration (GSA) as federal surplus. This removed certain restrictions from the vessel and opened up the possibility for civilian groups to actively search for the *Monitor*.

In 1955 Marine Corps diver Robert Marx, stationed at Camp Lejeune in North Carolina, announced that he had found the *Monitor* in shallow water off the coast of Cape Hatteras. "I found the thing," he said. He described seeing the wreck "buried in the sand, with the turret sticking out about four feet." He was sure it was the *Monitor*.[12] Marx claimed that his find was consistent with a story told by inhabitants of Hatteras Island in North Carolina, that shortly after the sinking several bodies of Union sailors had washed up onshore at Buxton and had been buried by the locals. Marx believed that this information indicated that the vessel had drifted toward land before sinking. Though he claimed to have found the ship with her distinctive turret in forty-five to fifty feet of water, he was unable to relocate the site again. Thus there was no evidence, other than his claim and that of his fellow diver, Keith Ingram, and their diving boat captain, Frazier Peele, that it was the *Monitor*.[13] A separate group, North Carolina Tidewater Services, used Marx's coordinates to search for the vessel in 1967 but found nothing.

Concurrent with these early efforts, Captain Ernest W. Peterkin of the Naval Research Laboratory in Washington, D.C., had begun collecting information about the *Monitor*'s final moments and plotting her possible course based on information he gleaned from firsthand accounts and the log of the USS *Rhode Island.* Begun as a personal project, Peterkin's study would intersect with his professional career as new technological developments in underwater photography became more viable. In 1970 the laboratory began testing a new system of underwater strobe photography, pioneered by Dr. Harold "Doc" Edgerton of the Massachusetts Institute of Technology, off the coast of North Carolina. Peterkin, through his research, had pinpointed a possible location for the *Monitor* and suggested testing the equipment on those coordinates. The location he proposed was well offshore in deeper water and beyond the easy reach of most search groups. While his initial calculations proved to be inaccurate, Peterkin continued to work on pinpointing the location based on his knowledge of the historical record, which did not indicate the shallow water location championed by Marx. By 1973 Peterkin had formulated a new theory of the wreck's location, sixteen miles southeast of Cape Hatteras.[14]

The lure of Marx's shallow-water theory was strong, however, and news items about each search for the elusive *Monitor* piqued the imagination of numerous groups. Michael O'Leary, with the USS *Monitor* Foundation, and Roland Wommack's Trident Foundation both mounted expeditions in the early 1970s using Marx's shallow-water theory. Neither group was successful, but news items of these searches convinced a group of midshipmen from the Naval Academy in Annapolis to take up the search in 1973, encouraged initially by the desire to do some wreck diving. However, their enthusiasm for the project grew, and they scheduled an expedition to Hatteras under the tutelage of Professor William M. Darden, of the Naval Academy's history department, and William Andahazy, of the Naval Research and Development Center in Annapolis. Ernest Peterkin provided them with his own research.[15]

The initial trip of the midshipmen in the spring of 1973 was disastrous, with high winds and heavy seas keeping them shorebound. They tried again in July, with the assistance of a navy research aircraft equipped with magnetometers. The group had two target areas they wanted to survey from the air: Marx's shallow-water site and a site farther offshore, based on the midshipmen's analysis of the historical documents and Peterkin's assistance. Returning with their data and film footage, the group turned their summer venture into a year-long academic project, entitled "Project Cheesebox."[16]

John Broadwater, a young electrical engineer who had recently decided to follow his passion for underwater archaeology instead, was also on the hunt for the ironclad. He was leading a team organized by Underwater Archaeological Associates and Marine Archaeological Research Services. The team spent time surveying the area near Marx's coordinates during that same summer, eventually teaming up with the USS *Monitor* Foundation.[17] Meanwhile, the National Geographic Society had agreed to sponsor a team from the Duke University Marine Lab in Beaufort, North Carolina. Led by John Newton, marine superintendent for the oceanographic program at the Duke Marine Lab, the group had enlisted the help of Harold "Doc" Edgerton of MIT. Edgerton, in addition to his work on strobe photography, had also been instrumental in the development of side-scan sonar technology since the 1950s, and he had used the system to assist in locating Henry VIII's lost warship *Mary Rose* in 1967.[18] Edgerton believed the *Monitor* would be a good target for testing improvements to his side-scan sonar. Besides Edgerton and Newton, the group consisted of Gordon Watts from the North Carolina Division of Archives and History; Dr. Robert Sheridan, a geologist from University of Delaware; Dorothy Nicholson, from the National Geographic Society; and Newton's daughter Cathryn. With these plus other researchers, Newton and Edgerton set out in the Duke University research vessel *Eastward* for a two-week survey of possible sites in the waters off Cape Hatteras, using the historical record rather than Marx's theories. Sheridan hoped to conduct a geological survey of the continental shelf off Hatteras and had secured the principal funding for the mission in part from the National Science Foundation.[19]

While Sheridan's work had gone reasonably well, none of the possible sonar or magnetometer targets had been promising, save for one, which turned out to be a fishing trawler.[20] However, on August 27, 1973, on the last day of the expedition, a "long amorphous echo" appeared on the side-scan recorder. Though the team was scheduled to return, they remained on-site for three additional days attempting to film and photograph the anomaly. Unfortunately, Edgerton's deep-sea camera became snagged on the wreck and had to be abandoned, leaving only blurry television footage and the side-scan information to help the team determine whether they had found the *Monitor*. Gordon Watts spent the next five months studying the tapes, trying to tease out any information that would positively identify the wreck as the *Monitor*. Knowing the interest of the midshipmen at the Naval Academy, he showed the film to them as well.[21]

There are hundreds of shipwrecks in the treacherous waters off Cape Hatteras. However, everyone who had been searching for the *Monitor* believed that the wreck would present a very distinctive and easily identifiable form to search for—in essence, the cheesebox (turret) on a raft (hull). No one had contemplated the possibility that the raft might be on top of

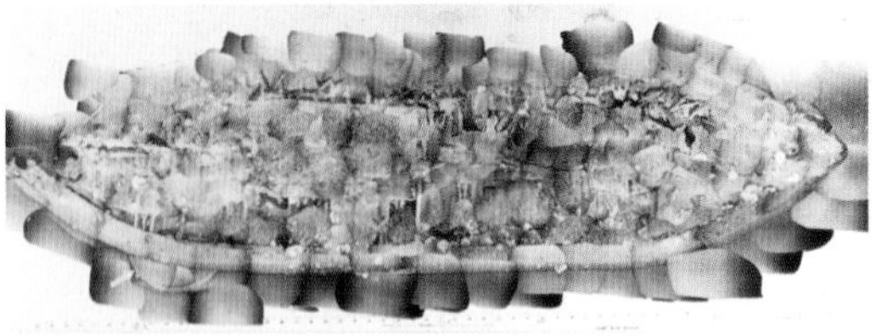

Fig 87. This photomosaic of the *Monitor* wreck site was produced in 1974. The turret can be seen at the lower left. (NOAA's Monitor National Marine Sanctuary)

the cheesebox: no one expected the *Monitor* to be upside down. Fortunately, Watts chose to change his expectations. Assuming that the ship could potentially be upside down, with the turret displaced underneath the hull, he found that the video began to make sense. He had pieced together a photomosaic from the video images, and he showed it to several colleagues, including John Broadwater. "When I looked at the mosaic," said Broadwater in a 2004 interview with the Newport News *Daily Press,* "I saw some similar elements. But I didn't see the *Monitor*—and I didn't think that anybody would have the nerve to say that it was. . . . Then Gordon asked me to pretend that the *Monitor* had landed upside down. . . . That's what did it. That's when everything in the picture fell into place and started to make sense. . . . That's when the *Monitor* was found."[22] Watts had shared his findings with John Newton in early 1974, but the two waited to announce the news.

The Naval Research Laboratory had scheduled a conference in Washington, D.C., on March 11, 1974, to bring together all of the groups who had been searching for the *Monitor.* The purpose was to assess all of their finds in order, first, to choose probable sites for study in the summer of 1974 and, second, to test the capabilities of the *Alcoa Seaprobe,* a research vessel outfitted specifically for photographing underwater features. Given the interest in the *Monitor,* this seemed the perfect mission to test the vessel. However, at a joint press event of Duke University and the North Carolina Department of Archives and History held a few days before the conference, on March 7, 1974, Newton and Watts announced that they had positively identified the wreck of the *Monitor.*[23] Though there were many skeptics at the subsequent Naval Research Laboratory Conference later that week, the navy agreed to take the *Seaprobe* to the newly announced site.

The *Seaprobe* departed for the *Monitor* in early April, having on board Newton, Watts, and Nicholson, along with naval personnel. During this expedition, the first still photographs of the ship were made and pieced together into the first full photomosaic of the wreck. Using 1,200 individual shots, this was the first full view of the vessel that the public would see.[24]

It was an impressive undertaking, and one that inspired the same sort of reverence that many expressed in January 1863. Upon seeing this image of the vessel, a member of the 1974 expedition team, Norman G. Cubberly, was moved to write the following sonnet:

> I saw the bones, a forlorn iron grave.
> The lonesome rusted wrack upon black sand.
> A cast off toy at peace beneath the wave.

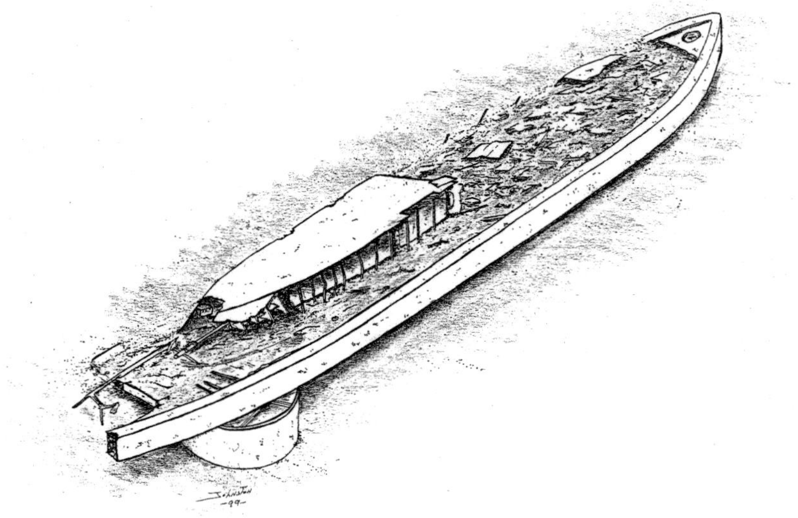

Fig. 88. Drawing of the *Monitor* wreck site by NOAA historian Jeff Johnston in 1999, prior to large artifact recovery. (NOAA's Monitor National Marine Sanctuary)

A weak thing flattened by a giant hand.
No trace is left of them that lived or died
But this, their song, forever haunts us all.
An engine built for death which has our pride.
A staunch defiant box so very small.
So fitting that we come revere these dead,
This small beginning, such a help to death!
Since all sea battles now from here were bred.
From these poor men great dragons draw their breath.

So let us cry and here at least release
A tear to bring us close to peace.[25]

Researchers assessed the condition of the ship and found that there was extensive damage to the stern. A large portion of the stern armor belt was missing, and the area surrounding the propeller and rudder assemblies showed extensive damage. This damage to the stern seemed to indicate that the vessel struck the ocean floor stern first. Analyzing the wreck, historians surmised that after wallowing in the storm-tossed sea the *Monitor*'s bow was lifted by a wave, causing all of the water to roll to the stern. This, combined with the tremendous weight of her thirty-ton steam engine, caused the ship to pitch stern first and then begin to sink vertically. The 173-foot-long ironclad did not have far to go to come to rest 240 feet below the surface and at some point turn in the water column, probably once to starboard. The stern quickly struck the bottom, causing the turret to dislodge from the brass ring and slide down the deck toward the stern. Then the massive turret fell off and landed on the ocean bottom. The port side of the *Monitor*'s armor belt came to rest over a portion of the turret, partly burying it in the sandy bottom.[26]

Finding the wreck of the *Monitor* was a true accomplishment, but this put the ship in more peril than she had been in during her battle with the *Virginia.* Geologist Robert Sheridan returned to the wreck for samples in May 1974. Using a rock dredge, he dragged it through the wreck in order to retrieve pieces for study. No cameras were used to assess the positioning of the dredge, nor were any lowered to assess the condition of the wreck afterward. He was dredging the wreck "blind." Though his mission had been coordinated with John Newton at Duke, this action was unauthorized. Sheridan defended it, saying it was in keeping with standard oceanographic practice. "Archaeologists want to preserve everything," he said to a reporter. But he wanted samples. It was a "value judgment" and Sheridan, who went on to say that he didn't "care about the criticism, really" felt that it was justified given that the "wreck is falling apart even as we study it." The ensuing press was not kind to Sheridan.[27]

The wreck site needed protection. One of the first steps was listing the site on the National Register of Historic Places, which occurred on October 11, 1974.[28] Though the National Register had no regulatory power, this step ensured that the historical significance of the wreck had been acknowledged and documented. But since the site had been announced, it was possible that unscrupulous wreck divers might strip the wreck. With this in mind, the governor of North Carolina suggested that the *Monitor* site might be a candidate for national marine sanctuary status.

Through the Marine Protection, Research and Sanctuaries Act of 1972 (often referred to as the "Ocean Dumping" Act), Congress authorized the secretary of commerce to designate specific areas as national marine sanctuaries in order to protect plant and marine mammal breeding grounds, coral reefs, cultural resources, and a variety of marine habitats. This federal protection would promote comprehensive management of their special ecological, historical, recreational, and aesthetic resources. Although the *Monitor* site was primarily a cultural resource, not a natural resource, the Monitor National Marine Sanctuary was the first sanctuary established under the act on January 30, 1975 (the 113th anniversary of the vessel's launch). The sanctuary was to consist of a vertical "column of water" one mile in diameter, from the seabed to the surface, located on the eastern continental shelf 16.1 miles southeast of Cape Hatteras.[29] The National Oceanic and Atmospheric Administration (NOAA) would oversee the sanctuary program.

Once federal protection was established for the wreck site under the Monitor National Marine Sanctuary, archaeologists began to explore and document the wreck and, eventually, recover portions of the Civil War ironclad. From 1974 through 1995 a series of thirty-four public and private expeditions collected a wealth of data and artifacts, including a high-profile visit to the wreck by Jacques Cousteau in 1979. Historian William C. Davis spent "an unforgettable hour 'touring' the *Monitor*" on one of these expeditions in August 1979. Twenty years later he recalled his impressions of the wreck site:

> Most evocative of all, however, was the turret, which has always been the focus of the *Monitor's* lasting grip on our imaginations. Though upside down and partially covered by the hull, which landed atop it when the vessel capsized in sinking, still much of the turret can be seen, and there still visible in its iron plating were the dents made by the *Virginia*'s shot during their epic duel. Those indentations are perhaps the most eloquent "first-hand" evidence of the Civil War that remain to us today.
>
> Most of all, and despite the dim light and limited visibility, there was the overpowering sense of majesty when this great iron wreck, at once both monument and living document, emerged from the gloom. It seemed to loom over the bare ocean bottom like a small iron mountain. Aboard the submersible all was silence, as four very terrestrial beings of our own time were stunned and speechless as we found ourselves in another world during those minutes in the presence of a great actor from another era.[30]

The first major artifact was recovered in 1977—the iconic red signal lantern, which, ironically, also happened to be the last thing seen by the rescued crew as the vessel went down in 1862. Amazingly, the hot glass in the lantern had not shattered when the *Monitor* sank beneath the Atlantic's waves that December night because the water of the Gulf Stream was 74 degrees, according to the abstract log of the USS *Rhode Island.*[31] A variety of small finds such as mustard and pepper bottles, wood paneling, hull fragments, and ceramics were also recovered during that time, as well as the unique, four-fluked anchor. NOAA was not a collecting agency, however, and conservation work as well as curation and storage of the artifacts were not centralized. Therefore, in 1986 NOAA issued a Request for Proposals to find a single institution that could serve as a repository for the objects, and in 1987 The Mariners' Museum in Newport News was selected to be the official repository.[32] The recovered artifacts were transferred there to be included in a permanent display.[33] This would become the principal way in which most people would be able to

Fig. 89. The *Monitor*'s red signal lantern was the last piece of the *Monitor* to be seen when she sank and one of the first artifacts to be recovered. (The Mariners' Museum, Newport News, Virginia)

experience the *Monitor* since the technical diving skills needed to visit the wreck site were beyond the reach of most people.

There were divers, however, with the training as well as a keen desire to visit the wreck site. In the 1980s professional diver Gary Gentile filed eleven applications for a permit to dive on the wreck. Each one was denied. Jacques Cousteau, however, submitted a single application that was immediately approved. Gentile filed a federal lawsuit against NOAA that was unsuccessful. In November 1989, however, Judge Hugh Dolan reversed the decision, opening up the *Monitor* site to more individuals through a free permitting process.[34] Many of the ensuing private dives resulted in important photographic imagery of the wreck site, as well as NOAA-directed artifact recovery.

Charting a New Course for the USS *Monitor*

By 1996 it had become evident that if there were to be a recovery effort for major artifacts from the wreck of the USS *Monitor*, it would have to occur within ten years. The wreck showed significant deterioration since it had been discovered in 1973. A major collapse of the hull appeared imminent.[35] The *Monitor*, as a cultural resource under the Sanctuaries Act, was thus deemed a "threatened resource" because cultural resources are considered "non-renewable."[36]

The wreck was endangered because it was situated in a dynamic environment. The confluence of cold water from the northern Labrador Current, and warm water from the southern Gulf Stream creates volatile conditions that often give rise to violent storms—the kind in which the *Monitor* sank. Strong bottom currents could scour out sections of the ship over time. The salty marine environment is also very corrosive to iron and other types of metal, of which the *Monitor* was largely constructed. Human interaction with the wreck was also a contributing factor in undermining the vessel's stability. In 1991 the U.S. Coast Guard found a private fishing vessel anchored on the wreck illegally. Evidence gathered later showed that this anchoring incident had placed an enormous amount of stress on the hull and had essentially broken the ship open, accelerating the oxidation and corrosion of the vessel. Commercial fishing gear entangled in the wreckage was another threat. NOAA had to make a decision to either allow nature to take its course or to recover some of the larger historically significant components in order to preserve as much of the *Monitor* as possible.[37]

In 1996 Congress issued a mandate to the secretary of commerce—Commerce being the department that oversees NOAA—to produce a long-range, comprehensive plan for the management, stabilization, and recovery of artifacts and materials from the *Monitor*. NOAA developed the plan, entitled "Charting a New Course for the *Monitor,*" which outlined a variety of options from physical stabilization and cathodic protection, to selective recovery of key components, to recovery of the entire ship, to even burial of the entire site. After weighing the advantages and disadvantages of each option, sanctuary staff made the recommendation to use a combined method of physically shoring up the wreck for stability in conjunction with recovering selected significant components.[38]

Since the adoption of the recovery plan in 1998, the primary goal of NOAA and the Monitor Sanctuary has been the protection of the wreck and safe recovery of artifacts.[39] While this has been primarily an archaeological process, not all aspects of the recovery have been purely archaeological. Some damage to the wreck was necessary to achieve the recovery of significant components. NOAA determined that some sacrifices were required in order to safely recover and preserve the most historically significant parts of the ship rather than let them deteriorate in the corrosive Atlantic environment. This process has been accurately termed "rescue archaeology."[40]

The first NOAA expedition to the Monitor Sanctuary after the adoption of the *Monitor* preservation plan was primarily to lay the groundwork for major artifact recovery on future expeditions. Experts gathered data and mapped and photographed the overall configuration of the wreck. The expedition focused on the stern areas of the wreck, including the engine room, turret, and area beneath the hull. Divers mapped and recovered exposed artifacts to protect them from possible damage. While propeller removal was slated for phase three of the preservation plan, when NOAA and the navy returned to the site in 1998 they found weather and bottom conditions perfect for recovery. Divers made the final cut through the solid iron shaft and brought the propeller to the surface, making it the first artifact recovered under NOAA's long-range plan. It was also the largest component recovered to date and was the first major artifact recovered since the anchor in 1983. On June 5, 1998, the propeller of the *Monitor* broke the surface of the water for the first time since 1862, when the ship was in the Washington Navy Yard.[41]

The NOAA/U.S. Navy expeditions to the Monitor National Marine Sanctuary in 1999 and 2000 set the stage for the engine recovery operation planned for 2001. In 1999 navy divers surveyed and assessed the lower hull and engineering spaces. Their work also facilitated plans for shoring up the hull with grout bags so that the engine, and eventually the turret, could be recovered without damaging the stability of the wreck. While on-site, archaeologists mapped exposed objects and gathered geotechnical data in the vicinity of the turret. This expedition was also a training opportunity in mixed-gas diving and salvage operations for personnel from the navy's Mobile Diving and Salvage Unit TWO, located at Little Creek in Norfolk, Virginia. Conditions at the wreck site presented an appropriately challenging training ground for these deep-sea divers.

During the summer of 2000, NOAA, the U.S. Navy, The Mariners' Museum, and other organizations embarked on a new series of expeditions to prepare for engine recovery. NOAA divers documented the engine, and with the help of navy divers, placed the system of stabilizing grout bags against the ship's deteriorating hull. They also raised the aft section of the propeller shaft and skeg to prepare the steam engine for recovery.[42]

The *Monitor*'s engine could not be rigged to be lifted directly to the surface. Extremely fragile after spending 140 years submerged in a volatile and corrosive marine environment, it required a protective structure during its lift to the surface and transfer to The Mariners' Museum, where it could begin its lengthy conservation. The Engine Recovery Structure, or ERS, contained three principal components: a bridge frame, a moveable spreader, and an engine lifting frame (ELF) suspended from the spreader. The bridge portion of the ERS was positioned over the *Monitor*'s engine during the 2000 expedition in anticipation of the engine recovery slated for the summer of 2001.

The 2001 field season consisted of five expeditions to the sanctuary conducted in three phases. Larger undertakings than previous missions, they involved personnel from NOAA, the U.S. Navy, The Mariners' Museum, the National Undersea Research Center at the University of North Carolina at Wilmington, the Maritime Studies Program at East Carolina University, and the Cambrian Foundation. In addition to recovery of the thirty-ton engine, the expeditions' goals included the removal of a section of the armor belt and, if possible, an initial archaeological excavation of the turret in preparation for its recovery in 2002.

Monitor 2001 was significant for its use of saturation diving technology. While the navy had developed the saturation diving technique in the 1960s, the service had abandoned it by the 1980s due to budget cuts. However, the sinking of the Russian submarine *Kursk* (K-141) in August 2000 was a cautionary tale that propelled Captain Chris Murray of the Mobile Diving and Salvage Unit to explore possibilities of bringing saturation diving back into the service. The *Monitor* expedition would be a perfect scenario to experiment with the deployment of commercial saturation systems and to train navy deep-sea divers in the technique.

Saturation diving is a method that allows divers to work at greater depths and for longer periods of time by remaining under pressure when they return to the surface. This requires saturation divers to live in a specially designed habitat. A saturation diving system (SAT) typically consists of two pressure chambers, a central mating chamber, and a personal transfer capsule or diving bell. The diving bell transports saturation divers between the surface pressure chambers and the work site.[43] Divers who are not working on the bottom live in one of the chambers and also decompress there. For the *Monitor* expedition, two SAT divers remained under pressure for a week or more and worked eight-hour shifts. Divers utilizing this system accomplished more involved tasks than surface-supplied divers, who were limited to thirty or forty minutes. The expedition used both methods.

Surface-supplied divers on the *Monitor* used a mixture of 85 percent helium and 15 percent oxygen, allowing them to descend up to three hundred feet without increased risk of nitrogen narcosis, or "the bends." The gas was supplied through umbilical hoses from the surface system. The umbilical also allowed for two-way communications. Video cameras and lights mounted on the helmets enabled those on the surface to see exactly what the diver saw and allowed NOAA archaeologists to supervise the divers.

More than seventy divers from twelve Navy Dive Commands worked on *Monitor* 2001. On a single day the expedition achieved a record twenty-six hours of bottom time, ten hours of surface-supplied diving, and sixteen hours of saturation diving. Thus the recovery of the *Monitor*'s unique "vibrating side lever" engine was one of the most complex underwater archaeological recovery projects ever conducted.[44] The mission contracted for the use of the Manson Gulf derrick barge *Wotan,* a 299 by 90-foot barge with a crane capable of a five hundred–ton lift. Crane operators more accustomed to working on oil rigs than shipwrecks were easily able to deploy the ELF, once it had been ascertained that the ERS had successfully remained in position over the stern of the wreck since the *Monitor* 2000 Expedition. The spreader assembly was used to position the ELF directly over the engine room. In order to safely recover the engine, navy divers worked around the clock for four weeks to remove the remnants of lower hull plating and free the engine from the wreck.

Because the engine was weakened by 140 years of corrosion, all of its components had to be secured to the ELF by dozens of cables and straps. Once the engine was rigged, divers severed all piping, supports, and connections in preparation for the engine to be hoisted. Once rigged, the entire engine unit was raised two feet, using hydraulic rams mounted on the spreader. Divers inspected the rigging and then slung heavy-duty cargo nets beneath the engine. The engine was then raised another four feet and inspected again. After a final check of the weather, divers attached steel lifting cables to the ERS, and the entire 120-ton structure broke the surface at 11:56 A.M. on July 16, 2001. The barge brought the engine to

Northrop Grumman Newport News, where it was offloaded to a smaller barge. After a slight delay caused by the need to alter portions of the ERS so that it could be used as a cradle during the conservation process, NOAA and U.S. Navy divers escorted the engine to The Mariners' Museum, where it arrived on August 7, 2001.[45] Apprentices from Northrop Grumman Newport News had built a tank to house the engine during the conservation process at the museum. They would shortly move on to building a larger tank for the turret of the *Monitor,* which would be the subject of the 2002 field season.

The written goals of the *Monitor* 2002 expedition seemed almost too simple, given the monumental task at hand. The few words describing each step of the process belied the hours of planning, the 24/7 operations needed to complete the task, and the sheer number of personnel required for the mission. The operations manual, revised shortly before the NOAA/U.S. Navy team left for Houma, Louisiana, where the *Wotan* was home-berthed, listed the nine goals associated with *Monitor* 2002 in laconic fashion:

- **Goal 1:** Remove deck and armor belt segments, as necessary, to provide sufficient access to the turret for the planned rigging and recovery operations.
- **Goal 2:** Excavate contents of the turret down as far as possible, mapping and photographing features and artifacts as they are encountered.
- **Goal 3:** Install the spider assembly atop the turret.
- **Goal 4:** Place the support platform on the seabed near the turret.
- **Goal 5:** Rig supports for the guns, carriages, port shutters and roof beams, as appropriate.
- **Goal 6:** Lift the turret assembly and secure atop the support platform.
- **Goal 7:** Raise the turret and contents and place them on the derrick barge.
- **Goal 8:** Transport the turret to Newport News and transfer to a smaller barge for delivery to The Mariners' Museum.
- **Goal 9:** Continue the navy program of realistic and challenging salvage training using surface-supplied saturation diving methodology.[46]

The manual also listed a timeline for the expedition that spanned from mid-May for loadout of the derrick barge *Wotan* in Houma to the final offloading at Naval Amphibious Base Little Creek on July 25. This would give the expedition a cushion of two weeks before the barge, navy personnel, and funding had to disappear. A notation in the manual pointed out that "all dates are estimated" and that it was subject to "equipment availability, weather, funding and other factors."[47] All would become issues before the recovery was over.

Historians and archaeologists believed that the recovered turret would reveal much about the final moments of the *Monitor*. Excavations done by navy divers while the turret still lay on the ocean floor revealed many features and artifacts that had been guessed at but not proven until the summer of 2002. The team had two principal questions: (1) had the guns remained within the turret; and (2), more soberingly, was the turret a grave site for any of the sixteen who had gone down with the vessel? Engineering expertise could deal with the first eventuality, which would necessitate additional supports to keep the gravity-mounted roof of the turret from giving way during the lift. Forensic anthropologist Eric Emery, from the military's Central Identification Laboratory at Joint Base Pearl Harbor-Hickam, Hawaii, was on board the *Wotan* to address the second issue.

Before the operation even began, there were problems. Instead of deploying at the wreck site as planned, the *Wotan* had to make an unplanned visit to Hampton Roads for emergency repair of its 500-ton capacity crane, throwing the schedule off by ten days before the first diver could enter the water. Finally, on June 24, NOAA and U.S. Navy personnel departed Norfolk, Virginia, aboard the *Wotan* for NOAA's Monitor National Marine Sanctuary. After arriving, they deployed eight 20,000-pound anchors to maintain position over the wreck. Next they removed debris from the *Monitor*'s stern. A 30-ton section of hull structure was removed after cutting through layers of iron and wood. After nine days the *Monitor*'s turret was completely uncovered for the first time since it sank on December 31, 1862.[48]

With the turret exposed, divers began to install the 57,000-pound lifting frame, known as the "spider," and began excavating the interior of the turret. Based loosely on the carnival claw machine, this engineering marvel, designed by a team led by Jim Kelly at Phoenix International, had hydraulic legs designed to grasp the turret all around its edges for the lift. "Stabbing guides" on the spider locked into receptacles on a solid platform, deployed next to the turret.

The turret was filled with layers of iron fragments, iron concretions, coal, and other hull debris. Excavation proceeded smoothly and was guided by the watchful eyes of NOAA team leaders John Broadwater and Jeff Johnston, who monitored the divers in a command van stationed on the deck of the *Wotan*. But on July 10 the weather turned; squalls, thunderstorms, and strong bottom currents slowed operations, and by four o'clock in the morning surface-supplied diving had to be suspended, although saturation diving continued.[49] The question of whether the turret roof had remained intact during the sinking was answered on July 12, 2002, when divers uncovered the distinctive gun carriages and the smooth iron of the guns themselves. This discovery signaled to the team that the turret could indeed be a time capsule.

Excavations on July 24 confirmed that the roof rails were in place, and on the twenty-sixth divers discovered bones, which analysis showed to be human. Eric Emery's presence was now crucial. The pace of the recovery necessarily had to slow. Though the divers were able to recover some of the remains, they found that a large portion of the bones was concreted to the roof rails. Given the timetable the team was working against, full recovery of the bones in situ on the ocean floor was not an option. Thus the remaining excavation of the turret occurred on board the *Wotan* and then continued at The Mariners' Museum throughout the summer and fall of 2002 and each summer thereafter. Ultimately, NOAA archaeologists recovered two sets of human remains, which were sent to the Central Identification Laboratory to await identification.[50]

The expedition crew worked twenty-four hours a day, in two twelve-hour shifts, as they raced against the clock to raise the turret. The *Monitor* expedition 2002 had funding enough only to work on the sanctuary for forty-five days. By August 1 only eight days of funding remained, and the weather over the Graveyard of the Atlantic was getting progressively worse. For two days currents, winds, and tidal surges prevented the lifting of the turret. A tropical depression (later to become tropical storm Cristobal) had developed just to the south of the wreck site, and the natural elements that had driven the *Monitor* to the ocean bottom 140 years before seemed to be conspiring to keep her in her grave.[51]

A break in the weather finally came on August 5. The bottom currents lightened and work resumed to connect cables from the lift-crane to the spider. Just before 5:00 P.M. the crane operator lifted the turret gingerly a few feet off the ocean floor and placed it carefully on a lift platform designed to support the base of the inverted turret, ensuring that the roof remained in place. At 5:45 P.M. the turret broke the surface of the Atlantic Ocean for the first time in almost 140 years. Cheers went up from the crew assembled on the deck of the *Wotan*. Captain Select Barbara "Bobbie" Scholley, the navy's on-scene commander for the expedition, said, "For a bunch of pretty tough, hoo-yah deep-sea sailors, there was an awful lot of hugging going on on the barge."[52] During the 45-day mission those "hoo-yah deep-sea sailors" completed 507 surface-supplied dives for 286 hours of bottom time. The SAT divers spent 213 man-days in saturation.[53]

On August 9, 2002, the *Monitor*'s turret, borne by the barge *Wotan,* made its way back to Hampton Roads. As the turret passed by Fort Monroe, the U.S. Army fired a twenty-one-gun salute. Morning traffic slowed on the Monitor-Merrimac Memorial Bridge-Tunnel as the turret passed near the site where it made history battling the CSS *Virginia*. Trans-

Fig. 90. This photomosaic shows the *Monitor* from the stern, prior to the recovery of the turret. (NOAA's Monitor National Marine Sanctuary)

ferred to a smaller barge at Newport News Shipbuilding's Virginia Advanced Shipbuilding and Carrier Integration Center, the turret continued the next day on its trip up the James River where thousands of spectators lined the banks or took to yachts, sailboats, and kayaks to watch the revolutionary naval icon make its way to The Mariners' Museum. The resemblance of the turret sitting amidships on the low-freeboard barge to the original *Monitor* was not lost upon the thousands assembled at the museum's Lion's Bridge to watch the turret come ashore on a multi-axle flatbed truck. Following a brief ceremony, the turret began its slow progress up Museum Drive as an impromptu escort of Union and Confederate reenactors, navy divers, NOAA and museum staff, and the general public formed around it. Crowds watched as it was placed in a 90,000-gallon steel tank for archaeological and conservation work.[54]

The turret recovery of 2002 was the last major recovery effort undertaken by NOAA on the *Monitor* wreck site, although smaller NOAA-led expeditions as well as several private dive groups have returned each year to document and monitor the condition of the site. A number of hurricanes, tropical storms, and nor'easters have passed over or near the site since 2002, and NOAA staff have documented further deterioration of the wreck, including the collapse of the midships bulkhead in 2004.[55] An expedition in 2006 focused on high-definition digital still and video imagery of the wreck site. On the same expedition, NOAA scientists and divers streamed live video from the site and engaged audiences around the country during a broadcast on the OceansLive.org web portal.[56] An expedition to take 3-D images and video of the wreck site began during the summer of 2015. Additional private dives have visited the site as well, documenting the wreck, sending reports to NOAA on the condition of the site, and sharing their photographs with the sanctuary.[57]

While no major recoveries are planned for the near future, there remain within the wreck site components of great significance. Much of the crew areas in the forward part of the ship have yet to be excavated.

They are believed to still contain many personal objects that belonged to the men serving aboard the *Monitor* in 1862. There is also much that could still be learned about the construction of the vessel. Of particular interest are the donkey engines and gears associated with the turning of the turret, the armor belt, and the underwater flushing toilets. Lack of funding for such a project, as well as lack of space for conserving additional items in the Batten Conservation Lab at the USS *Monitor* Center, mean that the more prudent and responsible means of resource protection will remain in in-situ preservation.

While the major recoveries are over, new information about the vessel's construction, the crew, and the *Monitor*'s final moments, continues to be found in the conservation process. Two hundred and ten tons of artifacts are housed on-site at The Mariners' Museum within the *Ironclad Revolution* exhibition, in climate-controlled storage, or in the Batten Conservation Complex. Here conservators, archaeologists, engineers, and historians work daily with the artifacts to extract both chlorides and information. Over a thousand artifacts have already been conserved and are on display at The Mariners' Museum or at other institutions around the country. While the deck plates and small machinery recovered speak to the fabric of the *Monitor* herself, the lived experience of the *Monitor* Boys themselves also emerges through personal artifacts. Shoes, boots, silverware, a gold ring, and a blue merino wool sack coat found in the turret remind twenty-first-century museumgoers of the human element that brought the *Monitor* to life. The coat is the most recent of such artifacts to go on display within the USS *Monitor* Center galleries. When first discovered in 2002, it looked like little more than a clump of mud, covered with debris, concretions, and microorganisms. But careful conservation and restoration work over the course of fourteen months produced 140 fragments of navy blue wool that had survived on the ocean floor. Now on display in a state-of-the-art $20,000 frame, visitors to The Mariners' Museum can imagine a sailor possibly wearing this coat on the cold night of the sinking before pitching it into the turret so that its weight would not cause him to drown if he were swept into the sea. (To date, the owner of the coat is unknown.)

There are, however, well over a thousand artifacts still undergoing active treatment. Of these the largest and most complex artifacts are the turret, condenser, and engine. While the objects are stable, they will need many more years of treatment before they can be displayed or stored safely outside of their chemical or water baths. Current estimates are that the project, as it is currently configured, will not be complete until 2029.

One of the principal goals of the Monitor National Marine Sanctuary's latest management plan, made final in February 2013, was to have the two sets of human remains found in the turret interred at Arlington National Cemetery.[58] Forensic analysis completed in October 2004 at the U.S. Army Central Identification Laboratory, Hawaii (now the Defense POW/MIA Accounting Agency) revealed a great deal of information about the two *Monitor* sailors, but not their names. One of the skeletons, designated CIL 2002–097-I-01, was that of a young Caucasian male between the ages of seventeen and twenty-four. He would have stood at five feet, seven inches. He had a broken, but healing, nose. The other individual, designated CIL 2002–097-I-02, was older, likely between the ages of thirty and forty. Also Caucasian, he was approximately five feet, six and one-half inches tall. One leg was a half-inch shorter than the other, which likely gave him a slight limp. A groove in his left incisor and canine teeth indicates he was a pipe smoker. He, too, had a broken nose with evidence of healing.[59]

Because the two were identified as Caucasian, the three African-Americans who perished in the sinking, Robert Howard, Robert Cook, and Daniel Moore, were far less likely to be possible matches. William Allen and Thomas Joice were within the appropriate age range for the younger man but were too tall. James Fenwick was too short. That left William Eagan, Samuel Augee Lewis, and Jacob Nicklis as the most likely possibilities. Wells Wentz (aka John Stocking) had been reported washed overboard, though that in itself would not have constituted a reason to rule him out. However, he was too tall to be the second individual. Robert Williams and William Bryan were the right ages and heights. The rest of the sixteen were outside of the age ranges indicated for the two sets of remains.[60] Mitochondrial DNA was present, but despite attempts to find modern relatives, the navy had no way of identifying them or determining next of kin, typically a prerequisite before the Accounting Agency releases the remains for burial. NOAA thus undertook a high-profile effort to locate additional relatives by bringing the two sailors back into the national spotlight.

Forensic anthropologists at the Forensic Anthropology and Computer Enhancement Services lab at Louisiana State University used casts of the skulls and hipbones (to help determine age) of the two men to create both clay and digital reconstructions of the faces of the two sailors. The faces were revealed at a press conference held at the Navy Memorial in Washington, D.C., on March 6, 2012, just days before the 150th anniversary of the Battle of Hampton Roads. The facial reconstructions and the genealogical work done by NOAA contractor Lisa Stansbury Morgan brought new family members to light, many of whom provided DNA samples. Unfortunately, there were no positive matches.

Thanks to a joint effort between NOAA, the U.S. Department of Veterans Affairs, The Mariners' Museum, and the U.S. Navy, however, work was soon underway to find a way to honor these sailors. On December

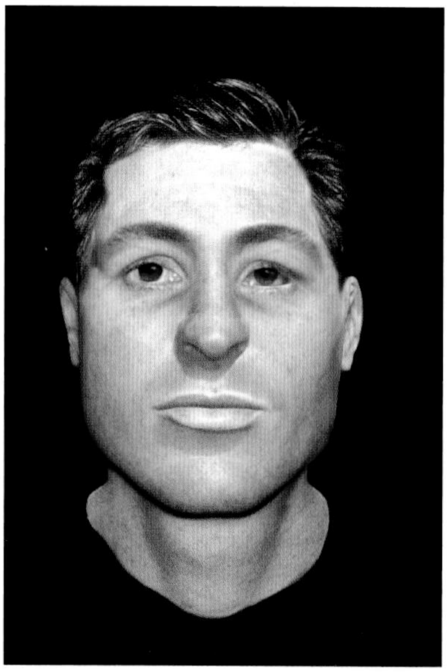

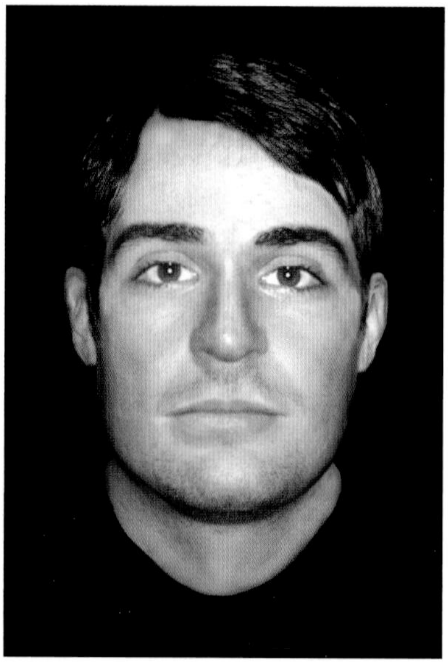

Figs. 91 and 92. Forensic facial reconstructions of the two sailors whose remains were discovered in the turret of the *Monitor*, created by the Forensic Anthropology and Computer Enhanced (FACES) Laboratory at Louisiana State University. The younger man (right) is possibly landsman William H. Eagan or seaman Jacob Nicklis; the older man (left) may be yeoman William Bryan or first class fireman Robert Williams. (NOAA's Monitor National Marine Sanctuary)

Fig. 91. Forensic facial reconstruction of the older sailor. **Fig. 92.** Forensic facial reconstruction of the younger sailor.

Fig. 93. Discovered during the excavation of the turret in 2010, this fragment of a flask, made at the Baltimore Glass Works, features a phoenix and the word "Resurgam," Latin for "I shall rise again." (The Mariners' Museum, Newport News, Virginia)

29, 2012, NOAA, the U.S. Department of Veterans Affairs, and the U.S. Navy placed a marker in the Civil War section of the Hampton National Cemetery, just yards from where the *Monitor* once lay moored in 1862. The desire was still felt among all the agencies that the men should be buried in Arlington. With no next of kin forthcoming, the navy stepped in to fulfill that role, and the remains were released to the navy in February 2013. Traveling from the lab in Hawaii with a military and NOAA escort, the remains were given the same respect and courtesy that a modern casualty would be afforded.[61]

On March 8, 2013, dozens of descendants of the *Monitor*'s officers and crew assembled in Arlington, Virginia, along with John Newton's family, members of various *Monitor* expeditions, historians, curators, conservators, and thousands of members of the general public to join the U.S. Navy in honoring the two *Monitor* sailors. Secretary of the Navy Ray Mabus, NOAA administrator Kathryn Sullivan, Civil War historian James M. McPherson, director of the Navy History and Heritage Command Captain Henry Hendrix, and navy chaplain Gary Clore made remarks during a private ceremony for *Monitor* family members and invited guests at the Fort Myer Memorial Chapel before the two caskets were placed on their flag-draped caissons for their brief journey to Arlington National Cemetery. They were laid to rest in Section 46, near the *Challenger* and *Columbia* space shuttle memorials, and in the shadow of the towering mast of the USS *Maine*, up a hill from the site. This was, as Secretary Mabus said during his remarks, possibly the last Civil War burial in history. Though the two men honored were buried as unknowns, family members of the sixteen expressed gratitude for the ceremony. Andrew Bryan, a descendent

Fig. 94. The *Monitor*'s engine register was the first artifact recovered from the wreck site that featured the ship's name. (The Mariners' Museum, Newport News, Virginia)

Fig. 95. These Goodyear rubber buttons from sailors' uniforms were manufactured by the Novelty Rubber Co. in New York. (The Mariners' Museum, Newport News, Virginia)

Figs. 96 and 97. On March 8, 2013, the two sailors recovered from the *Monitor's* turret were buried at Arlington National Cemetery with full military honors. A monument at the burial site honors all sixteen men who lost their lives the night of the sinking. (U.S. Navy photos by Mass Communication Specialist 2nd Class Todd Frantom/Released)

Fig. 96. Burial of two recovered *Monitor* sailors at Arlington National Cemetery. **Fig. 97.** U.S. Navy personnel preparing to drape a flag over one of the coffins.

of William Bryan, summed it up well when he said, "Even though it's 150 years later, it's not just old bones. It's people." He continued, "If it's not him, I'm OK with that."[62]

"Our Little *Monitor*"

The archival record, combined with artifacts recovered from the *Monitor,* gives historians a glimpse into this nascent world of American ironclad technology. Perhaps even more important, her story provides insight into how this experimental craft took on a character that caught the attention of the Union and, later, the nation. She first went by the names "Ericsson's Folly," "tin can," "rat trap," "a wash-tub on a raft," "a hat on a shingle," and "cheesebox." At the time of the battle many soldiers could not look past her peculiar appearance. One Massachusetts infantryman told his father, "I got a good view of the little Monitor she is not very hansome I can tell you . . . she looks as much like a couple of planks with a tar barrel set up in the centre."[63] Another Bay State soldier thought she looked like "a raft with a large crowned hat turned upon it."[64] But soon that strange-looking vessel would become known affectionately throughout the Union as "Our Little *Monitor.*" As one Union soldier lamented, in January 1863, "Our little Monitor lost, and none of our other iron-clads accomplishing anything."[65] Shortly after her sinking, patriotic tokens bearing the motto "Our Little Monitor" and an image of the ironclad firing her guns circulated throughout the North. They still appear regularly on eBay.[66] While there would be many other monitor-class vessels built, there would only ever be one *Monitor,* a fact that her officers and crew were quick to point out.[67] Her design informed the design of other vessels, providing several cautionary tales in the process, yet she remained unique among them, because she was the first.

The men who served aboard her were as unique as their vessel in the minds of the public. Lauded as heroes wherever they went, some found that they would not be allowed to spend their money once it became known that they were "Monitors." Though 108 men can be documented as having served aboard the original *Monitor,* countless others claimed to have served—their desire to be connected with the mythical qualities of this first turreted vessel was so great. Recognizing the historical significance of his invention, Ericsson donated his original model to the New-York Historical Society in June 1862. He would not be without one for long, though. A year later he was presented with a "golden model of the Monitor" at the Academy of Music.[68]

After March 9 both the Union and the Confederacy put their ironclad-building programs on the fast track. Just two days later, on March 11,

Ericsson sent a hurried note to Assistant Secretary of the Navy Gustavus Vasa Fox, underscoring the urgency and intensity of the moment: "Cannot spare one minute—plans of an impregnable twenty (20) mile ship with Turret of twenty six (26) feet & two (2) eighteen (18) inch guns detains me."[69] Over the course of the war the Union would lay down sixty-four monitors as well as nineteen other armored vessels. The Confederacy would lay down twenty-two casemate rams of the forty ironclads it built or bought. Some vessels were more successful than others—but most were plagued by problems in the same areas as their prototypes: speed, power, stability, seaworthiness, and draft. The design of the Passaic class monitors, which were under contract immediately following the *Monitor*'s success, improved on flaws found in the original *Monitor*. They had thicker hull plating, better steering, and an improved pilothouse, which was mounted on top of the turret. They carried a lopsided combination of one XI-inch and one XV-inch Dahlgren guns. The USS *Passaic* was traveling around Cape Hatteras the same night as the *Monitor*. Though she had difficulties, her design (and the decisions of her commanding officer) saved her from the same fate as the *Monitor*. The Canonicus class of Ericsson monitors followed in 1863. Larger still than the Passaic class, these monitors carried two massive XV-inch Dahlgrens in their turrets. The *Onondaga, Monadnock,* and *Miantonomoh* were double-turreted monitors, the latter two designed specifically for open ocean, with thirty inches of freeboard.[70] The USS *Roanoke* began her career as a steam frigate in 1857 and was present at the Battle of Hampton Roads. Steaming to New York after the battle, the *Roanoke* was decommissioned soon thereafter. Shipwrights at Novelty Iron Works in New York City then cut the *Roanoke* down to her gun deck and refitted her with three turrets and iron armor. Relaunched and commissioned in 1863, the *Roanoke* was the only monitor to carry three turrets.[71]

Other designers incorporated the monitor concept into their designs. James Eads had success with his riverine ironclads in the western waters, including sternwheel monitors. Others were not as successful, however. The Casco class, designed by Ericsson's former right-hand man and *Monitor* officer, Alban Stimers, was a disaster. These single-turret monitors with a turtleback deck were designed to operate in shallow rivers. The class had serious design flaws, and only four of twenty ships constructed were commissioned. The vessels had insufficient freeboard: one vessel only had three inches of deck above the waterline after the turret was installed. Several Casco class vessels were converted to turretless torpedo boats armed with spar torpedoes. A congressional inquiry into the construction of the Casco class monitors in 1865 came to the conclusion that the class would have been successful "had Mr. Stimers consulted with Mr. Ericsson as he had been instructed to do, and as he had done from the time the first monitor was contracted for."[72]

Regardless of their successes or failures, none of these later monitors would capture the imagination of the American public in the same way the original *Monitor* did. Her men were popular on the lecture circuit; her shape was popular in art, advertising, and home appliance design; and her designer, John Ericsson, was celebrated as a national hero on the occasion of his death in 1889, forty-six years after being maligned for the *Princeton* affair. A massive procession, including the majority of naval personnel from the Brooklyn Navy Yard, followed his coffin through the streets of New York as it was borne by several of the men who had helped build his unique vessel, the *Monitor.*[73] When a monument was dedicated to him in Washington, D.C., near the foot of the Lincoln Memorial in 1926, President Calvin Coolidge told the crowd that the monument "rededicate[d] America to the spirit which Ericsson represented."[74]

Surgeon Grenville Weeks wrote the most fitting epitaph for both the *Monitor* and her designer. It also serves as the unofficial mission statement for the USS *Monitor* Center. In March 1863, shortly after the loss of the *Monitor,* Weeks published an account of the sinking in the *Atlantic Monthly.* He recalled that within two days of the sinking the surviving officers and crew were back at Fortress Monroe—the reality of what had happened earlier in the week still "seeming . . . like some wild dream." He continued:

> One thing only appeared real: our little vessel was lost, and we, who, in months gone by, had learned to love her, felt a strange pang go through us as we remembered that never more might we tread her deck, or gather in her little cabin at evening.
>
> We had left her behind us, one more treasure added to the priceless store which Ocean so jealously hides. The Cumberland and Congress went first; the little boat that avenged their loss has followed; in both noble souls have gone down. Their names are for history; and so long as we remain a people, so long will the work of the Monitor be remembered, and her story told to our children's children.[75]

Edward M. Miller, one of the eight midshipmen to go looking for the *Monitor* in the summer of 1973, echoed Weeks's words when he wrote in 1978 that he hoped that the "complete story of the USS *Monitor* [could now] be written."[76] That story of "our little *Monitor*" is unfolding each day in the conservation labs and archives at The Mariners' Museum, and in the one-mile "column of water," sixteen miles off Cape Hatteras, that comprises the Monitor National Marine Sanctuary.

PART TWO

A Documentary Record of the USS *Monitor*

CHAPTER 9

The U.S. Gun Boat *Currituck* Escorts the *Monitor* to Hampton Roads, March 3–9, 1862

William F. Shankland of Philadelphia joined the Union navy as an acting master in June 1861. In 1862 he was commander of the USS Currituck, *the steamer that escorted the* Monitor *from New York City to Virginia. Following the Battle of Hampton Roads, Shankland spent time on blockade duty in the Chesapeake Bay and patrolled the James and York Rivers during General McClellan's failed Peninsula Campaign. He was honorably discharged from the navy in September 1867 and died in 1886.*

Shankland's journal—which is bound in a sailcloth cover with sailmaking stitches of hemp thread—still has the faint smell of having been on a ship. His account of the Battle of Hampton Roads blends the utter excitement of the two-day action with the nonchalant record keeping of an ordinary logbook. We have modified Shankland's punctuation slightly for the sake of readability. Each paragraph consists of a four-hour watch, and the quotation mark for each new time within a paragraph indicates that a new notation was being made within the same watch.[1]

Remarks on Board U.S. Steamer "Currituck"
Commanded by Wm. F. Shankland Esq. March 3rd 1862

At 12 Midnight light airs from the west. Weather clear. "At 2 A.M. Ship surrounded with ice, the remaining two hours the weather the same.

At 4 A.M. Light breeze from N.W. Weather clear and cold. "At 5.30 A.M. Wind hauled to the northward. "At 6 A.M. Wind N by W large quantities of drifting ice coming up with the tide. "At 7 A.M. the ice enclosing on the Ship causing a heavy strain on the after moorings. "At 8 A.M. Wind N.E. light and pleasant weather.

At 9.30 A.M. Received on board fresh meat and other provisions. "At 10 A.M. the U.S. Tug Boat got underway. Wind N.E. and weather cloudy and stormy. Continues so.

At 2 P.M. ceased raining weather cloudy. Wind from the N. East continues so during the Watch.

At 4 P.M. the weather the same. "At 5 P.M. the U.S. Ship "King Fisher" arrived at the Brooklyn Navy Yard. Wind N.E. cloudy & unpleasant weather.

At 6 P.M. The Ship clear from ice. And the weather the same. At 8 P.M. Thunder and Lightning. Wind East and squally and very unpleasant, all these four hours.

[Next page]
Remarks on Board U.S. Steamer "Currituck"
Commanded by Wm. F. Shankland Esq. March 4th 1862

This Day begins with rain and light winds from the N.E. "At 4 A.M. ceased raining, and wind hauled to the Westward. "At 6 A.M. Wind N.N.W. and blowing a brisk breeze. Continues the Same during the watch.

At 8 A.M. Strong Breeze, and cloudy weather. Wind N.W. "At 10 A.M. took on board a quantity of "Pursers Stores." "At 12 Noon Strong breeze and cloudy. Wind increasing from the Westward.

From 12 to 4 P.M. Wind and Weather continues the same. At 4 P.M. breeze rapidly increasing. Hauled taut the stern Moorings and made the Ship secure.

From 4 till 8 P.M. Wind Moderate inclining to the Southward—pleasant weather and clear.

From 8 till 12 P.M. Light Winds from West to South West by West. Weather fair but clouded. So Ends the 24 hours.

[Next page]
Remarks on Board U.S. Steamer "Currituck"
Commanded by Wm. F. Shankland Esq. March 5th 1862

Commences with light winds from the westward, cloudy and unfair weather.

From 4 to 8 A.M. Light air from the S.W. "At 6 A.M. Called all hands. "At 6.30 A.M. the U.S. Steamer "Oneida" came to anchor one pt on our port bow. "At 7 A.M. piped to breakfast.

At 8 A.M. Moderate breeze, and thick weather. Wind S.S.W. At 10 A.M. hoisted up and secured the 2nd Cutter and the Captain's Gig. Filled up water and got everything ready for Sea. Weather Continues thick and wind changeable these last two hours.

At 12 Noon Light breeze from E.N.E. cloudy and unpleasant. "At 1 P.M. hove up the Starboard Anchor and secured it, ready for sea at 1.30 P.M. thick Snow Storm. Continues so the Remainder of the four hours.

At 4 P.M. Slacked down the stern Moorings to let a powder boat pass. At 4.30 P.M. U.S. Steamer "Sachem" having hove up her Anchor and in steaming ahead, came down upon us and struck stern on our Starboard Quarter, shook the house but done no particular damage. "Wind light from the Eastward with Snow and sleet. "At 8 P.M. Wind hauled to the N.W. weather unpleasant, attended with Snow all the four hours.

[Next page]
Remarks on Board U.S. Steamer "Currituck"
Commanded by Wm. F. Shankland Esq. March 6th 1862

At Midnight light breeze from the Southward thick and cloudy weather with snow and sleet. "At 2 A.M. More Moderate, the clouds gradually decreasing. Wind light from N.W. "At 3 A.M. clear sky and cold continues so the remainder of the four hours.

At 4 A.M. Wind continues light from the west. Weather thick and hazy. And continues so during the Watch.

At 8 A.M. Fresh breeze from W.S.W. clear pleasant weather. "At 9 A.M. received on board three men for the U.S. Ship "St Lawrence" their names "George Senis, Thos. Harris, and Wm. Hasthings" all hands employed at clearing up decks. "At 11 A.M. hove up anchor and steamed down the East River in company with the Steam Battery "Monitor" and U.S. Steamer "Sachem."[2]

At 12 noon passed Fort William, distance ½ a mile, with the Battery "Monitor" one pt. on our Port Bow passed her when she was in the act of sending her hawser to the Tow Boat. Steamed down the harbour and joined the "Sachem" in the vicinity of Fort Richmond, hove too, and awaited the arrival of the "Monitor." At 2 P.M. passed Fort Richmond, dist ½ mile, went to the "Sachem" followed by the "Monitor." Crew Employed at clearing up deck and securing everything for Sea. Moderate breeze from N.N.W. fine pleasant Weather all these four hours.

At 4 P.M. Fine Pleasant weather. Wind N.N.W. steering in Company with the Steam Battery "Monitor" and U.S. Steamer "Sachem" all hands employed at clearing up decks and loading the Guns
"Continued to next page"

[Next page]
Remarks on Board U.S. Steamer "Currituck" continued
Commanded by Wm. F. Shankland Esq. March 6th 1862

At 6 P.M. Sandy Hook Light[3] bearing N.W. ½ W. distance 20 miles wind W.N.W. "At 6.15 P.M. Stationed the Lookout. Steering in Company with the Steam Battery "Monitor" and U.S. Steamer "Sachem" weather fine for the remainder of these 2 hours.

[Next page]
Remarks on Board U.S. Steamer "Currituck"
Commanded by Wm. F. Shankland Esq. March 7th 1862

At 1 A.M. Barnegat Light[4] bore N by W distance 12 miles. "At 2 A.M. made "Absecom light[5] bearing West distance 10 miles. Weather clear.

At 4 A.M. Weather clear. At 6 A.M. "Absecom light bearing N.W. Called all hands and washed decks. "A number of sail in sight.

At 8 A.M. Sighted a Barque steering W.S.W. at 9.50 A.M. Set the Foresail. At 10.30 A.M. Cape May Light[6] Ship bore W By N distance 6 miles. Strong breeze and heavy sea for the last 2 hours. Ship rolling heavily secured the boats by spans across the deck around the boats and davits. Vessel shipping large quantities of water.

At 1 P.M. Blowing a strong gale. Ship labouring heavy. At 2 P.M. reefed the Fore Sail and set it again. Made Indian River Light,[7] bearing W.S.W. distance 12 miles and hauled up for it. Ship Shipping large quantities of water. Wind N.W. and weather unpleasant.

At 4 P.M. Strong Breeze. Sea running high. Weather clear. At 4.30 P.M. made Cape Henlopen Light[8] bearing West.

"At 6 P.M. Sighted Indian River Light, Bearing W by N distance 8 miles. Strong gale and a heavy Sea. Vessel shipping large quantities of water & labouring heavily. "At 6.30 P.M. bore up for Indian River Light and passed it in Company with the "Monitor" and "Sachem" at 7.35 P.M.

"At 8 P.M. Weather clear and wind Moderating. At 10 P.M. Indian River Light, bore N.W. by N distance 12 miles. Wind N.W. and Continues so during the watch.

[Next page]
Remarks on Board U.S. Steamer "Currituck"
Commanded by Wm. F. Shankland Esq. March 8th 1862

At 12 Midnight clear weather breeze fresh. Sea getting more smooth. "At 1.30 A.M. hove to off shore. At 10 [P.]M. to 2 A.M. hove the lead no bottom at 10 fathoms the lights and everything secured at the end of these four hours.

At 4 A.M. Strong breeze and considerable sea. Ship rolling heavily. Following close after the "Monitor" 2 points on our Port Bow with the "Sachem" right to our port Stern.

At 6 A.M. Sighted a Sch[oone]r Steering W by S and several other vessels which could not be made out. "At 6.45 A.M. the "Monitor" shewing a signal of distress. Kept the Ship away, and ran under her Stern, when within hailing distance the Captain wished us to Stand in shore and keep close to him as his fires had repeatedly been extinguished by the Sea breaking over her. At 7 A.M. gale Moderated, and Sea going down vessel, considerably easier. "At 10 A.M. Made Hog Island Light[9] bearing S.W. by W distance 20 miles. Weather clear and pleasant, wind light from the westward. "At 11 A.M. spoke the "Sachem." At 12 Noon Hog Island Light bore N by W 1/2 W distance 12 miles. Weather continues the same.

"At 12 Noon Wind light clear and pleasant weather. "At 12.30 P.M. Sighted Smith Island Light,[10] bearing S.W. by S distance 10 miles. "At 1.30 P.M. sighted Cape Henry Light[11] bearing S.W. by S distance 15 miles. "At 2 P.M. passed Smith Island Light bearing N.W. by N distance 6 miles. "At 3 P.M. ran off and hailed the "Monitor" at 3.30 P.M. sighted the bouy on the Middle ground. Weather remains pleasant

"At 4 P.M. Kept the Ship away for Fortress Monroe Harbour perceived clouds of Smoke and heard heavy Cannonadeing which proved to be the Confederate Steam Ram Battery "Merrimac" in company with 2 Rebel Gun Boats

"Continued to next page"

[Next page]

Remarks on Board U.S. Steamer "Currituck"

Commanded by Wm. F. Shankland Esq. March 8th Continued

having attacked the U.S. Frigate "Congress, "Cumberland, "St Lawrence," "Roanoke," and "Minnessota" being engaged in the affray. "At 6 P.M. reached the harbour. Called all hands to Quarters, loaded the guns with shell and made the Vessel ready for immediate action. With the men at their Quarters.—Steamed up the harbour. Met the U.S. Frigate "St Lawrence" hailed and were informed that She had just left the scene of action and that the "Congress" had been taken by the Rebels and the "Cumberland" sunk the "Minnessota" aground at Newport news. "At 7.30 P.M. came to an anchor in 15 fathoms of water and 30 fathoms cable out on the Port Anchor, sent on board the "St Lawrence" the 3 men which we had brought from the Brooklyn Navy Yard. Secured the guns, and piped to Supper. "At 7.45 P.M. perceived the "Congress" on fire which rapidly increased and in a short time was completely enveloped in flames, fine pleasant weather. Wind N.W.

At 8 P.M. Weather clear and pleasant wind light from the S.W. "At 10.30 P.M. the Steam Battery "Monitor" past us Steaming up to New Port News. Weather continues fine during the entire watch.

[Next page]

Remarks on Board U.S. Steamer "Currituck"

Commanded by Wm. F. Shankland Esq. March 9th 1862

This Day begins with fine weather, light air from the N and Eastward. "At 6.45 A.M.[12] An Explosion took place on board the "Congress" and the once noble Ship was scattered all about the harbour, the remainder of these four hours are quiet, the "Roanoke" and "St Lawrence" having come too Anchor near the Fort, the "Minnessota" still aground the "Monitor" Steamed up the harbour and came too close by her.

"At 5 A.M. Wind light from the S. and Eastward, and weather misty. At 6 A.M. called all hands and washed down the decks. At 7 A.M. Saw the Confederate Steamers "Jamestown," "Yorktown," and the "Merrimac" coming down the River.

At 8 A.M. Weather clear and pleasant wind light from the South. "At 8.40 A.M. the Steam Battery "Monitor" and "Minnessota" engaged the Confederate Steamers "Yorktown," "Jamestown," and "Merrimac" at Newport News. "At 10 A.M. hove up our anchor and Steamed down past the U.S. Ship "Roanoke" and hailed her. "At 10.30 A.M. Wind hauled to E.S.E.

At 1.30 P.M. Took the U.S. Barque "Commanche" in tow and towed her out through the channel, left her at 2.40 P.M. and arrived back to the harbour at 3.45 P.M. and came to anchor with 25 fathoms of chain out. Weather fine and pleasant all these four hours. Wind E.S.E.

"At 4.30 P.M. Weighed Anchor secured everything for Sea and started from the harbour. the "Minnessota" all afloat, towing down towards the Fort. Strong breeze and clear weather Wind S.S.E.

At 7 P.M. Strong breeze from S.E. by S weather clear.
Remark Continued to next page

[Next page]
Remarks on Board U.S. Steamer "Currituck"
Commanded by Wm. F. Shankland Esq. March 9th Continued

At 8 P.M. Hailed a Schr bound to Hampton Roads proceeded at half speed steering E by N. "At 9 P.M. went about, heading W by S. "At 10 P.M. came to anchor in 6 fathoms of water with 60 fathoms of chain out. Cape Henry Light bearing S by W distance 4 miles.

CHAPTER 10

Firsthand Accounts of the Battle of Hampton Roads, March 8–10, 1862

Thousands of soldiers and civilians watched the Battle of Hampton Roads from the shorelines along the water. The following two letters offer very different perspectives of two men who witnessed the fight.

Henry Eaton Coleman to wife, March 10, 1862[1]

Henry Eaton Coleman was born in Halifax County, Virginia, in 1837. Prior to the war he studied civil engineering at the Virginia Military Institute and the College of William and Mary. When the Civil War began, he became captain in the 12th North Carolina Infantry. While stationed at Sewall's Point, near Norfolk, he observed the Battle of Hampton Roads. Coleman later rose to the rank of colonel of the 12th North Carolina, and fought at the battles of Second Manassas, Chancellorsville, Gettysburg, as well as the Overland Campaign and the defense of Petersburg. He was wounded five times in battle, and according to his son "was very severely wounded at Spottsylvania, Virginia [in May 1864]. A minie ball took off part of the top of his head so that his brain was visible. He fell perfectly unconscious and was supposed to be dead. However, after a time, he recovered consciousness and crawled to the shade of a bush. Late in the day he was taken up by his men." Remarkably, Coleman survived this injury, partially recovered, and on June 25, 1864, took a federal bullet in the right knee while defending a bridge near his home. Following the war Coleman worked various jobs, including as a civil engineer. He died on June 25, 1890, the twenty-sixth anniversary of his final war wound. The letter that follows is a remarkable record of the Battle of Hampton Roads, including two sketches by Coleman of the ironclads involved.

Camp Arrington
March 10th 1862.

My own darling wife

I have received your last letters, informing me that your Mother had gone to Cedar Grove & that you had gone back with her to Halifax. I should have written before, but have been putting off my letter in order to describe to you the "Merrimac's" debut. We had been expecting her for so long without seeing her, that I was very much surprised when she did come out.

On Saturday, March 8th, at 12 [P.]M, the "Merrimac" in company with the Gun Boats "Raleigh" & "Beaufort" (each of one gun) left her wharf in Norfolk & steamed directly to Newport News. At 2 P.M. The "Raleigh," Capt. Alexander, opened on the Blockading vessels; then the "Beaufort," Capt Parker, joined in, while the "Merrimac" quietly proceeded between the "Congress" & "Cumberland" (U.S. 40 gun Frigates) & gave it to them right & left. At 2.45 P.M. the "Cumberland" sunk, from the broadsides of the "Merrimac" & from her battering ram, & her whole crew (about 500 men) with the exception of a few who swam ashore, drowned. At 3 P.M. the "Congress" took fire, but was extinguished. shortly after taking fire she ran up a white flag at half mast in token of surrender & distress, & the commander of the "Merrimac" ceased firing & sent a boat to her assistance. This boat was fired on [from] shore several times, & then the "Merrimac" threw incendiary shells into her & burnt her to the waters edge with most of her crew aboard. She did not shew her flames however until about 8 P.M.

After winding up the "Congress" & "Cumberland" the "Merrimac" commenced firing on the Battery & Winter Quarters at Newport News. She anchored in 40 yds. of[f] the shore & gave them broadside after broadside, driving the gunners from their guns & setting fire to the Quarters. She also at this stage of the proceeding sunk a small steamer with a very heavy gun aboard. About 3 P.M. the "Minnesota" (U.S. 64 gun Frig.) came in from Old Point & as she passed Sewell's Point gave it her whole broadside (32 guns) at one crack; This was grand. All of her shot tho: fell short. About the time that the "Minnesota" hove in view, the "Patrick Henry" the "Jamestown" & the "Teazer" came down [the] James River, & got under Pig's Point battery. After the "Minnesota" got into position, our gun boats & the "Merrimac" pitched into her, & it was an incessant war of artillery, until darkness put an end to the scene.

At 4 P.M., the U.S. 40 gun Frigs. "St. Lawrence" & "Pensacola" came up to the assistance of the "Minnesota." One of these was hit from Sewell's Point & after getting nearly within range, they both pulled up short & one of them went back. About this time a very curious looking little concern came up from Old Point, supposed to be the "Ericson Battery" or the "Winan's Steamer." she didn't shew more than 6 inches above water & was iron cased. It is thought she had only one gun (a 100 pdr.) I saw one of her shots ricochet 24 times & Major [Augustus W.] Burton told me that he counted 40 odd ricochets (or rebounds on the water) from the same gun. This craft interfered with the "Merrimac" seriously. At about 6.30 P.M. the "Pensacola" put back to Old Point & the Merrimac overhauled her off Sewall's Pt., gave her a broadside & received a terrible one in return. This ended the action for the night. It was renewed at 10 A.M. Sunday morning by the "Patrick Henry" on the "Ericson Battery" & the "Merrimac" on the "Minnesota"—

at 1.20 P.M. our fleet retired to Norfolk. The "Merrimac" is not materially damaged, received one 100 pd. solid shot under the water line, broke off her ram in the "Cumberland" had her railing on the upper deck shot away & about 30 shots through her smoke stack. Her commander Capt. Buchanan remained on the upper deck through the fight. I enclose a rough sketch of the "Merrimac" & the "Ericson Battery"—

It is believed that the enemy lost on ship board & land together about 1500. The slaughter must have been awful. It was a long way the grandest sight I ever saw. The "Pensacola's" broadside at the "Merrimac" after dark was grand, but the "Congress" on fire was sublime. She presented the appearance of a red hot fire coal chiselled into the shape of a vessel—her masts & hull were all red hot at the same time. About 1 o'clock she exploded her magazine & the report sounded as if all the guns in this section had been discharged at one time. The column of flame seemed to go up a 1000 ft high. The "Merrimac" is in the dock now & will be out tomorrow I hope. I suppose our killed & wounded will not be more than 50. 2 were killed on the "Merrimac" by small arms from Newport News thro: her portholes. Capt. Buchanan (her Capt.) was wounded (not dangerously) & Lt. Miner (of the "M."[ )] badly. 6 or 7 men were wounded also on the wounded.[2]

At dark last night (Sunday) the "Minnesota" was aground, but this morning she is seen at Old Point in a disabled condition. The "Day Book" of today makes our list of killed & wounded smaller than I supposed. It is certainly a glorious victory. Different articles are floating on shore from the sunk vessel.

A private in the Artillery has a full suit of sailor's Rig & a great many letter that drifted ashore yesterday. He promised me one of the letters & if I can get it, I shall send it to you or keep it & bring it to you.

Our men are not enlisting rapidly. Lt. Taylor is endeavoring to raise a company & so is my O. Sergt. [orderly sergeant] They have split & are on their own hook.

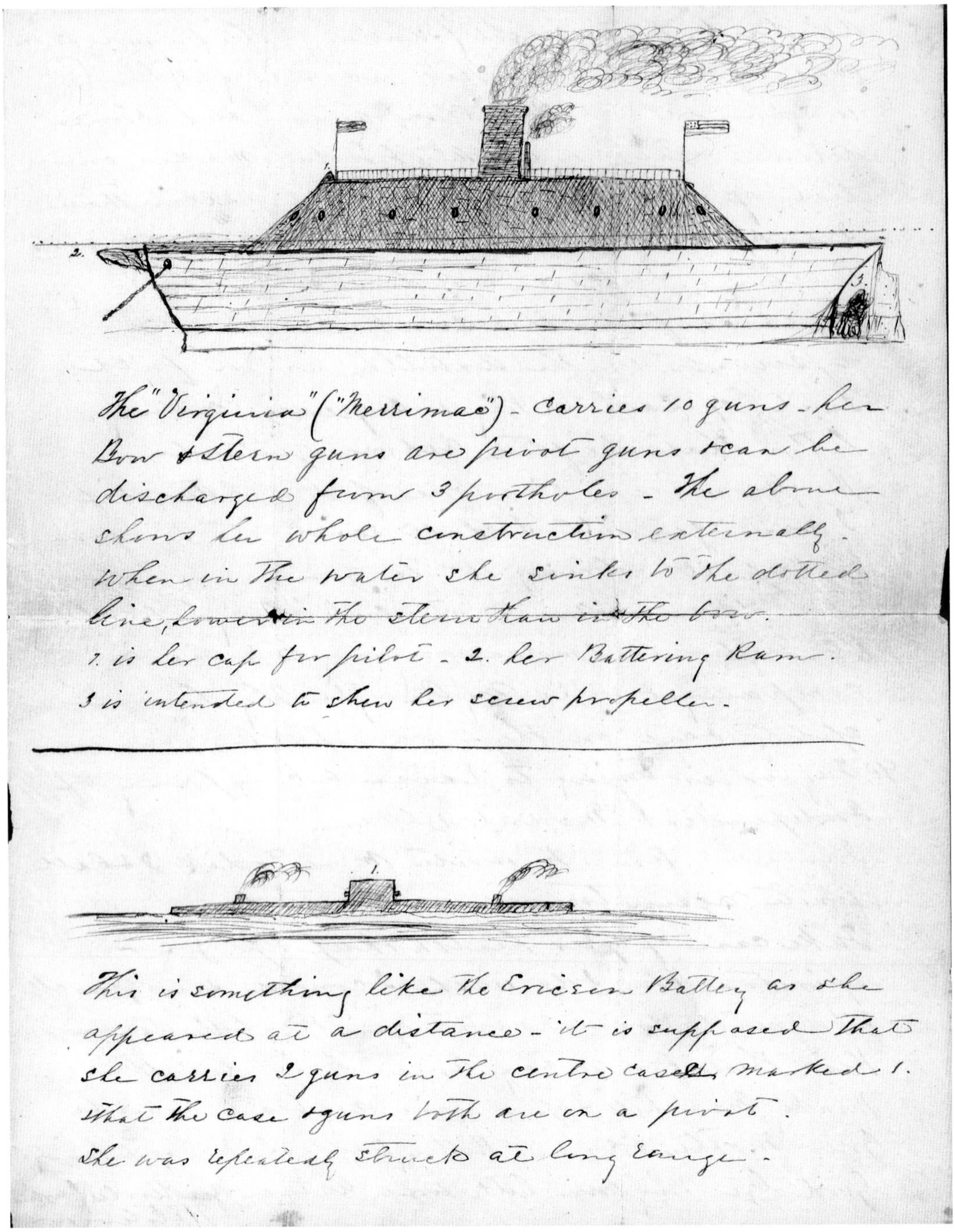

The "Virginia" ("Merrimac") - carries 10 guns - her Bow & Stern guns are pivot guns & can be discharged from 3 portholes - The above shows her whole construction externally. When in the water she sinks to the dotted line, ~~lower in the stern than in the bow.~~
1. is her cap for pilot - 2. her Battering Ram.
3 is intended to shew her screw propeller -

This is something like the Ericsson Battery as she appeared at a distance - it is supposed that she carries 2 guns in the centre ~~casett,~~ marked 1. & that the case & guns both are on a pivot.
She was repeatedly struck at long range -

Fig. 98. The final page of H. E. Coleman's letter included these beautiful pen and ink sketches of the *Monitor* and *Virginia.* (The Mariners' Museum, Newport News, Virginia)

Lt. Taylor is trying to raise a company of Independent Mounted Men.

I have n't time to write more today. I shall write again tomorrow or next day.

Take care of your health & keep up your spirits. How I do wish I could see you all I frequently dream about you & my little darlings. Kiss them for [me] many times. Don't let the "Monkey Man" kill "Top." Give my best love to your Mother & cousin Bettie & all the rest of the family. Good bye my own little wife. As ever Yr devoted husband

H. E. Coleman

Gustavus Vasa Fox to Alban Stimers, March 10, 1862[3]

The day after the engagement between the Monitor *and the* Virginia, *Assistant Secretary of the Navy Gustavus Vasa Fox sent a short note in pencil to engineer Alban Stimers offering encouragement and a bit of advice should the two vessels meet again.*

My Dear Stimers—

I notice with pleasure that you are on hand this morning. Please get every thing ready and keep her so for another fight. My impression is that the Merrimac is not much injured and everything depends upon the Monitor being in instant readiness to meet the enemy—You must stay by the vessel and I rely greatly upon your skill and judgement. I have ordered the frigates to go to sea and have sent for some of the small eleven inch gun boats of the Chippewa class to come here at once. Look out for coal enough and in all matters I feel safe with you on board. If she is disabled millions of property are lost. I may go up to night, if the frigates get off and will report well of you. Fire a little lower next time.

Yrs. truly

G.V. Fox

If you want more men apply to Capt Marston[4] there are plenty here.

My warm regards to all the officers for their gallant behavior yesterday

Fox

CHAPTER 11

President Lincoln's Mailbag, March 10–17, 1862

In the days following the Battle of Hampton Roads, anxious Northerners grappled for ways to defeat the CSS Virginia. *Believing that the* Monitor *was not sufficient to finish the job, inventors, crackpots, and imaginative citizens sent urgent letters to President Lincoln suggesting ideas for destroying the rebel monster. Some correspondents proposed different tactics that the* Monitor *could use the next time she encountered the* Virginia. *Nevertheless, few if any of these ideas were taken seriously. Writing more than a year later, one Washington lobbyist told Lincoln, "Immediately after the fight between the Monitor, & Merrimac—Mr Berny offered Ass. Sec. Fox, if he would allow it, that he, would, at his own expense, fit out the Monitor with his apparatus for throwing his Liquid fire & with that and his shell, go, himself, to Norfolk, destroy the Merimac, & burn or take the City. He was virtually laughed at, & denied every opportunity."*[1]

According to the lobbyist, some fifteen hundred proposals poured into the Navy Department following the Battle of Hampton Roads. The following letters are selected from the correspondence addressed to the Lincoln administration within a week of the battle. The fact that ordinary citizens felt confident enough to address their letters directly to president himself reveals the earnestness they were experiencing at this frightening moment as well as the familiarity they felt with their commander in chief.

John Brainerd to Abraham Lincoln, March 10, 1862[2]

Real Estate office of

JOHN BRAINERD,

No. 2 Montague Place,

Brooklyn, N.Y. Mch 10 1862

President Lincoln

Dear Sir,

I have just read of the havoc of the Merrimac upon our vessels and I hope a suggestion I have to make may be the means of destroying the monster—the fire Zuaves[3] can carry out the plan—scale her iron sides by some process and drop into her Smoke pipe a pill of Powder in some form that will finish her—like shooting an alligator in the eye—

Respectfully, Yours.

John Brainerd

[Postscript following the diagram:] I understand her to be shut in with an iron roof what resistance could be offer'd for 3 or 4 persons attempting to gain her smoke pipe at the same time with the powder pill? when in contact with the Cumberland or the Monitor to run into her prepared to administer the Pill

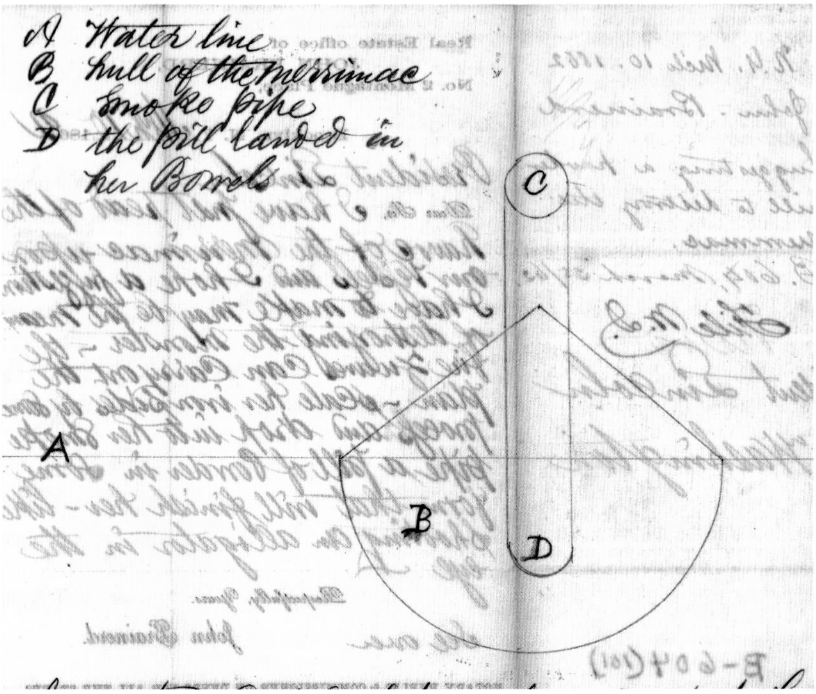

Fig. 99. Real estate agent John Brainerd's design for an explosive "pill of Powder" to drop down the *Virginia*'s smokestack and into "her Bowels." (National Archives)

Russell Sturgis to Abraham Lincoln, March 11, 1862[4]

New York March 11th 1862

To the President of the United States
Sir

I have the honor of handing you the enclosed copy of a Resolution passed at a meeting of the Harbor Commissioners this day—and to add that in case of need by the Government, ships and vessels can be procured all ready in ballast, that could leave this port at a few hours notice by telegraph.

With great respect
Your mo. obt Svt
Russell Sturgis—President

[Enclosure:]

New York March 11 1862

At a meeting of the Board of Harbor Commissioners of the Port of New York held this day the following Preambles and Resolution were unanimously adopted.

Whereas the "Merimack" has already left the Navy Yard at Norfolk and done great damage, and

Whereas she may again leave the port of Norfolk and do still further great damage to the cities on the Sea coast, bays and rivers of the United States, and

Whereas practical men have given it as their opinion that the port of Norfolk may be entirely closed by the sinking of vessels in the channel, therefore

Resolved, That the President of the Untied States be respectfully requested to cause said channel to be closed, if deemed expedient by the Authorities.

E. E. Morgan
Russell Sturgis
Commissioners } Robt L. Taylor
C H Marshall
Geo W Blunt

M. R. Fletcher to Abraham Lincoln, March 11, 1862[5]

Cambridge Mass March 12/62

To His Excellency

Abraham Lincoln

President of the United States

of America

&c &c &c

Washington

D.C.

Sir

I beg to state that soon after the fall of Sumpter, I communicated to the secretary of war the fact that I possessed a plan by which those Iron clad vessels, those Leviathan Monsters of England and France could be destroyed in case of interfereance with our Government and that too at trifling expense compared with the cost of building those or similar vessels. It was to my mind a fixed fact and I asked the opportunity to make it known to the government desiring compensation in the event of approval or trial

After several attempts I failed in obtaining any satisfactory reply—the reason assigned being the absence of plans, drawings explanations &c which I desired to give in person rather than by writing; and impressed with the belief of its value and of its importance during the struggle pending I communicated with Governor Andrew, Senators Hale and Wilson[6] to obtain their influence, but in vain. The daily reports of those who had visited Washington and returned without a hearing prevented me from adopting that course.

I volunteered my services to Gov Andrew as surgeon, quartermaster or agent in any capacity where my services might be valuable to the state or the country—hoping thereby to be brought in contact with Govt advisers—

That, like the other efforts was unheeded. Subsequently I obtained a package of letters from several persons holding positions of note, such as Mayor, Senators Representatives Merchants and Captain in the Navy certifying to my standing in the community and that any proposition I might make would be worthy the attention of Government[.] Those letters with a portion of my plan I forwarded to the Secretary of War, giving him my reasons for not explaining in writing, that, as traitors have been found in various departments the Navy might have a share—in which event the invention might be conveyed to the Rebels and the danger be reversed.

To my Letter accompanying said package and plans no reply as yet has been received and for ought I know they have reached the Confederates as their attempt at remodeling the Merrimack as near as I can learn so far as it goes, is a portion of my plan; and that badly executed. I am firmly of the opinion that had the Merrimack or even a much less bulky vessel been constructed upon my plan, the Moniteur could have done her no harm, and had she been in possession of the remainder of my mode of operation she would have destroyed all the steamers, Gunboats and the Moniteur besides—

Some of my friends advised selling the plan to whoever would pay the highest price—knowing that to be the Confederated states. I being a Doctor in Medicine, not in public life would never reap any reward otherwise. A gentleman from the south intuited the idea he received from my friend, adding "A Million of dollars are yours if it will do it." Soon after this remark the suggestion assumed another form viz If not go there, your right to sell to any one here to go to England France or other countries is unquestionable—You can sell to another, he giving a guarrantee to return to you with a half a million or half the proceeds. As an inventor I desired the fulfilment of my design, as an individual I felt the apparent indifference with which my proposals had been received and more than both, the want, *the need of money* was a strong argument—in favor of secession.

My answer was emphatically No! No! There is not money enough in the south to purchase my sense of honor, love of country and liberty. I preferred the Union to Rebellion, and to leave with my sons and their posterity that good name which we have inherited from our ancesters in the Highlands of Scotland

In fine I think my plan embraces all that is contained in the Merrimack the revolving Battery (Moniteur) and much more and that with it once alongside the Merrimack she could be sunk in a few minutes—while the operators would be out of danger comparatively speaking—Should the Government require new gunboats, or alterations in those in use so as to meet any emergency from domestic or foreign foes I shall be happy to devote myself to her interests in any capacity; and

I have the honor to be

Your Excellency's Most. Obt. Servt

M. R. Fletcher.

Axel Jorgensen to Abraham Lincoln, March 12, 1862[7]

St Paul Min March the 12 1862

Presedent Lincollen

Sir, upon reading the newes for yesterday and seing what a greet destruction the Merimac was to a part of our navy, I emedietly begun to think of a plan to sink that vassel weth les destruction of both life and property. The incloset is a drawing of the same plan. Betwin K K is a ingeruber [India rubber] boat 15 feet long and 5 feet high weth an Iron keel and botom in order to sink or if of wood Iron or lead ballast wood be nessesery to sink it sufitient, though barly enough to sink in order to make the ingeruber sylinder A of a so little sise as posibel so as not to be seen in a dark night in wich time it would be nessery to undertak the sinking operation.

C.C. is lines atach to the boat and the Buy [buoy] or floting Sylinder A and wich must be so constructet as to highten and lower the Baot at pleasur of the men ther is inside in the Baot B.B. is airetubs and the XE is a fanning mille so fittet as to draw aire in to suplay the men weth frish aire

G is a propelling whel behind h is the shaft I the Krang [crank] for one man to work at and to propel them to the plas of action M is an Iron Keel L is the rudder wich is to be manage by Lines insid of ingerubber tubs F is the plas wherin should be plaset an ager handel in watter tite Brac [brass] boxes turned well so as to go easy and admit of no water to pas trough and for each handel should be many Agers henging in a litle bag outside mede [made] so as to skru [screw] in easy and for to be able to do that wich nesseserely must be don from wethout ther should be med tow arms weth finger on out of ingerubber for eich Ager handel and weth thoughs [those] hands they would be able to highten and lower the boat by pulling or slacking the ropes C.C. at NN should be plast [placed] a skru or sharp bolt to fasten the boat to the side of the vessel to be sunk

On eich side of the baot may also be plaset an sylinder like A weth narow tubs to goe through to the inside weth litle Bracering on the ande of the tube and a airetite cap of Brac skrued an the tope of it to prevent the aire to eskape unles the managers a desire and thise airetubs could be blowen ful by the mouths of the men in order to lowt [float] lighter when they so desired.

For to prevent fatal accident to the men eich man should be drest like a diver exsept wethout lead an his feet, and an the brest should be an airetite bag to enable the men to flowt and to swim to theire starting point or headquarters, and eich man should be furnisht weth a sharp knive in order to rep or cut the side of the Baot in case of that water overtuck them so as to enable the men to eskeape through and save their lives.

If you think this is a good plan let no body know it but trustworty men or els befor you use it the South m[a]y not only make use of it against you but they may be an a sharper loocout and prevent the plan from excution

If you aprov of the plan and wont my assistens I am most willing to serv the country in that capaciety and you can tellegraf for me to com and I will com emedietly opon shuch [such] a cal my mens are smal and would need a travling pasport or ticket paid by the guvernment.

mine Adres is now and will be in tow weeks from now
St Paul Minnesota
I shal inquire at the telegraf ofice my selv—
Presedent A Lincolen

your humble servent
Axel Jorgensen

[Jorgensen's drawing is not included here.]

"J. B." to Abraham Lincoln, March 12, 1862[8]

Cold Springs N.Y.
March 12th 1862

To The President of U.S.
Sir;

I had occasion some time ago to address you upon the subject of iron-clad ships *and their manner* of destruction. It is hardly necessary that I should repeat the facts stated in my first letter, but my anxiety for the welfare if not indeed the safety of my country, prompts me to a step which I hope is not too presuming, at least I hope you will appreciate my motives.

I wish to state a few facts and to offer a few suggestions; and I address you instead of the Sec'y of War [Navy?], because although I have no personal acquaintance with either Mr Wells or yourself, yet I well know that you at least are a stranger to the petty pride which would tempt you to despise the opinions of your inferiors.

In the fierce contest of the little *Monitor* with its formidable adversary the *Merrimac;* had every shot or shell directed at the latter *penetrated* her armor she would have been totally destroyed. But such was not the case, but few of the heavy bolts penetrated, perhaps none fairly, hence the *long* and fierce contest of several hours duration which only resulted in slight damage to the Merrimac & its repulse (probably temporary).—I will now state a few well established facts. Had the Monitor posessed a single 15 or 20 inch gun, every *shell* alone would by its great weight and living force have crushed through the enemy's sides, and exploding or not would in *forty minutes* have sunk or captured her. Had each or any of our vessels at Hampton Roads posessed a single 15 inch gun the Merrimac would have been ours or the Ocean's. If these shells would not penetrate *both* sides of the enemy so much the better, they would then crush through one side and either explode directly in the vessel or *bury themselves in the other side* and *explode there.*

So much for simple *facts,* they are plain and need no fuller demonstration.

I am well aware that our harbors are about to be rendered "impregnable" by means of these monster guns. Though I think the number determined upon by the Board, by far too small.

There are at present but few perhaps but a single one of these guns, and that is at Fortress Monroe, just when it is wanted; I would respectfully suggest therefore in consideration of the above facts, that it be mounted if possible, upon the Monitor in place of one of the 11 inch inch [*sic*] guns which at present constitutes her armament. This however may be impracticable; if so, I suggest that the decks of one of the vessels (a *steamer* of course) be hastily and sufficiently strengthened and the Rodman 15 inch gun be mounted thereon. Then should the *Merrimac* appear as she threatens the [illegible word] vessel can choose and keep its own convenient distance, every shell will penetrate, but few of these *exploding mines* will be necessary to destroy the enemy and the contest will be *terminated* before the enemy can have time to greatly injure even a *wooden* vessel.

I am aware that som[e] of our new vessels are to be furnished with the fifteen or twenty inch guns of Cap. [Thomas Jackson] Rodman. But I think that the manufacture at least of a few of these guns might with propriety be hurried and the guns mounted on such vessels as are best adapted to the purpose. And *the gun only fired* when the targate is impenetrable to lighter projectiles[.] This will save the vessel unnecessary strain, if it be not well adapted to carry such heavy guns

Hoping you will not think me a very presuming youth, I subscribe myself with great respect

J. B.

"M." to Abraham Lincoln, March 13, 1862[9]

Philada. March 13th 1862

Hon Abraham Lincoln

Presdt U.S.A

Your Excellency

I had the honor to address you a letter dated 11th inst calling your attention to the superiority of a simple cylindrical iron bolt swaged & hammered say 8 in diam x 12 inches long with *flush corners* at the striking end for destroying *inclined* armor like that of the Merrimac, 1 over the spherical or round headed projectiles whose shape facilitates the object of inclined armor with the least possible tearing or concussion, while the flat headed cylinder strikes at a more favorable angle for cutting the plates, allows sufficient range and accuracy for the close engagements expected between Iron clad steamers or between such steamers and land batteries, and while it has greater weight of metal costs far less than lathe turned balls, besides being easily procurable. Without having intended to trouble you with a second communication on this subject, I have thus breifly reverted to it lest you may not have received my first letter, and further to propose (if the suggestion be adopted,) that a wash of lead, or even a cloth around the powder end, would be a great advantage. If for rifled guns the lead might be partly cut away, leaving a strap or feather for the grooves if such arrangement be now considered safe otherwise they might be hammered first to their greater diameter, and then with other sway [up] to the smaller, leaving nearly the desired feather for rifle purposes. Straps four or five inches long would perhaps do as well or even better than these along the whole length of the cylinder. Six inch *rolled* bars sawed off into lengths of ten inches, would be more effective against inclined plates at a horizontal fire than ten inch *balls* would. The following diagram represents a ball and a cylinder striking an incline of 52 degrees from the perpendicular.

M.

[M's diagram is not included here.]

George W. Knight to Abraham Lincoln, March 13, 1862[10]

Newbury port March 13th 1862

To the President of the United States

Dear Sir please excuse one of your humble Citizens to make the Following suggestions. If the Rebel Steamer Merrimac should make her appearance again & it should be necessary to atack her by the fleet, would it not be well to have some three or four of the small Steamers provided with a large Anchor and fifty fathoms of large chains slung under the bottom by small ropes in such away that they can be easely cut. The end of the chain well made fast to a good 3 in Hemp Rope Say fifty fathoms in length, Most of which can lay coiled upon the Deck near the stern. Then if the Commanders of the above fitted Steamers should be ordered to watch there oppotunity to Move close under her Stern, Drop the Rope on her Propeller, cut the lashings to the Anchor & Chain. The Rope would most certainly take the Propeller wind itself up untill it comes to the Chain and one or two turns would destroy the use of the Propeller and She would also be well Moored. Then the Fleet could take advantage of Position and destroy or disable the iron Monster

Yours Most Truly *Geo. W. Knight*

W. J. Thorn to Abraham Lincoln, March 15, 1862[11]

Saccarappa *Maine* March 15th 1862

Hon. Abraham Lincoln

President of the U.S.A.

Most respected & Dear sir,

Since the Rebel Steamer Merrimac made its appearance in Hamton Roads and has proved herself to be sutch a powerful agent of mischief and distruction to our Navy & Forts & Citties also of the North, I have been cogitating Some plan by which she might be sunk & distroyed. The plan as seen in the figures above Suggested itself to my mind to day, & Seemed to me to be practical, and I concluded at once to forward it to Washington & submit it to your consideration & also to that of the Navy department. I send also a copy to Hon W. P. Fessenden of the Senate.[12]

The red lines designed to show the out lines of the two crafts Merrimac & Monitor with the Monitor heading to the Broad side of the Merrimac.

The blue dotted line designed to show the waterline or surface of the water.

The Black line (fig 3) in the bottom of the Monitor designed to show a long Iron shaft of suitable dimentions & strength to stand all the pressure reqisite to come into forcible contact with heavy shiping with safety; and by a suitable cutter or borer attached to the outer end and a rapid revolution of the shaft by steam power on Board I am confident will cut a hole the size of borer almost instantly through the hull of a ship *where* it is not clad with Iron, & even Iron ships can be bored in this manner with a suitable instrument attached to the shaft.

It is obvious that if this plan could be made to operate effectually that the borer should be made to cut in all directions

In haste

Very respectfully Yours &c

W. J. Thorn

PS I think the shaft should traverse lengthwise so that it may be thrown out any needful distance or drawn in at the will of the Engineer or manager W. J. T.

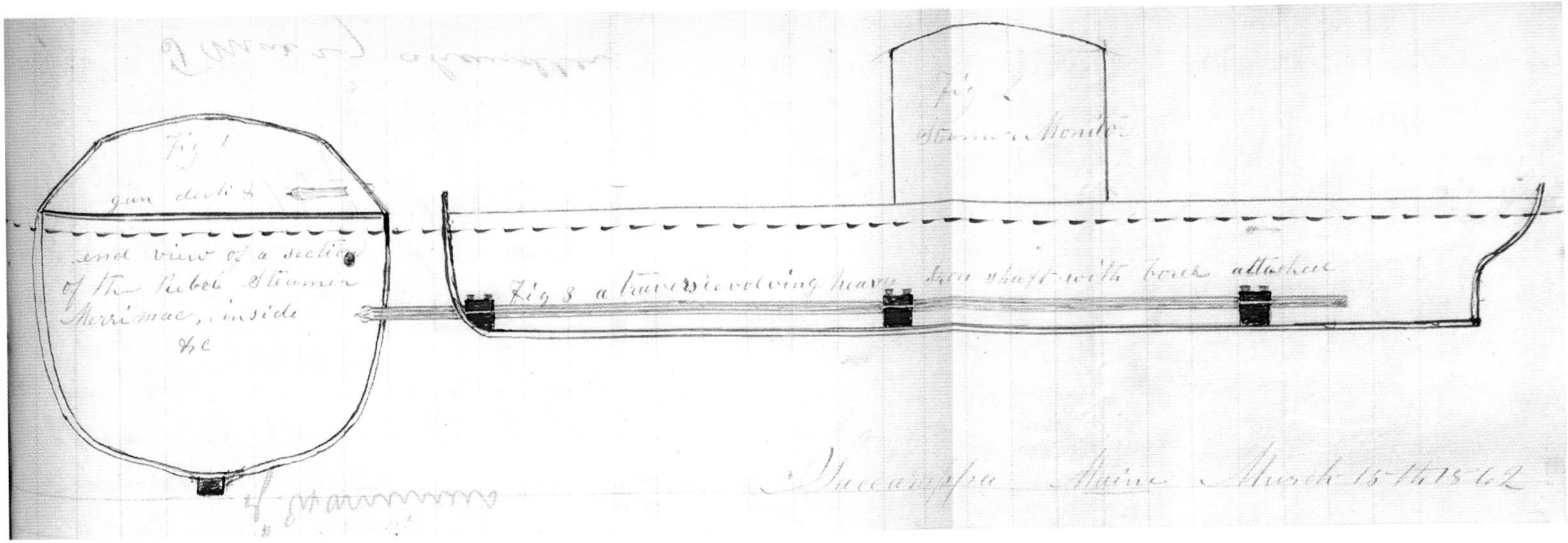

Fig. 100. W. J. Thorn's design for an iron bore to puncture the *Virginia.* (National Archives)

Joseph Masury to Abraham Lincoln, March 17, 1862[13]

Cleveland Ohio March 17/62

A Lincoln President of the United States

Dear Sir the great burden that is in the minds of loyal citizens is how shall the marrimack be destroyed I have a plan that will destroy here very quick and without loss of life on our part, It is this put on board the Monitor from 25 to 100 lbls of Rock Oil or Benzine of Light gravity in Iron tanks and place the tanks below decks make the tanks tight but leave a hole surficiant [sufficient] to admit the suction pipe atatch an Engine of surficant power to throw water from one to two hundread feet this Oil can be thrown full as well as water aproch the Marimack on the windard side and set the Engine to work and direct the hoes [hose] to the top of the merimack this being covered with R Road [railroad] Iron it will readily pass through and saturate the whole vessel and men and Furniture and the Oil will take fire from the discharge of their own guns and will stop thier fun in five minutes

every thing will be a fire it would be well to take along a few fire balls to through [throw] on if the Oil did not take fire from thier guns but I can asure you that if the oil comes in contact with any fire it will burn this Oil can be got in Pitsburg for from 3 to 4 Dollars pr bbl [barrel] and all you would want would be 25 bbls to rost out all the Rebbles that should be a board I should think this might be [illegible word] in a weeks time

Very Truly yours

Joseph Masury

If you wish to know any thing more of the nature of this oil Enquire Please enquire Proffesor J S Newbury[14] he is now on the Sanatory Comishion in your Imploy

J Masury

The following images depict some of the ideas that were submitted to Lincoln and his cabinet in the weeks after the Battle of Hampton Roads. Some are remarkable for their artistry and ingenuity; others are downright comical. Several writers suggested enhancements for the Monitor, *such as an improved pilothouse, while others devised methods for upending or otherwise sinking the* Virginia. *Several writers offered new ship designs or claimed that they could construct underwater cannons or iron-piercing artillery. A number of writers suggested designs for improved rams, some of which featured hydraulic power, saws, or torpedoes. Taken together, these designs reveal the genuine fear caused by the launching of the* Virginia *as well as the creative, patriotic—and opportunistic—responses of some innovative Northerners. The following images are all courtesy of the National Archives.*

Fig. 101. A suggested improvement to the pilothouse.

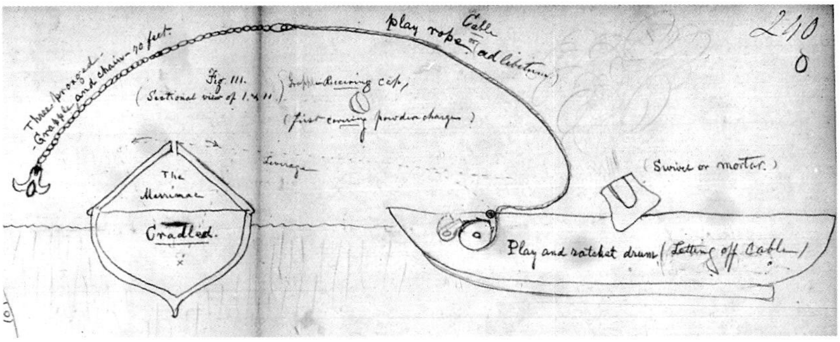

Fig. 102. A plan for cradling and tipping the *Virginia.*

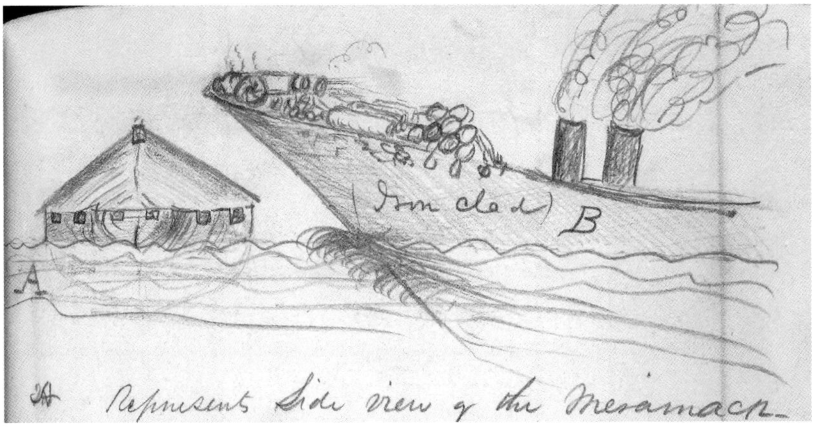

Fig. 103. A plan for sinking the *Virginia* (scene 1).

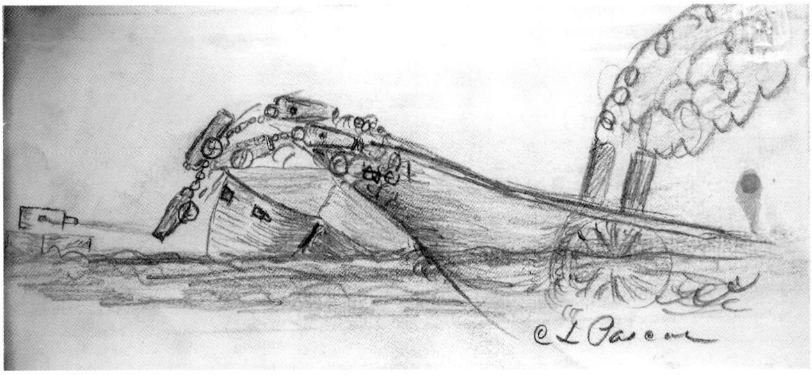

Fig. 104. A plan for sinking the *Virginia* (scene 2).

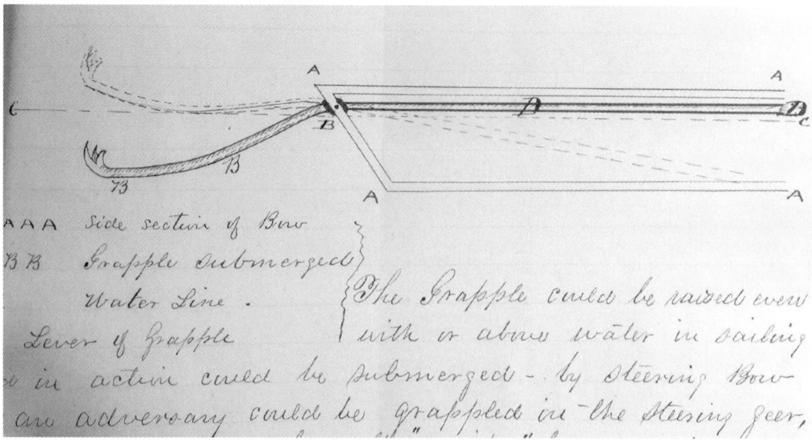

Fig. 105. Grappling hooks for grabbing the *Virginia.*

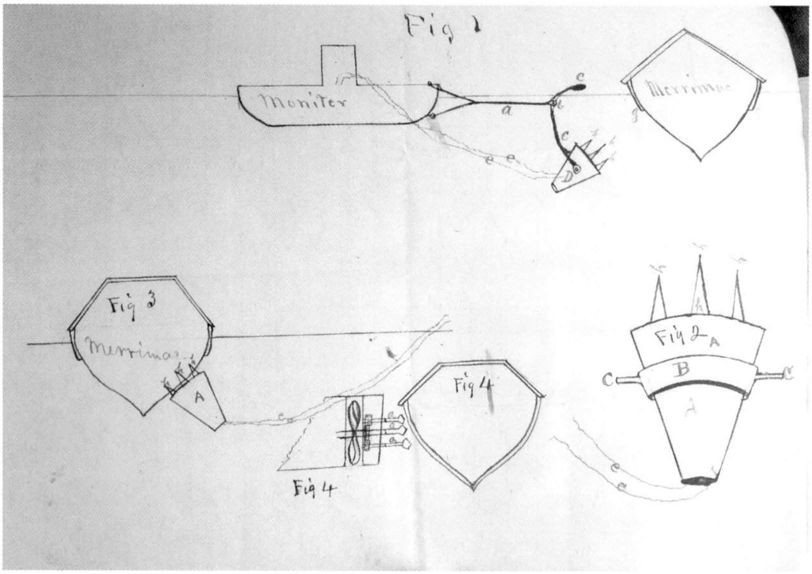

Fig. 106. Spiked grapple for puncturing the *Virginia.*

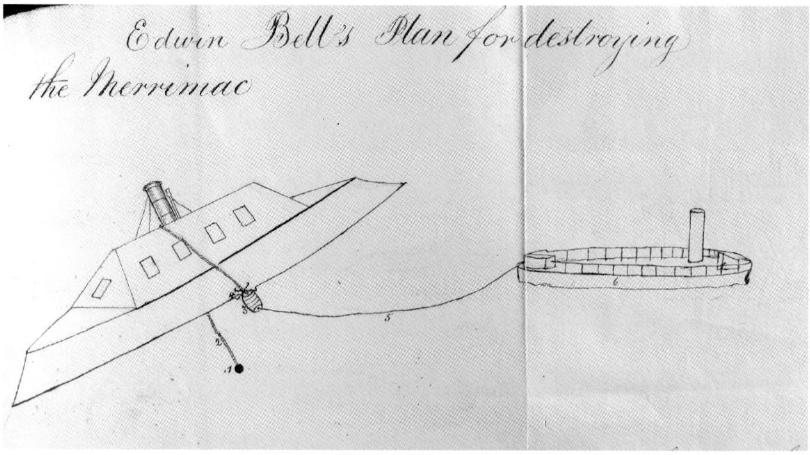

Fig. 107. A lasso to throw around the *Virginia.*

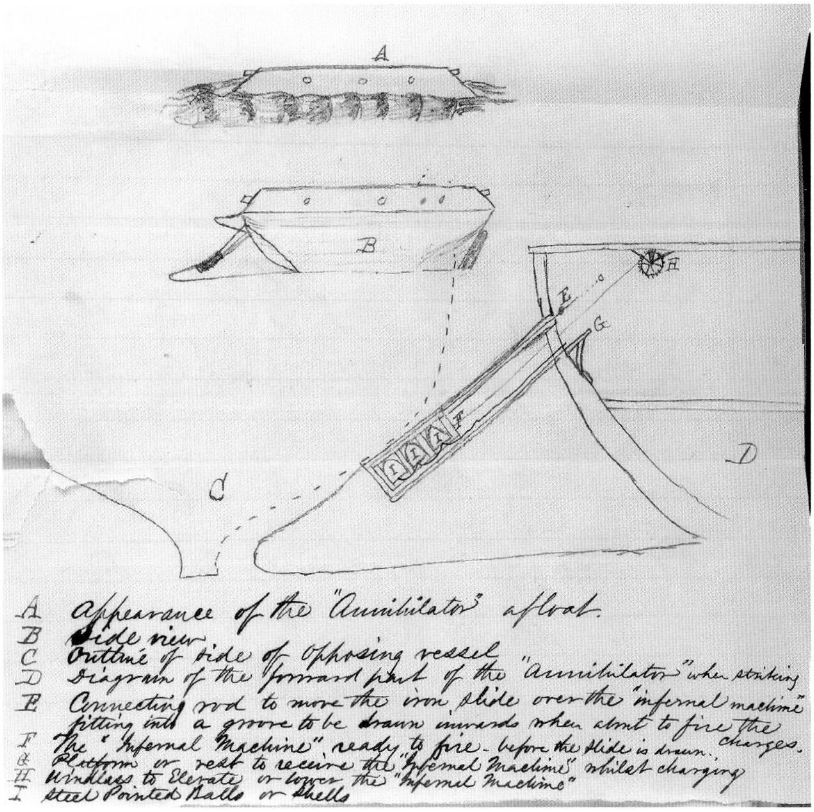

Fig. 108. Design for a ship with a casemate and two turrets. The designer apparently had not contemplated that the bow and stern guns were aimed right at the two turrets.

Fig. 109. Design for an ironclad ship called the *Annihilator*.

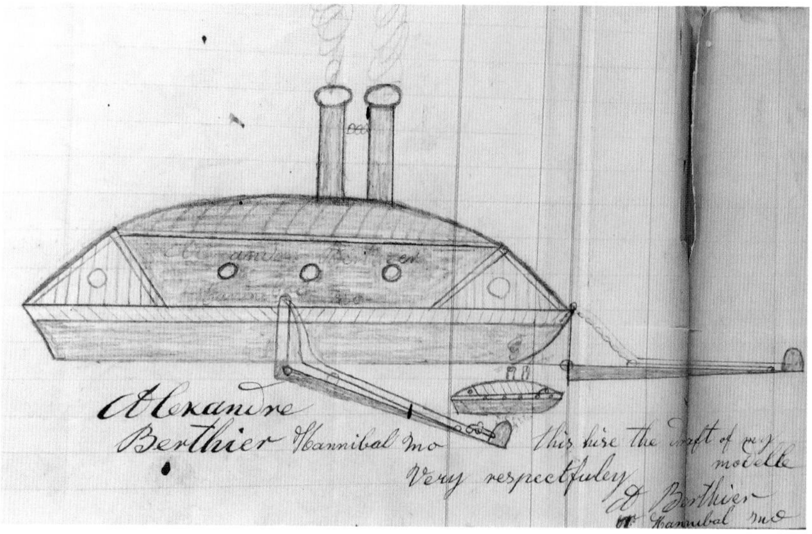

Fig. 110. Design for a large ironclad vessel.

Below: **Fig. 111.** Design for throwing smoke at the *Virginia*.

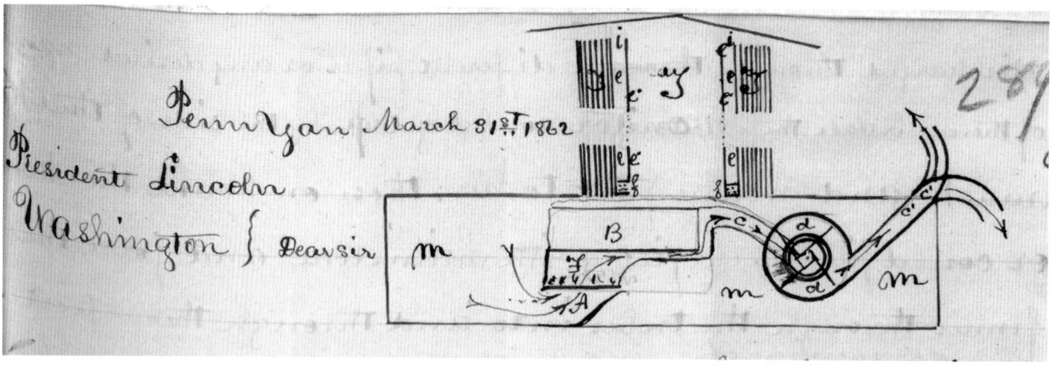

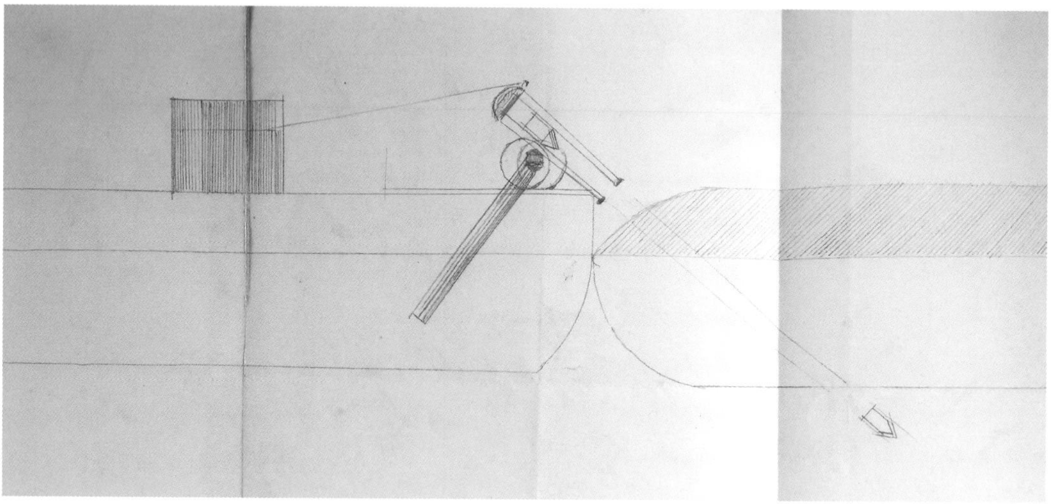

Fig. 112. Design for an iron-penetrating projectile.

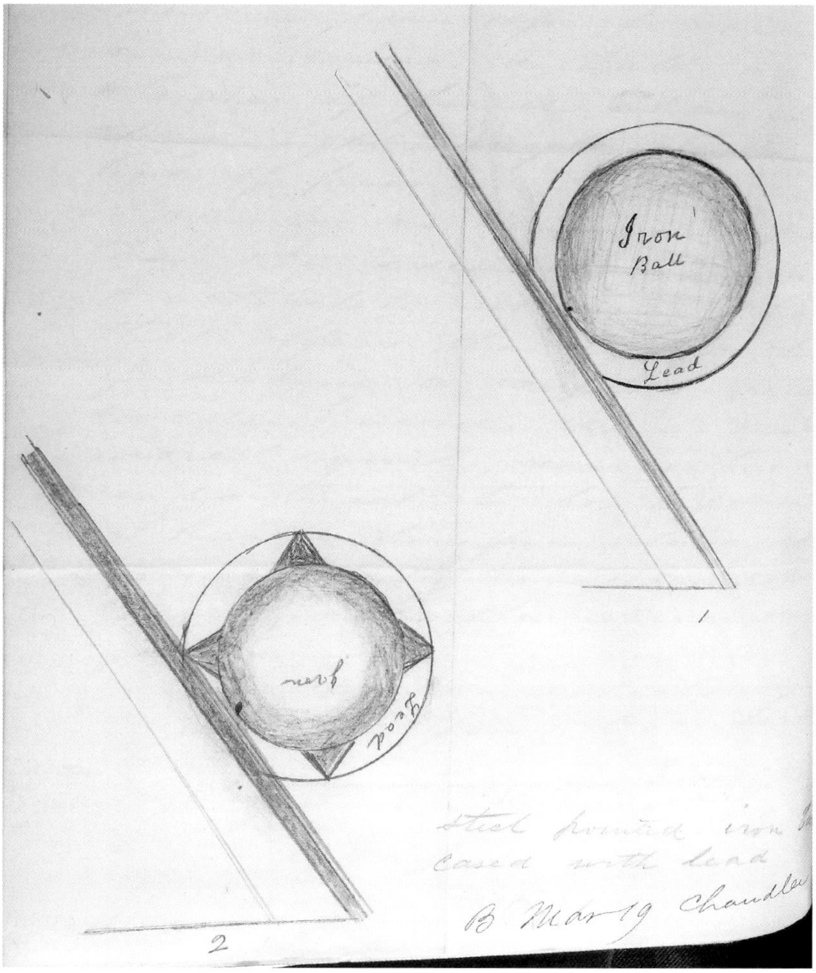

Fig. 113. Design for a spiked projectile.

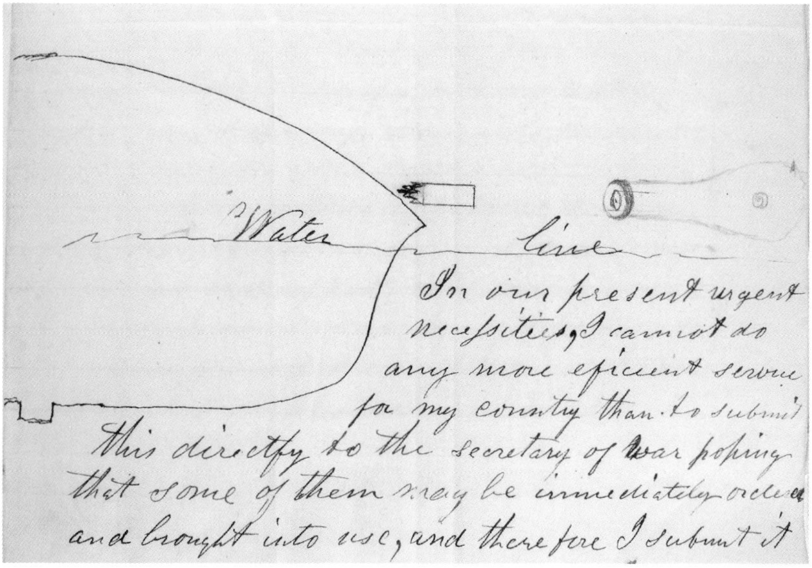

Fig. 114. Design for a new artillery shell.

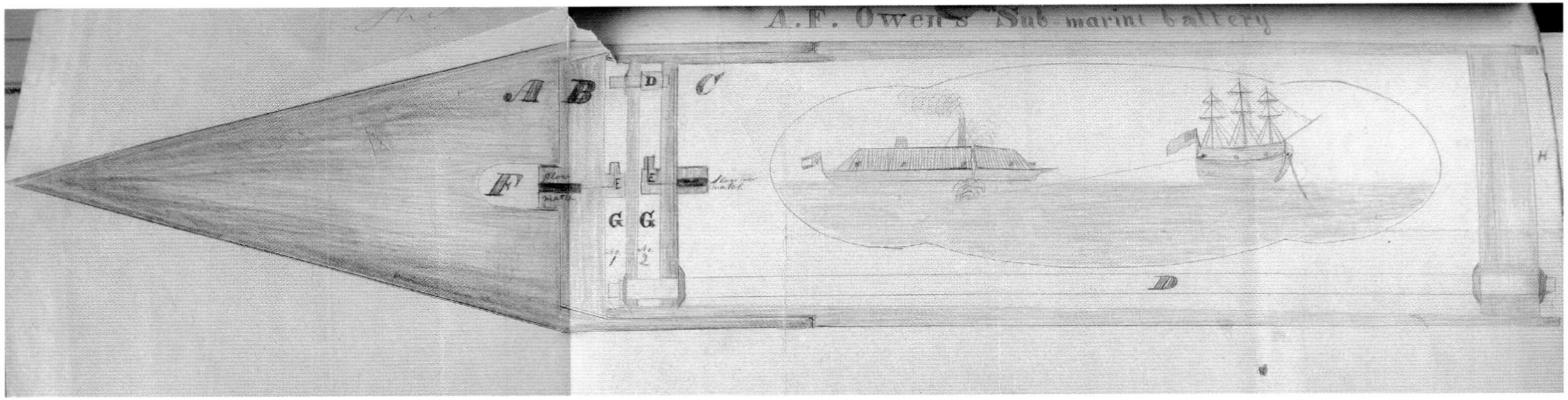

Fig. 115. Design for a submarine battery, featuring a scene from the Battle of Hampton Roads.

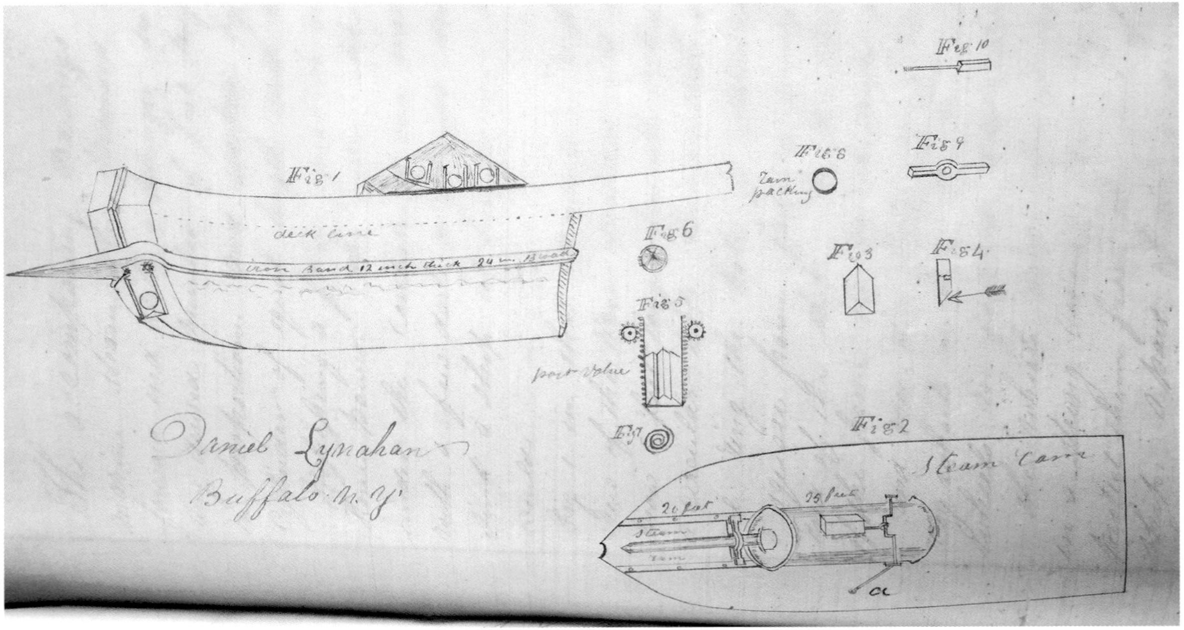

Fig. 116. Design for a steam-powered spike.

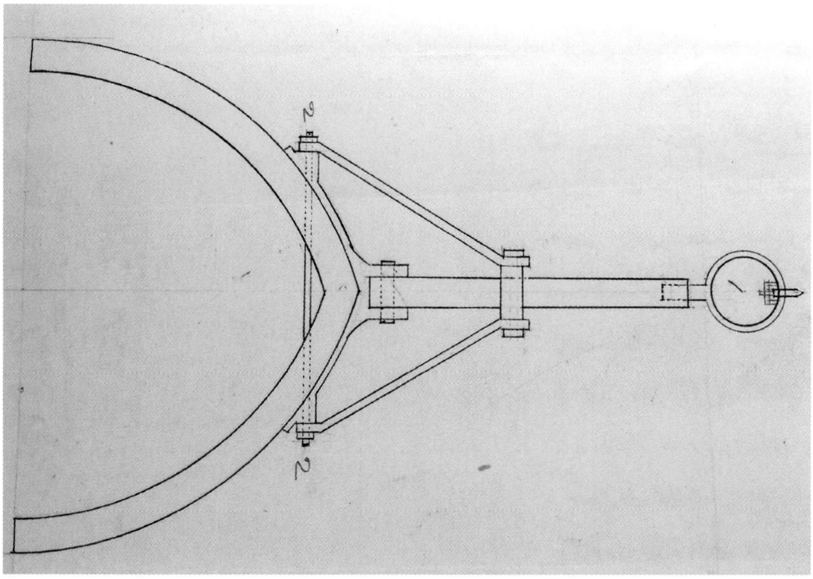

Fig. 117. Design for a ram with a spike.

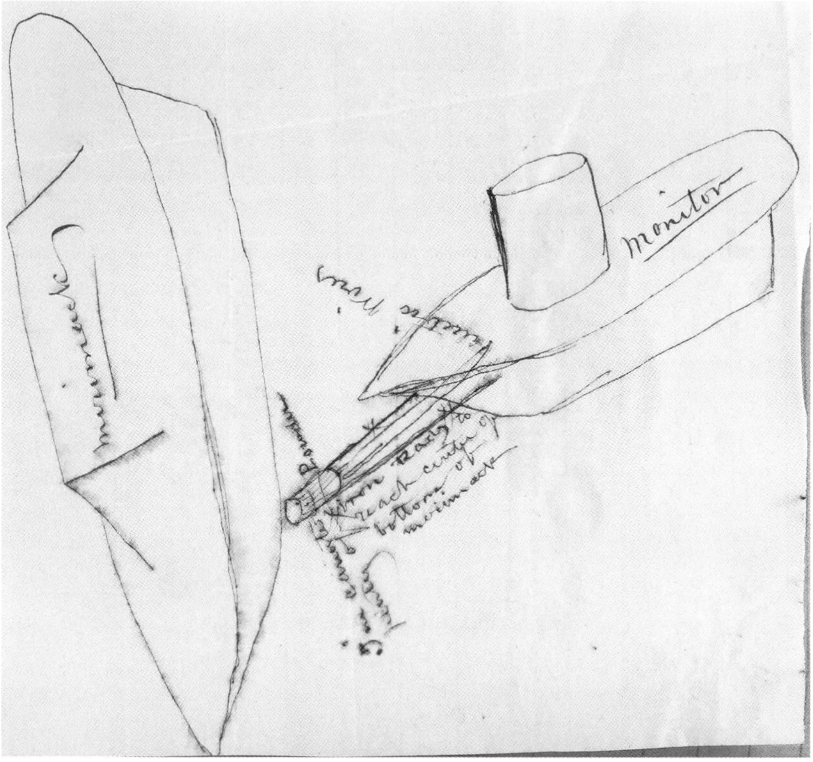

Fig. 118. Design for an explosive ram.

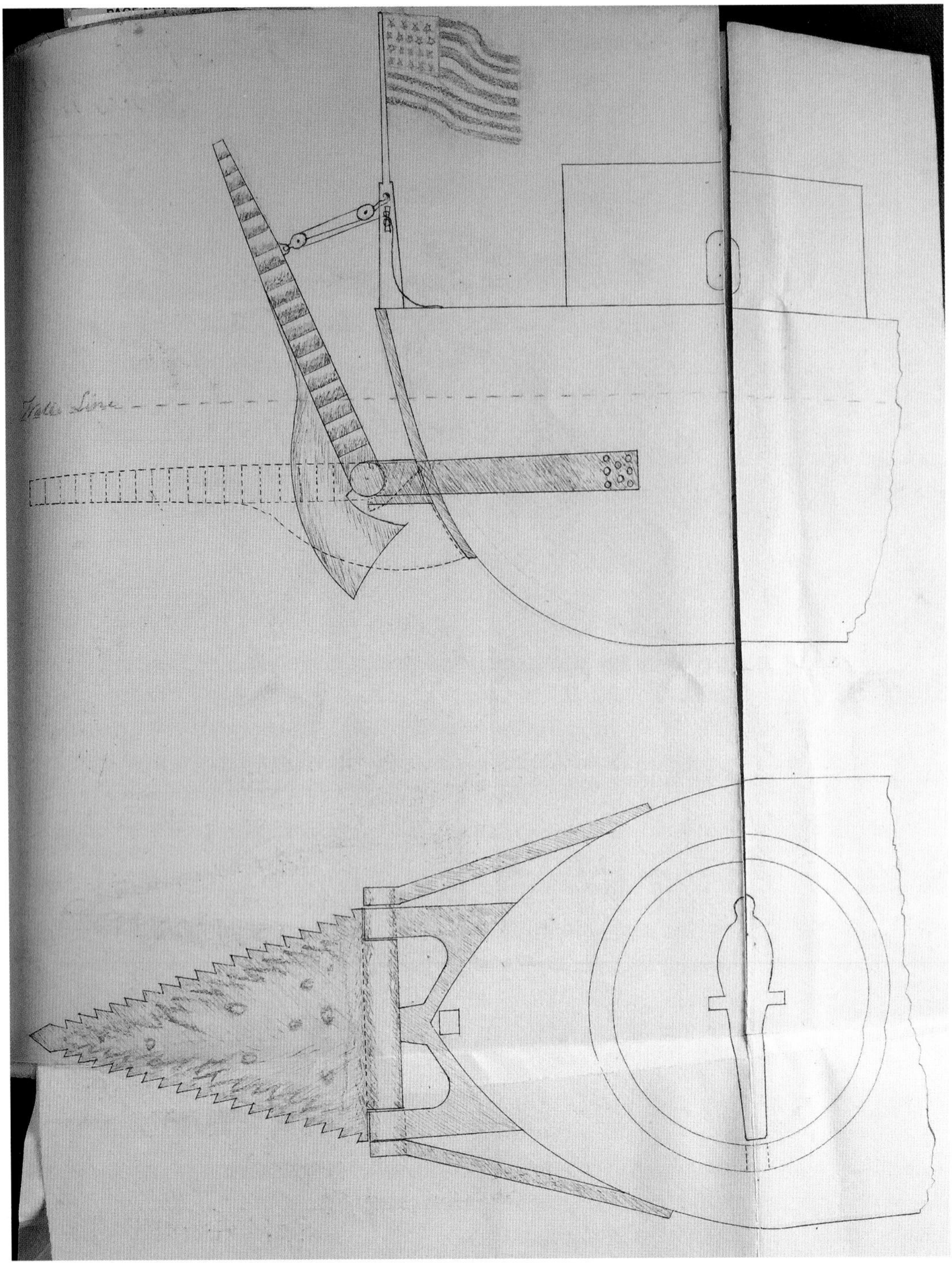

Fig. 119. A retractable saw.

Fig. 120. A torpedo buoy (scene one).

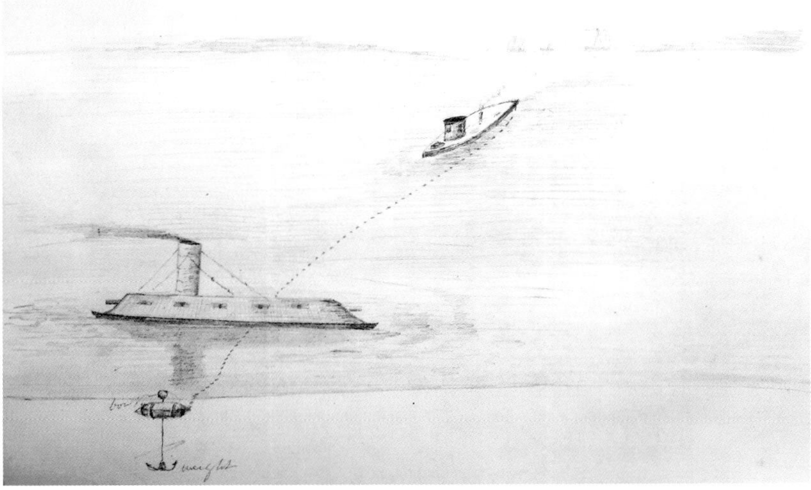

Fig. 121. A torpedo buoy (scene two).

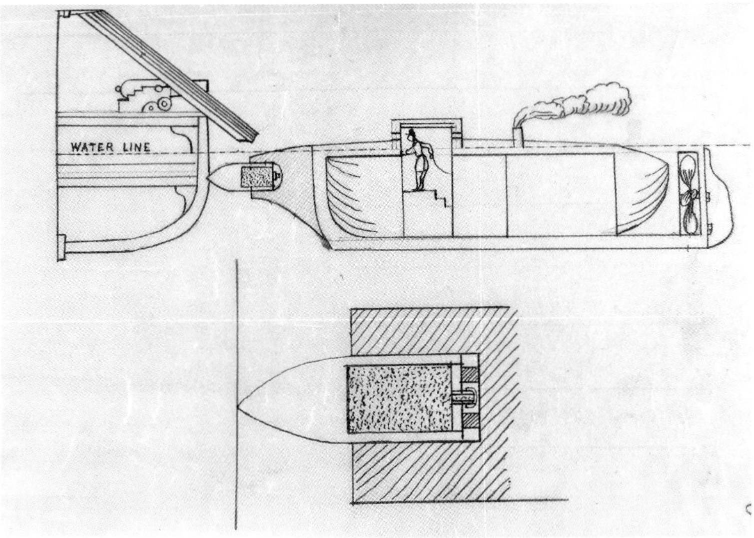

Fig. 122. A torpedo ram.

Fig. 123. A spar torpedo.

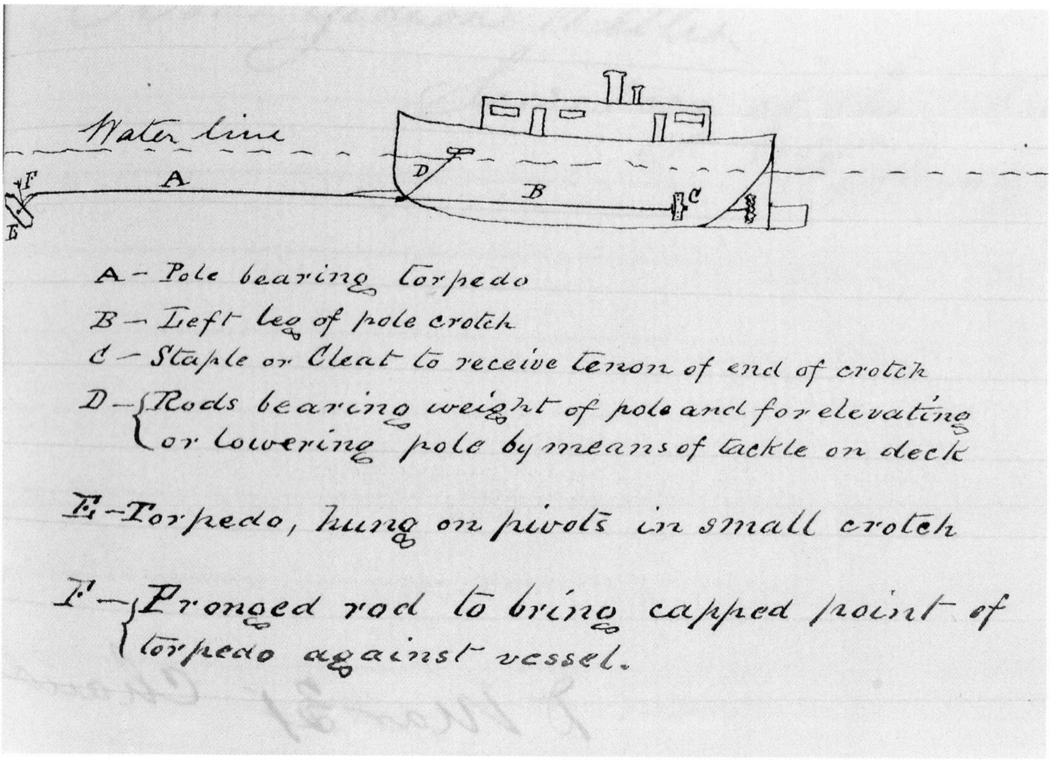
Water line
A
B
C
D
E
F
A – Pole bearing torpedo
B – Left leg of pole crotch
C – Staple or Cleat to receive tenon of end of crotch
D – Rods bearing weight of pole and for elevating
or lowering pole by means of tackle on deck
E – Torpedo, hung on pivots in small crotch
F – Pronged rod to bring capped point of
torpedo against vessel.

Fig. 124. Pole bearing a torpedo.

Fig. 125. Design for an underwater cannon.

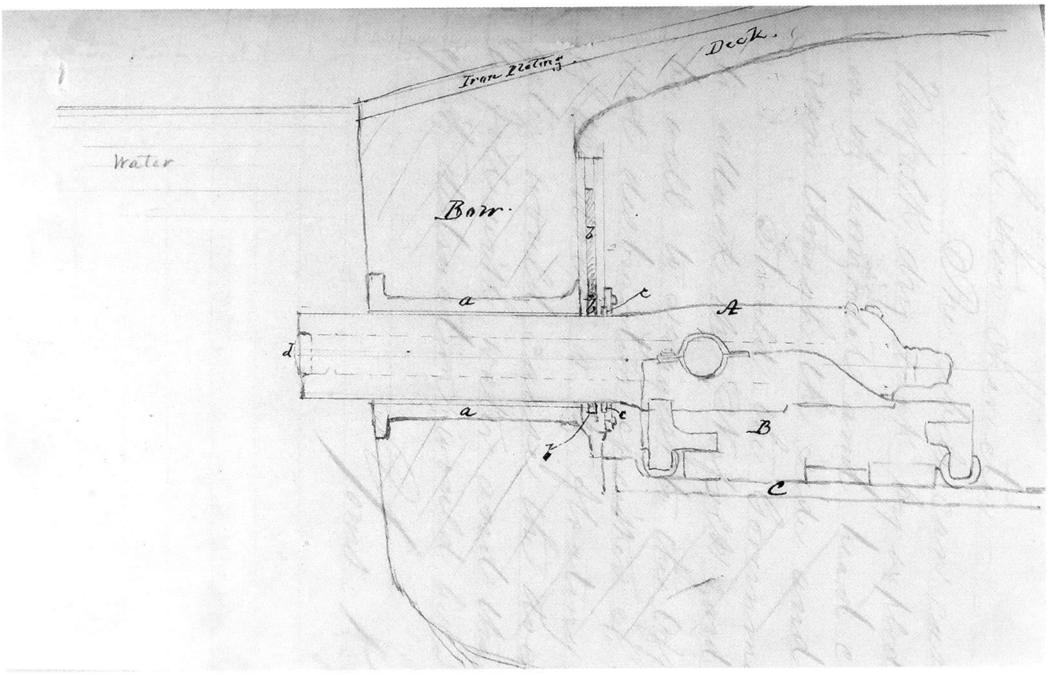

Fig. 126. Second design for an underwater cannon.

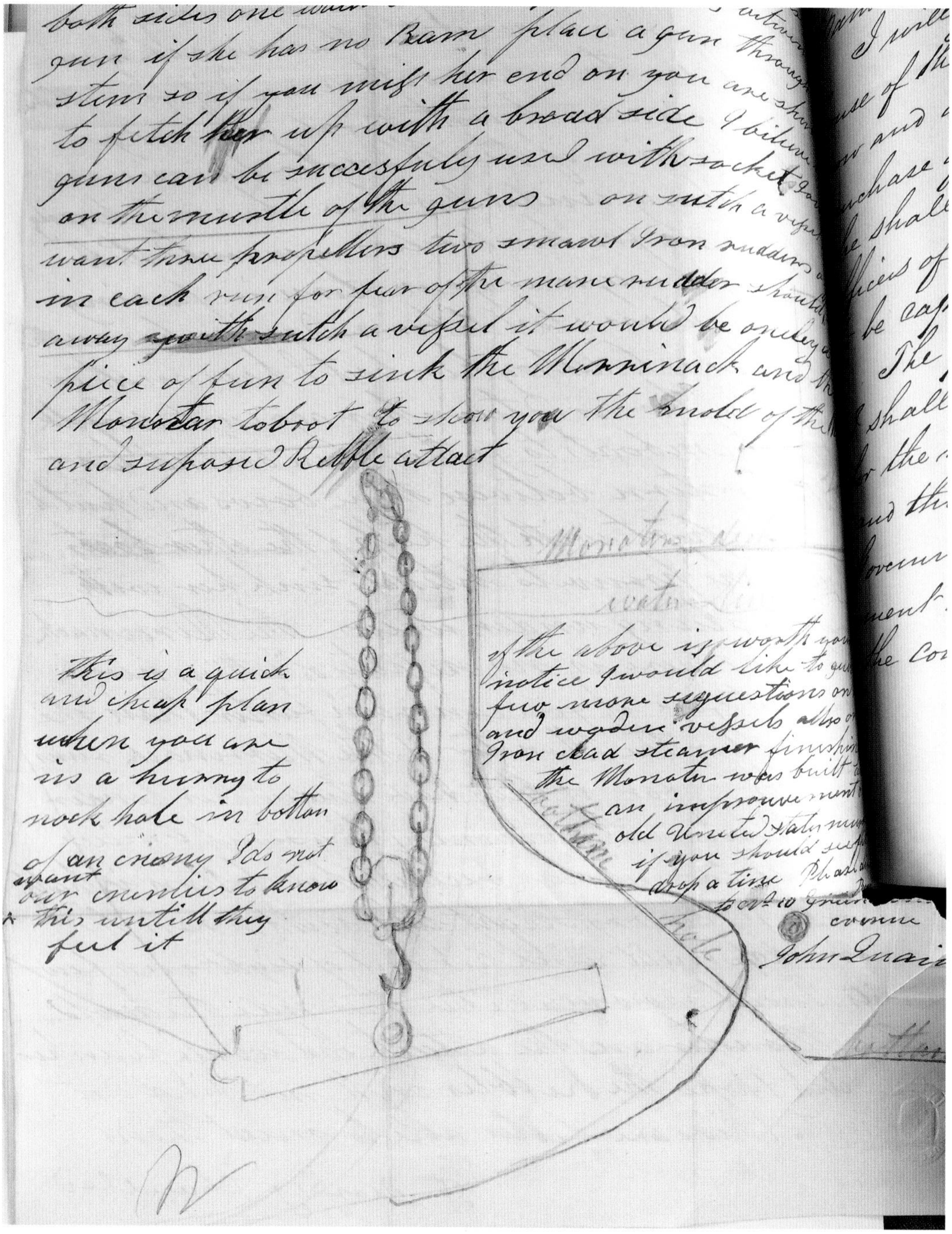
both sides one ...
gun if she has no Ram place a gun through
stern so if you miss her end on you are sure
to fetch her up with a broad side & ...
guns can be successfuly used with socket ...
on the muzzle of the guns on sutch a vessel
want three propellers two smawl Iron rudders
in each run for fear of the mane rudder should
away with sutch a vessel it would be onley a
piece of fun to sink the Marrinack and the
Monstar to brot to show you the model of the
and suposed Rebble attact

this is a quick and cheap plan when you are in a hurry to nock hole in bottom of an enemy I do not want our enemies to know this untill they feel it

of the above is worth your notice I would like to give few more suggestions on ... and wooden vessels also on Iron clad steamer finishing ... the Monator was built ... an improvement ... old United States ... if you should see ... drop a line Philad... ... John Quai...

Fig. 127. An underwater cannon that hangs by a chain.

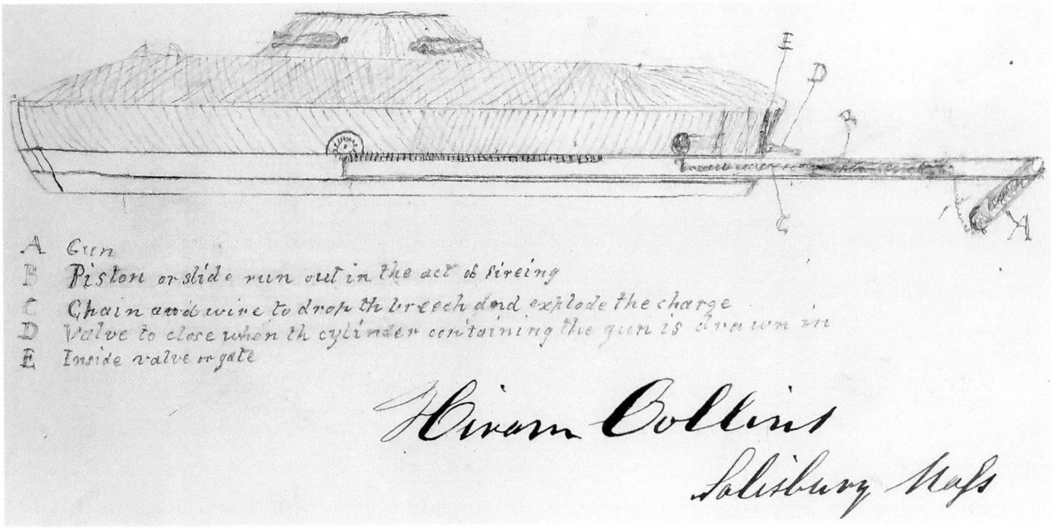
A Gun
B Piston or slide run out in the act of fireing
C Chain and wire to drop the breech and explode the charge
D Valve to close when the cylinder containing the gun is drawn in
E Inside valve or gate
Hiram Collins
Salisbury Mass

Fig. 128. Design for a retractable underwater cannon.

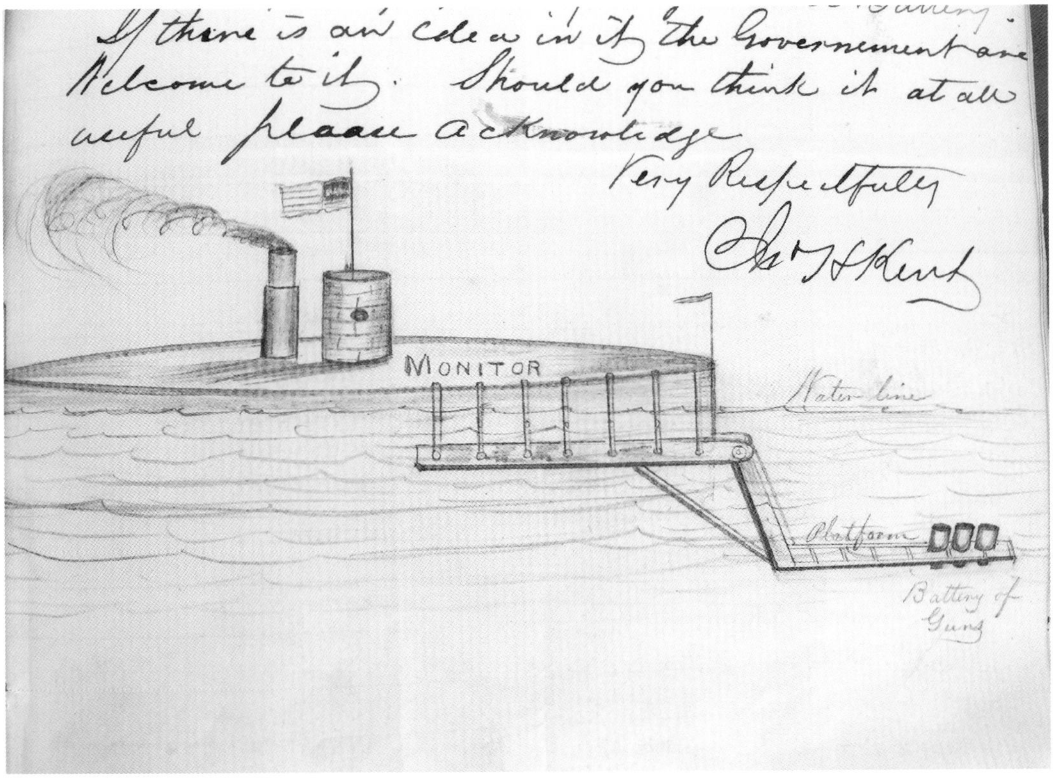
If there is an idea in it the Government are
Welcome to it. Should you think it at all
useful please acknowlidge
Very Respectfully
MONITOR
Water line
Platform
Battery of Guns

Fig. 129. Design for an underwater battery on a platform.

CHAPTER 12

An Engineer's View from the *Monitor*, May 14–June 30, 1862

Isaac Newton Jr. was born in New York City in 1837. He attended the Columbia College Grammar School at Hamilton College and then studied civil engineering at the University of the City of New York, earning his degree in 1856. Prior to the Civil War he worked at several ironworks and foundries, and later as an assistant engineer for two steamship lines.

In June 1861 Newton was commissioned a first assistant engineer in the Union navy and ordered to report to the USS Roanoke, *which was part of the blockade around Charleston. Aboard the* Roanoke *he served under chief engineer Alban Stimers. In November 1861 Newton was transferred to New York to assist in the construction of the* Monitor, *and in January 1862 he volunteered to serve as first assistant engineer aboard the ironclad.*

In August 1862 Newton became superintendent of construction for the Office of the General Inspector of Ironclads. He resigned from the navy in February 1865, and for the remainder of his career he held various appointments in the maritime and railway industries, as well as for the navy and the City of New York. Deep in debt, he died of an apparent suicide at the Century Club in New York City in 1884.

Newton's letters often reflected the frustrations of the men aboard the Monitor *during the summer months of 1862, when they saw little action and were confined below deck in sweltering heat.*[1] *In one letter written on June 18, 1862 (not reproduced here), Newton complained to a friend: "If any institution can twist and pervert the uses of a machine, that institution is the Navy Department or more properly in this case Commodore Goldsborough, to whom we are indebted for a month & more of* useless *misery cooped up in this vessel. The idea of the* Monitor *co-operating with the Army, in this river is simply* absurd."[2] *The following letters give a sense of life aboard the* Monitor *during that long, hot summer of 1862. We omitted words that Newton crossed out.*

U. S. S. *Monitor*
James River 12 Miles from
Richmond 14th May 1862

My dear Mother

I received your letter a day or so before we left Hampton Roads for the James River on our way to Richmond—

Last Thursday as you have probably heard by this time we in company with several wooden ship shelled the Fort on Sewalls point, this affair was a sort of exploring expedition on our part, the Merrimac kept up near the immense batteries on Craney Island.

I went in the pilot house during the Thursdays fight and happened to be looking in the direction of the turret when one of our guns was fired somewhat in the direction of the pilot house, the concussion was tremendous, some of the remnants of the powder got in one of my eyes making rather sore, so that I had to go around with a rag on it, however it is all right now—The next day Friday we went on a private reconoitering expedition, all alone in vicinity of Sewalls point, we hoped to entice the Merrimac out being alone but it was no go, she would not come, & of course red tape prevented us from going after her, we threw a couple of shell at the Fort where the rebel flag was still flying, in hopes that it would nettle them enough to make them venture down, but it did not; she was in a splendid place for us to fight her, the water was so shoal that it would prevent her from turning about while we could squirm about in every direction; however as I said before, we lost the chance because red tape tied our hands, we were quiet all day Saturday. The rebels blew up the Merrimac on Sunday morning at about five o'clock and at seven we started for Norfolk, reached there in about two hours, they had destroyed the Navy Yard, Dry Dock, &c, & all their steamboats—I should judge that not many of the regular inhabitants had left—

Troops were landed on Friday the day we made the reconnoitering expedition, the other side of the Rip Raps and reached Norfolk the next day at four o'clock P.M., just after the place had been evacuated by the Military.

Last Wednesday the Galena, Port Royal, & Aroostook went up the James River. Monday morning last at four in the morning we started after them accompanied by the Stevens trap,[3] when we passed a battery which fired this concern would run up under our lee to get out of harms way—at 11 o'clock we came up with the Iron clad Galena, Port Royal, & Aroostook all anchored at Jamestown about 40 miles up the river, after fooling for about four hours, the whole squadron started on up the river.

Just before we reached the Galena & co we saw two steamboats coming down the river full speed, they headed directly for us, we supposing they had designs upon us, loaded both guns with grape and pointed the turret to sweep their decks, on seeing our two big guns pointed towards them, they blew their whistles at a tremendous rate—They turned out to be flags of truce from Richmond with Union prisoners bound for Fort Monroe to be exchanged.

Fig. 130. Chief engineer Isaac Newton. (The Mariners' Museum, Newport News, Virginia)

We anchored Monday night about one mile below Fort Powhattan on the left bank of the river—The next morning at four started and found the Fort had been evacuated—we reached City Point at about 12 o'clock Tuesday afternoon, this place is called 45 miles from Richmond, there is a Rail Road to the latter place. At City Point white flags were flying in every direction, on our approach the RR warehouse containing about $25,000 worth of tobacco was set on fire, it belonged to a Bremen house,[4] the agent of it arrived just as our boat touched the wharf, he was in a terrible stew—Here we fooled away about four more hours of *valuable* time, old Rogers the Capt of the Galena,[5] went on shore to conciliate two common dirty white men & three or four yellow women—I forgot to remark that just before we arrived at City Point the two steamboats which we passed going down with prisoners, the Northampton & Curtis Peck, came up to us on their way up—That miserable old Rogers instead of detaining them & making them follow us, permitted them to go ahead full speed for Richmond, where of course they would arrive hours in advance of us—At last we started from City Point and after proceeding about twenty miles anchored again for the night, the next morning Wednesday started again at four and went ahead 'till 8 when the Galena got aground two miles below the obstructions and batteries at Wards Hill which is ten miles below Richmond—

May 16th The next morning Thursday we again got underweigh, we had not proceeded far before we saw the obstructions which consisted of about a dozen schooners, the *identical* steamboats which passed us with the flag of truce and the steam ships Yorktown and Jamestown sunk in the channel—we were now in close range of tremendous batteries planted on the bluff, of course if there had been no obstructions we would have sailed to Richmond in spite of all the batteries in the world—our Capt who is a military man saw at once the absolute folly of wasting powder & shell on these batteries because if they were silenced we having no force to occupy there, while the obstructions could be removed which would take a long time, it would avail us nothing—all this time a sharp fire of rifles was kept up at us from both banks of the river so that all hands had to keep below to avoid being picked off—However, at it we all went and fought for four hours nearly silencing the batteries at times by a well directed fire—Shortly before the action commenced the man who was at the lead on the Galena fell shot near the heart, by a Geurilla concealed in the bushes on the bank. The river is not *half* as wide as the river is at Albany.

The distance from the batteries was from 15 to 1700 yards 5 second fuze range—Every shot which struck that man trap the Galena went straight through, shortly before the action closed we thought a shell had penetrated her boiler and exploded it volumes of smoke poured on her port holes and the men were observed getting out of the ports from the side turned from the enemy, they got on the anchor and other places, they called out to us to come along side and take them off but it turned out that a shell had penetrated her side & burst inside, igniting a cartridge which was in the passing box carried by a powder boy, this created a dense smoke which we mistook for the bursting of her boiler—Shortly after this the Galena steamed out of the action, the rest of the vessels following.

It turned out just as we anticipated, that we could do nothing in way of proceeding to Richmond as long as the river was so thoroughly obstructed, without the assistance of a large land force to occupy the batteries after they had been silenced—

May 19 So we are now anchored at City Point about 45 miles below Richmond—The decks of the Galena was a frightful sight after the battle, brains, blood, arms & all portions of the human body were plastered about in every direction; some with shot through the body, some with half of their heads shot away, one shot carried away half of a guns crew—Most of those killed were killed outright and the wounded with but few exceptions were hurt but slightly—The number of killed was fourteen and the wounded about twenty, the powder boy who was carrying the cartridge which was set off by the explosion of a rifle shell was very badly burned, he was one of the Roanokes boys—It seems that wherever a shot struck her sides squarely it penetrated carrying fragments of her armor equal to the diameter the hole made by the ball, so that every shot which struck her was equal in effect to a shell exploding inside—The Monitor went up ahead of the Galena after she had anchored, but because we could not get elevation enough to the guns to reach the batteries which were on a bluff about 150 or 200 feet high we had to fall back to about 75 yards below her—

We were not struck very often, but those that did strike made severe dents but did no other damage, we were a mighty small mark to fire at and when struck no damage was done—Shot whistled over us incessantly for four hours—

The banks of the river after we got within three or four miles of the batteries were lined with sharpshooters, on hand to pick off men from the vessels, as I said before the river was not half as wide as the river at Albany is—This made it risky business to perambulate our decks much, one fellow annoyed the Captain very much during the action while he had his head out of the top of the turret by continually popping at him, he was so pertinaci[ou]s that one of the 11 inch was loaded with canister (1400 balls) and fired in the bush where he was concealed, that was [the last] that was seen of that rebel—

The voyage up the James River has in the main resembled a voyage into the interior of Africa more than any thing else I know off [of], nothing to be seen but nigger, nigger, nigger—The performanc[e]s of these darks was very amusing, they bowed, salaamed, waved handkerchiefs and made other demonstrations of delight, no doubt they suppose that their day of deliverance was at hand—The deliverance would probably consist of about one week away from the plantation and then hearty prayers for a speedy return to hog hominy and lolling about with scarcely anything to do—

We are now anchored opposite a most magnificent plantation, every thing looks bright and cheerful & no one would imagine that a great battle was about to commence within a few miles—

Remember me to all—It cannot be a great while before we will be at Fort Monroe, we cannot be wanted up here

I am quite well, but the Monitor is a mighty hot concern in warm weather—

Your aff son
I. Newton

"*Monitor*" City Point
June 30th 1862

My dear Mother,

I suppose you have seen the papers and read all the news about McClellan's retreat from the Chickahominy to the James River—

Last Thursday June 26th at about half past six the gunboats started on a bridge burning expedition up the Appottomox river which branches off to the left at City Point. The object was to burn a bridge over Swift creek, thereby destroying the Rail Road connection between Richmond & Petersburgh.

The plan of operations was, as follows, several vessels were to remain about City Point & blaze away indiscriminately about the country and on a given signal the warehouses & wharves at City Point were to be fired; the Appomatox or Appottomox river at 7 miles is divided by an island the left hand going to Petersburgh & the right goes by the mouth of this Swift creek where the [missing word?] was which was *to be* burned—Well one or two vessels were to go up the Petersburgh branch, while the bridge burning part[y] were to proceed up the left hand branch to the mouth of the creek at which place the small boats 10 in number were to be towed up by a steamboat of light draft as far as she could go, all the way to the bridge if possible, if not the small boats were to proceed alone—The boats which were to go up the Petersburgh branch were to blaze away indiscriminately also, (this was, that is the blazing away the only part throughly [*sic*] carried out)

Well now that I have told the plan, I will tell how it was carried out—as I said before the boats started at 6 P.M. Thursday June 26th—one or two of the boats got over the bar at the mouth of the river Apottomox without difficulty & proceeded up the river, but the inevitable Monitor (which was dragged along up this dirty shoal river, gracious only knows for what purpose expect to be stuck & abandoned) together with three gun boats got in a perfect mess on the bar, it was dark when we reached it, some were pointed one way & some another; the captains of each bawling out to one another. During this time, the vessels at City Point & the mixed up gunboats on the bar commenced the indiscriminate fire, some of them fired over our decks, nearly at one blowing one or two overboard. After squirming about on this bar about a couple of hours and getting aground two or three times, we got off & proceeded up the river, we went within about half a mile of the place where the river branches around the island and came to Anchor—The "Maratanza" went full speed up the Petersburgh side & plumped herself hard in the mud, the "Port Royal" tried to go up the Swift creek side where the bridge was and brought up on what they supposed to be rocks, but which turned out to be obstructions placed across the mouth—Thus ended the performance for the night, we would [have] gone back if the Maratanza could have been got off, but as she could not we had to wait—In the morning I had a good chance to see what sort of place we were in, it was a narrow river, a swamp on one and a high bank on the other with a fringe of trees a very good place for sharp shooters indeed; on top the bank was a house the inhabitants of which waved white rags, which I interpreted not so much a display of "Union" feeling as a desire that we would not put a shell through the house, they need apprehend nothing of the sort as long as they behave themselves—Between $5 and $6,000 worth of ammunition must have been fired away the night before in "indiscriminate firing"—We waited a good portion [of the] day for the Maratanza to get off so that we could all go down to City Point, it seems that the Maratanza got off early in the morning, but one of the small boats which were assisting got aground just as she came off, so this caused an additional delay—It was anticipated at one time that the Maratanza would have to be burned, for should a battery of field pieces and sharpshooters come from Petersburgh, as we expected every moment it would have been almost impossible to save her—On [the] next day Saturday June 28th in the afternoon, a tug boat came up from Fortress Monroe bringing despatches to the effect that General McClellan had met with a very extensive reverse and that he wanted the gun boats up the James River and the Chickahominy, immediately all the boats started for these two places, most of them the Monitor included going up the James River as far as Sturgeon town 25 miles *by the river,* here we anchored for the night, the next morning we were ordered to Turkey island about 6 miles above City Point, where it was reported part of McClellans army were expected every moment but they did not arrive, we saw the smoke of several explosions, which must have been caused by bridges &c being destroyed—Monday June 30 were ordered to go to City Point, on our way down we saw quite large parties of soldiers on the banks, many of them in bathing, poor fellows it was very refreshing to them after their hard march. They appeared to be in very good spirits indeed, calling out to us as we passed in a very familiar way, "Is that the Monitor," "How's your cheese" &c &c I heard one say, who must have been a New Yorker "I wish this was the East River" I have no doubt he did—At first we thought they were strglers [stragglers], or that the retreat had been very precipitate, but we afterwards ascertained this not to be the case; those we saw were probably part of the left wing of the army—July 1st Tuesday—Several transports with supplies have arrived from below.

I went on board the Canonicus the steamboat which used to run from Fall River to Newport & saw one of the Borden's sons who is captain,[6] he told me that he left the white house Saturday night at ½ past 10 & that we had succeeded in saving nearly all the Commissary stores, none of the provision vessels were lost; the captain of a coal schooner also told me pretty much the same thing—I have got confused by mistaking the day, on Monday afternoon that is yesterday, there must have been a large battle fought, the roar of artillery *was incessant* for nearly four hours, at first it was near but gradually receding, so we judged that the rebels had been driven back, we know none of the particulars, but I have heard that the loss was very heavy on both sides.

The gun boats opposite Turkey island partook in the battle, they threw shells at the extreme elevation of their guns—While I am now writing 3 P.M. the firing has commenced again and I very much fear the battle has commenced again; the roar of musketry was heard a short time since—I came below to avoid hearing it—I hope & pray that I may never hear the din of another battle, how they must have suffered, both the afternoon of yesterday and to day was sultry—The battle is probably caused by a division of the Army which protecting the retreat of the main army, however I have no idea how large a number are engaged, but there must have been a tremendous lot of artillery, yesterday the roar was incessant with scarcely a second of intermission—I suppose by this time the N. Y. papers are filled with details, we know nothing yet of details, all we know is that a large force came down one side of the "Pomonkey" (I believe thats the name) river, got in his rear cut off his communications and drove that portion, (about 18,000 I believe) of the army which had not crossed the Chickahominy, across, our army succeeded in destroying the bridges after them—You will remember not long ago Col Stewart[7] with a company of Calvary [cavalry] & artillery came down the same way & destroyed several provision boats; the rebels probably thus became aware that this was a week [*sic*] point—The universal opinion here is that Stanton is the man to blame, he is an enemy of McClellans & has to say the least *not* done all in his power to help him, his army was entirely to[o] small to contend with the overwhelming numbers the rebels have at Richmond—They, the rebels have at least 200,000 men, while McClellan has not had probably many more than 100,000—We have as I have said heard none of the details of the cause of the change of position of the army, it is a much better place to operate than they had before although farther off from Richmond, about 15 miles, but they avoid those extensive swamps they have had heretofore to contend with—

July 2d Wednesday I went on board the steamboat Express last night, I saw Lieut Harris, son of Senator H,[8] he has charge of all the ordinance stores & just arrived from White House; he told me the movement had been contemplated for some time, so he judged from the nature of the orders sent him from head quarters—the rebels obtained no supplies, those which could not be carried off were destroyed—Stonewall Jackson was killed in the fight the other side of the Chickahominy—In the battle of Monday we were rather worsted but yesterday the enemy were driven back with great slaughter, we could hear plainly the roll of the musketry—This morning a[t] ½ past 8 we started up the river from City Point and are now anchored about 6 or 7 miles above that place, we a[re] right opposite a wharf and plantation, the steamboat Delaware is here and has been taking on board some of the wounded, it has been a hard drizzly rain all the morning, the soldiers along the banks seem to take it as cool as possible, they are probably used to it by this time.

Gen McClellan slept on board the Galena last night, unquestionably he must have been nearly worn out with the work & anxiety of the last few days—His headquarters will probably be established at Harrison's House opposite Harrisons bar about 6 miles below City Point[9]—The army will now depend upon the James River as it did before on the York for supplies, it cannot securely be kept open as high as City Point, at least with the present number of gun boats—Now that so much depends upon this river two or three times as many gun boats as are now in it should be sent here, I sincerely hope they will be, but with such a man as Com Goldsborough in command of the squadron, it may be delayed too long, this man whose principal qualifications are immense size, big feet & the faculty of using neat, heavy round oaths when the occasion permits, is now I believe quietly rusticating on board the Minnesota in Norfolk harbor—

This gigantic man has the faculty of making members of congress & co believe that he possesses the "experience of the moderns & the wisdom of the ancients" combined and of swearing & bellowing to helpless subordinates and understrappers in a manner which scares them so that they scarcely know whether they are "afoot or horseback."

This is the man who has kept the Monitor of[f] here for nearly two months, notwithstanding the reports to him of the *absolutely necessary* repairs required, or that we were of no more use (nor half so much in fact) as a floating bethel,[10] since the fight at Fort Darling we have fired two (2) guns.

The richest incident happened this morning, Commander Rodgers (head man here now) sent orders to Capt Jeffers, for the Monitor to tow a couple of schooners over Harrison's bar, I regarded it as a very good joke, the idea of a concern like the Monitor towing schooners, it was probably from the fact that our [her?] speed is so *very very great* that the order was given; however we did *not* tow the schooners—It is believed on board here that the "*moral effect*" of the presence of the Monitor is the principal reason why we are kept here, if thats the case moral effect must be pretty well strewed along the river in these parts from the number of times we have passed up and down—One of these days if we keep on the moral effect will have to be towed about or stay in one place—One [On] the shore just opposite where we are anchored are a number of soldiers who must have strayed from their several regiments.

The steamboat Delaware took on board a number of sick and wounded—Just before the time arrived for us to go down the river a boat was sent on shore to take off any straglers who might be there; in a house a short distance from the shore three sick helpless soldiers were found, they were brought off, poor fellows, they had to be carried and seemed happy enough to be once more among friends under shelter. They were soaking wet it having rained hard all day long—Just as we were about leaving, we saw another soldier running towards the shore, a boat was sent & brought back three. They belonged to the 37th N.Y. & the 7th Michigan, the other was a boy about 15 who came on a visit to his brother & afterwards became cook to an officer—The Michigander informed us that in a house but a very little way back were a number of sick and wounded soldiers, in a shanty; however for some reason or other unknown to me we did not send after them, after we had proceeded a short distance farther down we espied two or three more soldiers in the bushes, we, so I understand understood [*sic*] them to say that, there was a train of wagons a short distance back, thereupon the three men we had taken off were sent on shore, in my opinion if they did not hurry mighty fast, they are by this time prisoners; the reason why these were landed is beyond my comprehension—

After we got down the river a short distance opposite the plantation of a rich old rebel named Carter,[11] this plantation is just on the bend of the river above City Point; well on the wharf nearly in front of his house we saw a large party [of] soldiers about a hundred in number many of them wounded, the steamboat Delaware was out in the middle of the river taking them off in small boats as this was a very slow process we got him to go along side the wharf, a farm wagon was sent off up the bank to bring down any wounded or sick in that direction.

I saw several wounded, hobbling along toward the boat, some were brought down in litters. For some reason or other, perhaps they saw or *thought* they saw the enemy, she started off, I saw two or three poor fellows running after her, I imagined how they must have felt.—A short distance below the dock in front of the Mansion, I saw a group of soldiers one in a litter or blanket together with Carter and several of his family, they waved but it was too late—I have no doubt but that Carter will give the wounded shelter—I have heard additional news of the battle of Monday & Tuesday (yesterday)[.][12] On Monday the rebels rather had the best of it, capturing nearly all our wounded, it is said that they approached our artillery, were mowed down like grass, would fill up the gap & continue the advance, be mowed down again, close up and keep on—The great gaps & alleys made in their lines we almost immediately filled up, but I believe the artillery was at last too much for them—In one case they attacked the position of Gen Robinson[13] three times, each time with entirely new bodies of men, but without success—Tuesday we beat them badly & drove them some distance—The slaughter was very great, but it stated that the rebels, I suppose on account of our artillery, lost two to our one—We are now anchored right opposite I think, the centre of the army, it looks like a city on shore, camp fires &c; it is about five or six miles below City Point, The place is called Harrison's and is the plantation on which President Harrison was born—The gun boats will now protect both flanks, so that

McClellan will only have one side to look out for—Reinforcements have arrived, some say 10,000, at any rate he *should be heavily reinforced immediately.* So had Gen Pope who has command of the combined armies of Banks, McDowell & Fremont. What a blessing to hear that that wretched blunderer Fremont has at last subsided—

Stanton is not a safe man, he is a bitter enemy of McClellan's and has interferred constantly with his plans—He was on board here when we were at Hampton Roads, I conversed with him, he wears spectacles and looks very much a Jew, a Chatham street Jew—Banks would make a good Secretary of War—Letters are a mighty scarce comodity with me now, to day I recd [received] two, one from you dated June 25th the other an envelope directed by Alice, enclosing a letter from Mr Stimers dated June 17th.

July 3d the shore for a long distance up and down last night looked like a large city—The hum of the camps can be heard on board here—Tell Harry that I am glad now he did not enter the Naval Academy, he can learn just as much were [*sic*] he is now, if *he only has a mind to,* he must pay particular to mathematics &c, must not pass over any thing without throughly [*sic*] understanding it—

I dont intend if I can help myself, to pass another summer penned up in this miserable manner, I had better stay at home and sit under the trees or in the grass; this makes two summers passed in this manner and I'm sick of it—

I suppose as soon as the Monitor is put out of commission I will be immediately bamboozled aboard of something else—Our cooking is now done principally on deck in an impromptu stove, sometimes in the furnaces of the boilers; the galley fizzled by setting the deck on fire sometime ago—This letter is intended to be kept *strictly within* the *family limits*—There is no war news whatever this morning.

There was a rumor at one time, that the enemy was advancing in force on the centre & both flanks, it turned out to be false, it was merely a sort of skirmishing parties, our gun boats threw a few shells at intervals this morning, toward the approach to the right flank. If McClellan has a few day[s] undisturbed he will again have his army in good condition, but he should immediately be heavily reinforced, he cannot be expected to make water run up hill—I heard the good news to day that Gen Buel with 50,000 men from Hallecks army was ordered to form a junction with Gen Pope, they must hurry up—The government must hurry up now is their chance, the rebels have concentrated every thing in Virginia whip them there and the jig is up—

Confound those silly expeditions on the coast, what do we want of Charleston & Savannah, we have more now than we can take care of.

So the Nashville is out again, great blockade, there must have been some old fossil in command—There may be a chance to send this in the morning so I'll close it up to night—

I wish you would send me the weekly Times, If you have any spare change and want something which will be good to keep, buy the "Rebellion Record" from the beginning—

We are now living on Salt Junk,[14] boiled about 8 hours, it can be got down—I am much better than I have been since we entered this river—I have within the past three days seen enough of the horrors of war to convince me that civilization is a humbug—Give my love to all, Remember me to Cally—Tell Harry he had better stick to his books during vacation, now's the time, if he don't learn he never will—

Your Aff son
I. Newton

CHAPTER 13

Repairing the *Monitor*

News Reports from October and November 1862

Most of the officers and crew were away from the Monitor *while she was undergoing repairs at the Washington Navy Yard in October and November 1862. As a consequence, newspaper reports are the best—and often most colorful—way to understand public awareness of the progress of repairs, including the perceptions of readers in the South.*

From the *Boston Evening Transcript*, October 3, 1862

THE WAR STEAMER MONITOR. This steamer, we see, is going up to the Washington Navy Yard for repairs, the Ironsides taking her place on James river,—but drawing too much water, probably, to go above City Point. The Monitor, we may as well say now, for it can do no harm, has her iron side plating shattered, if not in action, by use,—so that it is necessary for her, even thus early, in her life, to be repaired.

From the *Washington* (D.C.) *Evening Star*, October 3, 1862

THE "MONITOR" HERE.

As the fact has been stated in a Baltimore paper that the "Monitor" gunboat left Hampton Roads for this place on Monday last, there can be no harm in saying that she has arrived at the Navy Yard wharf, where she is an object of no little interest, just now. She was towed up the river for some distance by the tug Rescue, but steamed alone up the Eastern Branch. On the news of her arrival considerable stir was made by the employees of the yard, large numbers of them leaving their workshops to take a look at the "cheese box." The object of her coming up is that a few slight repairs may be made. She still bears the marks of her conflict with the Merrimac—dents being in her sides, but nowhere is she pierced. She came up along side of the wharf without difficulty.

From the Washington, D.C., *Daily National Intelligencer*, October 7, 1862

THE MONITOR continues to be the great object of attraction at the Navy Yard. It would save much trouble and annoyance, not only to the officers of the yard, but also to visiting parties themselves, if it were generally known that there is a positive order forbidding the landing of persons from small boats not only on the Monitor, but on the yard wharves. Quite a fleet of sail and row boats, including not a few steam-tugs, crowded with the curious, have sought a landing, but have, in every instance, been ordered away.

From the *Washington* (D.C.) *Evening Star*, October 8, 1862

NAVY DEPARTMENT. 7th Oct. 1862.

Passes will not be given to visit the Navy Yard during the time the "Monitor" is undergoing repairs. Upon the completion of the work upon that vessel, she will be thrown open to public inspection. Due notice of the time will be given.

From the Washington, D.C., *Daily National Intelligencer*, October 9, 1862

THE MONITOR has been visited within the past day or two by many distinguished officers, both of the army and navy. Among those whom we noticed were Rear Admiral Smith, Commodore Stribling, Brig Gen Whipple and Staff, and John Lenthall, Esq, Chief of the Bureau of Construction, Equipment, and Repair.[1] The Monitor now lies near the marine railway. Her hull, upon examination, is found to be in such good condition that it is now thought it will not be necessary to haul her out of the water in order to make the requisite repairs and improvements.

From the Washington, D.C., *Daily National Intelligencer*, October 11, 1862

It has been finally determined, in order to make assurance doubly sure that the hull of the Monitor is all right, to put that vessel upon the marine railway. She will therefore be hauled up this morning at high tide. Her two large guns (11-inch) have been placed in the centre of the yard.

From the *New York Evening Post*, October 14, 1862

A VISIT TO THE MONITOR.

. . .

WASHINGTON, October 11, 1862.

The Monitor has been here for five or six days, and is lying at the Navy Yard dock for repairs. It is pleasant to tread her deck and survey her almost impenetrable proportions. She bears the deep scars of twenty-five shots, but the heaviest have failed to penetrate half the thickness. In two places—one on each side, a ball struck her, splitting away two thicknesses of iron, and partially breaking the third. The outside is composed of five thicknesses of iron—then two feet of wood—after that another thickness of iron. The vessel does not look very large, but when we survey her we are struck forcibly with her formidable appearance. She draws about ten feet of water when ready for action.

At this time everything on board is in disorder—floors torn up, staterooms in confusion and showing the work of repair, which is going on very rapidly.

From the Monitor we went to various factories in the yard—the copper-rolling mill, anchor-factory, machine foundry and various other places, where our interest was enlisted in an intense degree.

In one of the buildings we saw the workmen moulding cannon balls; in another, drilling the cannon which have just been cast; in another, preparing cartridges, and so on through the whole yard.

From the *New York Times*, October 16, 1862

The *Monitor* was safely hauled upon the marine railway at the Washington Navy-yard on Monday. [L.] N. STODDER, sailing master of the *Monitor*, who has been on board of her ever since she left New-York, states that she has gone to Washington merely to have her boiler repaired. She is not injured at all in her frame or armor. She will be ready for sea in three weeks.

From the *Philadelphia Inquirer*, October 24, 1862

The United States war-steamer *Monitor*, now at the Washington Navy Yard, is to be made ready for active duty before the 1st prox. She has had the greater part of her defects remedied, her armor having hardly needed any repair. The ordnance officers are improving her battery, which will be very formidable. The *locale* of her next cruise is not known.

From the Washington, D.C., *Public Ledger*, October 24, 1862

The hull of the Monitor has undergone a thorough examination, and been found all right. The vessel has been scraped and painted, and she is now ready to be launched. Her machinery, both motive power and turret engines, will be put in complete order. Some improvements will be made in her interior for the comfort and convenience of her officers.

From the *Baltimore Sun*, October 27, 1862

The famous "Monitor" was successfully launched about noon today from the marine railway, at the navy yard. Various improvements—especially such as are conducive to more air and light in her interior—have been made. She will be fully prepared to hand [a nautical term for "haul"] within a few days. According to a recent official announcement from the Navy Department, the gates of the yard will be soon thrown open to visitors, to enable them to view this naval curiosity.

From the *Baltimore Sun*, October 28, 1862

The success with which the Monitor has been handled by our navy yard mechanics proves not only their capacity to execute well and promptly any work with which they may be entrusted by the authorities of the government, but also affords evidence of the enlarged facilities possessed by this important naval station for the rapid execution of any work which the wants of the service may require. It may be mentioned, as evidence of the skill and proficiency of our navy yard mechanics, that when the Monitor first came to the yard it was thought by the government authorities advisable to send to New York for an experienced iron boat builder (a foreman in Ericsson's establishment) to superintend the hauling up of the vessel, but when he got here, he found that there was really nothing to be done which the acting master carpenter (Talbert)[2] had not already done; and so he frankly admitted to the executive officer of the yard. The consequence was that he did not interfere in any manner with the arrangements for overhauling and improving the vessel—and the sequel has proved their entire sufficiency. . . .

Mr. Richard Carter, a watchman in the navy-yard, was drowned in the dock near the marine railway about nine o'clock last night. It is supposed that the deceased, in going his rounds, stumbled over one of the ropes used in launching the Monitor, and was precipitated into the dock. Mr. Carter was about 66 years of age, and formerly resided in Baltimore. He leaves an interesting family to deplore his sad fate. His body was recovered about then o'clock last night, and conveyed to his residence on I street south, near the navy-yard.

From the *Philadelphia Press*, October 30, 1862

FROM WASHINGTON,
Special Despatches to "The Press."

WASHINGTON, October 27, 1862. . . .

The Monitor was successfully launched yesterday, about noon, from the marine railway at the navy yard. . . . There are now about seventeen hundred mechanics and laborers employed in the yard, and great activity prevails. In some of the departments the employees are engaged both night and day.

From the *Washington* (D.C.) *Evening Star*, November 3, 1862

The Monitor is receiving her finishing touches, and will probably be ready for service this week. There will be no plates removed from her, as stated in a morning paper, as they are all sound. Some of the dents made by the Merrimac will, however, be straightened out.

From the *Philadelphia Inquirer*, November 3, 1862

The Monitor to be Open for Inspection on Thursday.

The stringent orders against admission at the Navy Yard will be removed about next Thursday, when the repairs to the *Monitor* will have been completed, and an opportunity will then be given to the public to witness this "cheesebox!" What alterations have been made in her is not intended to be made public, for fear the Rebels may be benefitted thereby, and we, consequently, refrain from mentioning it. Should the invention, however, work as well as the model, her triumph over *Merrimac, No. 2,* will be as certain and more decisive than that over *Merrimac, No. 1.*[3]

From the *Richmond Enquirer*, November 5, 1862

WASHINGTON, Tuesday. October 28, 1862.—

The Monitor now lies under the large shears at the navy yard to receive her heavy armament, &c. Passes to visit the yard will not, at present, be issued by the Navy Department under any circumstances. Nor will the Monitor be exhibited at the yard. So soon as she is placed in fighing [*sic*] trim, she will steam around to one of the city wharves, and there remain for a short time for public inspection.

From the *Milwaukee Sentinel,* November 7, 1862

The U.S. iron clad gunboat Monitor is to leave the Washington Navy Yard on Saturday for service. No one is allowed on board to see the nature of the alterations recently made in her.

From the *Washington* (D.C.) *Evening Star,* November 7, 1862

THE MONITOR UNDER INSPECTION.—Everybody went down to see the Monitor yesterday, per permission of the authorities, and the street railway folks had a time of it to accommodate the crowds moving Navy-Yard-ward through the afternoon. The little Monitor may have been a little astonished at the crowd thrown upon her so suddenly, but maintained a steady composure and presented an unvarying countenance of iron rigidity to all comers. Not a square inch of the "cheese-box" but was subjected to a forty-horse power force of inspection. Folks peeping up stairs and down stairs, into cannon muzzles, engine pits, pilot houses, shot holes, ventilation holes, and all sorts of holes, cracks and crevices; and there were "Peeping Toms" quite mean enough to take advantage of the embarrassments of the ladies in crossing the sieve-like deck and in ascending and descending the perpendicular ladders and gangways. But the ladies of Washington are rather famous for pretty ankles, and perhaps they didn't mind it.

And everybody inquired about everything of everybody, which gave an opportunity for some learned pundits, not exactly of the salt-water persuasion, but known amongst men as practical jokers, to run some saws upon those in quest of solid information: (and we regret to see that some of our contemporaries have been more or less taken in and done for thereby;) some of said saws being to the effect that the break-water recently placed about the pilot-house is a bran-new [*sic*] invention to catch the enemy's rifle balls and bullets; that the Monitor settles under water like a loon, on seeing the flash of the enemy's guns, to the discomfiture of said enemy; and that the recent "improvements" in the way of tall smoke stacks, tall ventilators, &c., will enable the Monitor to go into action with her decks ten feet under water; which, as the narrator informed his instructed and note-taking auditory, "would be a very important advantage."

Shall we insult out intelligent readers by telling them, for the fiftieth time, that the Monitor has a turret, that said turret revolves—has guns: that she is, moreover, an iron-clad, and has an engine: and that her crew are forced to "lay low and keep dark"! No, sir-ee. Bully for the Monitor!

From the Washington, D.C., *Daily National Republican*, November 7, 1862

Visiting the "Monitor."

Yesterday, a vast concourse of people, estimated at from five to six thousand, embraced the opportunity afforded by the Navy Department to visit the far-famed "Monitor." The crowd commenced entering the navy yard at one o'clock, and from that time until sunset a dense crowd was on the famous vessel all the time, though constantly changing.

The many objects of interest underwent the close scrutiny of all, particularly the ladies, a large number of whom were present, and took a lively interest in all that pertained to the "Cheese box."

Of course the greatest attention was paid to the round tower, which gave her the above name, and where the two black "dogs of war" are ready not only to "cry havoc," but when allowed to speak, "make havoc" with the objects of their wrath. We will not attempt a full description of an object which has been so often described by the press. The indentations made by the balls of the Merrimac, Minnesota and Fort Darling battery, are still visible on the plated iron turret, though it is covered to a thickness of 7 1/2 inches by eight thicknesses of wrought iron plating.

The places are marked by an engraving cut into the iron, designating the name of the vessel from which the shot came. On the turret were six impressions made by the Merrimac, two by the Minnesota, and one by the Fort Darling battery. On the larboard side of the vessel, just abaft the turret, was an indentation made by the prow of the Merrimac. This apparently did not effect as much as the shot, as the impression was only an inch deep, while on the bow, near the wheel house, the iron plating of the deck appears to have been penetrated by one of the Merrimac's shots. The wheel-house attracted a great deal of attention as being the scene of Lieut. Worden's wounding. This arranged just below the deck of the vessel, but as the man who steers must have his head above so as to see where his vessel is going, a heavily plated frame work is erected around him and his wheel, with crevices about three quarters of an inch in width left for him to take his observations. A heavy solid shot from the Merrimac broke one of the iron beams which support this house. In order to prevent the sharpshooters from injuring the pilot though his three quarter inch windows, a guard of plated iron has been securely fastened to the sloping sides of the wheel-house and turned up at right angles with those sides, thus catching any bullet or rifle ball which may be aimed at the windows of the wheel-house. This arrangement, we learn, has been affixed since the Monitor arrived at the yard. Several parts of the wheel-house bear evidences of the force of the Merrimac's shot.

The anchor and its steam-hoisting apparatus is below deck; so, also, is the propeller, which is aft and inside of the vessel, so that none of her motive power can be seen or reached by shot or shell.

The two guns in the turret are formidable monsters and attracted the greatest attention. The interior of the turret was visited. The machinery by which it is revolved is out of sight. The guns are placed on a track, and, as soon as discharged, they are run back to be reloaded. At the same time a heavy, plated beam drops down, thus effectually closing the port-holes. The guns are managed by sixteen men, each man having a particular work assigned him.

Below the deck are the accommodations for the inhabitants of this truly wonderful craft. They actually live below the surface of the water, as the vessel is only about fifteen inches above water. Here are the dining-room, kitchen, engineer's room, officers' quarters, sleeping bunks, &c.

When ready for service, the vessel carries only sixty men, including officers, engineers, gunners, sailors, servants, &c. She is now nearly ready for her next trip, and will sail in a day or two.

From the Washington, D.C., *Daily National Intelligencer*, November 8, 1862

THE MONITOR.—This invulnerable craft, to see which all the city flocked to the Navy Yard on Thursday, is getting on board her supplies, and will depart at an early day to make her mark somewhere.

From the *Alexandria* (Va.) *Gazette*, November 8, 1862

Yesterday, among the visitors to the Washington Navy Yard, was a man named R.P. Compton, said to be a clerk in one of the departments, but who gave his name as Smith, who, after he had been on board, went into one of the offices at the yard, and stated that he was a Southern man; that the South would be successful; and as for the Monitor, she was a d—d humbug. He was arrested and put in irons in the guardhouse, but he will likely be transferred to the Old Capitol.

From the *Hartford* (Conn.) *Daily Courant*, November 10, 1862

From Washington,
WASHINGTON, Nov. 9.—The Monitor left Washington Navy Yard last evening, and passed down the Potomac river.

From the Washington, D.C., *Daily National Republican*, November 10, 1862

THE MONITOR.—Those of our readers who visited this famous vessel last week, still retain a vivid picture of the wonderful capacity for the purpose designed by her constructor. Many would like to keep a memento of that visit. To such we would say that a spirited picture of the great naval engagement between the Monitor and Merrimac, has been published by Mr. S. C. A. Lotridge, which not only exhibits the two vessels with life-like accuracy, but gives at one view the Minnesota, the Congress and the Cumberland, with the rebel steamers Jamestown and Yorktown. As a border to the centre picture there are accurate representations of the internal arrangements of the Monitor, such as the engine room, wheel-house, ward room, berth deck, captain's cabin, interior of tower, and turret machinery, with a portrait of Ericsson, the builder. For sale at the bookstores in this city. Everybody ought to have a copy.

From the *Springfield* (Mass.) *Republican*, November 15, 1862

We have received from I.A. Heald a piece of the turret of the Monitor, taken from the part that was cracked by the striking of two balls. In repairing the Monitor at the Washington navy yard, one plate was taken off and cut up for relics, and it is one of these consecrated bits that we have before us.

From the *Richmond Examiner*, November 18, 1862

ADDITIONAL FROM THE NORTH.
MATTERS AND THINGS IN AND AROUND WASHINGTON

The Northern papers are filled with thousands of rumours of matters and things in and about the Yankee Capital. W[e] group together some of the most interesting extracts of their Washington correspondence . . .

The Monitor this afternoon is the great object of attraction. The gates of the navy yard are thrown open to the public, in order that all may gratify their curiosity by an inspection of this wonderful specimen of naval architecture. From one o'clock up to the present writing a continuous tide of people has been flowing eastward. The cars are literally jammed and the sidewalks crowded.

From the New Haven, Conn., *Columbian Register*, November 22, 1862

[From a soldier of the 15th Connecticut Volunteers]

During my stay [in Alexandria, Virginia], a large crowd assembled at the river front to see the Monitor pass by on her way to Fortress Monroe.— This "first of the iron clads" has been thoroughly repaired at the Washington Navy Yard, and has had some important improvements added, which it is said will add greatly to her efficiency, and is now returning to her post perhaps to try the vulnerability of Merrimac no. 2, or to protect the Northern cities from the formidable rebel rams which ex-Secretary [of War Simon] Cameron warns us of, as being built under the aid of *perfide Albion.* In either case, let us hope she may prove as before, invincible.

CHAPTER 14

Two Surgeons Observe the *Monitor*'s Final Moments

December 30, 1862, to January 11, 1863

Samuel Gilbert Webber was born in Boston in 1838. The son of a carpenter, he graduated from Harvard with a bachelor's degree in 1860. Two years later Webber joined the Union navy as an assistant surgeon, serving aboard the receiving ship Ohio *in 1862 and then on the* Rhode Island *in December 1862. He later served aboard the Passaic class monitor* Nahant, *resigning from the Navy in the spring of 1865. Following the war Webber received a medical degree from Harvard in 1865. He worked at the Boston City Hospital and was an instructor in nervous diseases at the Harvard Medical School until 1885. He was appointed a member of the faculty of the Tufts College Medical School about 1893, not retiring until 1917. He died nine years later, in 1926.*

Webber was aboard the Rhode Island *on December 31, 1862, as it towed the USS* Monitor *around Cape Hatteras. The letter that follows, which was written to Webber's future wife, Nannie (they would be married in 1864), describes the dangers faced by the* Rhode Island*'s crew the night the* Monitor *sank as well as Webber's interactions with the* Monitor *boys. Webber would amputate three of surgeon Grenville Weeks's fingers after they were smashed during his escape from the sinking vessel. In a subsequent letter (not reproduced here), Webber would tell Nannie of the admiration he had developed for Weeks: "My darling, I feel quite attached to Dr. Weeks. He has been so patient, so uncomplaining altho he has suffered much. He last night, in his sleep, groaned & moaned. I gave him considerable laudanum. To night he is sleeping quietly without the help of opim [*sic*]. I trust his fingers will not trouble him much."*[1]

Samuel Gilbert Webber to Nannie Sturtevant, December 30–January 4, 1862[2]

No 5

U.S. Str. Rhode Island
At Sea, December 30, 1862

My own, dear, prescious [*sic*] darling,

I suppose I may now tell you about our company. I did not in my last say any thing about who of us were going because I did not wish to worry you and make you feel too anxious, tho' I fear that the last part of my letter would have that tendency. That however was only doing something I have long tho't of doing. Another reason for not writing was that I did not wish that any one should have the least shaddow for saying that I had told anything to anybody which would have, even if known, any tendency to help the rebels. Rather particular perhaps; but that is the way I felt and these are the reasons I had for not telling you that yesterday afternoon the State of Georgia sailed from Hampton Roads having the monitor Pasaic in tow. About two hours after we left having the original Monitor in tow. I understand that at least one more monitor is coming after us, the Montauk, I suppose. It looks also as tho' the iron clad Galena was coming. The Colerado will probably sail before long and join us somewhere south. That will make about eight vessels, four of them iron clad. To be sure I am not certain that all these will join the expedition.

But where are we going? I dont know. There is a passenger on board for one of the vessels off Wilmington N.C. This has given rise to a rumor that we are going there. I rather doubt it. Some think Charleston, some Mobile is our stopping place. The truth is no one, unless perhaps the Capt., knows.

It looks rather dark in the horizon & the ship may put in at Hateras Inlet for the benefit of the Monitor. The M. is part of the time covered with water forward. The spray dashes almost as high as the turret.

My poor head feels the effects of the motion. It is heavy & my eyes do not feel perfectly right. I guess I read a little too long last night. Well I must rest them for a while to pay for it. I have not read much today.

Last night I lay thinking. I tho't to myself about death. I asked myself whether I was prepared to die. I questioned as to whether I was really a Christian. For a few minutes I felt rather singular. I could not very easily describe my feeling. I certainly did not relish the idea of death. Apart from leaving you, I did not feel as tho' I was fully ready. Yet after praying I think I felt easier & more willing to leave all with God. Now I feel quiet & less concerned. But am I a Christian? I asked myself that question. Should I not be more desirous of leading others to Jesus if I was? Should I not be more faithful. Such tho'ts came to my mind. I know I might be much more faithful. I dont want to make faith in Christ an excuse for doing nothing.

Darling, xxx you shall have this by & by. Pray for me. Oh, Nannie dear I have not been what I ought to have. I have done nothing. I seem to myself almost fast asleep in regard to religion. More at another time.

Wednesday Dec. 31st 1862. The last day of the year my dear Nannie, finds me safe & in health, except a *slight* heaviness of the head caused by the rough weather. Would that I could say the same of all. The Monitor has fought her last battle, fired her last gun, she is now, probably, resting quietly on the bottom somewhere near "frying pan shoals." Yesterday we made very good time & near sundown the State of Georgia & Pasaic were in sight also a steamer with a large sailing boat in tow. Cape Hateras light was passed in the afternoon. We were stearing for Beaufort. Cant write, too much motion.

New Years Day 1863. A happy new year to my own darling.

Before I do anything else, my Nannie, would like to know what I have done & what has been done during the last day or two. To begin where I left off. Night before last we were stearing for Beaufort. About 8 o'clk I was on deck & could see the waves dash over the Monitor. The spray flew about in front of the lantern which was on the turret. I have learned since that it washed over into the turret, sometimes almost a perfect stream of water. About 11 o'clk, I was awaked by noises overhead & at length heard a boy tell Mr. Field, who rooms next to me, that the Monitor was making signals of distress. Shortly after I learned that boats were to be sent off to her. I tho't I'd dress as some one might be injured. I then tho't that perhaps the Monitor would be poking her nose through the side of the vessel into my state room. Then it would not be pleasant to be in my room. I went on deck. To make matters short. Our boats were taking the crew off the Monitor. It seems that after the capt found the water was really gaining on the pumps, one of which threw 2000 to 3000 galls. per minute he signaled to us. Where so much water came from no one seemed to know, they think that she sprung a leak. There were many narrow escapes. One boat was caught between the Monitor & R.I. crushed a little, afterwards while hoisting it on board it was crushed much more. I saw one man washed overboard from the M. One man, the Surgeon, Dr. Weeks, had his hand caught by the fingers. Three of them were injured. Yesterday I shortened the bone and dressed them. It took rather longer than I tho't for, 1 ½ hours, & as I worked in the ward room, having Dr. W. on the table, dinner was delayed. He talked very much, & was very comical. We all had to laugh heartily. Last night I was with him a good deal. I began to brush back his hair from his eyes. He said, "That's right, play the woman for the present." I had the advantage of my practice with you during the last 7 months. Dr. W. gets along very well, excepting that he is weak & therefor sea sick. To return.—Our boats took off all the men on the M. except 16. One of our boats was along side of the Monitor, or near to her when we lost sight of her. I suppose there is no doubt that she sank. 8 of our men were in the boat. Yesterday we steamed around as near the spot as we could but no boat was seen. Mr. Brown[3] was in charge of the boat. He is a good officer and a fine boatman. We hope he has been picked up. He was rather in the track[4] of vessels & yesterday a great many were in sight. If he is lost 24 men have perished. I am surprised that so few were injured & none lost while tra[n]sferring them to our vessel. I have never seen a strong healthy man so exhausted as the Capt. & the Act Master were. Some of the men were too. The Capt. Commander Bankhead, The Lieut. Green, Act Master Stoddard, the paymaster, Senior engineer & one third asst. Engineer were saved. Four officers are not yet heard from. Once, the Monitor struck us two or three times, the wheel was caught on the center so that for a few seconds it would not move. No material injury was done to us. It is fortunate that we were able to save so many. We ought to be thankful & grateful that it is no worse. There was really some danger lest we should be seriously injured by the M. So far however we are safe. Will this loss break up the expedition? Is the Pasiac still floating? We are anxious to know. To day we have spoken a number of vessels & boarded one. We are 15–18 miles from Wilmington. I am nearly used to the motion. Now my head is a little uncomfortable, so that I cant go into exstacies about love &c. I could tell you what I want to say much better than to write it. The officers of the M. are nearly destitute. The Capt has one of my overcoats. Mr. Stoddard another. Dr. Weeks has my boots & shirt & drawers. I suppose I may in the confusion lose a little; but not much. I wished yesterday that you had been here to soothe Dr. W. To pass your hand across his forehead &c. He has a wife. He lost his cap & for a while I gave him the cap you knit me. He had some of your cakes to eat yesterday, I told him the same young lady made both & then showed him your photo. He said he liked the expression you seemed to be listening sympathetically to what I was saying. My dear darling, my own Nannie xxxx. By the way, I put your photo & letters in my pocket when I went on deck night before last. Whenever I think there is danger I secure them. Dr. W. saved his wife's letters. Enough now, perhaps I shall send this before long, If I can will write again. I have written an account to father. Possibly rather more connected than this; but about the same.

You may continue to send to Hampton Roads. My regards to all. Give Ada "all the love I have to spare" & what is left to the others, especially to Sadie.

As for yourself you may take all the love & xxx you wish & desire from your own Gilbert.

Friday Jan. 2d 1863. My own darling, I was in no condition yesterday to do much more than state facts. I was slightly unwell & now I have a headache. I was deprived of sleep one night & part of another, which with anxiety took away my appetite & made me a little feverish. My headache I thing [think] is partly from the same cause & partly from the motion of the vessel. The motion was a good deal. Yesterday we reached Wilmington. There were three blockading vessels there. We were ordered to Beaufort & are on our way thither.

Darling, I send you one part of an almond. I keep one part myself. When I came across it at the table I immediately wished to philopoene[5] with you. Then I tho't of sending it in a letter. Now, darling, I propose that we eat them on the 9th January some time during evening. I think you will have received this by that time.

Shall I receive letters at Beaufort? I hope there have been some sent from Fortress Munroe for me. If not I must wait. I am getting to be less impatient & better satisfied with simply thinking of you. Yet when I dont get a letter I expect I must say I am somewhat disappointed. I shall try to write you as often as I can so as not to disappoint you.

I amused myself this morning thinking how I might be able to surprise you when I return. I can imagine how you would meet me—with xxx & a hug, *so* long & *so* hard. Take some now from your Gilbert.

My dear Nannie. We are at Beaufort. I expect letters from you. That will be good. Yes, dearest, a letter from you. I feel better than I did. Less headache, shall send this as soon as possible. I was reading Essays of Elia[6] on Dec. 30 or 31st & came across one on New Years Eve. They were written by Lamb. You might find pleasure & possibly profit in reading them. He says "the birth of a New Year is of an interest too wide to be pretermitted by king or cobbler. No one ever regarded the first of January with indifference. It is that from wh. all date their time and count upon what is left."[7] There is much more wh. I wish I could quote for you. Darling, my dear, I want to write you more about the New Year. Dearest one, my own, I want you to write me about the past & present. One of your nice letters. My dear one, I suppose you have done so. xxx love & all that lovers desire your Gilbert sends to his darling Nannie.

Sun Jan 4, Received No. 4. wh. was written Dec. 24 & mailed Dec. 31 yesterday. We are at Hampton Roads again. Have writt[en] more wh. will send soon as another letter. God bless my darling to day. xxx your own Gilbert sends this.

Grenville Weeks to Antoinette Nicklis, January 11, 1862

One of the sixteen sailors to drown aboard the Monitor *was a twenty-one-year-old tailor's son from Buffalo, New York, named Jacob Nicklis. Nicklis had joined the crew of the* Monitor *on November 7, when the ship was at the Washington Navy Yard for repairs. Standing five feet, seven and a half inches tall, with gray eyes, light hair, and a ruddy complexion, Nicklis was not exactly pleased with the prospect of serving on this famous vessel. He had five years' experience aboard other ships, having served in the navy since he was sixteen years old. Upon first seeing the* Monitor, *he expressed some disappointment "on account of her accomodations," which, he wrote, "are very poor." After he'd had a chance to begin recovering from his own injuries, the* Monitor's *surgeon, Grenville Weeks dictated a brief but touching letter to Nicklis's sister informing her of her brother's death.*[8]

New York Jan 11th 1862

To Miss Antoinette Nicklis

I am too unwell to dictate more than a short sad answer to your note. Your brother went down with other brave souls, & only a good Providence prevented my accompanying him. You have my warm sympathies, & the assurance that yr brother did his duty well, & has I believe gone to a brighter world, where storms do not come. I remain

Yours most truly
G.M. Weeks
Late Surgeon
U.S. Str "Monitor"

Appendix

Specifications of the *Merrimack* and *Virginia* Before and After Conversion

The USS *Merrimack*, before conversion

Tonnage	3,200 tons
Length	305 feet
Beam	51 feet, 4 inches
Draft	23 feet (average)
Speed	9 knots (average)
Engines	Two horizontal, back acting; two cylinders; 72 inches in diameter, 3-foot stroke
Armor	None
Armament	Fourteen 8-inch smoothbore guns of 63 cwt Two 10-inch smoothbore guns Twenty-four IX-inch Dahlgren smoothbore guns
Complement	519

The CSS *Virginia*, after conversion

Tonnage	3,200 tons
Length	262 feet, 9 inches
Beam	51 feet, 4 inches
Draft	22 feet (average)
Speed	4–5 knots
Engines	Two horizontal, back acting; two cylinders; 72 inches in diameter, 3-foot stroke
Armor	4-inch iron plate (on the casemate)
Armament	Two 6.4-inch Brooke rifled cannon Two 7-inch Brooke rifled cannon Six IX-inch Dahlgren smoothbore guns (two modified for hot shot) Two 12-pounder howitzers on deck 1,500-pound cast-iron ram
Complement	320

Source: Sumner Bradford Besse, *C.S. Ironclad Virginia and U.S. Ironclad Monitor* (Newport News, Va.: The Mariners' Museum, 1996), 7–8.

Fig. 131. Not only was the *Monitor* the greatest invention of the Civil War, but it also featured more than three dozen patentable inventions, including the first-ever below-the-waterline flushing toilets. This image, created by Walt Taylor in 2013 for The Mariners' Museum, humorously depicts Abraham Lincoln having the experience of surgeon Daniel Logue, who accidentally turned this underwater toilet's valves in the wrong sequence, thus creating the world's first below-the-waterline bidet. While Lincoln visited the *Monitor* twice in 1862, his personal reaction to these subaquatic commodes remains a mystery. (The Mariners' Museum, Newport News, Virginia)

Notes

Abbreviations

Berent Papers	Irwin M. Berent Papers (MS164), TMM.
Geer Papers	George S. Geer Papers, 1862–1866 (MS10), TMM.
Logbook of the USS *Monitor*	Photostat copy of the Logbook of the *Monitor*, March–September 1862, The Mariners' Museum Library. The original is held in Record Group 45 (Naval Records Collection of the Office of Naval Records and Library), entry 392 (Journals and Diaries of Officers of the US Navy), National Archives and Records Administration, Washington, D.C.
NARA	National Archives and Records Administration, Washington, D.C.
Newton Papers	Isaac Newton Papers (MS13), The Mariners' Museum Library, Newport News, Va.
Nicklis Papers	Jacob Nicklis Papers, 1862 (MS363), The Mariners' Museum Library, Newport News, Va.
ORN	*Official Records of the Union and Confederate Navies in the War of the Rebellion.* Washington, D.C.: Naval War Records Office, 1894–1922.
RG 45	Record Group 45 (Naval Records Collection of the Office of Naval Records and Library), National Archives and Records Administration, Washington, D.C.
TMM	The Mariners' Museum Library, Newport News, Va.

Introduction

1. Edward M. Miller, *U.S.S. Monitor: The Ship That Launched a Modern Navy* (Annapolis, Md.: Leeward Publications, 1978), 1, 109.

1. The Origins of the CSS *Virginia*

1. *Journal of the Congress of the Confederate States of America, 1861–1865,* 7 vols. (Washington, D.C.: Government Printing Office, 1904–1905), 1:7.

2. William Merrick Bristol, "Escape From Charleston," *American Heritage* 26 (April 1975): 24–27, 82–88.

3. Abraham Lincoln, "Proclamation Calling Militia and Convening Congress," in Roy P. Basler, et al., eds., *The Collected Works of Abraham Lincoln,* 9 vols. (New Brunswick, N.J.: Rutgers Univ. Press, 1953), 4:331–33.

4. Edward McPherson, *The Political History of the United States of America During the Great Rebellion* (Washington, D.C.: James J. Chapman, 1882), 114.

5. Ibid., 149.

6. Bern Anderson, *By Sea and By River: The Naval History of the Civil War* (New York: Da Capo Press, 1962), 3–4.

7. *Harper's Weekly,* August 31, 1861.

8. Anderson, *By Sea and By River,* 4–5.

9. Donald Canney, *Lincoln's Navy: The Ships, Men and Organization, 1861–1865* (London: Conway Maritime Press, 1998), 17.

10. ORN, ser. 2, vol. 2, p. 51.

11. *Civil War Naval Chronology: 1861–1865* (1961–66; repr., Washington, D.C.: Naval History Division, 1971), 11.

12. Michael J. Bennett, *Union Jacks: Yankee Sailors in the Civil War* (Chapel Hill: Univ. of North Carolina Press, 2004), 163–64.

13. ORN, ser. 2, vol. 4, pp. 274–76.

14. Ibid., 276–80.

15. John V. Quarstein, *A History of Ironclads: The Power of Iron Over Wood* (Charleston: History Press, 2007), 67.

16. General J. Watts De Peyster, "A Military Memoir of William Mahone, Major-General in the Confederate Army," in *Historical Magazine: And Notes and Queries Concerning the Antiquities, History, and Biography of America, Volume II. Second Series* (Morrisania, N.Y.: Henry B. Dawson, 1870), 393.

17. ORN, ser. 1, vol. 4, pp. 288–98.

18. Ibid. From the French term *rasée,* which means "to shave close."

19. Daniel O'Connor, "Muzzle to Muzzle with the *Merrimack,*" *Civil War Times* 35 (June 1996): 22.

20. Gideon Welles, "Retrospective, March 6, 1861–July 1862," in William E. Gienapp and Erica L. Gienapp, eds., *The Civil War Diary of Gideon Welles, Lincoln's Secretary of the Navy: The Original Manuscript Edition* (Urbana: Univ. of Illinois Press, 2014), 665.

21. *New York Times,* May 23, 1869.

22. Senate Report 37, 37th Cong., 2nd sess., pp. 4–5 (April 18, 1862); Horace Greeley, *The American Conflict: A History of the Great Rebellion in the United States of America, 1860–'64,* 2 vols. (Hartford: O. D. Case, 1865), 1:477.

23. Welles, "Retrospective," 670–71. For Welles's full response (probably read at a cabinet meeting), see the manuscript draft "Remarks on Statement of John Parker Hale, Chairman of the Committee on Naval Affairs in the Investigation into the Destruction of the Navy Yard at Norfolk, Va., April 20, 1861," Gideon Welles Papers, Huntington Library, San Marino, Calif.

24. Quoted in the *New York Times,* May 5, 1861, from an article in the *Baltimore Exchange,* April 30, 1861.

25. *Richmond Daily Dispatch,* June 1, 1861. Brothers Barnabas and Joseph were not Confederate sympathizers, however. They were from Massachusetts and pro-Union. Unable to leave Norfolk before Virginia's secession, they were coerced into doing the job—though they were handsomely paid. Another member of their crew, Ebenezer Morgan Stoddard, was captured by Union forces the following day while salvaging a vessel on behalf of the B & O Railroad. He declared his loyalty to the Union, was allowed to proceed north, and immediately enlisted in the U.S. Navy, where he served as acting master of the USS *Kearsarge.* His firm may have raised the *Merrimack,* but he helped to take down the *Alabama.* For more information, see Anna Holloway, "Some Thoughts on Following a Dead Man," http://monitorkitty.com/?p=706 (accessed February 14, 2017).

26. John W. H. Porter, *A Record of Events in Norfolk County, Virginia, From April 19th, 1861 to May 10th, 1862* (1892; repr., Portsmouth, Va.: Edwards Brothers, 1996), 332.

27. ORN, ser. 2, vol. 2, p. 51.

28. George M. Brooke Jr., ed., *Ironclads and Big Guns of the Confederacy: The Journals and Letters of John M. Brooke* (Columbia: Univ. of South Carolina Press, 2002), 22, 25.

29. John L. Porter, "The Plan and Construction of the 'Merrimac,'" in *Battles and Leaders of the Civil War,* 4 vols. (New York: Century, 1884–1887), 1:717.

30. Sumner Besse, *C.S. Ironclad Virginia and U.S. Ironclad Monitor: With Data and References for Scale Models* (Newport News, Va.: The Mariners' Museum, 1996), 26–27.

31. John V. Quarstein, *C.S.S. Virginia: Mistress of Hampton Roads,* 2nd ed. (Appomattox, Va.: H. E. Howard, 2000), 37.

32. Brooke, *Ironclads and Big Guns,* 44.

33. William Norris, *The Story of the Confederate States' Ship "Virginia." (Once Merrimac.) Her Victory over the Monitor. Born March 7th. Died May 10th, 1862.* (Baltimore: John B. Piet, 1879), 21.

34. John Gross Barnard, *Notes on Sea-Coast Defense* (New York: D. Van Nostrand, 1861), 60.

35. John Mercer Brooke, *The Virginia, or Mer-*

rimac; Her Real Projector (Richmond, Va.: William Ellis Jones, 1891), 18.

36. Ibid.

37. Ibid., 70.

38. John Luke Porter, "Merrimac Gun Deck" and "U.S.S. Merrimac, June 1861 & 2," both in Collection of Battle of Hampton Roads Ships Plans (MS555), TMM.

39. The gun marked "Trophy No. 1," on display at The Mariners' Museum, was one of the *Virginia*'s IX-inch Dahlgrens. It clearly displays marks consistent with Tredegar.

40. Stephen Mallory, quoted in Brooke, *Ironclads and Big Guns*, 224.

41. A wheel that is believed to be the steering wheel of the *Virginia* is on display in the USS *Monitor* Center at The Mariners' Museum.

42. Craig Symonds, *Confederate Admiral: The Life and Wars of Franklin Buchanan* (Annapolis, Md.: Naval Institute Press, 1999), 137–38.

43. Quarstein, *CSS Virginia*, 67, 282. According to his service records, Walling joined Kevill's unit on April 19, 1861. He was detailed as a diver, however, "for benefit of [the] Confederate Government." See Porter, *A Record of Events*, 296–97; NARA microfilm M324 (Compiled Service Records of Confederate Soldiers), roll 869.

44. Chandra Manning, *Troubled Refuge: Struggling for Freedom in the Civil War* (New York: Knopf, 2016), 54; Owen Easley, "Library Gets Civil War Espionage Proof: Black Woman Gave Naval Secrets," *Virginian-Pilot and the Ledger Star*, July 2–3, 1982.

2. "The Navy Department Will Receive Offers . . ."

1. *New York Times*, August 15, 1861. The National Archives also holds the receipts for payment to run the ad in the Boston *Saturday Evening Gazette*, the *Boston Daily Journal*, the *Boston Daily Advertiser*, the *Providence Journal*, the *New York Commercial Advertiser*, the *Morning Courier and New York Enquirer*, the *New York Times*, the New York *Sunday Mercury*, the *Philadelphia Daily News*, the *Philadelphia Evening Journal*, the Philadelphia *North American*, the *Baltimore Clipper*, the *Baltimore Patriot*, the Washington *National Republican*, and the *Washington National Intelligencer*. See RG 45, entry 502 (Subject File, 1775–1910), AC (Construction), box 22, folder 2.

2. Donald L. Canney, *The Old Steam Navy, Volume Two: The Ironclads, 1842–1885* (Annapolis, Md.: Naval Institute Press, 1993), 8. Lenthall, like many, believed that the war would be over long before such vessels could even be completed. Union fortunes at Bull Run in July 1861 would alter that opinion significantly.

3. Horace Greeley, *The American Conflict: A History of the Great Rebellion in the United States of America, 1860–'64*, 2 vols. (Hartford: O. D. Case, 1865), 1:475–77.

4. Robert J. Schneller Jr., "'A State of War is a Most Unfavorable Period For Experiments': John Dahlgren and U.S. Naval Ordnance Innovation During the American Civil War," *International Journal of Naval History* 2 (December 2003) (published online).

5. Charles H. Davis, *Life of Charles Henry Davis, Rear Admiral, 1807–1877, By His Son* (Boston: Houghton, Mifflin, 1899), 4–9.

6. See *New York Times*, March 23, 1862. (The question mark in the quotation is McKay's.)

7. Renwick would best be known for his "thermostatic incubator," which revolutionized the poultry industry in 1884. See Edward Sabine Renwick, *The Thermostatic Incubator: Its Construction and Management, Together with Descriptions of Brooders, Nurseries, and the Mode of Raising Chickens by Hand* ([New York:] privately printed, 1884).

8. For some of the designs that came in, see David J. Gerleman, "Will That Thing Work?," *Civil War Times* 54 (February 2015): 46–51. For designs submitted after the Battle of Hampton Roads, see chapter 11.

9. Though rejected in 1861, the plans for this vessel were revised, and the result was the USS *Keokuk*, a hunchbacked ironclad with two stationary gun platforms. The *Keokuk* was commissioned in December 1862. See Canney, *Old Steam Navy*, 2:11.

10. Ibid., 15; *Abridgment . . . Containing the Annual Message of the President of the United States to the Two Houses of Congress . . . with Reports of Departments and Selections from Accompanying Papers* (Washington, D.C.: U.S. Congress, 1861), 1:748–52.

11. For a detailed explanation of the *Galena*'s armor, see Canney, *Old Steam Navy,* 2:20–25.

12. *Record of Service of Connecticut Men in the Army and Navy of the United States during the War of the Rebellion* (Hartford: Case, Lockwood and Brainard, 1889), 958; discharge papers reprinted in *The Story of the Monitor* (New Haven: Cornelius S. Bushnell National Memorial Association, 1899), 50. One ship buyer for the Navy believed that "Bushnell is a scoundrel" charging the Navy too much for ships. See George D. Morgan to Gideon Welles, September 2, 1861, Gideon Welles Papers, Huntington Library, San Marino, Calif.

13. "Negotiations for the Building of the 'Monitor,'" in *Battles and Leaders of the Civil War* 1:748–50.

14. J. Leander Bishop, *A History of American Manufactures: 1608—1860,* 3rd ed., 3 vols. (Philadelphia: Edward Young, 1868), 3:128–30.

15. William Conant Church, *The Life of John Ericsson,* 2 vols. (1890; repr. New York: Charles Scribner's Sons, 1906–1907), 1:242.

16. Ibid.

17. *Abridgment . . . Containing the Annual Message of the President,* 748–52.

18. *Story of the Monitor,* 20.

19. Church, *Life of John Ericsson,* 1:61.

20. Ibid., 116.

21. Ibid., 132, 134.

22. Jeff Kinard, *Artillery: An Illustrated History of Its Impact* (Santa Barbara, Calif.: ABC-CLIO, 2007), 202.

23. *Accident on Steam Ship "Princeton,"* House Rep. No. 479, 28th Cong., 1st sess., 3. For a discussion of the diplomatic ramifications of the *Princeton* disaster, see Matthew Karp, *This Vast Southern Empire: Slaveholders at the Helm of American Foreign Policy* (Cambridge, Mass.: Harvard University Press, 2016), 90–100.

24. Church, *Life of John Ericsson,* 1:141.

25. Olav Thulesius, *The Man Who Made the Monitor: A Biography of John Ericsson, Naval Engineer* (Jefferson, N.C.: McFarland, 2007), 64–65.

26. *Accident on Steam Ship "Princeton,"* 3.

27. Capt. Ernest W. Peterkin, *Drawings of the USS Monitor,* USS *Monitor* Historical Report Series, vol. 1, no. 1 (Washington, D.C.: U.S. Department of Commerce, 1985), 36–45.

28. Church, *Life of John Ericsson,* 1:246–47.

29. Cornelius Bushnell to Gideon Welles, March 9 and 23, 1877, Gideon Welles Papers, Huntington Library, San Marino, Calif. (also reprinted in *Project Cheesebox: A Journey Into History* 1 [Annapolis, Md.: United States Naval Academy, 1974]: 57); Welles, diary entry for January 3, 1863, in William E. Gienapp and Erica L. Gienapp, eds., *The Civil War Diary of Gideon Welles, Lincoln's Secretary of the Navy: The Original Manuscript Edition,* 116; Don E. Fehrenbacher and Virginia Fehrenbacher, eds., *Recollected Words of Abraham Lincoln* (Stanford, Calif.: Stanford Univ. Press, 1996), 72; William O. Stoddard, *Inside the White House in War Times: Memoirs and Reports of Lincoln's Secretary,* ed. Michael Burlingame (Lincoln: Univ. of Nebraska Press, 2000), 20. According to Stoddard, "Mr. Lincoln said he was like the fat girl when she put on her stocking—she thought there was something in it, and so he did, and the building of the *Monitor* was ordered, and is now quietly going on."

30. *Project Cheesebox,* 58.

31. Ibid., 59. To be sure, Ericsson also had his detractors. For example, Captain John Rodgers wrote,

> Mr Ericsson is in some respects a peculiar man—he is so full of faith in his own genius and his own inspirations that he has no room for doubt or distrust in matters which are unknown, and could be tried—He has ruined it is said nearly every man who has given implicit faith to his ideas and attempted to carry them out. . . . He has abundance of genius and resources—but he is not always sound in his conclusions—at the same time he is so confident and abundantly fortified in arguments that the danger of falling into his way of thinking is very great. . . . Like an adventurous traveller he scuns [shuns?] old and beaten paths—he delights in exploring new ones. . . . Every one knows that such deviations are very pleasant and as far as a journey is concerned, very hazardous. Before the government however shall embark its hopes in such new channels, those channels must be explored—or less figuratively, of all the men in the U.S. Mr Ericsson is the man who must be kept from doing harm, by insisting upon experimental proof of what he advances or proposes. The history of his life proves this.

See John Rodgers to Gideon Welles, May 2, 1863, Gideon Welles Papers, Huntington Library.

32. *Project Cheesebox,* 64.

33. Ibid., 64–65, 83.

3. Building the *Monitor*

1. Joseph Smith to John Ericsson, September 21, 1861, in RG 45, entry 502 (Subject File, 1775–1910), AD (Design and General Characteristics), box 51, folder 2.

2. John Ericsson to Joseph Smith, September 21, 1861, in RG 45, entry 502, AD, box 49, folder 10.

3. Elected mayor of Troy in 1855, he became a congressman in 1862. Winslow and business partner Griswold would later be instrumental in bringing the Bessemer process of ironworking to America, the two men holding the patent to the process.

4. John Flack Winslow to James Swunk, September 1891, reprinted in Francis B. Wheeler, *John Flack Winslow, LL.D. and the Monitor* (New York: F. B. Wheeler, 1893), 53–54.

5. John Ericsson to Joseph Smith, September 27, 1861, with enclosure to Cornelius Bushnell, September 23, 1861, in RG 45, entry 502, AD, box 49, folder 10.

6. USS *Monitor,* Contract Specifications, etc., RG 45, entry 502, AD, box 51, folder 10.

7. The documentary record is at odds with James Tertius deKay's assertion that Gideon Welles "allowed his staff to put together a remarkably mean-spirited contract for the ship, a business document that was totally out of keeping with the enthusiastic support he had shown Ericsson only a few days before." Any "harsh terms and arbitrary nature of the document" were penned with the full knowledge of the backers. See James Tertius deKay, *Monitor: The Story of the Legendary Civil War Ironclad and the Man Whose Invention Changed the Course of History* (New York: Walker, 1997), 95. The contract itself is held at the National Archives.

8. David Ellis, "The Story of the Monitor," unpublished manuscript and typescript, Battle of Hampton Roads Collection (MS359), TMM, 4.

9. Contract between Gideon Welles, John Ericsson, John Griswold, John Winslow, and Cornelius Bushnell, October 4, 1861 (MS341), ser. 2, TMM.

10. Ellis, "Story of the Monitor," 5. Many crew members were intimately acquainted with the details of their vessel's construction, some having participated in parts of the building process, while others were stationed on the receiving ships in Greenpoint, Brooklyn, while the construction was going on.

11. Bushnell to Smith, September 28, 1861, in RG 45, entry 502, AD, box 49, folder 10.

12. Ericsson to Smith, October 2, 1861, in RG 45, entry 502, AD, box 49, folder 10.

13. William N. Still Jr., *Monitor Builders: A Historical Study of the Principal Firms and Individuals Involved in the Construction of USS Monitor* (Washington, D.C.: National Maritime Initiative, Division of History, National Park Service, Department of the Interior, 1988).

14. Ellis, "Story of the Monitor," 9.

15. Drawings done by draughtsman Charles MacCord in October 1861 indicate a thickness of $^{15}/_{16}$ rather than one inch. From Capt. Ernest W. Peterkin, *Drawings of the U.S.S. Monitor,* U.S.S. *Monitor* Historical Report Series 1, no. 1 (Washington, D.C.: U.S. Department of Commerce, 1985), 448.

16. Stephen H. Muller and Jennifer A. Taylor, *Troy, New York, and the Building of the USS* Monitor (Troy, N.Y.: Hudson Mohawk Industrial Gateway, 2009).

17. Discovered on a brass valve, recovered in 2001. Discovered mark on a second brass valve in October 2011.

18. The *New York City Business Directory* of 1859 lists the firm as "iron merchants,"131.

19. *Trow's New York City Directory* of 1857 lists Benjamin Pike and Sons as "opticians, importers, & manufacturers of mathematical instruments." H. Wilson, *Trow's New York City Directory* (New York: John F. Trow, 1857), 658.

20. *Trow's New York City Directory* of 1857 lists Hidden as a "brassfounder." Wilson, *Trow's,* 381. It is possible that Hidden manufactured the brass for the deck lights. Though circumstantial, he did apply for a patent for a "new and useful Improvement in Deck Lights for Iron-Clad Vessels" on November 3, 1863. Patent # 40,479.

21. Lain's *Brooklyn City Directory* for 1862 lists a Jeremiah W. Atwater living in Brooklyn,

but with a business office on South Street in Manhattan. His occupation was listed as "towing." J. Lain, *The Brooklyn City Directory for the Year Ending May 1 1862* (Brooklyn, N.Y.: J. Lain, 1862), 11.

22. The Tax Assessment list for District 32 of the State of New York for October 1862 lists Thomas M. Shepard of Water Street as a manufacturer of "tin and sheet iron ware." RG 58 (Records of Internal Revenue Service), NARA. However, *Trow's New York City Directory* of 1857 as well as the 1860 census show that he also had a "caboose and stove warehouse." See *Trow's,* 750; 1860 U.S. census.

23. Discovered in 2008 on the inner workings of the engine room clock, recovered in 2001.

24. Discovered in 2011 on the valve assemblies and manometers, recovered in 2001.

25. Discovered in 2016 on the valve assembly, recovered in 2001.

26. Sands is listed in *Trow's* 1862 directory as House and Ship Plumber—232 Water Street (Sands later held a patent dated 1876 for "Improvements in water-closets for vessels"). Lain's 1865 Brooklyn directory lists Tooker as a plumber at the same address. *Lain's,* 416.

27. Stimers telegram to Smith, December 31, 1861, RG 45, entry 502, AD, box 49, folder 2.

28. Smith telegram to Ericsson, January 14, 1862, RG 45, entry 502, AD, box 51, folder 3.

29. Smith to Worden, January 15, 1862, RG 45, entry 502, AD, box 51, folder 3.

30. John Ericsson to W. R. Dorlan, August 20, 1874, Eldridge Collection, box 17, Huntington Library, San Marino, Calif.

31. John Ericsson, *Contributions to the Centennial Exhibition* (New York: "The Nation" Press, 1876), 493–94. Bushnell, upon receiving word that the vessel would be called *Monitor,* suggested to Smith that the Mystic River ironclad, initially called *Galena,* should be named *Retribution* instead. The navy kept the name *Galena.*

32. Ericsson to Smith, January 24, 1862, RG 45, entry 502, AD, box 51, folder 3.

33. *New York Times,* January 31, 1862; Frank Moore, ed., *The Rebellion Record: A Diary of American Events,* 12 vols. (New York: G. P. Putnam, 1861–1868), 4:57–59; *New York Tribune,* February 1, 1862.

34. Ericsson to Smith, January 31, 1862, RG 45, entry 502, AD, box 51, folder 3.

35. Smith to Ericsson, February 3, 1862, RG 45, entry 502, AD, box 51, folder 3.

36. Smith to Worden, February 6, 1862, RG 45, entry 502, AD, box 51, folder 4.

37. Smith to Worden, February 13, 1862, RG 45, entry 502, AD, box 51, folder 4.

38. Correspondent's letter dated February 16, 1862, in *Burlington Weekly Free Press,* February 28, 1862. The *Pittsburgh Gazette* of February 3, 1862, also provides a detailed description.

39. Stimers to Smith, February 17, 1862, RG 45, entry 502, AD, box 51, folder 4.

40. This is likely Commander John Jay Almy, who was stationed at the navy yard then.

41. Logbook of the USS *Monitor,* February 25, 1862.

42. *Specification of Cowper Phipps Coles: Apparatus for Defending Guns, &c., 1859* (London: Great Seal Patent Office, 1859). Coles continued to perfect his creation, and in 1866 the Royal Navy agreed to the construction of a low-freeboard turreted vessel called HMS *Captain.* Unfortunately, the need for auxiliary sails and rigging to make the *Captain* a seagoing vessel also made her unstable—and led to the death of Coles, who went down with his invention in 1870.

43. *New York Times,* February 16, 1887; *Brooklyn Daily Eagle,* June 24, 1900. Public interest in the war surged during the twentieth anniversary of the conflict in the 1880s. Popular magazines such as *Century* published articles written by the participants in famous battles, which sparked this new interest. The deaths of Ericsson and others associated with the *Monitor* also fueled this resurgence in interest. Interestingly, John Flack Winslow's memorial booklet, published after his death in 1892, contains a large section devoted to the exoneration of Theodore Timby and his contribution to the *Monitor.* See Francis B. Wheeler, *John Flack Winslow, LL.D. and the Monitor* (Poughkeepsie, N.Y.: Francis B. Wheeler, 1893), 54–66.

44. Peterkin, *Drawings,* 472.

45. This deficiency was fixed on April 17, 1862. The log indicates that during the first dog watch (4:00–6:00 P.M.) the crew "succeeded in getting both guns run out at once." See *Monitor* log, April 17, 1862.

46. Smith telegram to Navy Department, Washington D.C., January 21, 1862, RG 45, entry 502, AD, box 51, folder 3.

47. Peterkin, *Drawings,* 525–26.

48. Washington, D.C., *Daily National Intelligencer,* February 3, 1862.

49. David A. Mindell, *Iron Coffin: War, Technology, and Experience Aboard the USS Monitor* (Baltimore: Johns Hopkins Univ. Press, 2012), 75.

50. Brian Lavery, *Nelson's Navy: The Ships, Men, and Organization, 1793–1815* (Annapolis, Md.: U.S. Naval Institute Press, 2000), 207.

51. Keeler to Anna, March 5, 1862, in Robert W. Daly, ed., *Aboard the USS Monitor: 1862: The Letters of Acting Paymaster William Frederick Keeler, U.S. Navy, to His Wife, Anna* (Annapolis, Md.: United States Naval Institute, 1964) , 24–26. A portion of one of Keeler's bed curtains is on display at the U.S. Naval Academy Museum in Annapolis. It is blue and white with a floral pattern.

52. Keeler to Anna, March 5 and 26, 1862, in Daly, *Aboard the USS Monitor,* 26, 55–56.

53. E. V. Haughout & Co. to John A. Griswold, March 5, 1862, Battery Associates Records on *Monitor* Design and Construction (MS0335), TMM.

54. Keeler to Anna, March 14, 1862, in Daly, *Aboard the USS Monitor,* 48.

55. Keeler to Anna, August 19, 1862, in ibid., 210.

56. The sailors' workday was divided into six four-hour watches in which half the crew stood watch while the other half relaxed or slept, alternating every four hours. In order to keep the same men from having to stand the same overnight watch each night, the 4:00 P.M. to 8:00 P.M. watch was divided into two two-hour watches called the "first dog watch" and "last dog watch". There is no known etymological history of the name.

57. Geer to Martha, February 21 and April 27, 1862, Geer Papers.

58. Copy of Samuel Dana Greene letter to his mother, March 14, 1862, John Worden Papers (MS16), ser. 1, TMM.

59. USS *Monitor* Presentation Plan, Thomas F. Rowland Collection, 1861–1903 (MS376), TMM.

60. This resulted in an engine room that likely smelled of bacon, says *Monitor* engine expert Rich Carlstedt, in a research presentation at The Mariners' Museum, Spring 2011.

61. Logbook of the USS *Monitor,* March 3, 1862.

62. Keeler to Anna, March 4, 1862, in Daly, *Aboard the USS Monitor,* 21–23.

63. Church, *Life of John Ericsson,* 1:256.

64. Keeler to Anna, March 4, 1862, in Daly, *Aboard the USS Monitor,* 21.

65. Keeler to Anna, March 4, 1862, in ibid., 22.

66. Logbook of the USS *Monitor,* March 3, 1862.

67. *New York Times,* March 4, 1862.

68. ORN, ser. 1, vol. 6, p. 649.

69. Ibid., 681.

70. Samuel Dana Greene, "In the 'Monitor' Turret," in *Battles and Leaders of the Civil War,* 1:720; Alban C. Stimers to Father, May 5, 1862, in John D. Milligan, ed., "An Engineer Aboard the *Monitor,*" *Civil War Times Illustrated* 9 (April 1970): 30; *New York Tribune,* March 14, 1862; Keeler to Anna, March 6, 1862, in Daly, *Aboard the USS Monitor,* 30; Greene to Mary Greene, March 14, 1862, in Senate Report 1162, 48th Cong., 2nd sess., p. 4.

71. ORN, ser. 1, vol. 6, p. 687.

4. The Battles of Hampton Roads

1. H. Ashton Ramsay, "The Most Famous of Sea Duels: The Story of the *Merrimac*'s Engagement with the *Monitor* and the Events That Preceded and Followed the Fight, Told by a Survivor," *Harper's Weekly,* February 10, 1912. Unfortunately, many of the accounts of the battle were written several decades later, so the words of the men must be regarded as approximate at best and examples of poetic license with the passage of time at worst.

2. J. G. Gilmore to James F. Lawrence, March 12, 1862, in "Dear Friend Lawrence . . . ," *Cheesebox* 5 (February 1987): 7.

3. Hardin Littlepage, quoted in Quarstein, *CSS Virginia: Mistress of Hampton Roads* (Appomattox, Va.: H. E. Howard, Inc., 2000), 74.

4. Edward Shippen, *Thirty Years at Sea: The Story of a Sailor's Life* (New York: J. B. Lippincott, 1879), 280.

5. Gary W. Gallagher, ed., "'The Fight between the Two Iron Monsters': The *Monitor* versus the *Virginia* as Described by Major Stephen Dodson Ramseur, C.S.A.," *Civil War History* 30 (September

1984): 268–71. Henry Reaney, the acting master of the armed tugboat *Zouave,* claimed that his ship "fired the first shot at the *Merrimac,* and that but for her assistance the *Congress* would have been captured." See Henry Reaney, "How the Gun-Boat '*Zouave*' Aided the '*Congress,*'" in *Battles and Leaders of the Civil War,* 1:714–15.

6. Daniel O'Connor, "Muzzle to Muzzle with the *Merrimack,*" *Civil War Times* 35 (June 1996): 67.

7. See, for example, William H. Stewart, *A Pair of Blankets: War-Time History in Letters to the Young People of the South* (1911; repr., Wilmington, N.C.: Broadfoot, 1990), which tells the story of a Confederate soldier who recovered blankets from the wreck of the *Cumberland,* used them for the duration of the war, and still had them hanging on his wall when he wrote his memoir nearly fifty years later.

8. Martha Derby Perry, ed., *Letters from a Surgeon of the Civil War* (Boston: Little, Brown, 1906), 5–7.

9. Harriet Douglas Whetten, diary entry for August 1, 1862, in Paul H. Hass, ed., "A Volunteer Nurse in the Civil War: The Diary of Harriet Douglas Whetten," *Wisconsin Magazine of History* 48 (Spring 1965): 213.

10. Shippen, *Thirty Years at Sea,* 282.

11. Frank Stedman Alger, ed., "The *Congress* and the *Merrimac:* The Story of Frederick H. Curtis, A Gunner on the *Congress,*" *New England Magazine* 19 (February 1899): 689.

12. Court-Martial Case File KK-847, RG 153, Records of the Office of the Judge Advocate General (Army), NARA.

13. Louis Merz, "Diary of Private Louis Menz, C.S.A. of the East Point Guards (Co. D, 4th Georgia Regiment Volunteer Infantry, Doles-Cook Brigade)," *Bulletin of the Chattahoochee Valley Historical Society* 4 (November 1959): 26–27; Raleigh Edward Colston, "Watching the '*Merrimac,*'" *Century Illustrated Monthly Magazine* 29 (March 1885): 763–66. Others clearly heard the sounds of the battle from the shore. One Confederate soldier wrote that "the cannon roared like thunder." See Algernon Sydney Morrissett to father, March 10, 1862, in Leonora Dismukes Parish and Camillus J. Dismukes, eds., "A Confederate Soldier's Eye-Witness Account of the *Merrimack* Battle," *Georgia Historical Quarterly* 54 (Fall 1970): 430–32. For the recollections of the acting master of the gunboat USS *Mystic,* see R. F. Coffin, "The First Fight Between Ironclads," *Outing* 10 (August 1887): 416–21.

14. William Rattle Plum, *The Military Telegraph during the Civil War in the United States: With an Exposition of Ancient and Modern Means of Communication, and of the Federal and Confederate Cipher Systems; Also a Running Account of the War Between the States,* 2 vols. (Chicago: Jansen, McClurg, 1882), 1:139–40. George D. Cowlam was with the Fire Zouaves.

15. ORN, ser. 1, vol. 7, pp. 4–5.

16. Gideon Welles, in *The Annals of the War, Written by Leading Participants, North and South* (Philadelphia: Times, 1879), 24–25; Elizabeth Lindsay Lomax, diary entry for March 9, 1862, in Lindsay Lomax Wood, ed., *Leaves from an Old Washington Diary, 1854–1863* (Mount Vernon, N.Y.: E. P. Dutton, 1943), 190. Confederates hoped that the *Virginia* would be able to steam up the Potomac and shell Washington. See, for example, Abraham F. Leonard to Jefferson Davis, November 27, 1861, abstracted in Lynda Lasswell Crist, Mary Seaton Dix, and Kenneth H. Williams, eds., *The Papers of Jefferson Davis,* vol. 7: *1861* (Baton Rouge: Louisiana State Univ. Press, 1992), 430; Douglas F. Forrest to Jefferson Davis, February 28, 1862, abstracted in ibid., vol. 8: *1862,* 70.

17. Logbook of the USS *Monitor,* March 8, 1862.

18. Keeler to Anna, March 9, 1862, in Robert W. Daly, ed., *Aboard the USS Monitor: 1862: The Letters of Acting Paymaster William Frederick Keeler, U.S. Navy, to His Wife, Anna* (Annapolis, Md.: United States Naval Institute, 1964), 31.

19. Ibid.; Logbook of the USS *Monitor,* March 8, 1862; ORN, ser. 1, vol. 7, p. 5.

20. News reports quoted in "Report of Acting Volunteer Lieutenant Goodwin," in ORN, ser. 1, vol. 7, p. 31. Pilots were generally civilians and thus could refuse the assignment.

21. ORN, ser. 1, vol. 7, p. 31.

22. Logbook of the USS *Monitor,* March 8, 1862.

23. John Emmet O'Brien, *Telegraphing in Battle: Reminiscences of the Civil War* (Wilkes-Barre, Pa.: Raeder Press, 1910), 66–67.

24. ORN, ser. 1, vol. 7, p. 5.

25. Greene, "In the 'Monitor' Turret," 1:722.

26. ORN, ser. 1, vol. 7, p. 11.

27. Joseph McDonald, "How I Saw the *Monitor-Merrimac* Fight," *New England Magazine* 36 (July 1907): 548–53.

28. ORN, ser. 1, vol. 7, p. 71.

29. McDonald, "How I Saw the *Monitor-Merrimac* Fight," 548–53.

30. Alban C. Stimers to Father, May 5, 1862, in John D. Milligan, ed., "An Engineer Aboard the *Monitor,*" *Civil War Times Illustrated* 9 (April 1970): 32.

31. Keeler to Anna, March 6–9, 1862, in Daly, *Aboard the USS Monitor,* 40.

32. David Ellis, "The Story of the Monitor," unpublished manuscript and typescript, Battle of Hampton Roads Collection (MS0359), TMM, 25.

33. Ibid., 25–26.

34. Milligan, "Engineer Aboard the *Monitor,*" 32; Driscoll quoted in Irwin M. Berent, comp., *The Crewmen of the USS Monitor: A Biographical Directory* (Prepared for Underwater Archaeology Unit, Division of Archives and History, Department of Cultural Resources, State of North Carolina. Washington, D.C.: NOAA, United States Department of Commerce, 1985. USS *Monitor* National Marine Sanctuary Historical Report Series, No. 1, 24.

35. Keeler to Anna, March 6–9, 1862, in Daly, *Aboard the USS Monitor,* 32–33.

36. William R. Cline "The Ironclad Ram Virginia, Confederate States Navy," *Southern Historical Society Papers* 32 (January–December 1904): 243–49.

37. Berent, *Crewmen of the USS Monitor,* 24.

38. Sam McKee to Church McKee, March 10, 1862, in Hugh McKee, ed., *The McKee Letters, 1859–1880: Correspondence of a Georgia Farm Family during the Civil War and Reconstruction,* 2nd ed. (Milledgeville, Ga.: Boyd Publishing, 2001), 63–64.

39. Keeler to Anna, March 6–9, 1862, in Daly, *Aboard the USS Monitor,* 33.

40. Sallie Brock Putnam, "Memoir of Sallie Brock Putnam," in *Richmond During the War: Four Years of Personal Observation* (New York: G. W. Carleton, 1867), 389.

41. Keeler to Anna, March 6–9, 1862, in Daly, *Aboard the USS Monitor,* 34.

42. Ellis, "Story of the *Monitor,*" 26–27.

43. Keeler to Anna, March 6–9, 1862, in Daly, *Aboard the USS Monitor,* 33–34.

44. Greene, "In the 'Monitor' Turret," 723; Berent, *Crewmen of the USS Monitor,* 24; Geer to Martha, March 10, 1862, Geer Papers.

45. Keeler to Anna, March 6–9, 1862, in Daly, *Aboard the USS Monitor,* 40; Greene, "In the 'Monitor' Turret," 724.

46. Greene, "In the 'Monitor' Turret," 724.

47. This was akin to skipping stones across water but gave vessels line-of-sight firing capabilities with increased accuracy.

48. Keeler to Anna, March 13, 1862, in Daly, *Aboard the USS Monitor,* 34.

49. Greene, "In the 'Monitor' Turret," 723.

50. Keeler to Anna, March 9–13, 1862, in Daly, *Aboard the USS Monitor,* 35.

51. There seems to be no consensus on this, only that the *Monitor* was hit by friendly fire throughout the battle.

52. Milligan, "Engineer Aboard the *Monitor,*" 33.

53. Greene, "In the 'Monitor' Turret," 723.

54. Milligan, "Engineer Aboard the *Monitor,*" 33.

55. Albert Campbell to Clara, March 10, 1862, in *Perspectives on the Civil War* (Newport News, Va.: The Mariners' Museum, n.d.), 23.

56. Keeler to Anna, March 9–13, 1862, in Daly, *Aboard the USS Monitor,* 35. The temperatures inside the *Monitor* would become even more unbearable during the summer of 1862.

57. Greene, "In the 'Monitor' Turret," 725.

58. William Norris, *Story of the Virginia,* 8.

59. John R. Eggleston, "Captain Eggleston's Narrative of the Battle of the Merrimac," *Southern Historical Society Papers* 41 (1916), 166–78.

60. Greene, "In the 'Monitor' Turret," 723.

61. Keeler to Anna, March 9–13, 1862, in Daly, *Aboard the USS Monitor,* 35.

62. The forward pivot gun of the *Merrimack* was never moved out of its central position. Had the pivot been turned to where Curtis was kneeling, the battle would have had a very different outcome.

63. Memoir of Richard Curtis as quoted in *Perspectives on the Civil War,* 19. For the complete memoir, see Richard Curtis, *History of the Famous Battle Between the Iron-Clad Merrimac, C.S.N., and the Iron-Clad Monitor and the Cumberland and Congress, of the U.S. Navy, March the*

8th and 9th, 1862, as Seen by a Man at the Gun (1907; repr., Hampton, Va.: Houston Printing and Publishing House, 1957).

64. Norris, *Story of the Virginia,* 9.

65. Ellis, "Story of the *Monitor,*" 29.

66. Ramsay, "Most Famous of Sea Duels," 11–12.

67. H. Ashton Ramsay, "The Merrimac and the Monitor," in *The Monitor and the Merrimac: Both Sides of the Story* (New York: Harper and Brothers, 1912), 52–53.

68. McDonald, "How I Saw the *Monitor-Merrimac* Fight," 553. For more details on the *Dragon*'s role in the battle from the perspective of another man on the ship, see Alice Paula Perkins Mortensen and Edwin Hjalmar Mortensen, eds., *The Family of John Henry Taylor, Jr.: Featuring Family Letters Written During and After the Civil War* (Baltimore: Gateway Press, 1995), 16–24.

69. Greene, "In the 'Monitor' Turret," 726.

70. Keeler to Anna, March 9–13, 1862, in Daly, *Aboard the USS Monitor,* 38.

71. Worden "frequently asked from his bed of pain of the progress of affairs, and when told that the *Minnesota* was saved, he said 'Then I can die happy.'" See Greene, "In the 'Monitor' Turret," 727. Greene would be troubled throughout his life about the public perception of his actions that day. Northern newspapers initially excused the lack of pursuit. For example, the *New York Tribune* reported, just days after the battle, "The *Monitor* did not pursue, probably on account of the heating of her guns, or some other equally good reason." But questions would persist and become more shrill and minatory as time passed. The preparation of Greene's 1884 memoir apparently brought the old demons back. Greene shot himself before the article went to print.

72. Memoir of Richard Curtis, as quoted in *Perspectives on the Civil War,* 19.

73. William Lee Monegan to Joseph Monegan, March 10, 1862, William Monegan Papers (MS14), TMM.

74. William O. Stoddard, *Inside the White House in War Times: Memoirs and Reports of Lincoln's Secretary,* ed. Michael Burlingame (Lincoln: Univ. of Nebraska Press, 2000), 70; Michael Burlingame, ed., *Lincoln's Journalist: John Hay's Anonymous Writings for the Press, 1860–1864* (Carbondale: Southern Illinois Univ. Press, 1998), 231–32; John Hay, diary entry for March 1862, in Michael Burlingame and John R. Turner Ettlinger, eds., *Inside Lincoln's White House: The Complete Civil War Diary of John Hay* (Carbondale: Southern Illinois Univ. Press, 1997), 35.

75. Benjamin Brown French, diary entry for March 16, 1862, in Donald B. Cole and John J. McDonough, eds., *Witness to the Young Republic: A Yankee's Journal, 1828–1870* (Hanover, N.H.: Univ. Press of New England, 1989), 392. A few weeks later French sounded more optimistic: "Since the *Merrimack* came out 'on the rampage' three weeks ago, and was sent back into Norfolk like a whipped hound with his tail between his hind legs, the rebels have not dared to send her out. When she again makes her appearance in Hampton Roads, I prophecy [*sic*], from what I have heard, that she will be made as short work of as she made of the *Cumberland* and *Congress.* She will find more than one *ugly customer* to deal with. The next week must be full of events, it ought to settle the question of Union or Disunion, and I hope and trust that if it does settle it it will be Union forever!" See French, diary entry for March 29, 1862, in ibid., 392.

76. Julia Taft Bayne, *Tad Lincoln's Father* (1931; repr., Lincoln: University of Nebraska Press, 2001), 66–67.

77. According to Ericsson's chief draftsman, Charles W. MacCord, Ericsson was angry that the *Monitor* was not used more aggressively. He later wrote:

> The captain was disappointed that the 'Monitor' had not done her utmost during the engagement; by her subsequent inactivity he was simply enraged. . . . He had built his ship to *fight;* and I never heard him allude to the 'excessive caution' which kept her idle after her one battle, without scathing denunciations couched in language as fluent as it was vigorous, and more uncomplimentary than either.

MacCord also believed that if the federal government had supplied heavier guns that the *Monitor* could have sunk the *Virginia.* Charles W. MacCord, "Ericsson and His *Monitor,*" *North American Review* 149 (October 1889): 469.

78. Welles to Worden, March 15, 1862 in ORN,

ser. 1, vol. 7, p. 38; Welles, "Recommendation to Congress for Establishing a Dock Yard for the Purposes of an Iron Navy," June 1862, Gideon Welles Papers, Huntington Library, San Marino, Calif.

79. Stoddard, *Inside the White House in War Times,* 70.

80. Lord Lyons to Lord John Russell, March 11, 16, and May 6, 1862, all in James J. Barnes and Patricia P. Barnes, eds., *The American Civil War Through British Eyes: Dispatches from British Diplomats,* 3 vols. (Kent, Ohio: Kent State Univ. Press, 2005), 1:312–14; ibid., 2:38–42; Charles Francis Adams to son, April 4, 1862, in Worthington Chauncey Ford, ed., *A Cycle of Adams Letters, 1861–1865,* 2 vols. (New York: Houghton Mifflin, 1920), 1:123.

5. "The Pet of the People"

1. RG 11 (General Records of the United States Government), entry 6 (United States Government Documents Having General Legal Effect, Laws of the United States, Enrolled Acts and Resolutions of Congress, 1789–1962), NARA.

2. *Macon Daily Telegraph,* March 15, 1862.

3. *New York Times,* March 13, 1862.

4. *Philadelphia Inquirer,* March 11, 1862.

5. *Philadelphia Inquirer,* March 14, 1862.

6. Oak Hall was located on the southeast corner of Sixth and Market.

7. *Philadelphia Inquirer,* March 15, 1862. Towne Hall was located at 18 Market Street, Philadelphia.

8. Cleveland *Plain Dealer,* March 17, 1862.

9. *Zanesville* (Ohio) *Daily Courier,* March 17, 1862.

10. *Hunt's Yachting Magazine* 11 (May 1862): 231.

11. "The Merrimac," *Child's Paper* (October 1862).

12. John S. Wise, *The End of an Era* (Boston: Houghton, Mifflin, 1899), 203. For an example of how the *Congress* and *Cumberland* were commemorated, see Harold Earl Hammond, ed., *Diary of a Union Lady, 1861–1865* (1962; repr., Lincoln: Univ. of Nebraska Press, 2000), 116–17.

13. Sarah Emma Edmonds, *Nurse and Spy in the Union Army* (Hartford: W. S. Williams, 1865), 384.

14. *Vanity Fair* 5 (March 22, 1862): 142.

15. *Vanity Fair* 5 (May 17, 1862): 241. The same issue features a joke about the *Merrimac*—supposedly told by General McClellan to a fictitious reporter, McArone. McClellan refers to a previous *Vanity Fair* report by McArone and asks, "Why ought you to be swamped, and bust up at once?" The answer: "Because . . . aren't you a Merry Mac?"

16. Curiously, the New York–based Currier and Ives chose for one of their initial offerings an image of the events of March 8. It did not sell well. For a survey of depictions of the Battle of Hampton Roads in popular lithography, see Mark E. Neely Jr. and Harold Holzer, *The Union Image: Popular Prints of the Civil War North* (Chapel Hill: Univ. of North Carolina Press, 2000), chapter 4.

17. For an explanation, see Washington *Daily National Republican,* November 10, 1862, which is reproduced in chapter 13.

18. Elizabeth T. Porter Beach (lyrics) and Frederick Buckley (music), "The Last Broadside" (New York: Firth, Pond, 1862).

19. Thomas Buchanan Read, *The Poetical Works of Thomas Buchanan Read,* 3 vols. (Philadelphia: J. B. Lippincott, 1874), 3:275–79.

20. Oliver Wendell Holmes, *The Poetical Works of Oliver Wendell Holmes,* 3 vols. (Boston: Houghton, Mifflin, 1881), 1:251–52.

21. Anonymous, "The Cumberland," in Frank Moore, ed., *The Rebellion Record: A Diary of American Events,* 12 vols. (New York: G. P. Putnam, 1861–1868), 4:73.

22. Ossian Gorman, in William Gilmore Simms, ed., *War Poetry of the South* (New York: Richardson, 1866), 391–93.

23. Anonymous, in "Bohemian" (William G. Shepperson), ed., *War Songs of the South* (Richmond: West and Johnston, 1862), 202–3.

24. Stephen C. Foster, "Better Days are Coming" (New York: Horace Waters, 1862).

25. Stephen C. Foster, "That's What's the Matter" (New York: H. de Marsan, n.d.).

26. G Weingarten, "The *Monitor* Polka" (New York: H. B. Dodsworth, 1862); D. F. Geutbruck, "Secession Polka" (Macon, Ga.: John W. Burke, 1861); Edgar H. Munson, "The Fortress Monroe Polka" (New York: Firth, Pond, 1861); W. S. Crerar, "The Happy Contraband Polka" (New

Orleans: Louis Grunewald, 1865); A. G. Warner, "Southern Rights Polka" (Louisiana: N.p., 1861); Hermann L. Schreiner, "Battle Flag Polka" (Macon, Ga.: John C. Schreiner and Son, 1863); J. R. Boulcott (arranger), "Dixie Polka" (New Orleans: P. P. Werlein, 1860); C. S. Grafulla, "Manual of Arms Polka" (New York: Firth, Pond, 1862).

27. E. Mack, "Monitor Grand March" (Philadelphia: Lee and Walker, 1862); V. Tinans, "The Ericsson Galop" (Boston: Oliver Ditson, 1862); James W. Porter (music) and D. Brainerd Williamson (lyrics), "O Give Us a Navy of Iron" (Philadelphia: Lee and Walker, 1862); "Monitor and Merrimac—Air—Yankee Doodle" (Philadelphia: Johnson, Song Publisher, Stationer, and Printer, 1862).

28. *Columbus Crisis,* September 3, 1862.

29. "M.," "The Virginia's Knocking Around" (Baltimore: N.p., March 30, 1862).

30. Bob Zentz, "Ironclads Suite," on *Horizons,* audio CD (Sharon, Conn.: Folk Legacy Records, 2010); Eric Worden (lyrics) and Michael Goldberg (music), "Iron Is King," digital download for MAGIC education program, 2002, http://www.getmagic.net (accessed February 14, 2017); Justin Rice and Christian Rudder, "The Monitor," on *Bishop Allen & The Broken String,* audio CD (Austin: Dead Oceans Records, 2007); Patrick Stickles, Liam Betson, Ian Graetzer, and Eric Harm, "The Battle of Hampton Roads on *The Monitor,* audio CD (New York: XL Recordings, 2010); (Civil War, "U.S.S. Monitor," on *Gods and Generals,* audio recording (Eisenerz, Austria: Napalm Records, 2015).

31. Washington *National Republican,* March 31, 1862.

32. *San Francisco Evening Bulletin,* supplement, July 5, 1862.

33. Betsey Gates, ed., *The Colton Letters: Civil War Period, 1861–1865* (Milan, Ohio: McLane, 1993), 204; L. A. Gobright, *Recollection of Men and Things at Washington during the Third of a Century* (Philadelphia: Claxton, Remsen and Haffelfinger, 1869), 342; *Philadelphia Inquirer,* March 6, 1865; *New York Herald,* April 16, 1886; Omaha *World-Herald,* September 3, 1886; Tacoma *Daily News,* April 28, 1893 and July 2, 1895; *Trenton State Gazette,* April 27, 1898; Denver *Rocky Mountain News,* March 8, 1903; *Boston Herald,* June 18, 1925.

34. Twenty years later the builder of the model *Monitor* recalled building and testing it. "When completed she floated on an even keel with about two inches of freeboard," he wrote. "A trial trip was made of a quarter of a mile in the Allegheny river against the current on a June rise, under convoy of a fleet of skiffs, but unfortunately when rounding in her wharf she swung against the head of a raft, and sunk in twenty feet of water." The ship was dredged up, but her guns were never found and had to be made anew. Visitors to the fair could also see "machinery or manufactures" in Monitor Hall. See *Pittsburgh Gazette,* May 6, 20, 30, 1864; Boston *Daily Evening Traveler,* November 11, 1864; Rockford (Ill.) *Daily Gazette,* April 11, 1884; *Wheeling Register,* January 19, 1884.

35. *New York Evening Post,* June 28, 1862.

36. Ibid.

37. The information in the final five paragraphs of chapter 5 comes from "Up Pops the *Monitor*": The Battle of Hampton Roads in Popular Culture," exhibition curated by Anna Holloway, The Mariners' Museum, March 2011–August 2012; Anna Gibson Holloway and Jonathan W. White, "*Monitor* Pop!" *Civil War Times* 56 (February 2017): 26–33; *Los Angeles Herald,* November 25, 1883; *Trenton State Gazette,* April 27, 1898; Washington *Evening Star,* September 30, 1915; "So Sorry, My Island Now," season 1, episode 15 of *Gilligan's Island* (originally aired January 9, 1965); "Jamie's Project," season 2, episode 7 of *Wait Till Your Father Gets Home* (originally aired October 23, 1973). The label for "Short Fuse" can be seen in Jonathan W. White, "Beer Here!" *Civil War Times* 56 (February 2017): 6.

6. Aftermath of Battle

1. *New York Times* and *Philadelphia Inquirer,* March 10, 1862. This was the same "boisterous weather" that kept the *Virginia* in port on March 6 and nearly sank the *Monitor.*

2. ORN, ser. 1, vol. 7, pp. 6–7, 78.

3. *New York Times,* March 10, 1862 (early edition).

4. Ibid.

5. *New York Times,* March 10, 1862 (late edition).

6. *Philadelphia Inquirer,* March 10, 1862.

7. *Norfolk Day Book,* March 10, 1862, reprinted in the *Macon Daily Telegraph,* March 13, 1862.

8. *Macon Daily Telegraph,* March 11 and 14, 1862.

9. Reprinted in *Belfast* (Ireland) *News-Letter,* March 31, 1862.

10. *Dundee* (Scotland) *Courier and Daily Argus,* April 1, 1862.

11. Reprinted in *Belfast News-Letter,* March 31, 1862.

12. *Dundee Courier and Daily Argus,* April 2, 1862.

13. Keeler to Anna, March 9–13, 1862, in Robert W. Daly, ed., *Aboard the USS Monitor: 1862: The Letters of Acting Paymaster William Frederick Keeler, U.S. Navy, to His Wife, Anna* (Annapolis, Md.: United States Naval Institute, 1964), 39.

14. *Times* of London, reprinted in *Belfast News-Letter,* March 31, 1862.

15. Keeler to Anna, February 13, 1862, in Daly, *Aboard the USS Monitor,* 11

16. Keeler to Anna, March 9–13, 1862, in ibid., 34, 40.

17. Geer to Martha, March 10, 1862, Geer Papers.

18. Reprinted in the *Dundee Courier and Daily Argus,* March 26, 1862.

19. Nathaniel Hawthorne, "Chiefly About War Matters," in *The Complete Works of Nathaniel Hawthorne,* 12 vols. (New York: Houghton Mifflin, 1883), 12:336–38. Not all observers recognized the changing nature of heroism in combat. A few days after the battle Major General John E. Wool came aboard the vessel and told the officers, "Gentlemen you have made heroes of yourselves." See Keeler to Anna, March 11, 1862, in Daly, *Aboard the USS Monitor,* 42.

20. Keeler to Anna, March 18, 1862, in Daly, *Aboard the USS Monitor,* 53; Elizabeth Blair Lee to Phil, March 15, 1862, in Virginia Jeans Lee, ed., *Wartime Washington: The Civil War Letters of Elizabeth Blair Lee* (Urbana: Univ. of Illinois Press, 1991), 111.

21. Herman Melville, *Battle-Pieces and Aspects of the War* (New York: Harper and Brothers, 1866), 61–62.

22. H. A. Richardson to Kittie, March 27, 1862, H. A. Richardson Letter (MS317), TMM.

23. Alban C. Stimers to Father, May 5, 1862, in John D. Milligan, ed., "An Engineer Aboard the *Monitor," Civil War Times Illustrated* 9 (April 1970): 35; Keeler to Anna, March 31, 1862, in Daly, *Aboard the USS Monitor,* 65; Newton to William Kelly, March 31, 1862, Newton Papers.

24. Keeler to Anna, March 28, 1862, in Daly, *Aboard the USS Monitor,* 57.

25. Keeler to Anna, March 11, 1862, in ibid., 42. Historian William N. Still writes that Selfridge "had the unwanted distinction of being the only Union naval officer during the war to have three ships sunk under him." See William N. Still Jr., ed., *What Finer Tradition: The Memoirs of Thomas O. Selfridge, Jr., Rear Admiral, U.S.N.* (1924; repr., Columbia: Univ. of South Carolina Press, 1987), vii.

26. *Bangor* (Me.) *Daily Whig and Courier,* April 19, 1862.

27. Newton to William Kelly, April 7, 1862, Newton Papers.

28. Fox to Welles, March 10, 1862, in ORN, ser. 1, vol. 7, p. 83. On Lincoln's plan to use other vessels to ram the *Virginia* in April 1862, see Chester D. Bradley, "President Lincoln's Campaign against the *Merrimac," Journal of the Illinois State Historical Society* 51 (Spring 1959): 63–69. In the spring of 1862 Confederate soldiers believed that the *Monitor* was too afraid to engage the *Virginia* in another fight. See, for example, Herbert P. McNeal, ed., "Merrimac, Monitor and the War—A Soldier's View," *The Confederate Philatelist* 39 (July–August 1994): 129–33.

29. Keeler to Anna, March 30, 1862, in Daly, *Aboard the USS Monitor,* 63.

30. Keeler to Anna, April 15, 1862, in ibid., 83.

31. Keeler to Anna, May 7, 1862, in ibid., 106.

32. Thomas W. Smith to sister, April 8, 1862, in Eric J. Wittenberg, ed., *"We Have It Damn Hard Out Here": The Civil War Letters of Sergeant Thomas W. Smith, 6th Pennsylvania Cavalry* (Kent, Ohio: Kent State Univ. Press, 1999), 22.

33. Bradley, "President Lincoln's Campaign against the *Merrimac,"* 62–76. Of course, Jefferson Davis was also anxious during this time about the coming of Union gunboats up the James River to Richmond. See Jefferson Davis to Varina Howell Davis, May 13, 1862, in Lynda Lasswell Crist, Mary Seaton Dix, and Kenneth H. Williams, eds., *The Papers of Jefferson Davis,*

vol. 8: *1862* (Baton Rouge: Louisiana State Univ. Press, 1992), 174–75.

34. Repairs to the pilothouse were not fully complete until May 5, 1862, according to the logbook. See Logbook of the USS *Monitor,* May 5, 1862.

35. ORN, ser. 1, vol. 7, pp. 39–40. We have silently corrected most of the spelling, capitalization, and grammatical errors in this letter. The version in ORN is signed "The *Monitors* Boys," but we have rendered it "The *Monitor* Boys," which is how the signature usually appears.

36. Geer to Martha, July 1, 1862, Geer Papers.

37. Logbook of the USS *Monitor,* April 24, 1862.

38. Quoted in Keeler to Anna, May 4, 1862, in Daly, *Aboard the USS Monitor,* 102. Goldsborough reiterated this statement in his unofficial correspondence to Gustavus Vasa Fox following the Battle of Drewry's Bluff, dated May 21, 1862, in Robert Means Thompson and Richard Wainwright, eds., *Confidential Correspondence of Gustavus Vasa Fox, Assistant Secretary of the Navy, 1861–1865,* 2 vols. (New York: Naval History Society, 1918–1919), 1:272.

39. Logbook of the USS *Monitor,* May 3, 1862.

40. Kevin Dougherty and J. Michael Moore, *The Peninsula Campaign: A Military Analysis* (Jackson: Univ. Press of Mississippi, 2005), 82.

41. Fox to Goldsborough, May 7, 1862, in Thompson and Wainwright, *Confidential Correspondence of Gustavus Vasa Fox,* 1:266.

42. USRCS stands for United States Revenue Cutter Service, the forerunner of the U.S. Coast Guard. For Chase's account of this trip, see Salmon P. Chase to Janet Chase, May 7, 8, and 11, 1862, in John Niven et al., eds., *The Salmon P. Chase Papers,* 5 vols. (Kent, Ohio: Kent State Univ. Press, 1993–98), 1:337–44; ibid., 3:185–97.

43. Logbook of the USS *Monitor,* May 7, 1862.

44. For Lincoln's interest in technology and inventions, see Robert V. Bruce, *Lincoln and the Tools for War* (Champaign: Univ. of Illinois Press, 1989).

45. Keeler to Anna, May 7, 1862, in Daly, *Aboard the USS Monitor,* 107.

46. Newton to William Kelly, July 19, 1862, Newton Papers.

47. Keeler to Anna, May 8, 1862, in Daly, *Aboard the USS Monitor,* 110–12.

48. Keeler to Anna, May 9, 1862, in ibid., 114.

49. Richard Curtis, *History of the Famous Battle Between the Iron-Clad Merrimac, C.S.N., and the Iron-Clad Monitor and the Cumberland and the Congress of the U.S. Navy, March the 8th and 9th 1862, As Seen by a Man at the Gun* (Hampton, Va.: Houston Print and Publishing House, 1957), pt. 2. One Confederate sympathizer in Maryland lamented, "Merrimac destroyed. The greatest loss the South has so far sustained & sacrificed through mismanagement, which never could have happened had not [Franklin] Buchanan been wounded." See William Wilkins Glenn, diary entry for May 8, 1862, in Bayly Ellen Marks and Mark Norton Schatz, eds., *Between North and South: A Maryland Journalist Views the Civil War* (Rutherford, N.J.: Fairleigh Dickinson Univ. Press, 1976), 61. Confederate general Josiah Gorgas similarly lamented that "no one event of the war . . . created such a profound sensation as the destruction of this noble ship." Quoted in Crist, Dix, and Williams, *Papers of Jefferson Davis,* vol. 8: *1862,* 175.

50. Geer to Martha, May 11, 1862, Geer Papers.

51. Keeler to Anna, May 12, 1862, in Daly, *Aboard the USS Monitor,* 121; Chandra Manning, *Troubled Refuge: Struggling for Freedom in the Civil War* (New York: Knopf, 2016), 58–59; *Lowell Daily Citizen and News,* August 21, 1866.

52. Geer to Martha, May 15, 1862, Geer Papers; Newton to Mother, May 14–19, 1862, Newton Papers.

53. Jeffers to Goldsborough, May 22, 1862, in ORN, ser. 1, vol. 7, p. 27.

54. Newton to Mother, May 14–19, 1862, Newton Papers; Jeffers to Goldsborough, May 22, 1862, in ORN, ser. 1, vol. 7, p. 27.

55. Robert Alonzo Brock and Virgil Anson Lewis, *Virginia and Virginians: Eminent Virginians . . . History of Virginia from Settlement of Jamestown to Close of the Civil War,* (Richmond, Va.: H. H. Hardesty, 1888), 2: 437. Wood was the grandson of President Zachary Taylor and the nephew of Jefferson Davis.

56. Keeler to Anna, May 12–16, 1862, in Daly, *Aboard the USS Monitor,* 130–32; Geer to Martha, May 16, 1862, Geer Papers; Logbook of the USS *Monitor,* May 16, 1862.

57. Lieutenant William Jeffers in *Report of the Secretary of the Navy in Relation to Armored Vessels* (Washington, D.C.: Government Printing Office, 1865), 29.

58. Jeffers to Goldsborough, May 22, 1862, in ORN, ser. 1, vol. 7, pp. 27–29.

59. Logbook of the USS *Monitor,* June 2, 1862.

60. Ibid., June 1862.

61. Ericsson to Newton, June 24, 1862, Newton Papers. Ericsson also praised Newton's penmanship, saying that Newton was "quite an exception to the general rule that engineers write miserably."

62. Keeler to Anna, June 16, 1862, in Daly, *Aboard the USS Monitor,* 156.

63. Newton to Mother, June 30, 1862, Newton Papers.

64. Ibid.; Geer to Martha, July 1, 1862, Geer Papers; Keeler to Anna, June 23, 1862, in Daly, *Aboard the USS Monitor,* 162; Harriet Douglas Whetten, diary entry for July 15, 1862, in Paul H. Hass, ed., "A Volunteer Nurse in the Civil War: The Diary of Harriet Douglas Whetten," *Wisconsin Magazine of History* 48 (Spring 1965): 207.

65. Newton to Mother, June 30, 1862, Newton Papers.

66. Keeler to Anna, July 4, 1862, in Daly, *Aboard the USS Monitor,* 169–71.

67. Chuck Veit, "The Raid That Wasn't: The Navy Attack on the Petersburg Railroad, 26–28 June 1862," 2007, http://www.navyandmarine.org/ondeck/1862AppomattoxRaid.htm#_ftnref31 (accessed February 14, 2017).

68. Harriet Douglas Whetten, diary entry for July 15, 1862, in Hass, "Volunteer Nurse," 207. For other accounts of those who saw the charred remains of the *Congress* and *Cumberland,* see Augustus B. Sage to A. V. Sage, November 20, 1862, Augustus V. Sage Letter (MS332), TMM; Michael Guinan to Eliza Guinan, November 13, 1862, Michael Guinan Papers (MS73), TMM.

69. Keeler to Anna, July 4, 1862, in Daly, *Aboard the USS Monitor,* 183–84. The men of the *Monitor* had long feared the possibility of being boarded by enemy troops. On March 10, 1862—the day after the battle—Worden met with Lincoln, who recounted the meeting in a letter to Secretary of the Navy Welles: "I have just seen Lieut. Worden, who says the 'Monitor' could be boarded and captured very easily—first, after boarding, by wedging the turret, so that it would not turn, and then by pouring water in her & drowning her machinery. He is decidedly of opinion she should not go skylarking up to Norfolk." See Lincoln to Welles, March 10, 1862, in Roy P. Basler, et al., eds., *The Collected Works of Abraham Lincoln,* 9 vols. (New Brunswick, N.J.: Rutgers Univ. Press, 1953), 5:154. Other men expressed similar fears. "If on some dark night the enemy should succeed in approaching within a couple of hundred yards of us, in sufficiently large force say from 500 to 1000, the chance of being captured would be very much against us," observed Isaac Newton. He concluded that "boarding is our great danger, it is only the vicinity of other vessels which renders us safe." See Newton to William Kelly, June 18, 1862, Newton Papers. Some Confederates also hoped that the *Monitor* could be disabled by being boarded. See S. Thomas to Jefferson Davis, May 14, 1862, abstract in Crist, Dix, and Williams, *Papers of Jefferson Davis,* 8:177.

70. Keeler to Anna, June 3, 1862, in Daly, *Aboard the USS Monitor,* 145–46. Unfortunately, Rose O'Neal Greenhow's biographers have neglected Keeler's letters, which give a wonderful—almost comical—account of the dialogue between Greenhow and Jeffers.

71. ORN, ser. 1, vol. 7, pp. 548–63, 573–74, 581. Wilkes's flotilla would consist of the following vessels: *Wachusett* (Wilkes's flagship), *Galena, Cimarron, Mahaska, Tioga, Maratnza, Monitor, Delaware, Aroostook, Yankee, Sebago, Port Royal, Genesee, Jacob Bell, Commodore Barney, Southfield, Morse, Currituck, Satellite, Coeur de Lion, Dragon, A.C. Powell,* and *Stepping Stones.* The *Dacotah* would join the flotilla a few days later, replacing the *Sonoma.*

72. Logbook of the USS *Monitor,* July 9, 1862.

73. Keeler to Anna, July 25, 1862 (first letter), in Daly, *Aboard the USS Monitor,* 192–93; Wilhelm Durst file, box 1, folder 12, Berent Papers.

74. Keeler to Anna, July 25, 1862 (second letter), in Daly, *Aboard the USS Monitor,* 195.

75. ORN, ser. 1, vol. 7, pp. 583–84. General Order of July 14, 1862, read, in part:

> That from and after this first day of September, eighteen hundred and sixty-two, the spirit ration in the Navy of the United States shall forever cease, and thereafter no distilled spirituous liquors shall be admitted on board vessels of war, except as medical stores, and

upon the order and under the control of the medical officers of such vessels, and to be used only for medical purposes. From and after the said first day of September next, there shall be allowed and paid to each person in the Navy now entitled to the spirit ration, five cents per day in commutation and lieu thereof, which shall be in addition to their present pay.

76. George H. White to Mother, September 18, 1862, typescript in *Monitor* Collection Associated Records (MS390), TMM; Keeler to Anna, September 3 and 6, 1862, in Daly, *Aboard the USS Monitor,* 216–17; Logbook of the USS *Monitor,* September 2, 1862.

77. Logbook of the USS *Monitor,* August 18, 1862. Stevens continued the ratings of all petty officers on board save that of David Cuddeback, the captain's steward. Cuddeback took the tablecloth from the Captain's rooms, a maroon wool piece with the name *Monitor* embroidered on it in gold lettering. Cuddeback's descendants donated the tablecloth to the Virginia War Museum in Newport News in the 1990s, and it is currently on display at Lee Hall Mansion in Newport News.

78. Logbook of the USS *Monitor,* August 2, 1862.

79. Ibid., August 28, 1862; Keeler to Anna, August 3, 1862, in Daly, *Aboard the USS Monitor,* 213.

80. George H. White to Mother, September 2, 1862, typescript in *Monitor* Collection Associated Records (MS0390), TMM.

81. Keeler to Anna, September 8/11, 1862, in Daly, *Aboard the USS Monitor,* 218.

7. "The *Monitor* Is No More"

1. *Philadelphia Public Ledger,* October 4, 1862.

2. Washington *Daily Intelligencer,* October 7, 1862.

3. *Washington Evening Star,* January 7, 1863.

4. Keeler to Anna, October 6, 1862, in Robert W. Daly, ed., *Aboard the USS Monitor: 1862: The Letters of Acting Paymaster William Frederick Keeler, U.S. Navy, to His Wife, Anna* (Annapolis, Md.: United States Naval Institute, 1964), 228.

5. Benjamin Brown French, diary entry for October 10, 1862, in Donald B. Cole and John J. McDonough, eds., *Witness to the Young Republic: A Yankee's Journal, 1828–1870* (Hanover, N.H.: Univ. Press of New England, 1989), 412–13. Washingtonians toured the navy yard around this time to see other vessels as well. See, for example, Orville Hickman Browning, diary entry for December 10, 1862, in Theodore Calvin Pease and James G. Randall, eds., *The Diary of Orville Hickman Browning* (Springfield: Illinois State Historical Library, 1925), 1:594.

6. Baltimore *Sun,* October 28, 1862.

7. *Washington Daily Intelligencer,* November 6, 1862.

8. Louis N. Stodder (as told to Albert Stevens Crockett), "Aboard the U.S.S. 'Monitor,'" *Civil War Times Illustrated* 1 (January 1963): 35.

9. *Alexandria* (Va.) *Gazette,* November 8, 1862.

10. See Robert E. Lee to Jefferson Davis, December 8, 1862, in Lynda Lasswell Crist, Mary Seaton Dix, and Kenneth H. Williams, eds., *The Papers of Jefferson Davis,* vol. 8: *1862* (Baton Rouge: Louisiana State Univ. Press, 1992), 530–33.

11. Keeler to Anna, November 11, 1862, in Daly, *Aboard the USS Monitor,* 230.

12. *Milwaukee Daily Sentinel,* October 9, 1862; Keeler to Anna, November 17, 1862, in Daly, *Aboard the USS Monitor,* 232.

13. Wilhelm Durst would claim to have been "shanghai'd" while on a drunken spree and found himself unable to rejoin the *Monitor.* Nevertheless, he "remembered" the events of the sinking later in life.

14. Jacob Nicklis to Father, November 16, 1862, Nicklis Papers. Nicklis's entire correspondence is also available in Jonathan W. White and Christopher J. Chappell, eds., "Letters from the Monitor: The Civil War Correspondence of Jacob Nicklis, U.S. Navy," *Civil War History* 60 (December 2014): 436–52.

15. *Monitor* crew list, Berent Papers.

16. Keeler to Anna, November 17, 1862, in Daly, *Aboard the USS Monitor,* 232; *Monitor* crew list, Berent Papers.

17. ORN, ser. 1, vol. 7, p. 341.

18. Jacob Nicklis to Father, December 28, 1862, Nicklis Papers.

19. Keeler to Anna, December 25, 1862, in Daly, *Aboard the USS Monitor,* 250.

20. Geer to Martha, December 28, 1862, and Geer to Brother, January 13, 1863, both in Geer Papers.

21. Jacob Nicklis to Father, December 28, 1862, Nicklis Papers.

22. Copy of USS *Rhode Island* Logbook, Ernest Peterkin Collection (MS390), ser. 6, subser. 3, TMM.

23. Grenville Mellen Weeks, "The Last Cruise of the *Monitor," Atlantic Monthly* 11 (March 1863): 366–72.

24. ORN, ser. 1, vol. 8, 353.

25. ORN, ser. 1, vol. 8, 347.

26. "The Wreck of the *Monitor," Harper's Weekly* (January 24, 1863): 60.

27. Weeks, "Last Cruise of the *Monitor,*" 369.

28. Ibid.

29. Francis Banister Butts, "The Loss of the *Monitor," Century Illustrated Monthly Magazine* 31 (December 1885): 301.

30. ORN, ser. 1, vol. 8, p. 348; Weeks, "Last Cruise of the *Monitor,*" 369. Stephen D. Trenchard also recorded an account of the sinking and its aftermath in his manuscript journal, which is in RG 45, entry 392 (Journals and Diaries of Officers of the US Navy).

31. Keeler to Anna, January 6, 1863, in Daly, *Aboard the USS Monitor,* 258.

32. "Surgeon of the Monitor Tells of Night She Sank," *Idaho Daily Statesman,* November 8, 1906.

33. Weeks, "Last Cruise of the *Monitor,*" 370.

34. Ibid., 371.

35. "Narrative of the Sinking of the USS *Monitor,*" in *Project Cheesebox: A Journey into History* (Annapolis, Md.: United States Naval Academy, 1974), 2:476.

36. Keeler to Anna, January 6, 1863, in Daly, *Aboard the USS Monitor,* 258–59.

37. Butts, "Loss of the *Monitor,*" 300.

38. Weeks, "Last Cruise of the *Monitor,*" 372.

39. ORN, ser. 1, vol. 8, p. 348.

40. One eyewitness, however, hints at an additional life spared, though it cannot be corroborated through any official records. However, it is worth noting that E. W. Watson, who was master's mate on board the *Rhode Island* the night the *Monitor* sank, recalled that he saw "an old quartermaster with a large bundle under his arm." Though discouraged by Greene to try and save his personal possessions, the man "said nothing, but threw it into the boat. When the bundle was passed up over the side of the *Rhode Island* it proved to be a little messenger-boy—probably the smallest and youngest one in the service." E. W. Watson, "The Last of the Monitor" in *The Monitor and the Merrimac: Both Sides of the Story* (New York: Harper and Brothers, 1912), 70.

41. William Keeler in *Annual Report of the Secretary of the Navy* (Washington, D.C.: Government Printing Office, 1863), 27.

42. Keeler to Anna, November 17, 1862, in Daly, *Aboard the USS Monitor,* 232.

43. Butts, "Loss of the *Monitor,*" 300. Butts drew from Grenville Weeks's accounts published a few months after the sinking, as well as Samuel Dana Greene's account. Butts very likely embellished his account over time, but his is the only mention of Lewis during the sinking.

44. For more information on Nicklis, see chapter 15.

45. Webber to Nannie, January 2, 1863, in private collection (copy in possession of the authors).

46. Geer to Martha, January 2, 1863, Geer Papers.

47. Geer to Gilbert Geer, January 13, 1863, Geer Papers.

48. Keeler to Anna, January 6, 1863, in Daly, *Aboard the USS Monitor,* 253. Recent studies done by Dr. Jay Moore at The Mariners' Museum Library and Archives show that the "elements" were particularly brutal in the vicinity of the *Monitor* and *Rhode Island* while slightly less so just a few miles away, where the monitor *Montauk* and her escort *State of Georgia* struggled but did not succumb. Moore's analysis, based on weather reports from various regions in the days leading up to the sinking as well as the abstract log of the USS *Rhode Island,* leads him to believe that the *Monitor* encountered an "explosive cyclogenesis" or "weather bomb" the night she sank. The *Rhode Island*'s log shows a barometric pressure drop of 25.7 millibars in sixteen hours. Jay Moore, "The Gale that Sank the *Monitor,*" unpublished manuscript in possession of the authors.

8. Discovery and Recovery

1. Welles, diary entry for January 3, 1863, in William E. Gienapp and Erica L. Gienapp, eds., *The Civil War Diary of Gideon Welles, Lincoln's*

Secretary of the Navy: The Original Manuscript Edition (Urbana: Univ. of Illinois Press, 2014), 116. Even though Ericsson bore the financial risk in building the *Monitor,* Welles staked his reputation on the success of ironclad vessels. In December 1861 a ship buyer for the Union Navy wrote Welles, "I feel anxious about the Iron vessels lest Lenthal[l], Fox and Smith lead you into them and their failure is yours." See George D. Morgan to Welles, December 26, 1861, Gideon Welles Papers, Huntington Library, San Marino, Calif. Indeed, Ericsson praised Welles for his support of the ironclad program in a letter to James Gordon Bennett, the editor of the influential *New York Herald.* See Ericsson to James Gordon Bennett, April 25, 1862, in Charles O'Neil, "Engagement Between the *Cumberland* and *Merrimack," United States Naval Institute Proceedings* 48 (June 1922): 892–93.

2. *New York Times,* January 4, 1863; *New York Herald,* January 4, 1863; *Daily Milwaukee News,* January 4, 1863.

3. *New York Herald,* January 4, 1863.

4. *Providence Daily Evening Press,* January 5, 1863; Portland (Me.) *Daily Eastern Argus,* January 8, 1863.

5. *Hartford Daily Courant,* January 8, 1863.

6. *Providence Daily Evening Press,* January 10, 1863.

7. *New York Herald,* January 14, 1863. The January 24th issue of *Frank Leslie's* features the engraving.

8. ORN, ser. 1, vol. 8, pp. 345–49.

9. Robert Sheridan, *Iron From the Deep: The Discovery and Recovery of the USS* Monitor (Annapolis, Md.: Naval Institute Press, 2004), 37.

10. Student editors at the *Harvard Crimson* proclaimed (tongue in cheek) that they were part of an "American Students for Raising the *Monitor*" movement in April 1951 and wrote a poem rebuking the Navy for its decision. *Harvard Crimson,* April 14, 1951. The last verse reads:

> Let flounders man her silent gun,
> Let squid now grasp her wheel;
> For men once bold, have lost their nerve,
> And only ships are steel!

The students later reported a scheme to raise the vessel and tie up the salvaged *Monitor* at a pier on the Charles River where the city could sell orangeades from the deck for income.

11. Telephone call between Anna Holloway and McMullen's granddaughter, Margo Heiden, 2005.

12. *Eugene* (Ore.) *Guard,* July 18, 1955.

13. York (Pa.) *Gazette and Daily,* July 18, 1955.

14. Ernest W. Peterkin, "Movements of USS Rhode Island & Monitor plotted 19 May 1972," NOAA Associated Records (MS390), TMM.

15. *Project Cheesebox: A Journey into History* (Annapolis, Md.: United States Naval Academy, 1974), v–x.

16. Ibid.

17. John D. Broadwater, *USS Monitor: A Historic Ship Completes Its Final Voyage* (College Station: Texas A&M Press, 2012). See also John Broadwater, "A Search for the USS *Monitor," International Journal of Nautical Archaeology and Underwater Exploration* 4 (March and September 1974): 117–21.

18. Side scan sonar is a specialized sonar system for searching and detecting objects on the seafloor. It transmits sound energy in the shape of a fan and analyzes the return signal, or echo, that has bounced off the seafloor of other objects, such as shipwrecks. The strength of the return echo is continuously recorded creating a "picture" of the ocean bottom in which objects that protrude from the bottom create a dark image (strong return) and shadows from these objects are light areas (little or no return).

19. Sheridan, *Iron From the Deep,* x.

20. Later identified during the 2009 expedition, conducted by Monitor National Marine Sanctuary staff, as the YP-389, sunk during World War II by a German U-boat.

21. Gordon P. Watts Jr., *Investigating the Remains of the U.S.S. Monitor: A Final Report on 1979 Site Testing in the Monitor National Marine Sanctuary* (Raleigh: North Carolina Department of Cultural Resources, 1981), 30.

22. "Discovering the USS *Monitor," Daily Press* (Newport News, Va.), July 18, 2004.

23. *New York Times,* March 8, 1974. In his inimitable way, Watts said to a reporter at the *Washington Post,* "The problem is that everybody thinks they know what a shipwreck looks like.... They've seen them in the movies with the sails still flapping underwater and all that. And what

we have here instead looks to be an obvious pile of trash." *Washington Post,* March 8, 1974.

24. Bill Walsh, *Countermeasures* (April 1976); *Washington Post,* August 25, 1974. This mission was not without its controversy. Conflicting goals between the original *Monitor* team and the U.S. Navy resulted in the navy keeping all of the information gathered during the expedition, only releasing it later to Newton, Watts, and *National Geographic.*

25. Norman G. Cubberly, "MONITOR April 5, 1974," MIT Museum, Cambridge, Mass. HEE -SC-02562. MIT Museum Edgerton Digital Collections, http://edgerton-digital-collections.org (accessed August 26, 2015).

26. Watts, *Investigating the Remains of the U.S.S. Monitor,* 30; Harold Eugene Edgerton, "USS MONITOR Project, wreck site formation, 1975?," MIT Museum, Cambridge, Mass., HEE -SC-02590. MIT Museum Edgerton Digital Collections, http://edgerton-digital-collections.org (accessed February 14, 2017).

27. *Washington Post,* August 25, 1974.

28. The wreck was designated as a National Historic Landmark on June 23, 1986.

29. Marine Protection, Research and Sanctuaries Act, 16 U.S.C. § 1431–1445, October 23, 1972.

30. William C. Davis, "Foreword," in William Marvel, ed., *The Monitor Chronicles: One Sailor's Account: Today's Campaign to Recover the Civil War Wreck* (New York: Simon and Schuster, 2000), 8–9.

31. ORN, ser. 1, vol. 8, 353.

32. *Federal Register* 51, no. 171 (September 4, 1986).

33. Cooperative agreement between the National Oceanic and Atmospheric Administration and The Mariners' Museum, July 13, 1987.

34. Honorable Hugh J. Dolan, U.S. Department of Commerce Recommended Decision In the Matter of Gary Gentile, Respondent, Docket No. 951–193, November 20, 1989.

35. National Oceanic and Atmospheric Administration, Monitor National Marine Sanctuary, *Charting a New Course for the Monitor* (April 1998), 3.

36. *Federal Register.* 62, no. 233 (Thursday, December 4, 1997).

37. NOAA, *Charting a New Course for the Monitor,* 3.

38. Ibid., 28–36.

39. Ibid.

40. For a good explanation of the different sorts of underwater archaeology, see Joe Flatman and Mark Staniforth, "Historical Maritime Archaeology," in *The Cambridge Companion to Historical Archaeology,* edited by Dan Hicks and Mary Beaudry (New York: Cambridge Univ. Press, 2006), 168–88.

41. "Propeller of Civil War Gunship Rises Again," CNN.com (June 9, 1998), http://www.cnn.com/US/9806/09/monitor.dive/?related (accessed February 14, 2017).

42. The skeg supported the rudder and propeller shaft, which projected a distance of almost 30 feet from the stern. The 28-foot-long, 7,000-pound skeg was hauled up from the water at 11:00 A.M. and placed on the deck of the barge.

43. Brian Leshak, "SUPSALV Restores Diving Capability," *Undersea Warfare,* Winter 2013, issue no. 49, http://www.public.navy.mil/subfor/underseawarfaremagazine/issues/archives/issue_49/SUPSALV.html (accessed February 14, 2017).

44. David Alberg, *USS Monitor 2001 Project: Engine Recovery,* Department of Defense Legacy Program Information sheet, Revised February 29, 2008.

45. John Broadwater, "The *Monitor*'s Engine Reaches The Mariners' Museum: Special Update August 7, 2001" Online Log of *Monitor* 2001, http://oceanexplorer.noaa.gov/explorations/monitor01/logs/aug07/aug07.html (accessed August 26, 2015).

46. Monitor *Expedition 2002—Turret Recovery Expedition to the* Monitor *National Marine Sanctuary: Expedition Operations Manual,* Revised Draft, May 27, 2002. U.S. Department of Commerce, National Oceanic and Atmospheric Administration, National Ocean Service, Marine Sanctuaries Division, 6.

47. Ibid., 12–13.

48. John Broadwater, "Exposing the Turret, July 5, 2002," Online Log of *Monitor* 2002, http://oceanexplorer.noaa.gov/explorations/02monitor/logs/jul05/jul05.html (accessed February 14, 2017).

49. John Broadwater, "Strenuous Excavation, July 10, 2002," Online Log of *Monitor* 2002, http://oceanexplorer.noaa.gov/explorations/02monitor

/logs/jul10/jul10.html (accessed February 14, 2017). For Johnston's recollections, see Jeff Johnston, "Discovery and Recovery—The Modern History of the USS *Monitor:* A Personal Memoir," in Harold Holzer and Tim Mulligan, eds., *The Battle of Hampton Roads: New Perspectives on the USS Monitor and CSS Virginia* (New York: Fordham Univ. Press, 2006), 155–69.

50. John Broadwater, "Special Update: Possible Human Remains Located in Monitor's Turret, July 26, 2002," Online Log of *Monitor* 2002, http://oceanexplorer.noaa.gov/explorations/02monitor/logs/jul26/jul26.html (accessed August 26, 2015).

51. Paul Clancy, *Ironclad: The Epic Battle, Calamitous Loss and Historic Recovery of the USS* Monitor (New York: Koehlerbooks, 2013), 230.

52. The Mariners' Museum interview with Captain Bobbie Scholley, March 8, 2003.

53. Chief Warrant Officer Rick Cavey, MDSU2, "USS MONITOR Turret Recovery," *Faceplate: The Official Newsletter for the Divers and Salvors of the United States Navy* 6 (November 2002): 5.

54. Michelle Fox, "The Turret Completes Its Journey, August 10, 2002," Online Log of *Monitor* 2002, http://oceanexplorer.noaa.gov/explorations/02monitor/logs/aug10/aug10.html (accessed February 14, 2017); Anna Holloway, "Escorting History," August 11, 2002, *Food For Small Animals,* repr. at http://monitorkitty.com/?p=182 (accessed February 14, 2017).

55. "USS *Monitor* Suffers Severe Damage," Newport News (Va.) *Daily Press,* July 8, 2004.

56. *Monitor National Marine Sanctuary: State of the Sanctuary Report* (Washington, D.C.: Government Printing Office, 2008), 17–18.

57. See Joel Silverstein and Kathy Weydig, *USS* Monitor *2007 Expedition Final Report for Permit # MNMS-2007-001,* and *USS* Monitor *2008 Expedition Final Report for Permit # MNMS-2008-001,* Monitor National Marine Sanctuary Files, Newport News, Va.

58. U.S. Department of Commerce, *Monitor National Marine Sanctuary Final Management Plan* (Silver Spring, Md.: National Oceanic and Atmospheric Administration, Office of National Marine Sanctuaries, 2013), 87–94.

59. Forensic Anthropology Report: CILHI 2002-097-1-01 and I-02, U.S. Army Central Identification Laboratory, Hawaii (October 14, 2004).

60. For the most comprehensive listing of the crew, see John V. Quarstein, *The Monitor Boys: The Crew of the Union's First Ironclad* (Charleston: History Press, 2011), 265–98.

61. Private correspondence between Anna Gibson Holloway and Monitor National Marine Sanctuary Superintendent David Alberg, March 2013.

62. Rebecca Lurye, "For Civil War Sailors, Some Closure 151 Years Later," http://www.mcclatchydc.com/news/politics-government/article24746344.html (accessed Ferbuary 14, 2017).

63. George R. White to Father, April 19, 1862, in Robert C. Bartosz, ed., *Letters Home from Geo. R. White, Private, Co. G, 19th Reg., Mass. Volunteers* (Wenonah, N.J.: Robert C. Bartosz, 1991), 17.

64. R. B. Clarke, "*Monitor* and the *Merrimack,*" *Virginia Numismatist* (December 1969): 12–16.

65. Stephen W. Sears, ed., *Mr. Dunn Browne's Experiences in the Army: The Civil War Letters of Samuel W. Fiske* (New York: Fordham Univ. Press, 1998), 53.

66. The Mariners' Museum has several examples of these small copper coins in its collection.

67. George Geer, William Keeler, and Isaac Newton all reassured their relatives that the coming of other monitor-class vessels would do nothing to diminish their status as having served on the first.

68. Quarstein, *Monitor Boys,* 263–302; Keeler to Anna, March 11, 1862, in Robert W. Daly, ed., *Aboard the USS Monitor: 1862: The Letters of Acting Paymaster William Frederick Keeler, U.S. Navy, to His Wife, Anna* (Annapolis, Md.: United States Naval Institute, 1964), 42; Baltimore *Sun,* June 20, 1862; New York *Evening Post,* September 7, 1863.

Men made similar spurious claims about service aboard the CSS *Virginia.* For example, an alleged Confederate spy, captured in Illinois by Union detectives in April 1863, apparently claimed "that he lost his leg in the engagement between the Merrimac and Monitor, and that he was on the Merrimac." See Court-Martial Case File LL-777, RG 153, Records of the Office of the Judge Advocate General (Army), NARA.

69. J. Errickson [*sic*] to Fox, March 11, 1862, copy in Eldridge Collection, Huntington Library, San Marino, Calif. Another version of this letter is available in the Ericsson Papers, American-

Swedish Society, Philadelphia. For a Confederate who urged a stronger ironclad program, see Milton E. Bacon to Jefferson Davis, April 24, 1862, abstracted in Lynda Lasswell Crist, Mary Seaton Dix, and Kenneth H. Williams, eds., *The Papers of Jefferson Davis,* vol. 8: *1862* (Baton Rouge: Louisiana State Univ. Press, 1992), 152.

70. Following the war, the *Monadnock* undertook the longest sea voyage of any monitor up to that point when she steamed from Philadelphia to California in 1865–1866. The *Miantonomoh* crossed the Atlantic in 1866 and toured northern Europe, including Russia.

71. Paul H. Silverstone, *Civil War Navies, 1855–1883* (Annapolis, Md.: Naval Institute Press, 2001), 4.

72. Speech of James Wilson Grimes in *The Navy in Congress* (Washington, D.C.: Franck Taylor, 1865), 7.

73. "Captain Ericsson's Funeral," *New York Times,* March 11, 1889. Cornelius Bushnell, Cornelius Delamater, Thomas Rowland and Charles MacCord were among the pallbearers.

74. *Proceedings at the Unveiling of the Statue of John Ericsson, in Potomac Park, Washington, D.C. under the Auspices of the John Ericsson Memorial Commission* (Washington, D.C.: Government Printing Office, 1929), 46.

75. Weeks, "Last Cruise of the *Monitor,*" 372.

76. Miller, *U.S.S. Monitor,* 1.

9. The U.S. Gun Boat *Currituck* Escorts the *Monitor* to Hampton Roads

1. William F. Shankland Journal (MSS84475), Manuscript Division, Library of Congress, Washington, D.C.

2. Curiously, Shankland makes no mention of the steam tug *Seth Low.*

3. The Sandy Hook Lighthouse in New Jersey was built in 1764.

4. Barnegat Lighthouse, at the northern tip of Long Beach Island, New Jersey, was designed by George Gordon Meade and first lit in 1859.

5. Absecon Lighthouse in Atlantic City, New Jersey, was first lit in 1857.

6. Cape May Lighthouse, on the southern tip of New Jersey, was first built in 1859.

7. The Indian River is just south of Rehoboth, Delaware, along the Atlantic coast. The lighthouse does not appear to stand there today.

8. The Cape Henlopen Lighthouse, in Lewes, Delaware, was originally constructed in the 1760s; a replica stands on the site today.

9. The first lighthouse on Hog Island, Virginia, was constructed about 1852; it was replaced in 1896.

10. The Smith Island Lighthouse, in Cape Charles, on Virginia's Eastern Shore, was constructed in 1828 but was replaced a few years after the *Monitor* passed by it.

11. The Cape Henry Lighthouse, built about 1792 at the southern entrance to Chesapeake Bay, was replaced in 1881.

12. This time is likely an error, as the watch indicated is the Second Watch, i.e. 12:00 A.M. to 4:00 A.M.

10. Firsthand Accounts of the Battle of Hampton Roads

1. Henry Eaton Coleman Papers (MS319), TMM.

2. Coleman must have meant to name one of the other ships here instead of repeating the word "wounded."

3. Historical Collections of the National Oceanic and Atmospheric Administration (NOAA).

4. Captain John Marston (1795–1885) of the USS *Roanoke* was the Union naval commander in Hampton Roads at the time of the Battle of Hampton Roads.

11. President Lincoln's Mailbag

1. Oliver S. Halsted Jr., to Abraham Lincoln, April 25, 1863, Abraham Lincoln Papers, Manuscript Division, Library of Congress, Washington, D.C.

2. RG 107 (Records of the Office of the Secretary of War), entry 18 (Record Series Originating During The Period 1789–1889, Correspondence, Letters Received, Letters Received [Main Series], 1801–1889), NARA.

3. Zouave soldiers wore brightly colored uniforms patterned after French soldiers who were stationed in Africa.

4. RG 45, entry 36 (Correspondence, 1798–1918, Miscellaneous Letters Received, 1801–1884).

5. RG 45, entry 36.

6. Governor John A. Andrew (1818–1867) of Massachusetts, Senator John P. Hale (1806–1873) of New Hampshire, and Senator Henry Wilson (1812–1875) of Massachusetts, were all prominent Republicans of the Civil War era.

7. RG 45, entry 36.

8. RG 45, entry 36.

9. RG 45, entry 36.

10. RG 45, entry 36.

11. RG 45, entry 362 (Records of the Office of the Secretary of the Navy, 1798–1921, Records of Boards and Commissions, 1812–1890, Letters on Inventions Referred to the Naval Examining Board, 1861–1862).

12. William Pitt Fessenden (1806–1869) was a U.S. senator from Maine and later served as Lincoln's secretary of the treasury.

13. RG 45, entry 36.

14. Dr. J. S. Newbury, a geologist from Cleveland, was general manager of the Western Sanitary Commission. Following the war he taught at Columbia College in New York City.

12. An Engineer's View from the *Monitor*

1. Newton Papers.

2. Newton to William Kelly, June 18, 1862.

3. The *E.A. Stevens* (later the USS *Naugatuck*) was an ironclad vessel initially designed by brothers Robert L. Stevens and Edwin A. Stevens in 1841. She served for a brief stint with the North Atlantic Blockading Squadron's James River Squadron in April and May 1862.

4. On German merchants in Virginia during the Civil War era, see Andrea Mehrländer, *The Germans of Charleston, Richmond and New Orleans during the Civil War Period, 1850–1870: A Study and Research Compendium* (New York: De Gruyter, 2011).

5. Captain John Rodgers (1812–1882) assumed command of the ironclad *Galena* in April 1862 and commanded the James River Flotilla in May 1862. He would later command the ironclad *Weehawken* and participate in the federal assaults against Charleston in 1863.

6. William H. H. Borden (1840–1872) commanded the steamer *Canonicus,* transporting wounded soldiers from City Point to Point Lookout, Maryland, and Washington, D.C.

7. On June 13–15, 1862, Confederate general J. E. B. Stuart did his famous ride around General McClellan's army.

8. Ira Harris (1802–1875) was a Republican senator from New York; his son, William Hamilton Harris (1838–1895), served in the Army Ordnance Department.

9. Berkeley Plantation, home of former president William Henry Harrison (and future president Benjamin Harrison), is located on the James River in Charles City County.

10. A church or chapel for sailors.

11. Shirley Plantation, the residence of Col. Hill Carter, had been the home of Siah Carter, the runaway slave who joined the crew of the *Monitor.*

12. The Seven Days Battles took place outside of Richmond from June 25 to July 1.

13. Union general John C. Robinson (1817–1897) served with distinction in the Seven Days Battles and would later earn the Congressional Medal of Honor after being wounded at the Battle of Spottsylvania in May 1864.

14. Soldier slang for the heavily salted pork they received in their rations.

13. Repairing the *Monitor*

1. Admiral Joseph Smith (1790–1877), Admiral Cornelius Kinchiloe Stribling (1796–1880), General Amiel Weeks Whipple (1818–1863), who commanded the defenses of Washington, and John Lenthall (1807–1882), who was a shipbuilder by profession.

2. William Talbert.

3. These inscriptions are still visible on the guns today.

14. Two Surgeons Observe the *Monitor*'s Final Moments

1. Webber to Nannie, January 2–7, 1863, in private collection (copy in possession of the authors).

2. Samuel Gilbert Webber Papers, 1862–1864

(MS80), TMM. The bulk of Webber's papers is held in the South Caroliniana Library, Univ. of South Carolina.

3. Acting master's mate D. Rodney Browne of the *Rhode Island* was in command of the rescue boat that went back to the *Monitor* seeking survivors one last time. The boat got separated from the *Rhode Island* and was picked up by a schooner out of Maine. The schooner ran aground and had to be towed off by a Union navy vessel. Eventually they were reunited with the *Rhode Island.*

4. A ship's wake.

5. According to the *Oxford English Dictionary,* philopena is "a game or custom, originating in Germany, in which a gift or forfeit may be claimed by the first of two people who have shared a nut with two kernels to say 'philopena' at their next meeting; an occasion on which this is done; a gift or forfeit claimed in this way. Also: a nut with a double kernel, or a kernel from such a nut."

6. British essayist Charles Lamb first published *Essays of Elia* in the *London Magazine* between 1820 and 1825 and later as two books in 1823 and 1833.

7. These entertaining essays by Charles Lamb originally appeared in the *London Magazine* in the 1820s and were widely reprinted in American books and periodicals throughout the nineteenth century.

8. Jacob Nicklis Papers (MS363), TMM. For more on Nicklis, see Jonathan W. White and Christopher J. Chappell, eds., "Letters from the *Monitor:* The Civil War Correspondence of Jacob Nicklis, U.S. Navy," *Civil War History* 60 (December 2014): 436–52.

Selected Bibliography

Manuscript Sources

Huntington Library, San Marino, California
- Eldridge Collection
- Gideon Welles Papers

The Mariners' Museum Library and Archives, Newport News, Virginia
- Irwin M. Berent Collection (MS164)
- Franklin Buchanan Papers (MS81)
- Henry Eaton Coleman Papers (MS319)
- William deRohan Collection (MS8)
- George S. Geer Papers (MS10)
- Weldon B. Hester Clippings
- William Moneghan Papers (MS14)
- NARA USS *Monitor* Collection (MS341)
- Isaac Newton Papers (MS13)
- Jacob Nicklis Papers (MS363)
- Northrop Grumman Newport News USS *Monitor* Collection (MS336)
- Thomas F. Rowland Collection (MS376)
- Thomas H. Stevens Papers (MS358)
- J. W. Tynan Papers (MS77)
- USS *Monitor* Design and Construction Collection (MS335)
- Samuel G. Webber Letters (MS80)
- Gideon Welles Collection (MS311)
- John L. Worden Collection (MS16)

National Archives and Records Administration, Washington, D.C.
- Bureau of Yards and Docks (Record Group 71)
- Naval Records Collection of the Office of Naval Records and Library (Record Group 45)
- Records of the Office of the Judge Advocate General (Army) (Record Group 153)

NOAA *Monitor* National Marine Sanctuary
- USS *Monitor* Collection

U.S. Naval Academy Museum, Annapolis, Md.
- William F. Keeler Letters, Rosenbach Collection

Primary Sources

Published

Brooke, George M., Jr., ed. *Ironclads and Big Guns of the Confederacy: The Journal and Letters of John M. Brooke.* Columbia: Univ. of South Carolina Press, 2002.

Buchanan, Franklin. "The Fight Between the Virginia (*Merrimac*) and *Monitor.*" *Confederate War Journal* 1, no. 6 (September 1893): 82–85.

———. "Official Report of the Battle of Hampton Roads." *Southern Historical Society Papers* 7 (1879): 305–14.

Butts, Francis Banister. "The Loss of the *Monitor,* by a Survivor." *Century Illustrated Monthly Magazine* 31 (December 1885): 299–302.

———. *The Monitor and the Merrimac: Personal Narratives of Events in the War of the Rebellion, Being Papers Read Before the Rhode Island Soldiers and Sailors Historical Society.* Providence: N. B. Williams, 1890.

Cameron, William E. "The Battle in Hampton Roads as Viewed by an Eye Witness." *Southern Historical Society Papers* 32 (January–December 1904): 347–54.

Cannon, Legrand B. "The *Monitor* and *Merrimac.*" *Magazine of History* 15 (June 1912): 190–201.

Civil War Naval Chronology, 1861–1865. 6 vols. 1961–1996. Reprint. Washington, D.C.: Naval History Division, 1971.

Clopton, William I. "New Light on the Great Drewry's Bluff Fight." *Southern Historical Society Papers* 34 (January–December 1906): 82–98.

Coles, Cowper Phipps. *English Versus American Cupolas: A Comparison Between Capt. Cole's and Capt. Ericsson's Turrets.* London: E. Stanford, 1864.

Colston, Raleigh Edward. "Watching the 'Merrimac.'" *Century Illustrated Monthly Magazine* 29 (March 1885): 763–66.

Crockett, Albert S., ed. "Aboard the U.S.S. *Monitor.*" *Civil War Times Illustrated* 10 (August 1968): 147–49.

Curtis, Richard. *History of the Famous Battle Between the Iron-clad Merrimac, C.S.N., and the Iron-clad Monitor and the Cumberland and Congress, of the U.S. Navy, March 8th and 9th 1862, as Seen by a Man at the Gun.* Hampton, Va.: Houston Printing and Publishing House, 1957.

Davis, Charles H. "History of the U.S. Steamer *Merrimack.*" *New England Historical and Genealogical Register* 28 (July 1874): 245–48.

Eggleston, John Randolph. "Captain Eggleston's Narrative of the Battle of the *Merrimac.*" *Southern Historical Society Papers* 41 (September 1916): 166–78.

Ericsson, John. *Contributions to the Centennial Exhibition.* New York: "The Nation" Press, 1876.

———. "The Monitors." *Century Illustrated Monthly Magazine* 31 (December 1885): 280–99.

Greene, Samuel Dana. "An Eyewitness Account: I Fired the First Guns and Thus Commenced the Great Battle." *American Heritage* 8, no. 4 (June 1957): 10–13, 102–5.

———. "The Fight Between the *Monitor* and *Merrimac.*" *United Service* 12 (April 1885): 448–54.

———. "In the 'Monitor' Turret." *Century Illustrated Monthly Magazine* 29 (March 1885): 754–63; reprinted in *Battles and Leaders of the Civil War* 1: 719–29. New York: Century, 1884–1887.

———. "The *Monitor* at Sea and in Battle." *United States Naval Institute Proceedings* 49, no. 2 (November 1923): 1839–47.

Hawthorne, Nathaniel. "Chiefly About War Matters, By A Peaceable Man." *Atlantic Monthly* 10, no. 57 (July 1862): 43–61.

Hill, Jim Dan. *The Civil War Sketchbook of Charles Ellery Stedman, Surgeon, United States Navy.* San Rafael, Calif.: Presidio Press, 1976.

Jones, Catesby ap Roger. "The First Confederate Iron-Clad, the *Virginia,* Formerly the United States Steam Frigate *Merrimac.*" *Southern Magazine* 15 (December 1884): 200–207.

Keeler, William Frederick. *Aboard the USS Monitor: 1862; The Letters of Acting Paymaster William Frederick Keeler, U.S. Navy, to his Wife, Anna,* edited by Robert W. Daly. Annapolis, Md.: U.S. Naval Institute Press, 1964.

Littlepage, Hardin Beverly. "The Merrimac and the Monitor." *Southern Historical Society Papers* 11, no. 1 (January 1883): 32–34.

Marvel, William, ed. *The Monitor Chronicles: One Sailor's Account: Today's Campaign to Recover the Civil War Wreck.* New York: Simon and Schuster, 2000.

McDonald, Joseph. "How I Saw the Monitor-Merrimac Fight." *New England Magazine* [New Series] 36 (July 1907): 548–53.

Norris, William. *The Story of the Confederate States' Ship "Virginia." (Once Merrimac.) Her Victory Over the Monitor. Born March 7th. Died May 10th, 1862.* Baltimore: John B. Piet, 1879.

Official Records of the Union and Confederate Armies in the War of the Rebellion. 128 vols. Washington, D.C.: U.S. Government Printing Office, 1881–1901.

Official Records of the Union and Confederate Navies in the War of the Rebellion. 31 vols. Washington, D.C.: U.S. Government Printing Office, 1894–1922.

Ramsay, H. Ashton. "Wonderful Career of the Merrimac." *Confederate Veteran* 15, no. 7 (July 1907): 310–13.

Selfridge, Thomas Oliver, Jr. *Memoirs of Thomas O. Selfridge, Jr., Rear Admiral U.S.N.* New York: G. P. Putnam, 1924.

Symonds, Craig L., ed. *A Year on a Monitor and the Destruction of Fort Sumter by Alvah F. Hunter.* Columbia: Univ. of South Carolina Press, 1987.

Timby, Theodore Ruggles. *Beyond.* Washington, D.C.: n.p., 1889.

Weeks, Grenville Mellen. "The Last Cruise of the Monitor." *Atlantic Monthly* 11 (March 1863): 366–72.

Welles, Gideon. *The Civil War Diary of Gideon Welles, Lincoln's Secretary of the Navy: The Original Manuscript Edition.* Edited by William E. Gienapp and Erica L. Gienapp. Urbana: University of Illinois Press, 2014.

White, Ellsberry Valentine. *The First Iron-Clad Naval Engagement in the World: History of the Facts of the Great Naval Battle Between The*

Merrimac-Virginia, C.S.N. and the Ericsson Monitor, U.S.N., Hampton Roads, March 8 and 9, 1862. Portsmouth, Va.: E. V. White, 1906.

White, Jonathan W., and Christopher J. Chappell, eds. "Letters from the *Monitor:* The Civil War Correspondence of Jacob Nicklis, U.S. Navy." *Civil War History* 60 (December 2014): 436–52.

Wood, John Taylor. "The First Fight of Iron-Clads." *Century Illustrated Monthly Magazine* 29 (March 1885): 738–54.

Worden, John Lorimer, et al. *The Monitor and the Merrimac: Both Sides of the Story, Told by Lieut. J. L. Worden, U.S.N., Lieut. Greene, U.S.N., of the* Monitor *and H. Ashton Ramsey, C.S.N., Chief Engineer of the Merrimac.* New York: Harper and Brothers, 1912.

Secondary Sources

Books

Barto, Arnold, J. III, comp. *The 1987 Expedition to the Monitor National Marine Sanctuary: Data Analysis and Final Report.* Washington, D.C.: NOAA, 1991.

Battles and Leaders of The Civil War, 4 vols. New York: Century, 1884–87.

Berent, Irwin M., comp. *The Crewmen of the USS Monitor: A Biographical Directory.* Prepared for Underwater Archaeology Unit, Division of Archives and History, Department of Cultural Resources, State of North Carolina. Washington, D.C.: NOAA, United States Department of Commerce. USS *Monitor* National Marine Sanctuary Historical Report Series, no. 1. 1985.

Besse, Sumner Bradford. *C.S. Ironclad Virginia and U.S. Ironclad Monitor: With Data and References for Scale Models.* Newport News, Va.: The Mariners' Museum, 1996.

Broadwater, John D. *USS* Monitor*: An Historic Ship Completes Its Final Voyage.* College Station: Texas A&M Press, 2012.

Browning, Robert M., Jr. *From Cape Charles to Cape Fear: The North Atlantic Blockading Squadron During the Civil War.* Tuscaloosa: Univ. of Alabama Press, 1993.

Campbell, R. Thomas, and Alan B. Flanders. *Confederate Phoenix: The CSS Virginia.* Shippensburg, Pa.: Burd Street Press, 2001.

Canney, Donald L. *Lincoln's Navy: The Ships, Men and Organization, 1861–65.* London: Conway Maritime Press, 1998.

———. *The Old Steam Navy.* Vol. 2: *The Ironclads, 1842–1885.* Annapolis, Md.: Naval Institute Press, 1993.

Charting a New Course for the Monitor: A Comprehensive, Long Range Preservation Plan With Options for Management, Stabilization, Preservation, Recovery, Conservation and Exhibition of Materials and Artifacts from the Monitor National Marine Sanctuary. Washington, D.C.: U.S. Department of Commerce, National Oceanic and Atmospheric Administration, National Ocean Service, Office of Ocean and Coastal Resources Management, Sanctuaries and Reserves Division, April 1998.

Church, William Conant. *The Life of John Ericsson.* 2 vols. New York: Charles Scribner's Sons, 1890.

Clancy, Paul. *Ironclad: The Epic Battle, Calamitous Loss, and Historic Recovery of the USS Monitor.* New York: International Marine/McGraw-Hill, 2006.

Coombe, Jack D. *Gunsmoke Over the Atlantic: First Naval Actions of the Civil War.* New York: Bantam Books, 2002.

Coski, John M. *Capital Navy: The Men, Ships and Operations of the James River Squadron.* New York: Savas Beatie, 2005.

Davis, William C. *Duel Between the First Ironclads.* Garden City, N.Y.: Doubleday, 1975.

De Kay, James Tertius. *Monitor: The Story of the Legendary Civil War Ironclad and the Man Whose Invention Changed the Course of History.* New York: Walker, 1997.

Delgado, James P. *"A Symbol of American Ingenuity": Assessing the Significance of U.S.S.* Monitor. Historical Context Study for the Civil War Ironclad Warship U.S.S. Monitor. Washington, D.C.: National Park Service, 1988.

Dougherty, Kevin, and J. Michael Moore. *The Peninsula Campaign of 1862: A Military Analysis.* Jackson: Univ. Press of Mississippi, 2005.

Flake, Elijah Wilson. *Battle Between the Merrimac and the Monitor, March 9th, 1862.* Polkton, N.C.: printed by author, 1914.

Flanders, Alan B. *John L. Porter: Naval Constructor of Destiny.* White Stone, Va.: Brandylane, 2000.
Fuller, Howard. *Clad in Iron: The American Civil War and the Challenge of British Naval Power.* Annapolis, Md.: Naval Institute Press, 2010.
Gentile, Gary. *Ironclad Legacy: Battles of the U.S.S. Monitor.* Philadelphia: Gary Gentile Productions, 1993.
Harlowe, Jerry L. *Monitors: The Men, Machines and Mystique.* Gettysburg, Pa.: Thomas Publications, 2001.
Hill, Richard. *War at Sea in the Ironclad Age.* London: Cassell, 2000.
Holzer, Harold, and Tim Mulligan, eds. *The Battle of Hampton Roads: New Perspectives on the USS Monitor and CSS Virginia.* New York: Fordham Univ. Press, 2006.
Marx, Robert F. "The Halls of Montezuma." In *Always Another Adventure,* 30–90. Cleveland: World, 1967.
Miller, Edward M. *U.S.S. Monitor: The Ship That Launched a Modern Navy.* Annapolis, Md.: Leeward Publications, 1978.
Mindell, David A. *Iron Coffin: War, Technology, and Experience Aboard the USS Monitor.* Baltimore: Johns Hopkins Univ. Press, 2012.
Monitor Expedition, Turret Recovery 2002: Turret Excavation Manual: Museum Phase. Newport News, Va.: Monitor National Marine Sanctuary, 2002.
Muller, Stephen H., and Jennifer A. Taylor, *Troy, New York and the Building of the USS Monitor.* Troy, N.Y.: Hudson Mohawk Industrial Gateway, 2009.
Nelson, James L. *Reign of Iron: The Story of the First Battling Ironclads, the Monitor and the* Merrimack. New York: HarperCollins, 2004.
Nelson, Scott, and Carol Sheriff. *A People at War: Civilians and Soldiers in America's Civil War.* New York: Oxford Univ. Press, 2007.
Park, Carl D. *Ironclad Down: The USS* Merrimack–*CSS* Virginia *from Construction to Destruction.* Annapolis, Md.: Naval Institute Press, 2007.
Peterkin, Capt. Ernest W. *Drawings of the U.S.S. Monitor,* U.S.S. *Monitor* Historical Report Series 1 (no. 1), 1985. Washington, D.C.: United States Department of Commerce, 1985.
A Plan for the Conservation of Objects from the Ironclad USS Monitor. Newport News, Va.: The Mariners' Museum, 2003.
Quarstein, John V. *The Battle of the Ironclads.* Charleston, S.C.: Arcadia, 1999.
———. *CSS Virginia: Mistress of Hampton Roads.* Appomattox, Va.: H. E. Howard, 2000.
———. *A History of Ironclads: The Power of Iron Over Wood.* Charleston, S.C.: History Press, 2006.
———. *The Monitor Boys: The Crew of the Union's First Ironclad.* Charleston, S.C.: History Press, 2011.
Ringle, Dennis J. *Life in Mr. Lincoln's Navy.* Annapolis, Md.: Naval Institute Press, 1998.
Roberts, William H. *Civil War Ironclads: The U.S. Navy and Industrial Mobilization.* Baltimore: Johns Hopkins Univ. Press, 2002.
Sears, Stephen W. *To the Gates of Richmond: The Peninsula Campaign.* New York: Houghton Mifflin, 2001.
Sheridan, Robert E. *Iron From the Deep: The Discovery and Recovery of the USS Monitor.* Annapolis, Md.: Naval Institute Press, 2004.
Silverstone, Paul H. *Civil War Navies, 1855–1883.* Annapolis, Md.: Naval Institute Press, 2001.
Simons, Gerald, ed. *The Blockade: Runners and Raiders.* Alexandria, Va.: Time-Life Books, 1983.
Sloan, Edward William, III. *Benjamin Franklin Isherwood Naval Engineer: The Years as Engineer In Chief, 1861–1869.* Annapolis, Md.: United States Naval Institute, 1965.
Stern, Philip Van Doren. *The Confederate Navy: A Pictorial History.* Garden City, N.Y.: Doubleday, 1962.
Still, William N., Jr. *Iron Afloat: The Story of the Confederate Armorclads.* Columbia: Univ. of South Carolina Press, 1985.
———. *Ironclad Captains: The Commanding Officers of the USS Monitor.* Washington, D.C.: Marine and Estuarine Management Division, NOAA, U.S. Department of Commerce, *Monitor* National Marine Sanctuary Historical Report Series, 1988.
———. *Monitor Builders: A Historical Study of the Principal Firms and Individuals Involved in the Construction of the USS Monitor.* Washington, D.C.: National Marine Initiative,

Division of History, National Park Service, Department of the Interior, 1988.
Symonds, Craig L. *Confederate Admiral: The Life and Wars of Franklin Buchanan*. Annapolis, Md.: Naval Institute Press, 1999.
———. *Lincoln and His Admirals*. New York: Oxford University Press, 2008.
Wheeler, Francis Brown. *John F. Winslow, LL.D. and the Monitor*. Poughkeepsie, N.Y.: F. B. Wheeler, 1893.

Articles

Arnold, J. Barto III, et al. "U.S.S. *Monitor* Project: Preliminary Report on 1987 Field Work." In *Underwater Archaeology Proceedings: From the Society for Historical Archaeology Conference*, Reno, Nev., 1988, edited by James P. Delgado, 6–9. Pleasant Hill, Calif.: The Society, 1988.
Benedict, George Greenville. "Memorandum on the Civil War: The Builders of the First *Monitor*." *Century Illustrated Monthly Magazine* 39, no. 5 (March 1890): 798–99.
Bennett, Frank Marion. "The United States Ironclad *Monitor*." *Cassier's Magazine* 13, no. 6 (April 1898): 459–74.
Broadwater, John D. "A Search for the USS *Monitor*." *International Journal of Nautical Archaeology and Underwater Exploration* 4, no. 1 (March and September 1974): 117–21.
Bryan, Anna Semmes. "The *Virginia* and the *Monitor*." *Confederate Veteran* 32, no. 9 (September 1924): 346–47.
Campbell, Mrs. A. A. "The First Fight of Ironclads." *Confederate Veteran* 29, no. 8 (August 1921): 290–91.
Clayton, W. F. "In the Battle of Hampton Roads." *Confederate Veteran* 24, no. 10 (October 1916): 456–57.
Cline, William R. "The Ironclad Ram *Virginia*, Confederate States Navy." *Southern Historical Society Papers* 32 (January–December 1904): 243–49.
Coffin, R. F. "The First Fight Between Ironclads." *Outing* 10 (August 1887): 416–21.
Edgerton, Harold E. "The *Monitor* Found!" *Technology Review* 77, no. 4 (February 1975): 8–9, 67–68.
Farb, Roderick M. "Computer Video Image Digitization on the USS *Monitor*: A Research Tool for Underwater Archaeology." In *Underwater Archaeology Proceedings from the Society for Historical Archaeology Conference*, Kingston, Jamaica, 1992, edited by Donald H. Keith and Toni L. Carrell, 100–104. Tucson: The Society, 1992.
Farr, Arthur. "The Real Genius Behind the *Monitor*." *Civil War Times Illustrated* 36, no. 3 (June 1997): 34–36.
Fiveash, Joseph. "The Virginia's Great Fight on Water." *Southern Historical Society Papers* 34 (July 1906): 316–26.
Fuller, Howard J. "'This Country Now Occupies the Vantage Ground': Understanding John Ericsson's Monitors and the American Union's War Against British Naval Supremacy." *American Neptune* 62, no. 1 (2002).
———. "'The Whole Character of Maritime Life': British Reactions to the U.S.S. *Monitor* and the American Ironclad Experience." *The Mariner's Mirror* 88, no. 3 (2002).
Hess, Peter E. "The Battle for the U.S.S. [*sic*] *Monitor*." *Ships and Shipwrecks* 1, no. 2 (November 1990): 1–3.
Higgins, John F. "Brilliant Career of the *Merrimac*." *Confederate Veteran* 8, no. 8 (August 1900): 356–57.
Levy, Leo O. "Hawthorne, Melville, and the Monitor." *American Literature* 37, no. 1 (March 1965): 33–40.
MacCord, Charles W. "Ericsson and His Monitor." *North American Review* 149, no. 395 (October 1889): 460–71.
Newton, John G. "How We Found the Monitor." *National Geographic* 147, no. 1 (January 1975): 48–61.
Newton, Virginius. "The Ram Merrimac: Detailed Accurate History of Her Plan and Construction." *Southern Historical Society Papers* 20 (January 1892): 1–26.
Phillips, Dinwiddie B. "The Career of the Iron-Clad Virginia (Formerly the Merrimac), Confederate States Navy, March–May, 1862." *Collections of the Virginia Historical Society*, New Series 6 (1887): 193–231.
Preston, Robert L. "Did the 'Monitor' or 'Merrimac' Revolutionize Naval Warfare?" *William and Mary Quarterly* 24 (July 1915): 58–66.

Still, William N., Jr. "Confederate Naval Strategy: The Ironclad." *Journal of Southern History* 27, no. 3 (August 1961): 330–43.

Thompson, Richard H. "The Rise and Fall of the Monitor 1862–1973." *The Mariner's Mirror* 60, no. 3 (August 1974): 293–310.

Thompson, Stephen C. "The Design and Construction of USS Monitor." *Warship International* 27, no. 3 (1990): 222–42.

Tyler, Lyon Gardiner. "Virginia, Founder of the World's Navies." *Tyler's Quarterly Historical and Genealogical Magazine* 3, no. 2 (October 1921): 84–106.

Watts, Gordon P., Jr. "A Decade of Research: Investigation of the USS Monitor." In *The Underwater Archaeology Proceedings from the Society for Historical Archaeology Conference,* Savannah, Georgia, 1987, edited by Alan B. Albright, 128–39. Pleasant Hill, Calif.: The Society, 1987.

———. "Deep-Water Archaeological Investigation and Site Testing in the Monitor National Marine Sanctuary." *Journal of Field Archaeology* 12, no. 3 (Fall 1985): 315–32.

———. "The Location and Identification of the Ironclad USS Monitor." *International Journal of Nautical Archaeology and Underwater Exploration* 4, no. 2 (1975): 301–39.

Dissertations and Theses

Watts, Gordon P., Jr. "Monitor of a New Iron Age: The Construction of the U.S.S. Monitor." Master's thesis, East Carolina Univ., 1975.

Wegner, Dana M. "Alban C. Stimers and the Office of the General Inspector of Ironclads, 1862–1864." Master's thesis, State Univ. of New York College at Oneonta, 1979.

Index

Civil War in the North

Broken Glass: Caleb Cushing and the Shattering of the Union · John M. Belohlavek
Banners South: A Northern Community at War · Edmund J. Raus
"Circumstances are destiny": An Antebellum Woman's Struggle to Define Sphere · Tina Stewart Brakebill
More Than a Contest between Armies: Essays on the Civil War · Edited by James Marten and A. Kristen Foster
August Willich's Gallant Dutchmen: Civil War Letters from the 32nd Indiana Infantry · Translated and Edited by Joseph R. Reinhart
Meade's Army: The Private Notebooks of Lt. Col. Theodore Lyman · Edited by David W. Lowe
Dispatches from Bermuda: The Civil War Letters of Charles Maxwell Allen, U.S. Consul at Bermuda, 1861–1888 · Edited by Glen N. Wiche
The Antebellum Crisis and America's First Bohemians · Mark A. Lause
Orlando M. Poe: Civil War General and Great Lakes Engineer · Paul Taylor
Northerners at War: Reflections on the Civil War Home Front · J. Matthew Gallman
A German Hurrah! Civil War Letters of Friedrich Bertsch and Wilhelm Stängel, 9th Ohio Infantry · Translated and Edited by Joseph R. Reinhart
"They Have Left Us Here to Die": The Civil War Prison Diary of Sgt. Lyle G. Adair, 111th U.S. Colored Infantry · Edited by Glenn Robins
The Story of a Thousand: Being a History of the Service of the 105th Ohio Volunteer Infantry in the War for the Union, from August 21, 1862, to June 6, 1865 · Albion W. Tourgée, Edited by Peter C. Luebke
The Election of 1860 Reconsidered · Edited by A. James Fuller
"A Punishment on the Nation": An Iowa Soldier Endures the Civil War · Edited by Brian Craig Miller
Yankee Dutchmen under Fire: Civil War Letters from the 82nd Illinois Infantry · Translated and Edited by Joseph R. Reinhart
The Printer's Kiss: The Life and Letters of a Civil War Newspaperman and His Family · Edited by Patricia A. Donohoe
Conspicuous Gallantry: The Civil War and Reconstruction Letters of James W. King, 11th Michigan Volunteer Infantry · Edited by Eric R. Faust
Johnson's Island: A Prison for Confederate Officers · Roger Pickenpaugh
Lincoln's Generals' Wives: Four Women Who Influenced the Civil War—for Better and for Worse · Candice Shy Hooper
For Their Own Cause: The 27th United States Colored Troops · Kelly D. Mezurek
Pure Heart: The Faith of a Father and Son in the War for a More Perfect Union · William F. Quigley Jr.
"Our Little Monitor*": The Greatest Invention of the Civil War* · Anna Gibson Holloway and Jonathan W. White